D1112178

MEASURING EDUCATIONAL ACHIEVEMENT

McGraw-Hill Series in Education

HAROLD BENJAMIN, *Consulting Editor*

MAYS · Essentials of Industrial Education
MAYS · Principles and Practices of Vocational Education
MELVIN · General Methods of Teaching
MEYER · An Educational History of the American People
MICHEELS AND KARNES · Measuring Educational Achievement
MICKELSON AND HANSEN · Elementary School Administration
MILLARD AND HUGGETT · An Introduction to Elementary Education
MORT AND ROSS · Principles of School Administration
MORT AND VINCENT · Introduction to American Education
MORT AND VINCENT · Modern Educational Practice
MOUSTAKAS · The Teacher and the Child
MURSELL · Developmental Teaching
MURSELL · Successful Teaching
MYERS · Principles and Techniques of Vocational Guidance
PITTENGER · Local Public School Administration
PRESCOTT · The Child in the Educative Process
REMMLEIN · The Law of Local Public School Administration
REMMLEIN · School Law
SAMFORD AND COTTLE · Social Studies in the Secondary School
SCHORLING AND BATCHELDER · Student Teaching in Secondary Schools
SEARS · The Nature of the Administrative Process
SORENSON · Psychology in Education
THUT AND GERBERICH · Foundations of Method for Secondary Schools
WEBER · Personnel Problems of School Administrators
WELLS · Elementary Science Education
WILSON, STONE, AND DALRYMPLE · Teaching the New Arithmetic
WINSLOW · The Integrated School Art Program
YOAKAM · Basal Reading Instruction

MEASURING
EDUCATIONAL
ACHIEVEMENT

. . . .

by **WILLIAM J. MICHEELS, Ph.D.**

Professor of Industrial Education,
University of Minnesota

& **M. RAY KARNES, Ph.D.**

Associate Professor of
Industrial Education,
University of Illinois

. . . .

New York   Toronto   London
McGRAW–HILL BOOK COMPANY
1950

Measuring Educational Achievement

21 22 23 - M A M M - 7 5 4 3 2

ISBN 07-041770-9

4/5/73 Becker & Taylor 9.95

PREFACE

This is a book for teachers. We hope it can serve as a handbook to be used and reused in answering the numerous questions on testing and evaluation that besiege the classroom and shop teacher.

The basic ideas and many of the suggested procedures have grown out of our combined experience in preparing testing materials for classroom use. We have been guided by our additional experiences in presenting such materials to teacher-training groups.

Throughout the book we have tried to keep uppermost in mind the busy teacher and especially the inexperienced instructor. In certain instances this has meant sacrificing the completeness and preciseness that would be necessary in a book written for the specialist in measurement. For example, standardized tests have not been accorded the treatment that is afforded them in many books on educational measurement. This is not to disparage the use of standardized tests. On the contrary, we feel they are vital factors in any effective program of evaluation. However, real understanding of the nature of such instruments is gained only after handling and using them. The typical teacher uses few, if any, standardized tests. Our efforts have been aimed at gathering suggestions that can be used by the teacher in constructing classroom tests and other measuring instruments. The basic principles discussed herein should help him to use wisely any standardized tests that he may administer.

As we see it, the major value of a book of this kind is to present the "how" of making and using tests and other instruments of appraisal. We have tried not to neglect the "what" and "why"; in fact, the introductory chapters are devoted to such discussion, although largely in overview fashion. However, the history of the testing movement, like the history of Ethiopia, becomes much more meaningful after you have been there.

The focal point in many instances has been industrial education, primarily because we know that area of instruction best. To preclude the inhibiting aspects of subject-matter specialization we have added a rather large variety of examples from other subject-matter fields. Of course, the basic principles and procedures should be applicable in any teaching-learning situation.

We sincerely hope that this book will prove concretely useful and practically helpful both to the beginning and the experienced teacher who is desirous of making his evaluations more effective and meaningful.

We wish to express our sincere appreciation and thanks to the many students who have reacted to much of this material in draft form and have contributed a large share of the sample items; to John A. Butler, Walter W. Cook, Cyril Hoyt, John A. Jarvis, Verne L. Pickens, and H. T. Widdowson, who have read parts of the manuscript and offered valuable criticisms and suggestions; to Dean Horace T. Morse and Assistant Dean Alfred Vaughn of the General College, University of Minnesota, for permission to use selected items from the Comprehensive Examinations prepared for use in that college; to our colleagues in the Teacher-training Department, Armored School, Fort Knox, Kentucky, who provided much assistance in preparing certain preliminary materials that have been expanded or revised for inclusion herein; to the Bruce Publishing Company, publishers, and John J. Metz, editor, *Industrial Arts and Vocational Education,* for permission to use or adapt various articles prepared for that magazine by the authors and others; to David T. Ryans, executive secretary, and the Committee on National Teacher Examinations of the American Council on Education, for permission to adapt certain test items prepared by one of the authors for use in those examinations; to the other organizations and individuals, mentioned in footnote references, who allowed the use of cited materials; to Dr. Homer J. Smith and Professor Arthur B. Mays for advice and counsel as this project took shape and developed; and to Mrs. George E. DeVries and Mrs. J. B. Walden for their helpful assistance in the preparation of the manuscript.

WILLIAM J. MICHEELS
M. RAY KARNES

MINNEAPOLIS, MINN.
URBANA, ILL.
    July, 1950

CONTENTS

CHAPTER

ONE: AN INTRODUCTION
TO MEASUREMENT

Take a good look at the following line. How long is it? Just for fun write your guess on a piece of paper. Do not use a ruler.

Do you think you came within one-eighth inch of the correct dimension? You can check by turning to the next page.

THE foregoing may seem like an odd way to start a discussion of achievement testing. It is. But it illustrates some important concepts about measurement—some basic ideas that should be understood from the beginning.

What Measurement Is

When you wrote down a figure, you illustrated to yourself what measurement is. You determined the length of the line in terms of a specified unit of measurement (inch). Measurement of any kind is a matter of determining how much or how little, how great or how small. how much more than or how much less than.[1] This is

---

[1] In more refined terms, to measure means to "observe or determine the magnitude of a variate" (*Encyclopedia of Educational Research*, p. 713). It should be noted that enumeration (counting) and measurement are not one and the same thing. In simplest terms, enumeration answers the question "how many." Measurement answers the question "how much."

true whether you are trying to measure the weight of a sack of potatoes, the color of a person's eyes, the radioactivity of an "atom-
bombed" island, or the achievement of a student in the classroom.

Potatoes are usually measured in terms of *so many* pounds. A
person's eyes contain *so much* blue or hazel or other color. An
atom-bombed island is measured to determine *how much* radiation exists.

Achievement in the classroom is often stated in terms of *so many*
points on a test or similar device that is supposed to measure the
growth or achievement that has taken place.

Some of these things can be measured very accurately, others
only roughly; still other things cannot presently be measured at
all. This leads us to a basic precept of measurement and a consideration of what can be measured.

What Can Be Measured

*Anything that exists at all exists in some quantity, and anything
that exists in some quantity is capable of being measured.*[2]

In a sense this statement is an expression of faith. It does not
say that we are *now* able to measure all things. It does say that anything existing in quantity is capable of being measured. As a
beginning test maker, it is very necessary that you have an understanding of this concept. You will then realize that certain achievement may be impossible of fine measurement at the present time,
but you will also understand that the problem is one of devising or
improving measuring instruments so that the job can be done in a
better manner. In terms of teaching effort it is directly related to
the problem of developing tests and other devices that will do a
better job of measuring the outcomes of learning.

Fifty years ago there was no such thing as a Geiger counter for
measuring the radioactivity of an area. Seventy-five years ago we
had no standardized tests for measuring intelligence. One hundred
years ago who would have thought of measuring length in terms of

---

The length of the line on page one is $35/8$ inches.

---

[2] E. L. Thorndike, "The Nature, Purposes and General Methods of Educational Products," 17th Yearbook, National Society for the Study of Education, Part 2, p. 16.

millionths of an inch? In each instance, however, these things existed, even though they had not up to that time been measured with any degree of reliability. In the intervening years very positive strides have been taken in developing instruments that will measure radioactivity, intelligence, millionths of an inch, as well as many other things. Our present instruments for measuring achievement are crude in comparison with the various electronic devices used in physical measurements, but definite improvements are being made continuously. In the years ahead we shall be able to place more and more faith in the results of such tests. And just as the physical scientist is ever striving to improve the measuring instruments of his profession, so must we in teaching endeavor not only to make better measuring instruments but to make better use of those which are already available. This is not a job for the testing expert alone. It is a vital part of effective teaching.

In this discussion we are primarily interested in the measurement of achievement in the classroom, the shop, or the laboratory or on the job. You will be investigating and learning how to construct instruments for best determining relatively what a student has learned, how well he has achieved, how much he has developed, or to what extent he has changed. You will be learning how to use the measuring devices already available.

These goals are easy to understand. They are not so easy to attain. The point to be remembered is that achievement can be measured if adequate instruments are developed to do the job and if you use these instruments properly. Your responsibility as a teacher is to make or use measuring devices that are as accurate as it is now possible to obtain. This is a challenge that requires a thorough understanding of the progress that has been made to date as well as the problems and difficulties that still remain to be solved.

How Accurate Should Measurements Be?

You have just read that the measuring instruments of the teacher should be as accurate as possible. This statement might be tempered somewhat, in the following manner: The measurement should be as accurate as is necessary in terms of the objectives set forth. As an example of this modification, suppose that someone asked you for a piece of string "about 3 feet long." Your method of measurement would probably be somewhat different from that you would adopt if you were asked for a piece of string "exactly 3 feet long." The point is that in many instances an approximate figure would be sufficient. In other cases it would have to be more accurate. This can be illustrated further by two examples that have their setting in a teaching situation.

If a student were making a freehand pictorial sketch of an end table, you might tell him, in response to a question, that the length should be about 6 inches on the drawing paper. This might be sufficient for his purpose. If, however, he were making the detailed working drawings of the table, he would want the measurements to be more accurate and made with a scale. In this instance the use determines the degree of accuracy that is necessary. A similar situation would exist if a student's father were to meet you on the street and ask how his boy is getting along in your class. You might answer "fine," or "pretty good," or "not very well." At best this would be an approximation, but it might be sufficient for the purpose. On the other hand, if the father were to come to you at school and want to know in more detail about Joe's accomplishments, then conceivably your appraisal should be more detailed and more accurate. You should be able to show him some specific measurements of the boy's relative achievement. This is not always easy to do in an accurate manner.

Sometimes a very rough measure of achievement will suffice. In most cases this can be gained by brief, objective observation of the student at work. At other times you will want the measurement to be as accurate as possible. Then you look for the most precise instrument that can be obtained. A well-prepared test may help to provide such a measurement.

Another aspect of approximate measurement can be illustrated by considering the thickness of the page you are now reading. Suppose you were asked to measure the thickness. How would you proceed? Many readers would think of a micrometer because that measures in terms of thousandths of an inch. A micrometer would probably solve the problem, but suppose you could not read the scale and did not want to get outside assistance. A simple procedure would be to get enough sheets of paper to make a pile 1 inch high. By counting the number of sheets, you could determine roughly the thickness of a single sheet (in terms of a fraction of an inch). This measurement would be satisfactory for many purposes. It would not be as accurate as that determined with a micrometer, but it would be much better than a pure guess.

This example illustrates the point that some measuring instruments may be more accurate than others but may also be more difficult to use. Since achievement tests are measuring instruments (crude as they sometimes are), this likewise applies to them. Some tests, like the micrometer, cannot be used by the ordinary teacher because of complex procedures and "scales" which he does not understand or has not learned to use. But just as it is possible to use a ruler to obtain a rough measurement of page thickness, it is also possible for a teacher to learn how to devise instruments which will provide a measure of his students' achievement that is much better than a pure guess.

With further study and application he can learn to make or use tests that are more refined (although the measurement will still be crude in comparison with that obtained with a micrometer). The corollary can be carried one step further by stating that certain aspects of measuring achievement are similar to measuring the exact thickness of this page—sometimes it is a job for the testing expert, the person whose efforts are concentrated in this special field.

Steps in Developing a Measuring Instrument

Another fundamental of measurement can be introduced by referring again to the words and paragraphs you are now reading. Suppose a person has just asked you to measure the printing on this page. Suppose further that you have agreed to do this and have just sat down to comply with the request. Without doubt you would soon be wondering just what property the person wanted measured. If you were to jot down the possibilities on a piece of scratch paper, they might look something like the illustration on the next page.

This might be only a partial list of possible things to measure, but it would probably be sufficient for you to go back to the individual and ask him to state exactly what he wanted you to measure. Let's say he asks you to measure the length of the lines and the printing ink. This time you are not put off easily. We'll assume that you understand about measuring the length of lines, but not the printing ink. So you insist that he be more specific as to what he wants measured with respect to the ink. He decides that he is interested primarily in measuring the thickness of the ink on this page.

At this stage you may have determined to your satisfaction just what it is that you are supposed to measure (length of lines and thickness of ink). The next step is to do the measuring, and an invariable question will be to determine what instrument to use.

Things on this page that might be measured
1. *Length of lines*
2. *Space between lines*
3. *Height of the type*
4. *Width of the type*
5. *The printing ink*
6. *Page balance*
7. *Proportions*

With respect to the length of lines you would probably start out by using a rule. You would measure the line and find it to be $4\frac{5}{16}$ inches long. Suppose you then take this figure to your friend in evidence of your progress. He might be satisfied, or he might tell you that your answer is not satisfactory—he wanted the measurement in terms of picas (a standard measuring unit in printing). Your first reaction might be to tell your friend that this should have been explained to you at the outset. He did not do a good job of telling you "what" to measure with respect to length (that is, what scale or unit to use).

Perhaps you give your friend a lecture on the importance of describing *exactly what* he wants done. When that is finished, you still have to determine *how* to get the line measured in terms of picas. In this instance it is relatively easy because there is a standard instrument (line gauge) for measuring such units. Your problem then is to obtain a line gauge from a print shop and measure the lines. You would find them to be 26 picas long.

The second part of your assignment is to find out the thickness of the ink on the page. In this instance it is clear "what" is to be measured. Measuring the length of the lines was relatively easy after you had determined specifically "what" was to be measured. Now the problem is changed somewhat because you understand clearly what is to be measured, but the means for doing it presents a problem. If you are an amateur physicist or an ingenious individual, you *might* devise an instrument or a method for making the measurement. At best, this would take considerable research and experimentation. Your best bet would be to consult a specialist in physical measurement. He might decide to utilize or devise an instrument based on the principle of light reflection (this is one method that has been used in measuring thin films). The point is that a special means would have to be employed, and this would entail experiences that are not familiar to the ordinary individual.

The situation described above illustrates some important points with respect to measurement of any kind. In the first place it should clarify the two major steps to follow in developing an achievement test or any other measuring instrument.

1. Determine exactly *what is to be measured.*

2. Obtain or construct a measuring instrument that will best do the measuring.

This fundamental can be summarized by the words "what" and "how." It should be easy to understand what is meant by these two steps. Carrying them out is often a complex matter. We can justifiably say that the remainder of this book is devoted largely to helping you determine "what" to measure and "how best" to measure it.

With these thoughts in mind it might be well to reflect once again on the problems that were met in measuring the length of the lines and thickness of the ink on this page. Several difficulties arose in determining "what" to measure. This was narrowed down to length and thickness. However, before the length could be measured, the "what" had to be described more specifically. When that was accomplished, it became relatively easy to determine the number of picas by using the standard line gauge. In this instance the "what" took a little time, but the "how" was relatively easy. In measuring the thickness, it was simple to determine the "what," but "how" to do it presented some problems.

In measuring human achievement the procedure is exactly the same *but much more complex*. It is still a matter of determining "what" and "how," but it is considerably more difficult to state in precise terms the things that are to be measured and after that to construct measuring instruments that will do the job. Nevertheless, the same basic procedure is followed. By putting the "what" and the "how" into question form they become directly applicable to your teaching and testing in the classroom or shop: "What am I trying to measure and how can I best do the measuring?" *If you as an instructor will do nothing more than conscientiously ask and try to answer these two questions, the examinations you make and use will be bound to improve.*

Comparison of Physical Measurement and Achievement Tests

A ruler is a measuring instrument. An achievement test is also a measuring instrument. Just as some rulers are more accurate than others, some achievement tests are more precise than others. Rulers have been in existence for a very long time. They did not just happen. They had to be developed. Over the years they have been refined and improved in a variety of ways. In comparison with achievement tests rulers are used to measure a very simple property—length. On the other hand, human achievement is a much more complex property, and it is only in recent years that efforts have been concentrated on such measurement.

These few statements may appear digressive, but they are intended to serve a specific purpose—to make you think of an achievement test as a measuring instrument, just as a ruler is a measuring instrument, and also to emphasize the necessity of being careful in trying to carry the comparison any further than this. The logic of this suggestion can be justified by pointing out some significant ways in which these types of measurement differ.

Absolute and Relative Measurement

One important difference can be noted by a brief consideration of *absolute* and *relative* measurement. Absolute measurement answers the question "how much." A single expression given in such terms has definite meaning. It can stand by itself. It means the same in one part of the country as in another. We can say that a person is so many inches tall, or weighs so many pounds, or runs 100 yards in so many seconds. This has definite meaning in terms of certain prescribed standards.

Every reader will understand the statement "He is 6 feet tall." When we say that Junior received a score of 72 in a history test, however, the meaning is not similarly definite and in terms of well-defined and precise standards. The score will mean little until it is related specifically to the test (the number of items, the number of students, the type of students, the difficulty of the items, etc.). The phrase "6 feet tall" means 72 inches all over the country, but what does the score of 72 on the history test really mean? It has little meaning by itself. Before the test score can be interpreted wisely, it must be related to the test and those who were tested. This is an oversimplified way of saying that it is *relative* in nature.

Another differentiating aspect can be explained by considering the use of "zero." One meaning of the cipher, zero, is that it is the point from which measurements are made. Sometimes this point is chosen arbitrarily, as the zero on a thermometer or the point from which the meridians of longitude are computed. In absolute measurement, however, it is possible to establish zero so that it indicates a total lack of the property being measured. In the case of temperature, it is called "absolute zero" (—273.1° C.), a computed point that is believed to register the total absence of heat.

In the measurement of achievement we have not been able to establish a similar point that registers a total lack of the property. We do not have an "absolute" starting point upon which to base measuring scales. This can be illustrated further by comparing the measurement of length with that of achievement.

We can say with assurance that 4 inches is twice as much as 2 inches because zero on a ruler indicates a total lack of length. However, we cannot say that, since John gets a test score of 60 and Bill gets a score of 30, John has achieved twice as much as Bill, for zero on the test would not indicate a total lack of achievement. If a particular student had received a score of zero, it would only mean that he failed to get any of the items right. It would not mean that he had achieved absolutely nothing during the period covered by the test. Bill answered 30 items correctly, and Joe's score was 30 points "more than" Bill's, not twice as much. Achievement-test scores are relative, then. They indicate "how much more than" or "how much less than," rather than an absolute "how much."[3]

Fundamental and Derived Units

Measurement, as the reader is aware, is in terms of units (inches, pounds, points, etc.) . In order to be useful, these units must be definable in understandable terms and must be constant; that is, they must not mean one thing today and something else tomorrow.

Units are of two types, fundamental and derived. Fundamental units of measurement are those which have been arbitrarily defined, for the sake of convenience. A yard, for example, is the length of a metal rod in the U.S. Bureau of Standards. Before such units of measurement were standardized, they were usually thought of as the distance from the end of the nose to the finger tips of an outstretched arm. The foot was the length of the human foot. The inch was the length of the outer thumb joint. A mile was 1,000 paces. An acre was the amount of land a man could plow in one day with a yoke of oxen. Many other measuring units were similarly originated.

In order to make their meaning more precise, it became necessary to define and standardize the units arbitrarily and in terms that were more specific than, for example, the length of the human foot. In one sense, many common units of measurement just "grow'd," like Topsy, and were later standardized.[4] The point to remember is that such units of measurement have been determined arbitrarily, for the sake of convenience.

Derived units, on the other hand, are established on the basis of a specified relationship or set of conditions. The common example used to illustrate such units is the centigrade thermometer. Zero is the point at which water freezes and 100 the point at which water boils (in terms of specified conditions) . This scale is then divided into 100 parts, each of which is called 1 degree or 1 per cent of the

---

[3] For a full explanation of absolute and relative measurement, see B. O. Smith, *Logical Aspects of Measurement.*

[4] A scientific attempt to devise units of physical measurement resulted in the metric system, which is now used in many countries.

distance between the freezing and boiling points. The "volt" is a derived unit of electrical measurement, being defined as "the electromotive force which produces a current of one ampere when acting on a conductor of one ohm resistance."

Many other units of measurement have been derived, among them units of educational measurement. An example from educational measurement would be the units which are established on a specified basis, such as the average accomplishment of seventh-grade students. When such units are established properly, they have much more meaning than a raw test score. A score of 123 on a test may have little meaning by itself, but if it can be shown that this score indicates achievement exceeded only by the upper 10 per cent of seventh-grade students, it begins to take on meaning. A detailed treatment of the subject is not warranted at this point, other than to indicate that units of measurement can be derived in the field of achievement. Such units are relative in nature—keep that in mind—but they have meaning which is not found in a raw test score.

Direct and Indirect Measurement

The length of a piece of wood is measured directly. This is accomplished by placing a ruler *directly* on the board and counting off the number of units (inches). On the other hand, the amount of heat in a room is not measured in a comparable manner. It is done *indirectly,* by noting what happens to a column of mercury or alcohol in a small glass tube (thermometer). We cannot put heat on a bench or table and measure it directly; rather, we note the effects of the heat by observing the expansion or contraction of the column of mercury. In still other words, we do not measure heat in terms of what it is but in terms of what it does. When the mercury expands and rises in the tube, we can say with assurance that the room is getting warmer.

A long time ago, when this phenomenon was first noted and put to use, it was not possible to say in precise terms how warm or cold a room had become. At that stage, the observer could state only that the mercury had risen in the tube; therefore, the room must be warmer. Through a scientific approach, however, it was possible to define the properties of heat clearly, to *derive* constant units (degrees), and to meet the requirements of absolute measurement (absolute zero). With these accomplishments, the question of "how much heat" could be answered in very specific terms. Today, we do not have to be satisfied with saying that the mercury has risen and therefore the room must be warmer. Even the amateur can quickly note the relative amount of heat as registered on the thermometer. Before leaving this example it should be pointed out that the measurement of heat and other physical properties is not a closed book. Scientists are ever striving to improve and refine the instruments so that even more accurate and meaningful measurements can be obtained.

In one sense the measurement of achievement is very similar to the measurement of heat—it must be accomplished in an *indirect* manner. We cannot put a person's achievement on a table and measure it directly as we can a piece of wood. We have to measure the effects or outcomes of achievement rather than the property itself. It is intangible in nature. We cannot reach out and put it in our hands. What we do is try to develop situations (test items) to which an individual responds. The test items are somewhat similar to the mercury in a thermometer. The more an individual is able to respond correctly to the situations, the more he is assumed to have achieved.

The point to remember, in this instance, is that these attempts at measurement are *indirect* in nature. We endeavor to measure achievement by what it does. A further observation should note the crudeness of mental measurements in comparison, for example, with measurement of heat. In many respects achievement measurement is little more advanced than was heat measurement at the stage when it could be shown only that mercury in a glass tube would go up and down in the relative presence and absence of heat. In fact, our efforts to date have not produced a standard substance (in the form of standard situations) that can be likened to mercury. That is, we cannot reach in a drawer for a standard set of test items (like mercury) that will indicate the relative presence or absence of achievement in exactly the same way each time the set is used and with any person. This is a sobering thought, but one that should be well understood by the beginning test maker. The problem is a complex one, more so than might be implied by the few paragraphs here devoted to the subject. The intent has been primarily to emphasize the limitations in the measurement of mental traits—limitations that should be comprehended even by the person who is just beginning a study of achievement testing.

With this understanding firmly in mind, the reader will appreciate not only the problems that remain to be solved but the healthy strides that have already been made in this field of measurement, a field that is still in its early childhood. There are many teachers in our schools whose undergraduate college training included no experience whatever with the construction and use of objective examinations.[5] That is another way of saying that it is only in the last two or three decades that the trend toward objective measurement has become widespread to any degree. Is it any wonder that perfection is still a long way off?

The Testing Movement

While the scientific approach to measuring achievement is in its infancy, achievement testing, as such, is not a new development. The Old Testament contains a favorite example of a simple achievement test. Jephthah (Judg. 12:5) used the password "shibboleth" because he knew the enemy could not pronounce the sound "sh." All those fugitives at the Jordan fords who said "sibboleth" were promptly killed. It was a very effective test. The early Chinese (about 200 B.C.) are credited with having used tests in the selection of their civil servants,[6] and reference is made to the use of oral examinations in the twelfth century at the University of Bologna.[7] In fact, it may be said that Socrates, 400 years before Christ, used oral achievement testing in a manner that is all too seldom emulated in our schools today. He "quizzed" his listeners, not primarily to find out how much they knew, but rather to provide a basis upon which the individual's knowledge and understanding could be clarified, strengthened, and broadened. It is in

[5] The first college course in Educational Measurements was offered at Columbia University in 1902, with Dr. E. L. Thorndike as the instructor.

[6] Paul F. Cressey, "The Influence of the Literary Examination System on the Development of Chinese Civilization," *American Journal of Sociology*, 35:250–262 (September, 1929).

[7] *Columbia Encyclopedia*, p. 595.

the efforts to attain a similar goal that we find the most important uses to which achievement tests can be put.

Written examinations in the schools are of more recent origin. They were not generally used in this country until after 1850. Horace Mann suggested the use of written examinations in 1845. It is interesting to note that he advocated the use of a large number of questions and commented on the desirability of standardization.[8] At about this same time the Boston schools began to administer written examinations. A few years later (1865 to 1878) the Regents' Examinations were inaugurated in the State of New York. In 1900 the College Entrance Examination Board was organized and the next year provided a few broad essay questions that were taken by approximately 1,000 private school graduates who wanted to enter colleges cooperating with the Board.

Almost as soon as their use became widespread, written examinations began to be criticized. School superintendents, as well as college administrators, gave impetus to the growing discontent. Almost parallel to these subjective voices being raised was the emergence of the scientific movement in education. In 1890, F. Y. Edgeworth was writing in the *Journal of the Royal Statistical Society* about "The Element of Chance in Competitive Examinations."[9] Though this was one of the first articles to appear on the subject, it was but the start of a veritable flood of "objective evidence" on the unreliability of essay tests, as ordinarily constructed and used. Together with these criticisms came a growing awareness that educational problems could and should be approached in a scientific manner.

As a result the testing movement was born. A great many antecedents and converging forces played parts in the birth and initial development of the testing movement. The work of Thorndike and his students is usually accepted as the start, although it must be remembered that many previous educators, psychologists, mathematicians, and others had made important contributions that were necessary to the development of new concepts and tech-

[8] O. W. Caldwell and S. A. Courtis, *Then and Now in Education: 1845–1923.* Yonkers, N.Y.: World Book Company, 1923, pp. 37–41.

[9] F. Y. Edgeworth, "The Element of Chance in Competitive Examinations," *Journal of Royal Statistical Society,* 53:460–475 (1890).

niques.[10] The first standardized tests (scales) were in the fields of arithmetic (1908) [11] and handwriting (1910) .[12] Soon other standardized tests made their appearance, and by 1928 the number had grown to almost 1,300, as catalogued by Monroe and his associates.[13] Several years ago Lee was writing, justly proud, about the 6 million standardized tests used in the schools in 1931.[14] More recent figures show that during 1944 approximately 60 million standardized tests were administered to approximately 20 million people in this country.[15] Though military uses were included in these figures, they indicate the phenomenal growth that has taken place in the use of standardized tests.

It should be noted that these "standardized" tests (many of the earlier ones were that in name only) differ from the ordinary informal achievement tests made and used by the teacher in the classroom. The test items used in the two types are similar, but the methods of construction and the later use of the test results are more refined in the standardized versions of tests. In the informal test, the teacher often constructs a number of questions or items and immediately gives the test to the students, usually as a means for helping to determine a final mark in the course. The competent maker of standardized tests proceeds in a manner that is more scientific. He is more specific in defining what he hopes to measure, but the major difference is that he tries out the items before they are put into the final test. He finds out ahead of time whether each item is satisfactory by giving one or more pretests to a carefully selected group of students classified from very bright to very dull.

[10] For a succinct summary of the more important contributions, see W. W. Cook, "Achievement Tests," *Encyclopedia of Educational Research,* pp. 1283–1286.

[11] C. W. Stone, *Arithmetical Abilities and Some Factors Determining Them,* Contributions to Education, No. 19. New York: Teachers College, Columbia University, 1908, pp. 102.

[12] E. L. Thorndike, "Handwriting," *Teachers College Record,* 11:83–175 (1910).

[13] W. S. Monroe *et al., Ten Years of Educational Research.* Urbana: University of Illinois Press, Bureau of Educational Research, *Bull.* 42, Vol. 25, No. 1, 1928, pp. 267.

[14] J. Murray Lee, *A Guide to Measurement in Secondary Schools.* New York: Appleton-Century-Crofts, Inc., 1936, p. 3.

[15] *The American Psychologist,* 2:26 (January, 1947) .

Following this tryout, each item in the test is scrutinized from every angle. The biography of the item is recorded in detail on a card. If the best students answer it correctly and poor students "muff" it, the item is ready for inclusion in the final test. If the poor students get the right answer more often than the good students, the item is thrown out or revised and tried again.

The final test is composed of items that have proved to be satisfactory. It has been standardized on the basis of the carefully selected group of students, mentioned above. Their scores are recorded in terms of typical achievement levels, called "norms" (derived units of measurement, see page 10) so that the scores of any person (or class) taking the test can be compared with the attainments of the standard group. In other words, the scores on a carefully prepared standardized test have more meaning and can be interpreted more objectively than those obtained on an ordinary informal classroom test. However, because a test is said to have been standardized does not provide automatic assurance that it is a good test. Many of the early examinations of this type were inferior in quality and caused more harm than good. Often they were standardized in name only and were based on an improper tryout group or used items that were proved "good" by superficial or artificial standards. These were the tests prepared by individuals whose main desire was to "climb on the band wagon."

Closely related to the early development of standardized tests was the appearance of testing bureaus, usually on a state-wide basis. The major functions of these bureaus were to prepare and distribute tests, as well as to orient school people with reference to the proper methods of administering the examinations and using the results. Such centers were established as early as 1913 (University of Oklahoma), although the largest number came into being just after World War I (more than 100 in all). In the late twenties state-wide testing programs were introduced. One of the first of these was the University of Iowa every-pupil scholarship testing project (1929). By 1939 twenty-six states had similar systematic testing programs.[16] In 1930 the American Council on Education organized the Cooperative Test Service,[17] an organization that is

[16] Cook, *op. cit.*, p. 1285.
[17] Now a part of the Educational Testing Service.

still active in the construction and distribution of standardized achievement tests.

Coincident with, or perhaps closely related to, this earlier rash-like outburst of standardized tests was the discovery or application of statistical methods for handling the mass of data being accumulated. The statistical concepts and techniques of the 1920's are now commonplace and elementary, but they were the single most important factor in giving impetus to the newborn science of measuring human traits and abilities. These new statistical methods were developed or adapted in order to handle and interpret the vast amount of data being collected. Even more important is the fact that these new techniques were the means for illustrating and emphasizing the inferiority of many tests that had previously been considered satisfactory. In passing, it should be noted that, while the 1920's saw the widespread acceptance and use of simple statistical techniques, their derivations and fundamental theses were often based on the findings and assertions of men who had lived many years before.

In this text, your authors have perhaps outwardly minimized the importance of proper statistical treatment by including only a few of the simpler techniques (Chapter Fifteen). In reality these few techniques have been included only for the use of those readers whose prime need is to secure a simple understanding of some basic and elementary procedures. Proper treatment of even an introductory nature now requires a complete text entirely devoted to the subject.

These few paragraphs of a scattered historical nature should be sufficient to emphasize the comparative recency of this movement to put the measurement of human traits on a more scientific basis. Many of the men credited with "firsts" in the field are still living. This should help to make clear why the millennium is not yet discernible. Giant strides have been made. Many obstacles have been overcome, but numerous problems remain to be solved. As an experienced instructor or as a teacher in training you have an obligation to your students to learn about and understand the progress that has been made as well as the problems that remain. You will constantly be measuring the achievements of your pupils. It is in your interests and theirs to make these measurements as accurate and as meaningful as possible. The competent machinist knows how to use a micrometer. The expert carpenter is thoroughly familiar with the scales on a framing square. The grocery clerk learns early how to read the scales for weighing groceries. In like manner you, as a teacher, must learn to use intelligently the measuring tools of your occupation. You will not be working primarily with wood or metal or weighing sacks of potatoes. You will be working with the most valuable resource we have—people. It is only logical to expect that you should learn how to measure the results of your efforts.

You and Measurement

Before leaving this brief introduction to measurement we should take a quick look at its effect on our daily lives. Your alarm clock helps you to get up in the morning—it measures time. By glancing at a thermometer you determine whether a room is too warm or too cold. The speedometer on your car helps you to obey the speed regulations. You purchase food by the pound. You check your tires with a pressure gage. You may check your work with a micrometer. Your utility bills are based on readings taken from watt-hour meters, gas meters, and water meters. If it all becomes a bit overwhelming, your blood pressure is measured by using a sphygmomanometer.

On and on we could go; in fact, it is difficult to think of an activity in our daily life that is not influenced directly or indirectly by some form of measurement. If, perchance, measuring instruments were suddenly denied us, we should revert to an uncivilized status almost overnight. By the same token the development and refinement of measuring techniques will play an integral part in whatever new advances we are able to make, socially as well as technologically.

An understanding of measurement is not something that is needed by only a privileged few. It can provide information and insight that will prove useful and interesting in all phases of our daily lives.

SUMMARY

To measure means to determine the magnitude of a property in terms of a suitable unit. This is true in measuring human achievement as well as physical properties. "Anything that exists at all exists in some quantity, and anything that exists in some quantity is capable of being measured." This precept explains, in part, the position of persons in educational measurement who are ever striving to devise new instruments of appraisal or improve those which are already in existence.

The accuracy of a measurement is closely related to the objective being measured. Approximate measurements will sometimes suffice. At other times it is necessary to have a measurement that is as precise and accurate as possible. Constructing a measuring instrument is basically a twofold process: (1) determining exactly what is to be measured; (2) obtaining or constructing an instrument that will best do the measuring. This process can be further summarized by the words "what" and "how." These words, and all they imply, should be considered constantly by the person who is constructing tests or other instruments of evaluation.

Educational tests are, in some respects, similar to the instruments used in measuring physical properties. In other respects they differ significantly. An achievement-test score answers the question "how much more than" or "how much less than" rather than an absolute "how much." Human achievement is measured indirectly and in a manner similar to that used in measuring heat by means of a thermometer.

Educational measurements are crude in comparison with such physical measurements as length and weight. The reason for this is understandable, however, when it is realized that achievement is a very complex property and that it is only in recent years that the scientific method has been applied broadly to the solving of educational problems. The testing movement did not become widespread until the second and third decades of this century. The growing pains that were evident then have not yet been eliminated, although significant strides have been made. The many problems that remain will demand, if they are to be solved, the in-

genuity, imagination, and hard work both of teachers and specialists for many years to come.

SOME THINGS TO DO AND QUESTIONS TO ANSWER

1. As an instructor starts on his first teaching assignment what
should he know about measurement? Stated in other words, what
should he know about measurement in order to be successful as a
teacher?

2. Suppose that a friend has just approached you for advice on constructing a test in a field about which you know little. On the basis of
your experience to this point, how would you counsel your friend as to
the procedure to be followed?

3. Have your ideas about tests and testing been changed as a result
of reading this introductory chapter? Without looking back at the
chapter it might be fun to jot down some of those thoughts or ideas.
If this suggestion could be carried one step further, it would be interesting to compare your statements with those of a friend or other class
members who have likewise just read the chapter. The object of this
suggestion is to have you do some thinking on your own. It would be a
good assignment preceding a class discussion.

4. Another interesting procedure would be to spend a minute or two
jotting down the types of test items with which you are now familiar.
Perhaps you would want to include a comment or two along with each
one. File these in your notebook. It will be fun to look at them later
to see whether or not your ideas have changed.

5. In your own words explain the difference between a standardized
test and an informal test. Imagine that you are explaining the difference to a parent who knows little about formal education.

6. What does the term "statistics" mean to you when used in connection with tests and measurement in the schools?

7. Suppose that you were asked to speak briefly to a group of teachers
or college students on the topic "Educational Tests as Compared with
a Craftsman's Tools." Jot down the points that you would want to
cover in this talk.

8. Do you think it is right to say that oral tests are of little value?
Why?

9. How would you explain the term "norm" by talking about the
height of people? How would you relate this to test norms?

10. When an instructor announces that your class is going to have a

test, what are some of the questions that come to mind? What use can you make of these questions in your teaching?

SELECTED REFERENCES FOR ADDITIONAL READING

Ayers, Leonard P. "History and Present Status of Educational Measurements," *The Measurement of Educational Products,* 7th Yearbook, National Society for the Study of Education, Part II. Bloomington, Ill.: Public School Publishing Company, 1918. Chap. I.

Caldwell, Otis W., and Stuart A. Courtis. *Then and Now in Education.* Yonkers, N.Y.: World Book Company, 1923.

Cook, Walter W. "Achievement Tests," *Encyclopedia of Educational Research.* New York: The Macmillan Company, 1941. Pp. 1283–1301.

Greene, Harry A., Albert N. Jorgensen, and J. Raymond Gerberich. *Measurement and Evaluation in the Secondary School.* New York: Longmans, Green & Co., Inc., 1943. Chaps. I, III.

McCall, William A. *Measurement.* New York: The Macmillan Company, 1939. Chap. I.

Ross, C. C. *Measurement in Today's Schools.* New York: Prentice-Hall, Inc., 1947. Chaps. I–II.

Smith, B. Othanel. *Logical Aspects of Educational Measurement.* New York: Columbia University Press, 1938. Chaps. I–IV.

Tolley, William P. "American Education and the Testing Movement," *Educational Record,* 29:86–96 (January, 1948).

CHAPTER

TWO: KINDS AND TYPES OF EVALU-
ATING INSTRUMENTS

Measurement and Evaluation

In the previous chapter you were introduced to
the subject of measurement, with emphasis on its use in teaching
situations. This brief treatment, while introductory in nature, was
for the purpose of setting forth several fundamentals that should
be understood by the beginning test maker. Your understanding
of these fundamentals will be reflected in the measuring instruments you devise and use. In large part the success of your evaluating efforts will be dependent upon your ability to apply these
several principles.

Before proceeding further a distinction should be made between "measurement" and "evaluation." *Measurement* implies a
precise, quantitative value which can be placed on a physical property or an outcome of instruction (a board is so many inches long
or a student received so many points on a particular test). *Evaluation,* a newer term in educational circles, is more comprehensive
in nature and includes values which result from the exercise of
judgment and more subjective appraisals (as well as from the use
of strictly objective techniques). In the words of Wrightstone,
"Evaluation is a relatively new technical term introduced to designate a more comprehensive concept of measurement than is implied in conventional tests and examinations."[1]

[1] J. Wayne Wrightstone, "Evaluation," *Encyclopedia of Educational Research,* p. 468.

In terms of teaching efforts you will be evaluating when you take into consideration the many factors that are inherent in student growth—proper attitudes toward others, safety habits, manipulative skills, acquisition of knowledge, appreciation, understandings, and the like. Certain of these traits can be measured with rather precise devices. Others will require the careful exercise of judgment based on effective observation. In other words, you cannot rely on a pencil and paper test for a complete picture of your students' growth and development. Other measures and appraisals are also necessary.

While a major part of this text is devoted to the construction and use of achievement tests, the other instruments of appraisal are equally important. Later chapters contain suggestions and examples of various devices that should be used to supplement the written achievement tests you will be making and administering. This chapter reviews briefly the several types of evaluating instruments which may be made by others but with which you should be familiar.

Classification of Evaluating Instruments

Tests and other instruments of evaluation can be classified in several ways. Sometimes they are segregated in terms of individual and group tests, that is, whether the test can be given to a group of people at the same time or must be administered to each person individually. In other instances the differentiation is in terms of rate tests and power tests. Rate tests are those on which a time limit is set and speed of response is an important factor. Power tests allow the student to work until he is finished or until he can go no further. Still another classification uses the headings "traditional, or old-type, examination" and "new-type objective tests." This is primarily a differentiation between the subjective type of essay test and the several types of objective-test items (true-false, multiple-choice, etc.) .

Perhaps the best general classification is that based on the uses or the kinds of abilities being measured, as shown in the following headings:

1. Achievement tests.
2. Scholastic-aptitude (intelligence) tests.

3. Special-aptitude tests.
4. Interest inventories.
5. Character or personality instruments.

This is the classification we shall use to consider briefly the several types of instruments with which you should become familiar.

Achievement Tests

An achievement test is an instrument designed to measure relative accomplishment in a specified area of work. There are two main types, general-achievement tests and diagnostic tests. There is no fine line of demarcation between the two. The general-achievement test,[2] as the name implies, samples the entire field of work being tested and yields a single score indicating relative achievement. A diagnostic test is designed to reveal a person's strengths and weaknesses in one or more areas of the field being tested. It assists the teacher in determining exactly where the learning or teaching has been successful and where it has failed.

Most teacher-made tests are of the general-achievement type. They yield a single score that is of little value for diagnostic purposes. However, a careful analysis of the results of such tests may provide important information for diagnostic purposes, especially if the results on individual items are scrutinized thoroughly. Not many teachers take the time or make the effort to do this.

Although later chapters will discuss the construction of achievement tests in more detail, it might be well to pause briefly at this point and consider the several types by means of various examples. The Cooperative General Mathematics Test for High School Students[3] measures information acquired in algebra, plane and solid geometry, and trigonometry. It has three parts, which use short-answer- and multiple-choice-type questions. The test is given to high school students who have had 2 years of mathematics. The results are useful to college counselors in determining how much

[2] Lindquist has defined a general achievement test as "one designed to express in terms of a single score a pupil's relative achievement in a given field of achievement." Herbert E. Hawkes, E. F. Lindquist, and C. R. Mann, *The Construction and Use of Achievement Examinations.* Boston: Houghton Mifflin Company, 1936, p. 23.

[3] Published by the Cooperative Test Service (Educational Testing Service)

mathematics the student has retained and at what level he might start his college mathematics. This test, then, provides a relative measure of what a person has achieved in these several areas of mathematics, either in or out of school. Keep in mind that this is but one illustrative example of a wide variety of similar achievement tests now available.

The USAFI[4] Tests of General Educational Development (GED tests) have been taken by many returning servicemen as a means of obtaining high school or college credit for their previous educational experience, both in and out of military service. These are general achievement tests designed to measure the educational development of the individual or his ability to profit from a program of general education at the high school or junior college level. They are somewhat different from the usual achievement tests given at the end of a course. Detailed facts are minimized. The tests endeavor to measure the individual's acquisition of broad generalizations, ideas, and concepts and his ability to comprehend, evaluate, and think clearly. The battery is composed of nine separate tests, five on the high school level and four on the college level.[5]

High School Level

Test 1. Correctness and Effectiveness of Expression.

Test 2. Interpretation of Reading Material in the Social Studies.

Test 3. Interpretation of Reading Material in the Natural Sciences.

Test 4. Interpretation of Literary Materials.

Test 5. General Mathematical Ability.

College Level

Test 1. Correctness and Effectiveness of Expression.

Test 2. Interpretation of Reading Materials in the Social Studies.

Test 3. Interpretation of Reading Materials in the Natural Sciences.

Test 4. Interpretation of Literary Materials.

[4] United States Armed Forces Institute.

[5] Description taken from catalogue of Science Research Associates, Inc.

Each test consists of a number of short reading passages taken from textbooks and other materials in the field, followed by multiple-choice questions based on the passages. Each test is published in a separate booklet with which individual answer sheets are used. While the special answer sheets are designed for hand scoring, standard IBM[6] sheets may be used if machine scoring is desired.

Norms[7] for each of the high school level tests are presented for six geographical regions and for the country as a whole. Norms for each of the college level tests are given for three types of institutions, classed according to the scholastic aptitude of their entering freshman classes. The test is nontimed, but each test takes approximately 2 hours to administer.

General-achievement Batteries. Various batteries of general-achievement tests are available for surveying achievement in broad areas of subject matter. When such tests are given to students in the elementary or secondary school, it is possible to identify areas of weakness or strength that a student may possess. On the basis of the tests given to all students, each teacher is able to obtain information that can add materially to the effectiveness of instruction.

The Iowa Tests of Educational Development, for example, endeavor to measure more than the attainment of skills and knowledge. The following test titles indicate the nature of the materials:

1. Understanding of Basic Social Concepts.
2. Ability to Do Quantitative Thinking.
3. Ability to Write Correctly.
4. General Proficiency in the Natural Sciences.
5. Ability to Interpret Reading Materials in the Social Studies.
6. Ability to Interpret Reading Materials in the Natural Sciences.
7. Ability to Read Literary Materials.
8. Ability to Use Important Sources of Information.
9. Ability to Recognize Important Word Meanings.

[6] International Business Machine.

[7] Remember that "norms" are used in interpreting an individual's test score on the basis of similar scores made by a carefully selected group of persons.

The Cooperative Achievement Tests of the Cooperative Test Service[8] are for high school classes in the following subject-matter areas: English and reading, social studies, natural science, and mathematics. The Stanford Achievement Tests have been constructed especially for the primary and intermediate grades. Many other similar batteries have been developed for the several school levels, and in a variety of subject-matter areas.

The mathematics test mentioned above measures achievement in a special field. The GED battery covers a broad area of educational development, using tests that are different from those usually given at the end of a course of instruction. They are still general achievement tests. The tests which you make and use in your teaching will, for the most part, also be of the general achievement type. There will be one main difference. The instruments mentioned above have been standardized—yours will be informal. Remember that a standardized test is one in which the items have been carefully prepared and then tried out on a carefully selected standardizing group. By the time the test is printed and distributed, each item has proved its value. You may be able to develop such an examination, but for the most part your tests will be of the informal type.

This same distinction can be made with respect to diagnostic tests. The Basic Skills in Arithmetic Test by Wrinkle, Sanders, and Kendel[9] is an example of a standardized test of this nature. This diagnostic test "measures skill in dealing with whole numbers, fractions, decimals, and percentages, and points out a student's difficulties in dealing with those fundamental arithmetical operations which are of greatest use in solving everyday problems. Designed to be used primarily in junior and senior high schools, the test can serve as the basis for individualized instruction in mathematics review classes." This is a nontimed test with the norms based on the administration of the test to more than 3,000 students.

These several examples of general achievement and diagnostic tests have been of the pencil-and-paper variety. Both standardized and informal versions require the students to write their answers

[8] Now called Educational Testing Service.
[9] Distributed by Science Research Associates, Inc.

on the test paper or on special answer sheets. Achievement tests may also be oral in nature; that is, the person doing the testing states each question orally. The person taking the test may give his reply orally or may write down his answer, or a combination of these two methods may be used. In one sense, the daily questioning of students at work is a very informal type of oral achievement test. The questions are often poor and seldom prepared in advance, but the purpose is similar to that of other achievement tests—to determine what the students have accomplished or where they are having difficulty. Instructors would do well to consider carefully this aspect of their teaching. Time spent in preparing effective oral questions of this type and a simple method of recording responses or observations would be very useful in implementing other measures of achievement.

A more formal approach to oral achievement testing is that used by the U.S. Employment Service in its oral trade tests. When a person registers for employment, he is interviewed with respect to his previous training and experience. Since the interviewers cannot possibly have an intimate knowledge of the hundreds of occupations, some method was necessary whereby they can ascertain readily and rapidly whether a person who registers as a plumber, for example, really knows something about plumbing. After careful and thorough study a standard set of oral questions has been developed for a large number of trades. By using these questions and noting the responses the interviewer can quickly determine whether an individual is acquainted with a particular trade. Perhaps the best use is to ferret out those persons whose experience has been meager or very limited. For the others, a more refined type of measurement is often necessary.

Upon reflection it will be noted that such achievement tests are used primarily for prognostic purposes—for determining whether a person will be likely to succeed on a given job. Technically such tests might better be classified as aptitude tests. They are still instruments that measure accomplishment or achievement. This should not cause consternation, for, as will be repeated later, any test is an aptitude test if it provides a good indication of a person's potentialities in a given field of work. In other words, if you know how well an individual has achieved up to a certain point, you have a good basis for predicting his achievement beyond that point.

The performance test is still another means for measuring achievement. While it is literally true that any test should be a test of performance, this name is usually applied to those instruments which measure manipulative skills primarily. Instead of writing answers on a piece of paper or answering oral questions, the student taking a performance test is required to perform an operation or carry out a job under careful direction, with an objective basis for marking. The section on Special-aptitude Tests contains several photographs of simple performance tests, and a later chapter (Chapter Twelve) is devoted entirely to the development of manipulative-performance tests for use in technical and shop classes.

Scholastic-aptitude Tests

Perhaps the most important factor related to success in schoolwork is the ability to do abstract thinking—the ability to understand and manipulate abstract symbols such as word meanings or verbal relationships. This is not the only factor, to be sure, but it is probably the most important single factor. For this reason most tests that have been developed for the purpose of predicting school success or ability to learn have endeavored primarily to measure the person's abilities in this respect. Such tests have commonly been called "intelligence tests" (and still are), although the present trend is to use the terms "scholastic-aptitude" or "educational-aptitude tests." Undoubtedly this is a more accurate indication of the real nature of such tests.

Very few persons graduate from high school without adding the term "I.Q." to their vocabulary, and many other persons use it freely, but very few understand the real meaning of the term. Even some teachers talk about I.Q.'s loosely and unwisely. It is well to keep in mind that the term I.Q. (intelligence quotient) is a ratio, as the name implies—a ratio between a person's mental age and his chronological age (I.Q. = M.A./C.A.). Thus, if an eight-year-old receives a score of 83 on an intelligence test and the average score of all eight-year-olds is 83, it is said that his mental age is 8 and his chronological age is 8. This gives a ratio of 1

(I.Q. $= \frac{8}{8}$, or 1). In order to avoid the use of numbers less than 1, the quotient is multiplied by 100 (I.Q. $= \frac{8}{8} \times 100 = 100$). The individual in our example is said to be average in his ability to learn: he has an I.Q. of 100.

If, in this same test, another individual receives a score of 106, which is the score of the average twelve-year-old, he has a mental age of twelve with a chronological age of 8. His I.Q. is 150, indicating an individual with superior ability in whatever the test measures, presumably the ability to learn (I.Q. $=$ M.A./C.A. $= 1.5 \times 100 = 150$). Such tests *do not* indicate that a student with this score *will* learn rapidly, or that he will be interested in his work, or that he will have determination to learn, or that he will have the proper attitudes toward his teacher. The score is merely an indication of capacity or potentiality.

All tests of scholastic aptitude *are not* scored in terms of an accomplishment-age ratio. For that reason they should not be called I.Q. tests, as is so often done. The present trend seems to be away from indicating "learning ability" in terms of a single, general score, especially at the upper levels. Differential tests are now being constructed that help to indicate a person's specialized potentialities. Such tests provide an indication of a person's verbal facility, linguistic ability, mathematical aptitude, spatial visualization, and the like. On the basis of these differentiated scores, the prediction of educational success becomes more meaningful. The Yale Educational Battery, described later, is an excellent example of such tests.

Scholastic-aptitude tests may be individual in nature or they may be of the group type. The most widely used individual test is the Stanford Revision of the Binet-Simon Scale. This scale, administered individually, consists of a group of tests arranged in age levels from 3 to 18. It was originally developed by the Frenchmen Binet and Simon, in 1905, as an instrument to be used in estimating a student's probable rate of progress and to pick out those persons who would be unlikely to profit from formal school instruction. Although Binet made several revisions, the test did not come into common use in this country until the appearance of Terman's Stanford Revision in 1916 (revised again by Terman and Merrill in 1937). It should be pointed out that the process is a

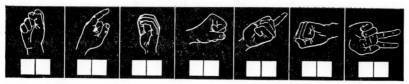

Fig. 1. Space thinking (i.e., the ability to visualize solid objects and to see their relationship to each other) is tested by the time required to determine whether each of the hands is a right or a left. To take this test the reader should check the appropriate box under each of the pictures: left for left hands, right for right hands. Thirty seconds should be sufficient to identify them all correctly. Answers are given at the end of the series of examples. Space thinking is important in professions like engineering, architecture, and dressmaking.

technical one and that this particular test should be administered only by persons thoroughly trained in the methods used.[10]

There are many group tests which measure scholastic aptitude or general intelligence. The Army General Classification Test (AGCT), developed for use during World War II, is an example of one such test. The test was designed to classify soldiers on the basis of their ability to learn army duties. One of the several equivalent forms of the test was administered to all inductees who could read and write the English language. On the basis of the test, men were sorted into five broad groups: I, very rapid learners; II, rapid learners; III, average learners; IV, slow learners; V, very slow learners. By using the test results, it was possible to select men for army duties in accordance with the ability required to learn those duties. This test was not perfect in its predictive qualities, but it saved much time and effort in pointing out the general learning ability of individuals. In passing, it should be noted that this is not the only test used by the military. All branches make effective use of many types of tests.

A further insight into this type of testing can be gained by reviewing some types of problems that are utilized. The following

[10] For a detailed description of the test and its administration, see L. M. Terman and Maud Merrill, *Measuring Intelligence* (Boston: Houghton Mifflin Company, 1937). Another individual test used widely for adolescents and adults is the Wechsler-Bellevue Intelligence Scale; see D. Wechsler, *The Measurement of Adult Intelligence* (Baltimore: The Williams & Wilkins Company, 1939) p. 229.

illustrative examples (and that on the previous page) have been taken from a *Life* article, "Factors of Intelligence,"[11] which describes the work done by Drs. L. L. and Thelma Gwinn Thurstone of the University of Chicago, authorities in the field of testing.

SHAPE RECOGNITION

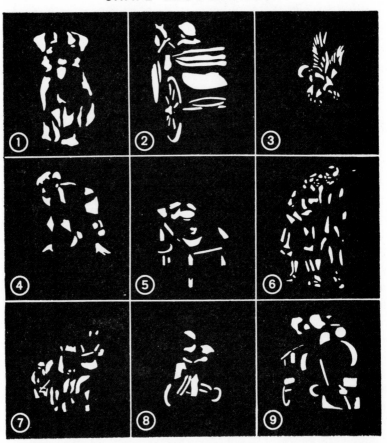

Fig. 2. Mutilated pictures test ability to see sense and unity in a group of apparently jumbled and disjointed elements. Successful administrators should be able to recognize subjects of most of these pictures almost immediately.

[11] June 9, 1947, used with permission. (Drawings reproduced by permission of Thelma Gwinn Thurstone.)

PERCEPTION

Fig. 3. Identical pairs of objects are hidden in each of these boxes. File clerks and copyreaders will probably be able to spot them all in less than the normal 60 seconds since they exercise the faculty of perception constantly in their work.

33

Fig. 4. (See legend on facing page.)

Fig. 4 (Cont.). Unrelated object in each line is out of keeping with the rest. In the top line containing several hats all but fedora are party hats. This is a test of reasoning power, which is important in intellectual occupations. Time: 3 minutes.

WORD FLUENCY

Fig. 5. Naming pictures with words which all begin with the same letter (in this case P) measures fluency of vocabulary. This quality is indispensable to writers, teachers, lecturers. Average person takes 2 minutes to name all 18.

VERBAL UNDERSTANDING

1. JUVENILE____AWKWARD	YOUTHFUL	DEPENDENT	BASHFUL
2. FAMOUS____FLUVIAL	RENEWED	FAITHFUL	RENOWNED
3. OVERT____RICH	OPEN	TRIFLING	QUIET
4. WANTON____GAINFUL	UNRESTRAINED	EXTENSIVE	SOFT
5. REMOTE____INIMICAL	DISTENDED	SPARSE	FAR
6. POTENT____GAY	THICK	TIRESOME	STRONG
7. OPULENT____WEALTHY	ELECTIVE	CONTRARY	HATEFUL
8. SERE____WITHERED	CHEAP	HELPFUL	SINGLE
9. ECCENTRIC____EMPHASIZED	WARY	AWFUL	STRANGE
10. VOLUBLE____EDIBLE	ENLARGED	DREAMY	FLUENT
11. ANONYMOUS____RECONDITIONED	DESTRUCTIVE	NAMELESS	SYNONYMOUS
12. ACOUSTIC____MELODIOUS	AUDITORY	SELDOM	ECSTATIC
13. INEBRIATE____KINGLY	WEARY	FRISKY	DRUNKEN
14. SUPERB____GILT	MAGNIFICENT	IMMENSE	MINUTE
15. FLAGRANT____NOTORIOUS	PATRIOTIC	INFLATED	SUITABLE
16. CAPACIOUS____HUNGRY	SAVAGE	ROOMY	ODOROUS
17. FETID____AMUSING	FEVERISH	PUTRID	CONTAGIOUS
18. GROTESQUE____LIVELY	RECUMBENT	BIZARRE	TRAGIC
19. MALIGNANT____STOLID	HARMFUL	WORN	POOR
20. INNATE____DRUNK	INHERENT	IMPERATIVE	PASSIVE
21. PRODIGAL____LOST	BELOVED	EXTRAVAGANT	YOUNG
22. FRANK____POPULAR	QUEER	BRUTAL	OPEN

Fig. 6. Synonym for each word at left can be found among the other words in same line with it. Ability to pick them out shows extent of word understanding, which is a vital factor in learning process. Most high school graduates get 15 right.

NUMBER FACILITY

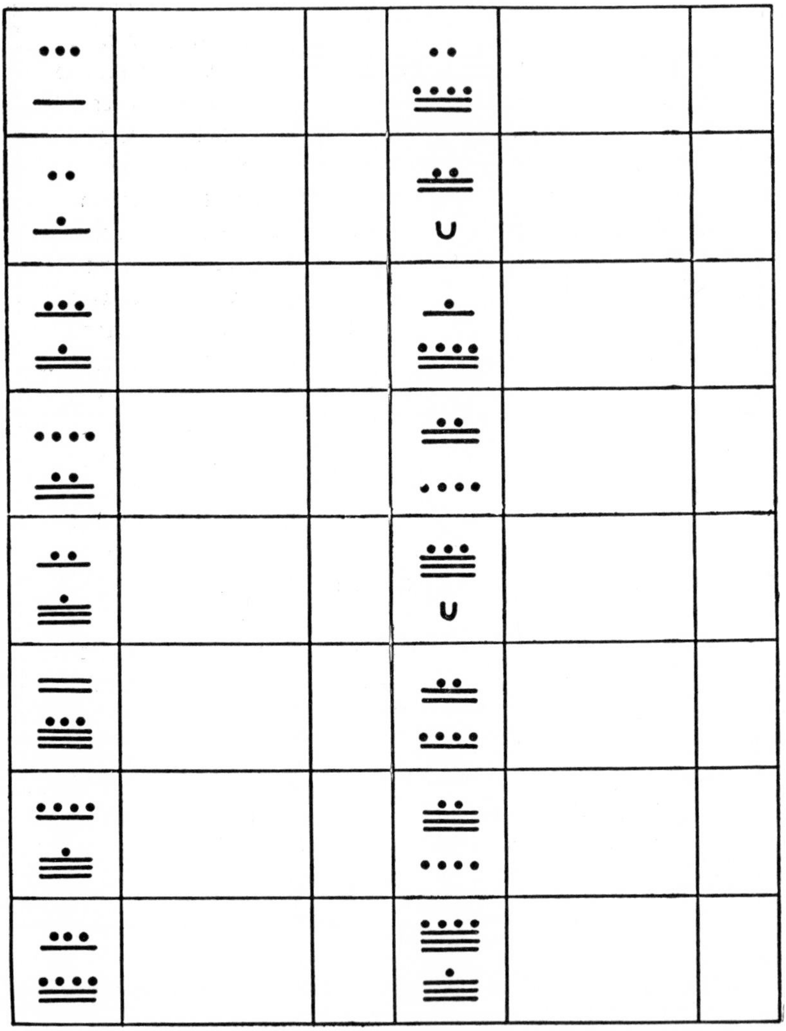

Fig. 7a. Ability to calculate, tested by this exercise, is one of the most specific of the primary mental functions. It is essential to clerks, cashiers, and accountants, valuable in many other professions. To take the test, which should require 5 minutes, write equivalents of Maya numbers in boxes at right. [The Maya code and two examples are given on the opposite page.]

0	1	2	3	4	5	6	7	8	9
U	•	••	•••	••••	——	•⁄—	••⁄—	•••⁄—	••••⁄—
10	11	12	13	14	15	16	17	18	19
══	══•	══••	══•••	══••••	═══	═══•	═══••	═══•••	═══••••

Fig. 7b. Number code is based on numerical system of ancient Maya. To prepare for test, study Maya numbers 0 to 19 (above). Numbers 20 and over, expressed by combining symbols one above another, are deciphered by multiplying the bottom symbol by 1, top symbol by 20, and adding.

EXAMPLE 1   EXAMPLE 2

$$\text{••}\underline{} \times 1 = 7$$

$$\text{•}\underline{} \times 20 = 120$$
$$\text{••}\underline{} \times 1 = \underline{7}$$
$$127$$

ANSWERS

HANDS. Left to right: R,L,L,L,L,L,R.

MUTILATED PICTURES. 1. dog 2. carriage 3. hawk 4. sprinter 5. kitchen table 6. young couple 7. man plowing 8. child on tricycle 9. locomotive

IDENTICAL PAIRS. Finding correct pairs is simply a matter of time.

UNRELATED OBJECT. Position in each row is 4,3,2,1,4,4,1,3,1,2,2

NAMING PICTURES. Here is one set of answers (there are other correct ones): peppermint, pauper, padlock, primate, prints, pussy cat, popgun, poultry, pottery, pachyderm, prince, perambulator, plaything, profile, peddler, portfolio, punishment, pixie

SYNONYM. 1. youthful 2. renowned 3. open 4. unrestrained 5. far 6. strong 7. wealthy 8. withered 9. strange 10. fluent 11. nameless 12. auditory 13. drunken 14. magnificent 15. notorious 16. roomy 17. putrid 18. bizarre 19. harmful 20. inherent 21. extravagant 22. open

NUMBER CODE. Lefthand column: 65, 46, 171, 92, 156, 218, 196, 174. Righthand column: 54, 240, 134, 244, 360, 249, 344, 396

A group test that has been in wide use for many years is the Otis Self-administering Test(s) of Mental Ability. There are several equivalent forms, each of which contains seventy-five items of various kinds arranged in order of difficulty. The total test has a time limit of 30 minutes, which means that it can be administered to many people in a short period of time. It has been used in industry as an easy means of obtaining one measure of the mental "brightness" of job applicants.

The Otis test is omnibus in nature, that is, it provides a single score. The newer approach to scholastic-aptitude testing is exemplified in the Yale Educational Aptitude Battery. The intent of this series of tests and other similar instruments is to determine the specific branch (es) of collegiate study for which an individual is best suited. This battery is developed on the logical basis that different types of "thinking abilities" are required in the various fields of study. There is some overlapping, to be sure, but success in engineering, for example, necessitates a type of thinking somewhat different from that employed by the successful student of literature. Some students possess high abilities in both of these, as well as other fields. Other students are low in one and high in the other. This series of tests is an attempt to *differentiate* between various areas of ability and in a manner that is not possible when only a single score is obtained on the total test. The battery is composed of seven tests, measuring the following elements:

1. Verbal facility.
2. Linguistic aptitude.
3. Verbal reasoning (logical inference, deductive judgment, etc.) .
4. Quantitative reasoning.
5. Mathematical aptitude.
6. Spatial visualizing.
7. Mechanical ingenuity.

The following excerpts from the sample practice booklet will illustrate the type of items used to measure these several abilities. For the purpose here intended, a study of these sample items will be more illuminating than would a detailed discussion of the construction and use of the battery.

PRACTICE BOOKLET FOR YALE EDUCATIONAL
APTITUDE BATTERY [12]

The following material has been abstracted from the practice booklet
and is presented for illustrative purposes. Though not reproduced here
in full, the booklet contains detailed instructions for marking a separate answer sheet, and a larger number of examples.

TEST I—VERBAL COMPREHENSION

Part I: Paragraph Reading.

DIRECTIONS: Each sentence or paragraph below contains one word which
spoils its meaning. This incorrect word is one of the *five* words which
have numbers printed just above them. You are to find the incorrect
word and strike out its number.

Answers

Example: "The sale of fur in the tropics is an important
       1   2
business, made so by the lack of need for clothing which
       3   4
will ward off the cold."
       5   1 2̸ 3 4 5

The meaning is spoiled by the word "important," which
is number 2 of the five words. Therefore, number 2 is the
correct answer, as indicated.

Now, answer these problems in the same way.

1. The rapid increase of natural knowledge, which is the
                          1
   chief characteristic of our age, is brought about in vari-
                2
   ous ways. The main army of science moves to the con-
        3
   quest slowly, never ceding an inch of the territory lost. 1 2 3 4 5
        4   5

2. China, and much later, Western Europe and the United
                          1
   States, invented systems of examinations which admit-
        2   3
   ted the unsuccessful candidates to one or another kind
        4   5
   of preferment.   1 2 3 4 5

[12] Taken from Albert B. Crawford and Paul S. Burnham, *Forecasting College Achievement* (New Haven: Yale University Press, Appendix A). Used
by permission.

PRACTICE BOOKLET (*Cont.*)

Part II: Word Relations.

DIRECTIONS: In this test, the symbol # will be used to indicate *opposite in meaning to*. For example:

Find NOUN # Verb "grieve": 1-help, 2-joy, 3-sense, 4-charity, 5-image

This means that you are to find a noun among the five words given which conveys a meaning opposite to that conveyed by the verb "grieve." The answer is "joy," number 2.   1 2̸ 3 4 5

Work these problems:

1. Find NOUN # Verb   1-punishment, 2-open,
   "chastise"   3-praise, 4-movement,
                       5-curse   1 2 3 4 5

2. Find ADVERB #   1-falsely, 2-costly,
   Adjective "sufficient"   3-carefully, 4-illegally,
                       5-inadequately   1 2 3 4 5

Part III: Synonyms.

DIRECTIONS: In each line below, the word in CAPITAL letters is followed by two words in smaller letters. Sometimes only the *first* of these two means the same, or nearly the same, as the capitalized word, and in this case the answer is number 1. If the *second* word only is a synonym, number 2 should be indicated. Likewise, if *neither* word means the same as the capitalized word, the answer is number 3; and if *both* are synonyms of the capitalized word, the choice is number 4. The first two are correctly answered.

			First	Second	Neither	Both
1. ABSURD	ridiculous	tedious	1̸	2	3	4
2. GORGEOUS	intricate	eccentric	1	2	3̸	4
3. IMMUTABILITY	probability	inability	1	2	3	4
4. GARRULOUS	loquacious	ornate	1	2	3	4

PRACTICE BOOKLET *(Cont.)*

TEST II—ARTIFICIAL LANGUAGE

This test is an attempt to measure the ability underlying facility in learning new languages.

DIRECTIONS: Study the vocabulary and rules of the artificial language given below. Then work the practice sentences in the order in which they appear.

VOCABULARY:

I—vlu	to be —jahviz	good—zeyt
he, it (nom.)	to read —skraliz	book—stetsleit
—wes	to have—dromiz	word—gleit

RULES

1. Articles are not used in the artificial language.

2. Verbs are not conjugated for person and number.
e.g., *jahviz* is used for *am, are, is.*

3. Future—prefix *bli* to the verb.
e.g., to read—*skraliz;* will read—*bliskraliz.*

Word order—as in English where possible.

SAMPLE EXERCISE:

A	B	C	*Answers*
I	have	a book	

A. (1) Wes   (2) Polvlu   (3) Vlu   (4) Polwes   (5) Vlul   1 2 ∦ 4 5
B. (1) dromiz (2) jahviz   (3) amdiz   (4) somiz   (5) binotiz   ∤ 2 3 4 5
C. (1) gleit   (2) zepoldeit (3) zeyt   (4) stetsleit (5) oveit   1 2 3 ∦ 5

The correct translation of the sample sentence is: *Vlu dromiz stetsleit.* The correct choice for "A" is then (3); for "B" it is (1); for "C" it is (4).

PRACTICE SENTENCES:

A	B	C
1. Vlu   jahviz   zeyt.

A. (1) He   (2) I   (3) We   (4) It   (5) to read   1 2 3 4 5
B. (1) read   (2) have   (3) will be   (4) will have (5) am   1 2 3 4 5
C. (1) book   (2) word   (3) he   (4) good   (5) it   1 2 3 4 5

A	B	C
2. The book   will have   a word.

A. (1) Gleit   (2) Vlu   (3) Stetsleit (4) Wes   (5) Zeht   1 2 3 4 5
B. (1) Blidromiz (2) jahviz (3) dromiz   (4) blijahviz (5) skraliz   1 2 3 4 5
C. (1) zeht   (2) gleit   (3) wes   (4) stetsleit (5) vlu   1 2 3 4 5

PRACTICE BOOKLET (*Cont.*)

TEST III–VERBAL REASONING

This is a test of ability to think logically, i.e., to arrive at valid conclusions and work out relationships from given data.

Part I: Logical Inferences.

DIRECTIONS: Each of the following questions has two parts—a *statement of fact* which is always assumed to be true, and a *conclusion* from that statement of fact. Five possible judgments can be made for each conclusion. They are as follows:

1. Necessarily true
2. Necessarily false
3. Probably true
4. Probably false
5. Undetermined

You are to examine each question carefully, make your judgment of the conclusion and then record the *number* of your judgment in the regular manner. Judgment number 5 (undetermined) is to be used when you believe that the statement of fact does not give you sufficient information to enable you to judge the conclusion at all. In each case, *assume that the statement of fact is true.*

Answers

EXAMPLE: Most thunderstorms are accompanied by lightning, rain and a high wind.
Conclusion: There will be a high wind with our
next thunderstorm.   1 2 $\not{3}$ 4 5

Work the problems below:

1. John is older than Jim. Jim is older than Bob.
   Bill is older than Bob.
   Conclusion: Bill is older than John.   1 2 3 4 5
2. It is known that only five persons have had this book and
   it is improbable that four of them would have written
   these new marginal notes in it.
   Conclusion: James, the fifth person, wrote these notes. 1 2 3 4 5

PRACTICE BOOKLET (*Cont.*)

Part II: Interpretation of Experiments.

Although this test deals with scientific observations, it assumes no previous study of the subject-matter involved. Each question itself provides all information necessary for selection of the correct answers. It is therefore a test not of knowledge but of ability to reason logically from the facts presented and of judgment in forming conclusions. Note that the "evidence" presented is hypothetical and *may be* contrary to fact.

DIRECTIONS: In each of the following exercises, certain data are presented. Below the descriptions of the data are several statements which have been suggested as possible interpretations. Assume that the facts given in the description and in the results are correct. Then on the basis of *these facts only,* consider each statement. One of five possible judgments can be made for each interpretation:

1. The evidence is sufficient to make the statement necessarily true.
2. The evidence is sufficient to make the statement necessarily false.
3. The evidence suggests that the statement is probably true.
4. The evidence suggests that the statement is probably false.
5. There is insufficient evidence to make a decision concerning the statement.

EXAMPLE: In studying the habitats of red maple trees, they were found growing only in swamps, along rivers and in bogs. In studying the habitats of American elm trees, they were found growing only in swamps, along rivers and in bogs. In all of these different habitats, the leaves of the maples were always opposite on the branches and the leaves of the elms were always alternate on the branches.

Answers

INTERPRETATIONS:

a. The habitats in which the two kinds of trees grew did not affect the position of leaves on the branches.   1̸ 2 3 4 5
b. A certain amount of water was necessary for both kinds of trees to grow.   1 2 3̸ 4 5
c. American elms were affected more by the environment than were red maples.   1 2 3 4̸ 5
d. The leaves were always opposite on the branches of American elm trees.   1 2̸ 3 4 5
e. Cedar trees are also found growing in swamps, along rivers and in bogs.   1 2 3 4 5̸

PRACTICE BOOKLET (*Cont.*)

Part III: Word Analogies.

DIRECTIONS: In each of the following items, notice the relation between the first two words, then cross out the numbers of the TWO WORDS having most nearly the *same relation as the two given* words. Remember to cross out the numbers corresponding to TWO WORDS, as no partial credit is given for one number correctly marked.

Answers

EXAMPLE: execution: lynching   (1-order,   2-command,
              3-obedience, 4-society, 5-lawlessness, 6-savage) 1̸ 2 3 4 5̸ 6

Work the problems below:

1. marrow: bone   (1-fist, 2-gist, 3-boxing, 4-argument,
     5-millstone, 6-neck)   1 2 3 4 5 6
2. infringement: copyright   (1-sin, 2-trespass, 3-wrong,
     4-faith, 5-property, 6-statutes)   1 2 3 4 5 6

PRACTICE BOOKLET (*Cont.*)

TEST IV–QUANTITATIVE REASONING

This is a test of ability to think logically and to arrive at conclusions through processes of induction and deduction from quantitative data.

Part I: Discovering Principles.

The student should note that in this part he must write out his answers rather than select them from a group of possibilities.

You are to examine *imaginary* series of observations. You will then be asked to draw certain conclusions from these observations and to discover relationships and laws.

In principle, these problems are similar to those which confronted our earliest scientists. Since these observations are imaginary, however, the relationships and laws which can be discovered from them are *not* those with which scientists are actually familiar. Therefore, success on this test does not depend upon knowledge of sciences such as physics and chemistry, but rather on your ability to study observations and draw logical conclusions from them.

To fix these ideas in your mind, study the following easy example:

Observations

A	B
6	12
9	18
17	34
7.5	15
8	16

What is the value of B when A equals 13? Answer: 26.

EXPLANATION: It is quickly seen that each number in column B is exactly double the corresponding number in column A. Therefore, when A is 13, B must equal 26. Note that the simplest way of stating this relationship is in the form of an equation. When thus stated, it becomes:

$$B = 2A \text{ or } A = \frac{B}{2}.$$

PRACTICE BOOKLET *(Cont.)*

Work the problems below:

A	B	
8	2	1. When A = 72, what is the value of B?
32	4	2. When B = 0.7, what is the value of A?
18	3	
200	10	3. State the formula in algebraic terms.
50	5	

(Though not stated in the Practice Booklet, this formula is: $A = 2 \cdot B^2$)

Part II: Number Series.

The numbers in each problem are arranged according to some particular scheme. The following example shows you how to proceed. You are to indicate the numbers which come next in the series.

7   14   28   56   112   <u>224</u>   <u>448</u>

Work the problems below:

1.   1   3   5   7   9   ——   ——

2.   2   4   8   16   32   ——   ——

3.   1   4   9   16   25   ——   ——

Part III: Relationships.

Study the symbols below. They are commonly used to stand for certain relationships.

= means "is equal to"
< means "is less than"
> means "is greater than"

Using the information under GIVEN FACTS, find the symbol which expresses the most exact relationship between the two letters under CONCLUSION. Then cross out the number corresponding to that symbol. Work the problems below. The first one is done correctly.

GIVEN FACTS	CONCLUSION	=	<	>	
1. A = B; C = B	therefore A	~~1~~	2	3	C
2. A = B; C < B	therefore A	1	2	3	C
3. A > B; C = B	therefore A	1	2	3	C

PRACTICE BOOKLET (*Cont.*)

TEST V—MATHEMATICAL INGENUITY

This is a test to measure aptitude in mathematics.

Part I: Solve for x.   *Answers*

1. $\dfrac{4}{x} = \dfrac{x^2}{2}$ x = ?   0, 1, $\not{2}$, 3, 4

2. $2x + \dfrac{4x^3y}{2x^2y} = 8$ x = ?   0, 1, 2, 8, 16

Part II

In the problems below, you are given a sentence which expresses a certain relationship, with five equations written after it. *One* of these equations correctly expresses the relationship stated in the sentence. Find this equation and mark its identifying key number.

                                                                         Answers

1. The area (A) of a rectangle is equal to the product of the two sides (s_1 and s_2).

   (1) $A = 2s_1 s_2$ (2) $A = s_1 + s_2$ (3) $A = s_1 \cdot s_2$

   (4) $A = s_1$ (5) $A = s_2$ 1 2 $\not{3}$ 4 5

2. The energy (E) of a moving body is equal to one-half the mass (m) times the square of the velocity (v).

   (1) $E = \frac{1}{2}(mv)^2$ (2) $E = \frac{1}{2}m^2v$ (3) $E = \frac{1}{2}mv^2$

   (4) $E = mv^2$ (5) $E = \frac{1}{2}m$ 1 2 3 4 5

PRACTICE BOOKLET (*Cont.*)

Part III: (Note: Figures in this section are not necessarily drawn to scale.)

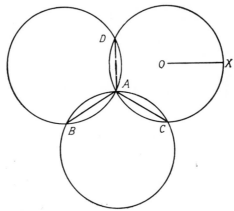

Given: AB = AC = AD   *Answers*

Radius OX = $\sqrt{3}$

The three circles   Hence: AB = ?   1   2   3   4   5

have equal radii   (1)   (1.15) (1.73^{+}) (1.75) (2)

Part III of the secondary school Mathematical Ingenuity Test represents a learning problem which cannot well be illustrated in advance.

TEST VI–SPATIAL RELATIONS

Part I: Each pile of blocks below has been made by gluing together CUBES of the same size. After being glued together, each pile was *painted on all sides except the bottom.* You are to examine each figure and determine HOW MANY CUBES have, respectively: none of their sides painted; just one of their sides painted; just two of their sides painted; just three of their sides painted; just four of their sides painted; just five of their sides painted.

PRACTICE BOOKLET (*Cont.*)

EXAMPLE:

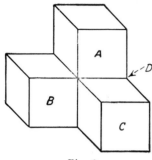

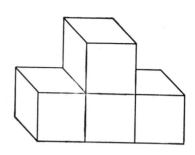

Fig. 0.   Fig. 1.

In Fig. 0, how many CUBES have:	*Answer*
1. none of their sides painted?	0
2. just one of their sides painted?	0
3. just two of their sides painted?	1
4. just three of their sides painted?	0
5. just four of their sides painted?	2
6. just five of their sides painted?	1

EXPLANATION: There are four cubes in Figure 0. Cube A has just five painted sides. Similarly, Cube B and Cube C have just four painted sides each. Cube D, hidden from sight by the others (underneath Cube A), has only two painted sides. There are, then, no cubes with none of their sides painted, nor are there any with just one or just three painted sides. There are, however, one cube with two painted sides, two with four, and one with five, and the answers would be as shown.

PROBLEM: In Fig. 1, how many CUBES have: *Answer*

1. none of their sides painted?
2. just one of their sides painted?
3. just two of their sides painted?
4. just three of their sides painted?
5. just four of their sides painted?
6. just five of their sides painted?

PRACTICE BOOKLET (Cont.)

Part II

DIRECTIONS: The pictures that follow (except for B and D which are drawn in perspective) are "orthographic" views of various solid objects. That is, the projection of the object looking *down* on it is shown in the upper left-hand corner; the projection looking at it from the *front* is shown in the lower left-hand corner; and the projection looking at it from the *end* is shown in the lower right-hand corner. These views are *always* in the same positions. Figure A is an orthographic view of a simple block. The conventional perspective view is shown in Figure B. If there were a square hole in the block, the views would look like C and D. Lines that cannot be seen *on the surface* in any view are dotted.

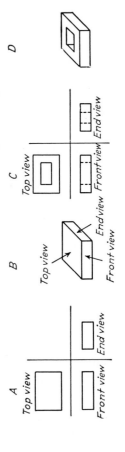

PRACTICE BOOKLET (*Cont.*)

In problem E, two views are shown, with four alternatives to complete the set. You are to select the correct one. Since the front and top views are given, it is the end view that must be missing. The front view shows that there is a smaller block on the base and that there is no hole. The top view shows that the block is round and in the center of the base. The answer, therefore, must be number 2.

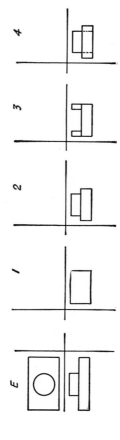

PRACTICE BOOKLET (*Cont.*)

Part III

Look at Figures 1 through 6. They are made up of Figure A, which appears in the left-hand margin, plus one of the figures shown at the top. Study each figure until you can identify the parts from which it is made. If you wish, you may draw lines dividing the figures into their parts. Now compare the parts with their original positions at the top and in the left-hand margin and see whether or not they have been *turned over* so that the face of the figure not seen in the original position is now facing toward you. In the case of each figure, decide *how many of its parts must necessarily have been turned over* (not how many COULD have been). Note that a figure can be *turned around* without being *turned over*. Now decide how many parts, if any, in each figure have necessarily been *turned over*. Note that the correct answers to the first four figures have been placed in answer boxes beneath the figures to help you study them.

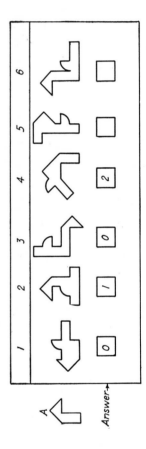

PRACTICE BOOKLET (*Cont.*)

TEST VII–MECHANICAL INGENUITY

DIRECTIONS: Read the following description of the diagram and then answer the questions.

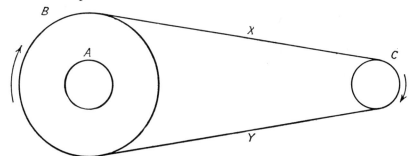

DESCRIPTION: Pulleys A and B are jointed firmly so that they turn together. XY is an elastic belt. C is the driven pulley.

1. In order to make C revolve in the direction opposite from that which is shown, would you

Answers

   (1) put the belt around A?
   (2) reverse one end of belt?   1 2 3
   (3) leave it as it is?

2. If B is larger than C, which turns faster?

   (1) B
   (2) C   1 2 3
   (3) Both turn at the same rate

3. If belt XY were replaced by a belt connecting A and C, will C move

   (1) faster?
   (2) slower?   1 2 3
   (3) at the same rate?

Before leaving the topic of scholastic-aptitude, or intelligence, tests, it should be repeated that the few samples included here are only illustrative of a wide variety of tests that have been developed in an effort to determine the probable learning abilities of individuals. Such tests must be used and interpreted wisely. Some of them must be administered individually and by trained persons. Others, of the pencil-and-paper variety, can be given to groups of people at the same time. As a classroom teacher you may have little to do with the administration of such tests, but your effectiveness as a teacher will be improved if you are able to interpret wisely the results that are made available to you.

If you have a record of the scholastic aptitude of each student in your classes, this will serve as a helpful indication of the level of achievement to be expected in each case. Remember to interpret such measures wisely. They are but one means of getting a total picture of the individual student. Such test scores should be only a starting point in your efforts to have each student develop to the greatest extent possible while under your guidance.

Perhaps the best advice would be to suggest that before trying to make use of any such test results you study carefully the manuals accompanying the tests. This is not often done by individual teachers, but it is nothing more than a logical approach to the problem. If you were a competent shop teacher, you would make it a point to become intimately acquainted with each new machine or piece of equipment that is placed in your shop. Keep this thought well in mind as you come in contact with the scores made on tests with which you are unfamiliar. They are among the most important of the tools placed at your disposal. Treat them properly, and develop skill in using them.

Special-aptitude Tests

We pass now to a brief discussion of other types of aptitude tests—those pertaining to special abilities. In a sense any test is an aptitude test if it provides a measure that is useful in predicting probable success in a specified field of work. When we speak of a person's aptitudes, we refer to his *potentialities*. They may be high, but his success is not therefore guaranteed. Rather, we say, "he has what it takes to be successful." It follows that a high score on an aptitude test is not a guarantee of success but a carefully determined *estimate* of what the individual should be able to do.

Scholastic aptitude, as described in the previous section, pertains to potential learning ability. Scholastic-aptitude (intelligence) tests provide scores by means of which we estimate a person's probable success in various learning situations. Such tests have sometimes been called "general-aptitude tests" in the sense that they measure general learning ability. For comparative purposes this term is useful although the inference should not follow that scholastic aptitude is therefore general in nature. We saw how the newer tests are differential in nature; that is, they provide information about several specialized learning abilities.

A great variety of so called "special-aptitude tests" have been designed to measure *relative fitness* for special types of work. Such things as manual dexterity, visual acuity, musical ability, and clerical aptitude are illustrative of the areas in which special-aptitude tests operate. It should be understood that such tests do not endeavor to measure future accomplishments. Rather, they are designed to find out systematically what a person can do *now*. On the basis of these present abilities it is possible to *estimate* future success (in terms of probabilities, not certainties). It follows that the making of an aptitude test is more than a process of assembling a group of test items or performance tasks. The test has little value until its predictive qualities have been proved. Bingham tells of a mechanical-ability test that was more closely related to future progress in clerical work than many tests designed expressly for that purpose. Similarly, a particular aptitude test for office workers was more useful in predicting the progress of apprentice machinists than was the mechanical-ability test mentioned above.[13] The name is sometimes misleading.

Let us consider this point from a slightly different angle. Suppose that you have constructed a set of ten wooden puzzles ranging from very simple to very difficult. Suppose further that for several years you have had a considerable number of freshman engineering students try to work the puzzles, keeping a careful account of the scores. You then watch closely the progress of the students. It might be that ability to work your puzzles is in no way related to

[13] W. V. D. Bingham, *Aptitudes and Aptitude Testing*, p. 9.

success in the school of engineering. For purposes of illustration, however, let us assume that there is a very striking relationship. You find that nearly all the students who fall by the wayside are those who were unable to complete more than five of your puzzles. You find further that no person who was able to complete seven puzzles was later dropped for scholastic reasons. You would then

Fig. 8. Spatial-relations test, sometimes called "wiggly-block test." Accuracy of visualization and speed are factors measured by this type of test.

have a very useful aptitude test for counseling with prospective engineering students. Any person unable to complete five puzzles would be likely to have difficulty in the school. Any person who could complete seven puzzles would be likely to have sufficient ability to be a successful student. This oversimplified example illustrates again that any test is an aptitude test if it provides an accurate and useful measure of relative fitness for a particular calling.

The accompanying examples (Figs. 8 to 17), adapted from *Life*,[14] show several types of special-aptitude tests used by the

[14] Feb. 1, 1943. Used by permission.

U.S. Employment Service. There are many others. The point to keep in mind is that these tests have been developed to aid in determining whether a person has certain special abilities that fit him for a particular type of work.

Fig. 9. Block test consists in picking up small disks of wood and putting them into the holes in the board. Sometimes the disks must be turned over. In other tests they must form a particular pattern. This is a fairly simple test with the results judged largely on speed alone.

Interest Inventories

An interest inventory is an organized method of listing or inventorying a person's likes and dislikes (his interests). These interests are then related to those of other persons in specific groups of occupations or areas of activity. In other words, if you were to complete an interest inventory, you could find out whether your interests are similar to those of teachers or more closely related to the business group, the science group, or other groups of occupations.

Fig. 10. Tweezer-dexterity test requires the person to pick up the pegs with tweezers and put them into holes. Various tasks are possible. This test helps to determine aptitude for working with small tools.

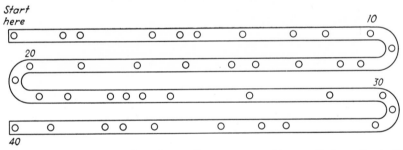

Fig. 11. Dotting test requires the applicant to move his pencil along the path in which the circles lie and put a dot in the middle of each circle. The circles are spaced irregularly to make it harder. A good scorer would finish these accurately within 10 seconds.

Interest inventories are not tests in the usual sense of the word. There are no right or wrong answers. There is no passing or failing score. The individual merely checks whether he likes, dislikes, or is indifferent to a variety of situations. The response to a single point may mean little, but the several hundred reactions help to

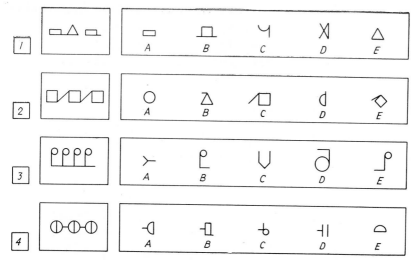

Fig. 12. Geometrical-design problems call for shape recognition. Design shown in small box is composed of one element repeated plus element labeled A, B, C, D, or E in box at right. Object is to tell which element is used to continue design. In No. 1, answer is E.

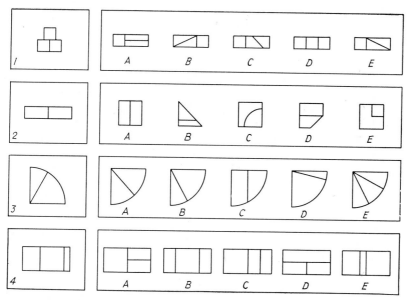

Fig. 13. Scrambled designs are shown here. The object is to find which of the elements (A, B, C, D, E in big boxes) are used to make designs shown in the small boxes at left. Answer for No. 1 is D. Good scorer would answer all these within 10 seconds.

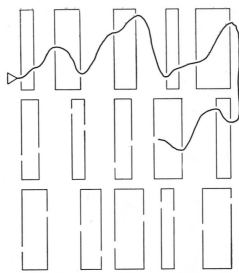

Fig. 14. Maze problem is not hard to understand but requires a steady hand. Applicant starts at triangle in upper left-hand block and draws line through openings in blocks, being careful not to touch the printed lines. Good time for complete problem: 20 seconds.

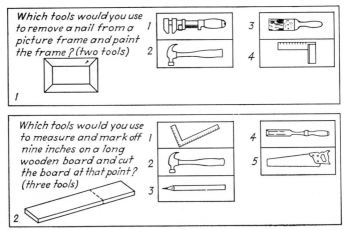

Fig. 15. Tool-recognition test is given to find out what the applicant might know about the uses of tools. Poor performance would show that the applicant had little or no knowledge of carpentry. Good time in which to answer these two problems: 20 seconds.

indicate a pattern of interests—the direction in which a person's interests lie. The final outcome provides a good indication of whether a person would be happy or satisfied in specified types of work. An interest inventory does not specify the extent of success, although interest and ability are undoubtedly related in a positive manner.

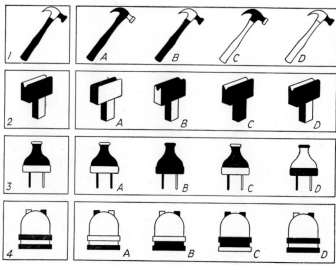

Fig. 16. Another recognition question asks the applicant to look at the picture in the box on the left-hand side, then quickly pick out the matching picture from among those in the group shown at the right. Good time for answering these questions: 15 seconds.

Bingham[15] provides four reasons for trying to measure a person's vocational interests. The first has been mentioned already: to determine whether a person would be satisfied in doing a particular type of work. A second reason is to ascertain whether an individual is likely to be interested in the same things as other people in the work—whether the personal relationships will be congenial. Third, a person will tend to do better at those things which interest him most, although it does not follow that high interest indicates high ability (the relationship is positive, but not necessarily close) . Finally, a measurement of interest may call attention to a field of activity about which the individual has given little thought.

[15] *Op. cit.,* p. 61.

In other words, his attention could be called to a certain occupation or group of occupations that had been overlooked or never considered.

Interest inventories are relatively easy to administer. Some of

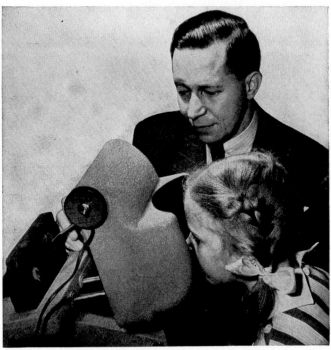

Fig. 17. This instrument, a telebinocular, is used in measuring aptitudes related to visual acuity.

them are difficult to score and must be handled by a trained person. Among the most widely used interest inventories are the following: Strong's Vocational Interest Blank for Men, Cleeton's Vocational Interest Inventory, Kuder's Preference Record, and Thurstone's Vocational Interest Schedule. The following sample taken from Cleeton's inventory[16] indicates the nature of the items used in such measuring devices (pages 65 to 68).

[16] Published by McKnight & McKnight, Bloomington, Ill. Used by permission.

FORM A   **MEN**

Cleeton
VOCATIONAL INTEREST INVENTORY
Compiled by
GLEN U. CLEETON
Professor of Industrial Psychology
Carnegie Institute of Technology; Pittsburgh, Pennsylvania

NAME (Print) ....
        (Last Name)   (First Name or Initials)

STREET ADDRESS .... SCHOOL...........,....

CITY .... STATE ....,..

AGE: Yrs. .... Months .... TELEPHONE...................

Grade completed in elementary school: 1 2 3 4 5 6 7 8

Years completed of high school: 1 2 3 4 Of college: 1 2 3 4

Other educational qualifications ....
Types of jobs at which you have worked:

1. ....

2. ....

3. ....
What kinds of work do you feel you are best prepared to do at present?

1. ....

2. ....
If you were financially able, and free to choose without restriction, what

kind of work would you like to prepare for? ....

....

Do you have any physical handicaps which might interfere with work in

any field? Indicate nature ....

....

Indicate any special skills which might have vocational value.

1. ....

2. ....

3. ....

Turn This Page and Study Directions Carefully
Fig. 18a.

*Fig. 18. The Cleeton Vocational Interest Inventory. A sample of the type of
material included in such a measuring device.*

65

How to Mark Answers on Machine Scoring Form

If your teacher gives you a separate answer form DO NOT MARK ANYTHING ON YOUR QUESTION BOOKLET. In that case fill out blanks and mark answers on the special form. Your answer form will be scored by an electrical test-scoring machine. This machine will score your test accurately if you observe the following directions carefully:

1. Study each item or question and decide which answer you wish to make. Remember that "+" is to indicate that you like the thing mentioned or that you wish to answer *Yes,* and "O" is for things you dislike and when your answer is *No.*

2. Find the pair of dotted lines numbered the same as the questions you are answering and indicate the answer you wish to make by blackening the space between these lines under either "+" or "O" with a soft pencil. **Be sure that the line you mark is in the row numbered the same as the question you are answering. Misplaced answers are counted as wrong answers.**

3. Indicate each of your answers with a *solid black pencil mark.* Solid black marks are made by using an extra soft pencil, by going over each mark two or three times, and by *pressing firmly on your pencil.*

4. If you change your mind, erase your first mark completely.

5. Keep your answer sheet on a hard surface while marking your answers.

6. Make your marks as long as the dotted lines.

The machine will not give you a correct score unless you indicate answers with solid black pencil marks. Do not leave any stray marks on the answer sheets; erase all marks except those intended for answers.

A sample is given on page 4 that shows the way in which you are to mark your answers on the separate answer form. Turn to page 4 and study the example and remaining instructions carefully.

Fig. 18b.

Personality Instruments

Personality is an inclusive term. There have been many definitions. For our purpose we can think of personality as being "the whole person in action."[17] Perhaps the simplest approach to an

[17] Willard C. Olson, "Personality," *Encyclopedia of Educational Research,* p. 794.

Men's Vocational Interests PAA

GROUP A

1. Astronomer .... (.+.)
2. Bacteriologist .... (.O.)
3. Carpenter .... (.+.)
4. Chemist .... (.+.)
5. Dentist .... (.O.)
6. Drug manufacturer .... (.O.)
7. Explorer .... (.O.)
8. Hospital laboratory
    worker .... (.....)
9. Instrument maker .... (.....)
10. Nerve specialist .... (.....)
11. Optician .... (.....)
12. Pharmacist .... (.....)
13. Physician .... (.....)
14. Specialist in mental
    diseases .... (.....)
15. Public health officer .... (.....)
16. Scientific research
    worker .... (.....)
17. Sculptor .... (.....)
18. Ship's officer .... (.....)
19. Surgeon .... (.....)
20. Watchmaker .... (.....)

GROUP B

21. Anatomy .... (.....)
22. Botany .... (.....)
23. Cabinetmaking .... (.....)
24. Hygiene .... (.....)
25. Nature study .... (.....)
26. Physiology .... (.....)
27. Zoology .... (.....)
28. Pet monkeys .... (.....)
29. Cowboy movies .... (.....)
30. Side show freaks .... (.....)
31. Animal zoos .... (.....)
32. National Geographic
    Magaz ne .... (.....)
33. Detective stories .... (.....)
34. Sick people .... (.....)
35. Nervous people .... (.....)
36. Luther Burbank,
    plant wizard .... (.....)
37. Laboratory work .... (.....)
38. Health resorts .... (.....)
39. Gardening .... (.....)
40. Applying antiseptics .... (.....)

GROUP C

41. Working for yourself instead of others .... (.+.)
42. Emphasis on quality of work .... (.+.)
43. Can you meet emergencies quickly? .... (.+.)
44. Work which is interesting with modest income .... (.+.)
45. Do you usually drive yourself steadily? .... (.+)
46. Do you have few intimate friends? ....
47. Work requiring technical responsibility ....
48. Giving first aid assistance ....
49. Being a member of a professional soci
50. Similarity in work ....
51. Do you dislike taking ord
52. Operating a small busi
53. Small pay with opp
54. Being chairman
55. People who pr
56. Repairing
57.

Fig. 18c.

introductory understanding of personality tests is to consider them as instruments that endeavor to measure the personal adjustment and the social adjustment of an individual. This is an oversimplification, but it will suffice if you keep in mind that personality measurement is a complex matter and cannot presently be approached by means of a single test or similar device.

DO NOT WRITE ON THIS PAGE

If you have filled in all the answers to the bottom of page 14, you have completed the test. Hand in your booklet. This page and the one which precedes it are to be used by your teacher or counselor.

INTERVIEW RECORD
(See Manual of Directions)

Teacher or counselor will record here the results of interview with student.

Favorite subjects: 1.................................... 2....................................

Chief sports and recreations: 1.................................... 2....................................

Hobbies: 1.................................... 2....................................

Health: Excellent.... Above Average.... Average.... Below Average.... Poor....

Work preferences:

    Preference for work with PEOPLE

      ....Directly: As in selling, personal service, or professional contacts.

      ....Indirectly: As by writing or advertising where people are influenced without direct contact.

    Preference for work with THINGS

      ....Directly: With materials themselves, in producing, handling, storing, transporting, etc.

      ....Indirectly: With symbols of things, as in accounting, research, designing, and solving problems.

Results of other tests. Record name of test, score, and rated standing.

1.................................... 2....................................

3.................................... 4....................................

5.................................... 6....................................

RECOMMENDATIONS

Record here advice or recommendations made to student on th
all available information.

1. Vocational: ....

....

....

2. Educ

Fig. 18d.

Personality is unique. It represents the sum total of everything about an individual that makes him adjust in his own way to his environment. The best approach to personality measurement would be a careful and thorough study of the individual, using every measuring device that would be helpful. This approach has been used in certain instances, but it can be seen readily that time and money are inhibiting factors which preclude widespread application of this method.

A wide variety of group tests and similar instruments have been devised in an effort to measure how well an individual is adjusted personally and socially. Before describing one or two measures of this type, it might be well to consider the major traits that have received most attention. Teachers, as well as psychologists, will be interested in these traits, since they are related to classroom behavior. Among the more important are the following (listed in terms of comparative extremes) :[18]

Introvert—extrovert	Careful—careless
Ascendant—submissive	Fearful—fearless
Unsocial—social	Lazy—industrious
Unreliable—reliable	Suspicious—trustful
Dishonest—honest	Rude—courteous
Noncooperative—cooperative	Cold—affectionate
Shy—bold	Sluggish—overactive
Quiet—talkative	Slovenly—neat
Even-tempered—hot-tempered	Carefree—worrying
Calm—excitable	Unhappy—happy
Cautious—impulsive	Dependent—independent

Even a casual glance at this partial list of traits will help to indicate the complexity of a "total personality." It is doubtful if any trait exists independently of the others. There is an overlapping, close relationship that makes it difficult to isolate particular traits for systematic study. There are numerous problems that lie in the path of a scientific approach to the measurement of personality, although these need not be considered in our effort to obtain an introductory acquaintance with the nature of this broad subject.

Every normal individual makes an attempt to measure personality when he uses his unaided senses to classify people with whom he comes in contact. Each time you say, "He's a nice person, but my! what a temper" or "She is very attractive, but she never says anything," you are utilizing a crude form of evaluation. You have

[18] Taken from Monroe, *Encyclopedia of Educational Research*, p. 788. Copyright, 1941, by American Educational Research Association. Used by permission of The Macmillan Company, publishers.

observed another individual's personality from a subjective point of view. You have given an over-all statement with respect to total personality and have selected a specific trait for particular emphasis. You will be making similar estimates of the various students in your classes. For the most part your method will be subjective observation. Psychologists also use observation in measuring personality traits, but they have refined the technique so that objective reports can be obtained. Objective, scientific observation is one of the important methods used in personality measurement.

Other means have also been used in an effort to evaluate the various traits mentioned above. Rating scales, projection tests, attitude scales, personality inventories, and free association are among the more common types used in this connection. Traxler[19] estimates that nearly 500 tests and inventories of personality have been produced. For the purpose here intended it is not necessary to describe any of these appraisal devices in detail. Rather an attempt has been made to present a few typical examples of the various types of instruments with only a brief introduction to indicate the nature of the device. No attempt has been made to present an evaluation of the several instruments.

The California Test of Personality is a group test, similar to several others that have been developed in this field. In the words of a coauthor, it is

based on the thesis that the desirable individual is adjusted within himself and that he is also capable of adapting himself satisfactorily in a variety of social situations. An effort is thus made to measure *personal adjustment* in terms of (1) self-reliance, (2) sense of personal worth, (3) sense of personal freedom, (4) feeling of belonging, (5) freedom from withdrawing tendencies, and freedom from nervous symptoms; also *social adjustment* in terms of (1) social standards, (2) social skills, (3) freedom from antisocial tendencies, (4) family relations, (5) school relations, and (6) community relations. All of these related categories . . . may be measured in from forty to fifty minutes. The results secured are graphically represented on a diagnostic profile which makes possible the immediate detection of undesirable personality trends. . . . It is possible to determine objectively . . . the way an individual

---

[19] Arthur E. Traxler, *Techniques of Guidance*. New York: Harper & Brothers, 1945, p. 98.

feels, thinks and acts about many of the so-called intangible factors of personality adjustment.[20]

An interesting approach to the measurement of personality is the projection test, wherein the subject is given an unfamiliar task to which he presumably reacts in the same way as he would approach an unfamiliar situation in actual life. Each task is apparently meaningless, as will be seen, although the person being tested is asked to give a meaning in his own personal way. When this has been done the trained observer is able to interpret each person's reactions in terms of established personality patterns.

Perhaps the best known of these tests is the Rorschach (Ink Blot) Test developed several decades ago by the Swiss psychiatrist Hermann Rorschach. In recent years such tests have received an increasing amount of attention in this country and have caught the public fancy, as evidenced by the *Life*[21] illustrations and captions, shown here (pages 72 and 73) to portray the nature of the tests.

The Rorschach test is difficult to apply. It must be interpreted by experts who know how other people have reacted to a given series of ink blots. Following the two examples are the comments of four individuals, a lawyer, an executive, a producer, and a composer. They were asked to react to four ink blots (two not shown here). At the right is an interpretation of these reactions as made by Thomas M. Harris, who teaches a course at Harvard in adapting the Rorschach to job selection.

Purdue Personnel Tests for Technical and Vocational Use

To this point we have investigated very briefly the more common types of evaluating instruments with which a teacher should have some acquaintance—achievement tests, scholastic-aptitude tests, special-aptitude tests, interest inventories, and personality instruments. The several references at the end of this chapter provide a specific and detailed treatment of each type of test and in such manner as is not possible within the few pages of a single chapter. The best way to become thoroughly familiar with these

[20] Louis P. Thorpe, "Diagnosing War Neuroses," *Education,* 63:553 (May, 1943).

[21] Oct. 7, 1946, p. 55. Used by permission.

What Ink Blots Show in People

Below is how Harvard's Thomas Harris interprets the personalities of LIFE's four subjects by their ink-blot responses. Rorschach blot responses are judged not so much by their actual content as by how they compare with the responses in thousands of tests previously given.

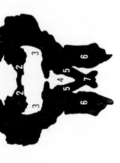

Women at a Table (Whole Blot)
Dog Profiles (1)
Half Moon (White Area) (3)
Stormy Sky (3)
A Building (6)
Legs (7)

Godey's Ladies (1)
Ballet Dancers (2)
Praying Nun (2)
Shoes (2)
Cameo (3)
Smoke (3)
Pine Trees (4)
Santa Claus (5)
Pleading Man (6)
Two Birds on a Branch (6)
Daniel Boone (7)

Russian Eagles (1)
Whelks (4)
B-29 Wings (4)

Dunce-capped Bears (1)
Touching Fingertips (2)
Large-headed Screw Sunk in Wood (3)

Lawyer: Very discriminating kind of mind which can make accurate, fine and detailed observations. She sticks to the facts, is concrete. Has good grip on reality. Self-assertive. Excellent judgment in dealing with people; she has a great sensitivity to their needs and feelings. A liberated mind with ability to adapt. Mind of her own, yet in no way arbitrary. Very persistent, pleasantly aggressive.

Executive: Mind is flexible, not limited to any single approach. He can keep his thoughts in one direction without getting in a rut. Good

Rhinoceros Beak on Hound's Head (5)
Heads of People as Heads on Maces (7)

Fire Tongs (7)
Hedge Clippers (7)

organizer, he sees details in perspective. Pattern has much in common with records of certain types of very high-level industrial personnel. Not easily frustrated, he is a steady sort with great drive and energy. Can adapt well to others while keeping his own independence.

Two Dancers (2)
Series of Clowns' Heads (3)
Two Scotch Terriers Fighting (4)
George Washington Heads (5)
Two Deer Heads (6)
Two Heads (7)

Two Dancers Seated in Tableau (Whole Blot)
Profiles Suggesting Heads (Outer Edge) (1)
Face of Moose (White Area) (4)
Army Insignia (White Area) (4)
Two Heads with Peaked Caps (5)
Two Oriental Heads, Statues (5)

Producer: Remarkable originality, looks at things from an unusual point of view. An excellent observer, discriminating and critical. Brilliant rather than thorough, spasmodically energetic. Very strong self-will, hard to deflect. Extraordinary persistence, especially in the face of difficulties. May actually work better under pressure. Very self-assertive. High in sensitivity.

A formal dance. At top are two women in ruffles (1). Between them are two columbines in ballet skirts embracing (2). Below that are two scrawny stags' heads (4). At each side of a stag is a deformed elder (3). And at bottom are two men in pigtails telling stories (7).

Two demons or dwarfs whose beards are touching (2). They are laughing softly. The protuberances on their heads are like horns (1). Their knees are misshapen. Their feet interlocked (7). They are both seated atop the blades of cleavers (6).

Composer: Does not fall into any of the common Rorschach classifications. Amazingly complex and individualistic, little in common with "ordinary" people. Some elements of this pattern resemble the records of people whose work requires the most difficult and complex intellectual effort. Something uncompromising and rather daring about his record. He will maintain personal integrity at all costs, will not deviate from his subjectively important goals.

several types of evaluating instruments is to obtain sample copies, study the manuals, take the tests, score them, and interpret the results.

Before concluding this overview of various evaluating devices it seems appropriate to include a section which describes several selected tests that will be of special interest to workers in the field of technical and vocational education. Although there have been many published examinations in these fields, few have stood the test of time and careful scrutiny. The following examples, developed at Purdue University, are among those which have been constructed on a scientific basis and have proved useful for the purposes intended. It should be kept in mind that these descriptions are not complete. The complete test manual, together with sample forms, should be obtained and studied by anyone interested in using the tests as a part of his training program.

Adaptability Test[22]

Purpose. The Adaptability Test is designed to measure mental adaptability or mental alertness. It can be used as an employment aid in selecting and identifying not only persons who should be placed on jobs that require rapid learning but also those who do not readily adapt to new situations but who might be satisfactory (or even superior) employees on simple, routine jobs such as packing, inspecting, or assembling or in operating simple, repetitive machines.

The Purdue Mechanical Adaptability Test[23]

Purpose. The Purdue Mechanical Adaptability Test, Form A, is designed to aid in identifying men or boys who are mechanically inclined and who, therefore, are most likely to succeed on jobs in training programs calling for mechanical interests and abilities.

It is essentially a test measuring one's experimental background in mechanical, electrical, and related activities. Its construction is based on the fact that, other things being equal, men who have

[22] Joseph Tiffin and C. H. Lawshe. Published by Test Service Division, Science Research Associates, Chicago, Ill.

[23] C. H. Lawshe and Joseph Tiffin. Distributed by Division of Applied Psychology, Purdue University, Lafayette, Ind.

profited from previous experiences with electrical "gadgets," as demonstrated by knowledge assimilated, make significantly better progress in a course in practical electricity than do those who previously have shown little interest in electrical appliances and simple wiring problems.[24]

Purdue Industrial Training Classification Test[25]

Purpose. The Industrial Training Classification Test is designed to select those persons who are most likely to profit from an industrial-training program. It is designed to evaluate an individual's ability to read simple measurements and solve simple arithmetical problems involving fractions, decimals, and the conversion of decimals to common fractions. These simple but basic skills are essential to success in any vocational school, in the industrial arts, or in industrial-training programs. Combined with manipulative-dexterity and sense-of-space-relations tests, it possesses high predictive significance for school, industrial, and war-work training programs.

This test was originally designed to aid in the selection of applicants for admission to an eleventh- and twelfth-grade-unit trade school. Further experiments indicated that such a test might be useful in the selection and classification of adult trainees, particularly on the preemployment level. Consequently, the test has been adapted to apply in this broader area.

Purdue Blueprint Reading Test[26]

Purpose. The Purdue Blueprint Reading Test is designed to aid industry and vocational schools in determining the ability of applicants or students to read blueprints. The test samples a wide variety of principles and practices in common use. The score made on the test furnishes a reliable index of mastery of these principles.

---

[24] C. H. Lawshe, Jr., and G. R. Thornton, "A Test Battery for Identifying Potentially Successful Naval Electrical Trainees," *Journal of Applied Psychology,* 27:399–406 (1943).

[25] C. H. Lawshe and A. C. Moutoux. Published by Test Service Division, Science Research Associates, Chicago, Ill.

[26] Joseph Tiffin. Published by Test Service Division, Science Research Associates, Chicago, Ill.

The test is self-administering. After carefully reading the title page, the examinees are instructed to open the booklets and begin the test. Thirty minutes of testing time is allowed. The time is sufficient to permit practically everyone to finish the test.

The Purdue Industrial Mathematics Test[27]

Purpose. The Industrial Mathematics Test is designed to measure achievement in simple and basic arithmetic and computational skills required of men in the various skilled trades and also of men on such jobs as setup, layout, maintenance, and design. The test is also recommended for use in formal apprenticeship, trade-extension, and other similar training programs.

Purdue Test for Electricians[28]

Purpose. The test for Electricians is designed to aid industry and vocational schools in determining the amount of knowledge of electricity and electrical operations possessed by applicants or students. This knowledge is of primary importance in the selection of an industrial-plant electrician. This test also serves as a terminal achievement examination in vocational and trade schools and in formal training programs.

Purdue Test for Machinist and Machine Operators[29]

Purpose. The test for Machinists and Machine Operators is designed to aid industry and vocational schools in determining the amount of machine-shop knowledge possessed by applicants or students. The test yields a total over-all score for general achievement in machine-shop practice and separate subscores for the operation of the lathe, planer and shaper, grinder, and milling machine and for general benchwork. The test is particularly useful in the selection of new machinists or machine operators. In addition, the "profile" resulting from the test subscores provides a basic consideration for promotion or transfer or in the formation of a "utility unit." In vocational and trade schools, as well as in formal

[27] C. H. Lawshe, Jr., and Dennis H. Price. Distributed by Division of Applied Psychology, Purdue University, Lafayette, Ind.

[28] Joseph Tiffin. Published by Science Research Associates, Chicago, Ill.

[29] *Ibid.*

training programs, it serves as a terminal achievement examination.

The content of this test was determined from an analysis of a report of the committee on the machine-shop course of study of the Indiana Industrial Education Association, entitled Course of Study, Machine Shop Practice and Instruction.

SOME THINGS TO DO AND QUESTIONS TO ANSWER

1. What type of test would you use to measure the understandings that have been acquired through reading this chapter?

2. Imagine that you have been asked, on five minutes' notice, to talk about different kinds and types of tests before a parent-teacher meeting. On a piece of paper, jot down the names of the various types you would mention. Then add a few notes after each name that would serve as the key points for your talk.

3. Explain how the student results on a scholastic-aptitude test could be helpful to you in your teaching. Where will you obtain such information?

4. Suppose that you were in a school that has just given the Iowa Tests of Educational Development to all the students. Explain what you would do to find out more about the tests and how you could use the results in your teaching.

5. Why is it necessary to make a distinction between measurement and evaluation?

6. Do you think students should be allowed to see their scores on a scholastic-aptitude, or intelligence, test? Why?

7. Outline a simple diagnostic test that you could use in your teaching.

8. Is it necessary for you to have an understanding of aptitude tests? Why?

9. How can you make use of the results obtained on attitude scales in your teaching?

10. Describe the evaluation procedure you would use if you wanted to predict whether or not a vocational school graduate would be successful on the job.

11. Suppose an adult comes to you and asks for assistance in trying to find out the kind of job for which he is best suited. What would you say to him, or how would you proceed?

12 Do you think industry should make more use of tests in selecting and advancing workers? Why?

SELECTED REFERENCES FOR ADDITIONAL READING

Bernreuter, R. G. "The Present Status of Personality Tests," *Educational Record, Supp. 13,* 160–171 (1940).

Bingham, Walter Van Dyke. *Aptitudes and Aptitude Testing.* New York: Harper & Brothers, 1937. Pp. 390.

Buros, O. K. *The Third Mental Measurements Yearbook.* New Brunswick, N.J.: Rutgers University Press, 1949. Pp. xiv and 1047.

Cooperative Achievement Tests (descriptive pamphlet and catalogue). New York: The Cooperative Test Service, American Council on Education. (This is now the Educational Testing Service, New York.)

Crawford, Albert Beecher, and Paul Sylvester Burnham. *Forecasting College Achievement, A Survey of Aptitude Tests for Higher Education,* Part I. New Haven: Yale University Press, 1946. Pp. 291.

Darley, John G. *Testing and Counseling in the High-school Guidance Program.* Chicago: Science Research Associates, 1943. Pp. 222.

Flanagan, John C. *Scaled Scores.* Bulletin of the Cooperative Test Service. New York: The Cooperative Test Service, American Council on Education, 1939. (A useful bulletin for discussion and interpretation of other types of scores. Can be understood by a person with little statistical training.)

Fryer, Douglas. *The Measurement of Interests.* New York: Henry Holt and Company, Inc., 1931. Pp. 448.

Greene, Harry A., Albert N. Jorgensen, and J. Raymond Gerberich. *Measurement and Evaluation in the Secondary School.* New York: Longmans, Green & Co., Inc., 1943. Chaps. 6, 9, 11, 13, 24.

Likert, R. "A Technique for the Measurement of Attitudes," *Archives of Psychology,* 140:1–55 (1932).

Remmers, H. H., and N. L. Gage. *Educational Measurement and Evaluation.* New York: Harper & Brothers, 1943. Pp. 580.

Stuit, Dewey B., ed. *Personnel Research and Test Development in the Bureau of Naval Personnel.* Princeton, N.J.: Princeton University Press, 1947. Pp. 513. (This is a significant publication for specialists in technical and vocational testing.)

Terman, L. M., and Maud Merrill. *Measuring Intelligence.* Boston: Houghton Mifflin Company, 1937.

Thurston, L. L., and E. J. Chave. *The Measurement of Attitudes.* Chicago: University of Chicago Press, 1929. Pp. 96.

Traxler, Arthur E. *Techniques of Guidance.* New York: Harper & Brothers, 1945.

Wechsler, David. *The Measurement of Adult Intelligence.* Baltimore: The Williams & Wilkins Company, 1944. 3d ed.

CHAPTER

THREE: PURPOSES OF
EVALUATION

IN Chapter One it was stated that measurement is fundamentally a two-step process: (1) determining exactly *what* is to be measured; (2) selecting or developing an instrument that will best do the measuring. The process was further simplified by using the two words *what* and *how*. Throughout this book these two words will be repeated again and again. If the authors are successful, you will have them well in mind each time you make a test or each time you devise a test item. You will be asking yourself these two questions: Just what am I trying to measure? How best can I do the measuring? This chapter is devoted partially to a discussion of the first word, "what." The intent is to describe what it means with respect to educational measurements generally and achievement tests specifically.

Some readers will already have been thinking that the word "why" ought to be included as well as "what" and "how." To this point the "why" has been implied. It was assumed that when a person determines *what* he wants to measure he knows also *why* he wants the measurement, or what he is going to do with it. This implication cannot always be accepted. In fact, too many teachers have a very narrow conception of *why* they give tests. For that reason the first part of this chapter will treat briefly the several purposes of measurement in the school with emphasis on the implications for classroom or shop teachers. Following this broad overview the "what" will be considered in terms of several specific points that should be evident in every well-made measuring instrument.

The over-all purpose of evaluation is to improve the work of the school. Keep in mind that the word "evaluation" is comprehensive in nature; that is, it includes all types of measuring instruments (tests, rating scales, interviews, etc.), together with the exercise of judgment. In this and several succeeding chapters the major emphasis is on achievement examinations, but it must be remembered that there are other means of evaluation, albeit they have not been used extensively by classroom teachers. The point to be emphasized is that any evaluating instrument must aid in the work of the school, or it has little value. This means that there is no value in giving a test unless constructive use is made of the results. Every item should reflect what it is endeavoring to measure. With this thought in mind we pass to a brief discussion of the several uses of tests in the school.

Administrative Uses of Tests

In the past, tests were used almost entirely for administrative purposes. Teachers used the results as a basis for assigning marks and promoting students from grade to grade. Administrators scanned the scores when they were interested in rating the effectiveness of their teachers. In certain instances these are still the major reasons for giving tests. The schools in which this practice persists are usually those which conceive their job to be one of pushing students from grade to grade with the hope that by accumulating numerous facts from textbooks the pupils will become acceptable citizens. Such a philosophy is becoming more and more outmoded: the well-prepared teacher of today knows that his job is much more than one of "dishing out" a lot of facts and testing to see whether or not the students remember them.

It should not be inferred from the above paragraph that school marks and promotions must be abolished. Some people might argue for this extreme, but a more intelligent approach would be to strive to put school marks in their right perspective, to make them more meaningful, and to make sure that they are considered as means to an end rather than ends in themselves.

The present-day administrator uses tests broadly to improve the work of his school. Where necessary and when possible, test results will be the basis upon which students are classified or classes are grouped. In some schools it is often possible and desirable to segregate the very bright students or the very dull students into separate classes. The purpose here is not to condemn or uphold this practice but rather to point out that this is one administrative use that is made of test results. Another important use is in the transferring of students from school to school within a system or between systems. In the past some schools prided themselves on the rigidity of their transfer standards and were prone to retard incoming students until they could prove their worth. With the use of good tests and accurate records it is now possible to minimize the ill effects of transferring from one school to another. Of course, some schools are still backward in the tests they give and the records they keep. Yet it is safe to say that positive strides have been made in the right direction and that more and more administrators are making good use of tests in an effort to get an accurate and complete picture of the students entrusted to their care. This departure is closely allied with the growing awareness of the importance of adequate guidance, which is discussed in an ensuing section.

Another important use of tests for administrative reasons is in justifying certain educational expenditures. Boards of education and groups of citizens are justly interested in the facts that underlie the spending of public monies for educational purposes. All of us tend to be creatures of tradition, and it is sometimes difficult to make the public realize the necessity of spending money for a new program or the extension of an old service. Test results are sometimes very helpful in justifying such ventures. For example, remedial-reading specialists are being employed by more and more schools. This costs money, but it can easily be justified on the basis of tests given before and after the program has been introduced.

Supervisory Uses of Tests

The only real reason for having supervision and supervisors is that they aid in the improvement of instruction. This is also the only sound reason for using tests in the classroom. In this sense supervision and testing are very closely related.

The supervisor is a guide and helper. His is a service enterprise, if properly conceived and carried out. He is constantly evaluating in an effort to determine how well the instruction is proceeding and where it might be improved. In accomplishing these goals he uses observation, which is a method of evaluation (a method that could be made much more objective than is usually the case). In order to supplement his observations he also makes use of quantitative measures, such as test results. Effective supervision is more than a process of observing teachers and collecting a number of test scores, but these are the important tools of the supervisor who is genuinely interested in improving the instruction of his teachers. Test results can be useful in evaluating the accomplishments of individual students and classes, in comparing different methods of teaching, in helping to provide for individual differences, and in finding out where the supervisory program needs adjustment or change.

Tests in a Guidance Program

Educational guidance, vocational guidance, social guidance—such terms are receiving more and more attention in the literature of education and in the activities of the school. Administrators, teachers, students, and parents are becoming more and more cognizant of the need for an expanded guidance program which uses every possible means to know the individual and understand him better. In doing this it is necessary to employ a variety of tests and other measuring instruments.

The present-day specialist in guidance is also a specialist in measurement. He is thoroughly familiar with each of the several types of evaluating instruments mentioned in the preceding chapter. He knows how to use them. He knows how to interpret the results. A guidance center is, per se, a testing center. Adequate records are kept for each student. Data on his learning ability, his achievement, his interests, his personal difficulties, and any other significant information are collected, recorded, and interpreted in an effort to obtain a better understanding of the individual. A single, end-of-the-year test score is not enough. There must be many tests and of different kinds. An effective guidance program endeavors, in one sense, to obtain a large number of candid cam-

era shots from every conceivable angle, rather than a single portrait. Added all together the candid shots have much more meaning than a single posed portrait.

Though more and more schools are employing trained guidance workers, this service only supplements the work of the
teacher. Guidance specialists will be the first to state that the classroom instructor continues to have a most important place in the
guidance of individual students. This is another way of saying that
every teacher must use every means at his disposal to know and
understand his students better. Guidance counselors can be useful
to teachers in helping them interpret the results of tests and other
instruments that provide a picture of each student's potentialities
as well as his limitations. Teachers can be of much service to counselors in keeping them informed of student accomplishments, reactions, and difficulties. In either case the accuracy of the evaluating efforts will help determine the effectiveness of the guidance.

Curriculum Development

Well-prepared measuring instruments can be very useful in determining the effectiveness of a particular curricular pattern. On
the basis of test results it is sometimes possible to determine the
changes that should be made in order more completely to attain
the goals that have been set. This approach assumes that tests are
devised in terms of the objectives that have been established. It is
more than a matter of determining how much subject matter has
been assimilated. This is an important point, for it is somewhat
at variance in emphasis from the ordinary tests that are used in
classroom teaching.

The ordinary approach to building a course of study is to have
the instructor, the supervisor, a group of "experts," or the teachers
themselves prepare the course. On the basis of their opinions they
decide what is to be taught, when it should be taught, the order of
presentation, and how much should be accomplished in a given
period of time. There may be nothing wrong with this approach
if all useful data are considered and if the results of the course are
continually evaluated. If this or any similar process is followed, it
is obvious that tests and other measuring instruments will have
to be utilized. They should help to indicate such things as where

changes need to be made, how much should be learned at different levels, and how difficult the subject matter is. In short, the measuring instruments should be devised in such a manner that the real objectives of the course are being measured. This is not easy to do, and it cannot be done entirely by pencil-and-paper achievement tests. The other instruments of evaluation will provide important information.

Tests in Research

Evaluating instruments are used for research purposes having to do with administrative problems, guidance, supervision, curriculum, and all other aspects of the school. If it is true that research deals with the investigation of problems, then it should be clear that it reaches into every part of the school. Scientific research is ordinarily concerned with quantitative measures. Objective tests provide such measures for many types of research problems. For example, one such problem might be to determine the best method of teaching students how to read the micrometer. Suppose that three methods were to be investigated: (1) reading about it in a book; (2) seeing and hearing a teacher demonstration; (3) seeing and hearing a sound motion picture. Several important steps must be followed in setting up such an investigation on a scientific basis, but in this instance we are interested only in the use of tests.

In the first place it would be necessary to have three groups of students that are directly comparable. They must have similar abilities, backgrounds, and so on. It should be immediately apparent that before the teaching methods are tried out there must be a measuring program to determine the similarities and differences within the groups and between the groups. It would be necessary to give intelligence tests and perhaps several types of achievement tests in order to select comparable individuals. This may take more time and effort than measuring the effectiveness of the actual teaching methods being investigated. It may be necessary to find out ahead of time if any of the students know how to read a micrometer. A pretest would have to be given. As the teaching goes forward, it might be desirable to give a series of tests in order to determine the speed of comprehension, the amount of repetition needed, the permanency of the learning, and so on. This description is not a complete explanation of how such a research project should proceed, but it should illustrate several of the uses of tests in conducting research of this kind. This example provides one illustration of why the present-day specialist in educational research must also be a specialist in educational measurement.

Tests and the Classroom Teacher

We come, finally, to the uses of tests by the classroom teacher. This does not mean that the other uses of tests are more important than those of the teacher. On the contrary, this heading would come first if the list were in the order of importance. In this instance the subject has been placed at the end of the list because the remainder of the chapter is devoted to a discussion of tests as used by the instructor.

For teachers, as well as others, the main use of examinations lies in the improvement of instruction. A teacher is a guide. Through his efforts he endeavors to bring about constructive changes in his students. He wants them to grow, to develop, to be able to respond correctly to new situations. This is true of the teacher of English, the teacher of industrial arts, the teacher of office workers, the teacher of part-time evening extension students, the foreman or supervisor on the job, and any person who assumes a teaching role. It is by means of tests and other evaluating instruments (observation, questions, interviews, etc.) that the instructor finds out whether the changes have taken place. In this instance we are studying particularly the uses of achievement tests, and hence the emphasis will be in that direction, although it should be repeated again that there are other means of evaluation that must also be used.

If you were to pause at this point and review several textbooks on the place of measurement in education, you would find a rather extensive and somewhat detailed list of uses by the classroom teacher. For the purpose here intended it has been possible to group the various uses of measurement under three main headings as follows: (1) to aid in improving instruction; (2) to provide a basis for assigning marks; (3) to provide an incentive for application. In considering these several broad headings the approach will be in the second person, since *you*, the reader, are now a teacher, or will soon be using tests to measure the results of your instruction and guidance.

Tests Can Aid in the Improvement of Instruction. This is the first use of tests, and the most important one. The other two major headings that follow are closely related to this use; in fact, they have been grouped separately only as an aid in clarification.

By studying the results of good tests (plus information obtained from other evaluating devices) you can obtain a fairly accurate picture of the way your students learn. You can soon discover what the typical student can be expected to learn. You can determine the relative effectiveness of various methods of teaching your materials. Weaknesses in your instruction will be revealed. You may find that certain parts of your course need added emphasis and that your methods of teaching need to be modified or augmented by other methods. Each of the above points might be illustrated by a variety of examples, but that does not seem necessary at this stage. *The important consideration is to emphasize the necessity for studying the results of your tests in order to make your instruction more effective.*

As you plan your program of instruction, you will presumably be keeping in mind the needs of all your students. This means that you must know as much as possible about each one. One method for obtaining preliminary knowledge is to review the accumulation of data in the central office. By being able to interpret the test scores and other information found there it will be possible to obtain a good picture of each student's potentialities in your subject, together with other information that will be useful in your classwork. Then, through your evaluating efforts you will be able to ascertain whether each student is achieving in accord with his abilities. As you study the test results of students who are having difficulty, you will be better able to locate the source and reasons for the difficulties.

Tests should be used as teaching devices. Many of the short daily instructional tests are more important for the teaching done in connection with them than for the test scores that are made by individual students. The very nature of tests can make students think about things and state their reactions in a manner that is not always possible with the traditional recitation approach. If you make use of such tests, it might be found desirable occasionally to insert deliberately ambiguous items or controversial questions solely for the purpose of motivating student reaction and discussion. Such tests should not be considered as achievement examinations, naturally, but they can be very useful in a teaching-learning situation. Some teachers who use tests for this purpose also make it a practice to give the tests during the first few minutes of the period, as one means of getting boisterous students calmed down and immediately at work. The implication does not follow that tests will take care of discipline problems entirely, but they can be useful in this respect if properly prepared and administered.

In this connection it is always good policy to return the tests to the students after the corrections have been noted. This general rule applies also to the longer achievement tests. In the first place it seems only fair that the students be allowed to see the extent to which they have been successful together with the items on which they have fallen down. This also provides a good opportunity to reemphasize important points and to do a certain amount of reteaching where necessary. Such a procedure has to be handled properly, with no place for argument just for the sake of arguing. There will be students who try to back the instructor into a corner, but this is not a valid reason for refusing to let the students see their test papers. If time can be justified for the giving of a test, some means should be devised so that the students can review their efforts after the papers have been corrected.

In studying test results in an effort to improve your instruction one precaution must always be observed. If your students make consistently high marks on your tests, this is not necessarily evidence that you are doing an outstanding job of teaching. Before coming to such a conclusion there are several things that must be considered. It is true that the success of a teacher can be judged by the accomplishments of his pupils, but high test scores do not always signify positive achievement. In the first place a test may be so easy that even the poor students get high marks. In another instance a test may be fairly difficult but will yield high scores obtained only by those students who take the time and make the effort to memorize certain things found in the textbook. Such a test may measure memorizing ability with no allowance made for the student's ability to apply the material. Students often concentrate on those things which will enable them to make high marks on tests instead of learning so that they can use and apply the things being taught. Such students learn the testing habits of their instructor and know how to get ready for examinations. There is also the type of instructor who "teaches his tests." He tends to neglect those points which are not included in the tests and thus enables students to make high scores which are not a real indication of achievement.

These several paragraphs can be summarized by stating once again that tests can aid in the improvement of instruction, but only if they are carefully made and if *you* study the results to determine where improvement might be forthcoming.

Tests Provide a Basis for Assigning Marks. Students learn different amounts. In so far as possible you, as a teacher, will be endeavoring to determine the relative amount that each student has learned. You will be endeavoring to rank your students on the basis of their accomplishments. In most teaching situations you will be required to assign a mark to each student. In arriving at these marks you will most probably use test results as an important means of evaluation. In certain training situations you will have to determine which students have reached the minimum standards of performance and which have not. In other instances it will be necessary to mark on a five-point scale. Still other schools continue to mark on a percentage basis, while some institutions have abolished marks in the traditional sense and have resorted to a more comprehensive statement regarding the students' development and achievement. Whatever method of marking is used, its effectiveness will be closely related to the accuracy of the teacher's evaluation.

The reliability and usefulness of traditional school marks have formed a debatable subject for some time. It is not within the province of this discussion to argue pro or con for a particular type of marking system. Rather, it seems logical to expect that we will have school marks of some kind for a long time to come. If these marks are to be more meaningful than in the past, a first consideration will have to do with the development of more accurate measures of achievement. You must learn to make and use tests in such a manner that the resulting marks will be truly indicative of relative achievement. This is a challenge that will call for your best efforts.

Tests Provide an Incentive for Application. In order to gain an understanding of the interest of students in test results, one has only to observe their reactions when test papers are returned for review and discussion. If there is any question about this point, consider your own experiences when you were on the receiving end of tests. Think of the times you have put forth extra effort in getting ready for a test. Some readers will still be very much concerned with their ability to pass the tests that are constructed by their instructors. They will agree with the authors that knowledge of a forthcoming test is a powerful motive to start studying.

It would be nice (perhaps) if all students in a school were interested in learning all they possibly could whether or not a check were made on their progress. This, however, is not the case. A few will put forth their best efforts whether or not tests are given. But the majority will work harder if they know that they are to be held accountable for what has been taught. Generally, the instructor who administers the most rigid program of evaluation gets the greatest amount of work out of his students.

There is one danger in using tests and test results as an incentive to students to apply themselves to work and study. Their interest in marks can be a superficial one, which easily leads to efforts to "hit the test" rather than learn the subject matter for its value now and in the future. Students who study primarily to pass tests usually forget the material much faster than those who are interested in learning because of the values to be derived. A positive suggestion is this: Give rigid tests; give them frequently; *but design tests that require your students to make application of what has been taught.*

What to Measure

To this point we have touched briefly upon a variety of uses for tests in teaching-learning situations, as well as in the other activities of the school. These rather general statements should be sufficient to give an indication of "why" tests are used, especially by the classroom teacher. Details have been held to a minimum in the belief that the remainder of the book will provide a working knowledge of how you can make effective use of tests in your teaching efforts. There still remains the question of "what" to measure, in terms of the purpose that has been established. From now on the "why" will be considered as an integral part of the "what."

In the next few paragraphs an effort will be made to impress *you* with the importance of asking a question each time you prepare a test. In fact, it should be asked each time you start to devise a single test item. You have seen the question before, and it will be repeated again. It is this: *Just what am I trying to measure?*

In physical measurement it is usually easy to state what is to be measured. There will seldom be disagreement in deciding on what is to be measured. At the same time, physical properties can usually be described in specific, unambiguous terms (how much a person weighs, length of a board, etc.) . It was pointed out in Chapter One that this same procedure cannot be followed readily in educational measurement. The need is the same, but the task is much more complex. To take an actual example, it is easy to say that we want to measure the length of a board in terms of inches. Making such a measurement is clear and simple. There is no question about the "what." In an effort to parallel this example let us imagine that we want to measure the achievement of a class in drawing. The first questions would be likely to be, "What kind of drawing are you talking about, at what level, and what constitutes achievement at this level?" Rather than measure in terms of inches we have to measure in terms of many things, and teachers do not always agree among themselves what those things should be.

An investigation of drawing tests would show that some teachers emphasize the copying of drawings from textbooks; others dwell on sketching activities; still others concentrate on problems of visualization; and so on. In a drawing class, or any class, there is a variety of things to be measured. Teachers differ in the things they teach and the goals they endeavor to attain. Even when they can agree on the desirable outcomes they want for their students, it is often difficult to describe these outcomes in specific, meaningful terms. Unless this is done, however, it becomes even more difficult (perhaps impossible) to devise test items that really measure the extent to which the outcomes have been achieved. This leads to a discussion of course objectives which are directly reflected in any good program of measurement.

Unless you, as a teacher, have a clear understanding of the objectives you are trying to attain, you cannot expect to develop tests that will do a good job of measuring those objectives. Looking at it in another way, many of the criticisms that have been heaped upon objective tests and their emphasis on straight facts are justly criticisms of the teaching and learning objectives. If a teacher conceives of his job as one in which he causes his students to memorize numerous facts and remember many steps of procedure, with little else thrown in, then it is to be expected that his tests will reflect this philosophy. There are altogether too many teachers who continue to teach in this manner. Some of them give lip service to the development of understandings, proper attitudes, ability to apply facts, and so on, but these positive goals seldom mean much because no real effort is made to achieve the objectives.

This is an indictment that cannot be taken lightly. It is a justified and valid criticism of many teachers and their teaching efforts. Conceivably, the goals of a course should be well understood and described before any tests are developed, but some teachers may not see the wisdom and practicality of this approach until they ask themselves the question "Just what am I trying to measure?" Of itself this question will not guarantee the automatic development of acceptable objectives, but it will serve to underline the close relationship that exists between the goals that are to be striven for and the tests that endeavor to measure the extent of attainment. Once this is understood, it will be easy to see why the building of a course of study necessitates a constant consideration of the methods of evaluation that are to be used throughout the course.

In the simplest possible terms this means that before you can do very much about making good tests you must know why you are teaching the course and what you expect the students to get out of it. Many teachers would have a hard time explaining this satisfactorily. They are not sure themselves. Is it any wonder that they usually produce tests that are little better than nothing? Without belaboring the point further, the question of *what to measure* can be summarized in a few brief paragraphs.

An effective instructional program has specific, well-defined objectives. These specific objectives are usually expressed in terms of certain desirable skills, understandings, and attitudes to be acquired by the student. The resourceful teacher will allow his students to have an important part in determining these objectives. Measuring and evaluating devices should be designed to determine the extent to which these objectives are being realized. Instructors, supervisors, and administrators must obtain an accurate picture of what the student knows about the subject, what he can do, what kind of attitude he has toward the work, plus any other information that may help to indicate growth and achievement.

The ability to *use* and *apply* the things taught is the important outcome of practical instruction. The instructor must *teach* and *test* for application. A student's ability to write certain facts on paper or list steps of procedure is not sufficient proof that he understands, that he will be able to use and apply the information, or that he will be able to perform the work in a practical situation. Although certain things may be taught in the program which cannot be applied by the student until later, such situations make it even more important that the teaching and testing be in terms of application.

Unless your students are to make use of the things you teach, there is little value in your teaching. Unless your tests measure the students' ability to apply what has been taught, there will be little of real value in your tests.

There is no need to go further into detail as to "what" to measure. *You* are the person who will decide that. The important consideration is that you become fully aware of the necessity for determining the "what" in clear, unmistakable terms. The next section describes several steps that will be helpful in this process.

Steps to Follow in Setting Forth the Test Objectives

In any effective teaching-learning situation the student must be the focal point—the center of attention. The teaching is done to help bring about constructive changes on the part of the student.

It follows then that instructional objectives can best be stated in terms of changes that should occur in the pupils. This is especially true in formulating test objectives since the evaluation must be in terms of student changes.

What are some of the objectives that should be considered? One classification[1] includes eleven major types, of which the last was added by the authors. They are reproduced here to serve as a starting point and check list in considering the objectives that are to be measured:

1. The development of effective methods of thinking.
2. The cultivation of useful work habits and study skills.
3. The inculcation of social habits.
4. The acquisition of a wide range of significant interests.
5. The development of increased appreciation of music, art, literature, and other aesthetic experiences.
6. The development of social sensitivity.
7. The development of better personal social adjustment.
8. The acquisition of important information.
9. The development of physical health.
10. The development of a consistent philosophy of life.
11. The development of useful manipulative skills.

These objectives are stated in general terms. The curriculum builder and, in our case, the test maker must express each objective in terms of the specific changes that are expected in the students. This leads us to the first step in considering the objectives to be measured.

1. List the Major Objectives for Which an Appraisal Is Desired. For a comprehensive achievement test there may be several such objectives. In other instances a single objective may be the point of reference.

As an example of this step let us consider a set of objectives for a beginning course in drawing (junior high school level).

As a result of experiences gained in this course, each student should:

1. Develop the ability to express ideas graphically and solve certain everyday problems through the use of drawings.

[1] Eugene R. Smith, Ralph W. Tyler, *et al., Appraising and Recording Student Progress.* New York: Harper & Brothers, 1942, p. 18.

2. Develop the ability to visualize relationships between a total object and its parts as represented by working drawings.

3. Develop an understanding of the place of drawings in the world of work.

4. Develop an understanding of some of the occupational opportunities in this area of work.

5. Develop a critical attitude toward his own accomplishments (he should be given learning experiences in evaluating his own work).

6. Develop an understanding of the necessity for, and the importance of, planning in drawing and in all the industrial-arts activities that will follow.

In respect to measuring the attainment of these objectives we should probably ask ourselves just what they mean in terms of tests and other evaluating devices. Perhaps this would be clarified if a series of tentative general questions could be formulated to put the objectives into problem form, as follows:

1. Has the student acquired the important facts and principles related to beginning drawing?

2. Has he developed a real understanding of the technical terms and expressions that have been introduced?

3. Is he able to apply the elementary principles of drawing in solving actual problems?

4. Has he developed simple skills in executing the techniques of drawing?

5. Has he developed habits of neatness and accuracy?

6. Has he developed proper concepts and understandings as related to shape and size description?

It will be readily apparent that these several outcomes cannot be measured adequately by using a single type of test. A pencil-and-paper test might be helpful in trying to answer several of the questions, but in item four, for example, a manipulative-performance test would be necessary. Still another type of evaluating device would be needed in determining the extent to which habits of neatness and accuracy have been developed (item #5). Perhaps the instructor would want to devise a simple check list to assist him in this appraisal.

At this point we may not be certain that the above questions constitute all the outcomes in which we are interested. This leads to the next step in the process.

2. Examine the Course Content for Additional Objectives. This is a checking step. It is a means of ascertaining that all the significant objectives are being considered. In reality, it is a part of the first step, but important enough to be emphasized by itself.

The procedure is to consider each unit or topic in the course and ask the questions "Just what is the purpose of this topic?" or "What should the student get from this unit?" Very often this brings to light important objectives that might otherwise be slighted.

When the above drawing course of study was examined in this manner, it was found that the first teaching unit contained an activity in which the students were asked to make simple pictorial sketches (cubes or rectangles). Then, using their imagination, they were to create something different by drawing additional lines. A study of this activity brought forth the following question (objective) to be added to the above list:

7. Has he (the student) developed his creative ability and his ability to use imagination?

This single example is sufficient to illustrate the desirability of this step. Perhaps a similar study of succeeding teaching units would bring forth additional objectives worthy of measurement.

We are now ready for the third step, in which each objective is narrowed down still more.

3. Analyze and Define Each Objective in Terms of Expected Student Outcomes. This is the inventorying step. You list the various elements that are part of each objective. You give meaning to each element by defining it in terms of student behavior. That is, what characterizes a student who has achieved a particular element? How does he differ from a person who has not achieved to the same extent? In other words, you make a sort of job analysis of each objective.

Teachers of technical and vocational subjects will find the traditional trade and job analysis useful in inventorying and defining the elements relating to manipulative skills and related knowledge. Such instructors must not forget, however, that there are other equally important outcomes of instruction—outcomes that also need analysis and definition if their attainment is to be evaluated effectively.

Let us consider question 1 above as an example of how this should be carried out.

Has the student acquired the important facts and principles related to beginning drawing?

The first step would be to list (inventory) all the facts and principles that students are expected to remember. A second step would be to list misconceptions or misstatements of fact that are likely to be made by students who have not acquired the necessary understandings. The proper student behavior might be defined by saying that students who have accomplished this objective will be able to remember and state the facts without having to look them up. They will also be able to recognize misstatements of fact and misconceptions. Perhaps this procedure would be made more systematic and orderly by employing a simple chart with the following headings:

Facts and Principles	Common Misstatements or Misconceptions
1.	1.
2.	2.

An example of a more detailed analysis work sheet is shown in Table 1. It has been taken from testing materials utilized by the U.S. Civil Service Commission. The job in question is that of tracer, an occupation in the drawing field, but on a higher level than the seventh-grade drawing course mentioned above.

It should be repeated that the purpose of this step is to give meaning to each objective and to inventory the elements contained in the objective. It is a laborious process. It takes time. But it is necessary to effective test construction. When completed, this analysis will form the basis for a complete program of evaluation. When tests are made without carrying out this step, they are almost bound to be incomplete instruments.

4. Establish a Table of Specifications for the Test (s). After the objectives have been listed, checked, and analyzed, a table of specifications should be prepared for the test or tests that are to be developed. In essence this table is similar to a blueprint used in

Table 1. Occupational Survey for Test Questions*
Job: Tracer IV C-48.31

Job duties (column A)	Operations (column B)	Knowledge factors (column C)	Characteristics of incompetence (column D)
I. Selects materials.........	1. Selects tracing sheet	Tracing cloth should be used for permanent work Tracing paper is suitable only for rough copying Thin paper is best for quick work Thick paper is best for slow but permanent tracings The three essential qualities of tracing sheets are (1) transparency; (2) erasability; (3) ink absorption Glazed side of cloth may be used for practice Dull side must be used for regular work Vellum is the smoothest type of paper	Selects wrong sheet for purpose Wastes sheets Practices on dull side, places regular work on glazed side
	2. Selects pencils or pens	Pen may be used on vellum Smooth paper has little tooth A soft (3H) pencil should be used on paper with little tooth A very hard (5H) pencil may be used on paper with good tooth Pencil work is ordinarily done on paper Tracing cloth ordinarily requires use of ink	Makes errors in selection for given purpose

* Dorothy C. Adkins, and associates, *Construction and Analysis of Achievement Tests.* Washington, D.C.: Government Printing Office, 1947, p. 25.

building construction. It serves as a guide to the test maker. It shows the emphasis that is to be given to each objective being measured. It aids in the construction of actual test items.

The table of specifications can be prepared in considerable detail. However, for most teacher-made tests the greatest use will be in assigning the number of items that should be prepared for each objective. An example, for a subject-matter test in the field of statistics, is shown in Table 2.

Table 2. A Sample Test Outline*

Broad Outline for a Subject-matter Test for Statistician (*P*-1)

Area of subject matter	*Number of items*
a. General	25
b. Frequency distributions	15
c. Charts, graphs, and index numbers	15
d. Measures of central tendency	15
e. Measures of dispersion	20
f. Measures of correlation	20
g. Other	15
Total	125

Detailed Breakdown of Area *d*, Measures of Central Tendency

d. Measures of central tendency	*Number of items*
(1) Definitions of common measures	3
(2) Advantages and disadvantages of common measures	4
(3) Computation of common measures	4
(4) Other	4
Total	15

* Dorothy C. Adkins, and associates, *Construction and Analysis of Achievement Tests.* Washington, D.C.: Government Printing Office, 1947, p. 28.

The four steps to follow in setting forth the test objectives will be mentioned again in Chapter Five, which describes the entire process of constructing a test. In reading that chapter you may want to come back to these pages and study the method of listing and analyzing test objectives. In fact, you may find it helpful to re-read these few suggestions each time you start to construct a test. They are basic.

SUMMARY

The major purpose of evaluation is to improve the instruction that is being given. An instrument of evaluation will be of little use unless it aids in such improvement. This means that the instructor must learn how to make constructive use of tests and other measuring instruments.

Tests are employed administratively for such things as assigning marks, promoting students, judging the effectiveness of teachers, and justifying educational expenditures. The efficient supervisor utilizes test results as well as observation in evaluating the teaching program under his direction. An effective guidance program in the school implies that tests and other evaluating instruments are used broadly for many measures that will help in gaining a better understanding of individual students. If a guidance program is to be successful, it demands the wholehearted cooperation of all instructors. They must work closely with the guidance specialist and must understand and be able to use the information that he provides about individual students.

Tests can also be useful in curriculum development if they are constructed properly to measure the extent to which objectives are being realized. In many types of educational research well-prepared tests will be an important means for obtaining quantitative measures that bear on the problem being studied.

Classroom teachers, generally, can make more effective use of tests in their teaching efforts. The major purpose, again, should be to improve the instruction that is being given. Tests will also provide one basis for assigning marks; they will be useful in giving individual guidance; and they will serve as an incentive to many students.

These general statements help to indicate why tests are used in the classroom or shop. The word "why" should be considered as an integral part of the "what." Before a successful test can be constructed, the test maker must be able to answer the question "Just what am I trying to measure?" A consideration of this question invariably produces a consideration of the objectives that have been established—the two are closely related. Both the teaching and the testing should be concerned primarily with the application of things learned.

In setting forth test objectives four steps will be found helpful:

1. List the major objectives for which an appraisal is desired.

2. Examine the course content for additional objectives.

3. Analyze and define each objective in terms of expected student outcomes.

4. Establish a table of specifications for the test (s) .

SOME THINGS TO DO AND QUESTIONS TO ANSWER

1. Think of yourself in an actual teaching situation. You are on the job. In what ways can tests be helpful in improving your instruction?

2. What would you like to know about each student that comes into your classes? Be specific. Jot down a list of the things that would be useful to you.

3. Using the list that you have just made, indicate, in each instance, where this information can be obtained. You might carry the process one step further and check those items of information that will be readily available.

4. Suppose that an individual student in one of your classes does not seem to care whether or not he learns anything. In your teaching role, what steps would you take with such an individual? Think this through carefully, and be specific, for you are likely to encounter quite a few individuals of this type. In this instance you are primarily interested in evaluating devices, but do not be concerned if it is necessary to consider other aspects of teaching.

5. What should you know about the guidance program carried on in your school or training establishment? How can you learn about these things? In your opinion, how many teachers know and understand these things? Why?

6. Consider the topic "Pencils." Jot down some objectives that you might wish to achieve if you were called upon to teach "Pencils." Preface your list of objectives with the statement:

"As a result of studying about 'Pencils' the student should

"1.

"2.

"Etc.

Be specific. It will be interesting to compare your list with that prepared by others.

7. In connection with the above list of objectives, consider the ques-

tion of "what to measure." How will you measure the attainment of these objectives? How will this procedure apply in your particular field of interest?

8. How will you make sure that your students are able to apply the things they learn in your classes?

9. Prepare a simple test of two or three items that could be used in introducing a new topic or in developing a class discussion. If facilities are available, it might be well to duplicate the items and try them out on your fellow students in this course. The purpose of this suggested activity is to develop some ways in which tests can be used strictly for teaching purposes.

10. What do you think about using short tests at the start of each period of instruction? Why?

11. Do you think that test results should be the major basis upon which marks are assigned? If not, how would you assign marks?

12. Consider the several major types of objectives listed on page 93. Are you sure of what is meant in each case? What could be done to give more meaning to each of these objectives? In other words, if a school-board member asked you for a written statement on what is meant by any one of these objectives, how would you proceed?

13. List the objectives for a test that might be given in your special field of interest. Then put the objectives into question form. As you do this, jot down the questions that come to mind. They will form the basis for an interesting class discussion.

14. Now, select just one of the objectives mentioned above. Prepare a characterization of a person who has accomplished this objective. What will he do? What will he be like? How will he differ from a person who has not achieved the objective? By carrying this out in considerable detail you will begin to understand the value of such an approach. It will make the job of test construction a much easier one.

SELECTED REFERENCES FOR ADDITIONAL READING

Adkins, Dorothy C., and associates. *Construction and Analysis of Achievement Tests.* Washington, D.C.: Government Printing Office, 1947. Chap. I.

Brown, Clara M. *Evaluation and Investigation in Home Economics.* New York: F. S. Crofts & Co., 1941.

Greene, Harry A., Albert N. Jorgensen, and J. Raymond Gerberich. *Measurement and Evaluation in the Secondary School.* New York: Longmans, Green & Co., Inc., 1943. Chap. VIII.

Henry, Nelson B., ed. *The Measurement of Understanding.* 45th Yearbook, National Society for the Study of Education, Part I. Chicago: University of Chicago Press, 1946. Pp. xi and 338.

Remmers, H. H., and N. L. Gage. *Educational Measurement and Evaluation.* New York: Harper & Brothers, 1943. Chaps. I, II.

Ross, C. C. *Measurement in Today's Schools.* New York: Prentice-Hall, Inc., 1947. Pp. 104–113.

Smith, Eugene R., Ralph W. Tyler, and Evaluation Staff. *Appraising and Recording Student Progress.* New York: Harper & Brothers, 1942. Chap. I.

Tyler, Ralph W. *Constructing Achievement Tests.* Columbus, Ohio: The Ohio State University Press (reprints from the *Educational Research Bulletin*), 1934. Pp. 14–23.

CHAPTER

FOUR: WHAT MAKES A
GOOD TEST

WHEN the question of what to measure has been determined satisfactorily, the next problem is that of devising a test (or other instrument) that will do the best job of measuring. The next few chapters will be devoted to this problem, with emphasis on the procedure to be followed by the teacher in the shop or classroom.

If you were told to construct a fine piece of furniture according to the highest standards, you would naturally be expected to know and understand those standards. If you were not sure of some of the requirements, you would want to find out about them right away. This is also a basic step in learning about achievement tests, how they are built and how they can be used. What makes a good test? What are the characteristics and requirements that must be kept in mind? These are the questions to be answered first.

If a general statement would suffice, these questions could be answered in one sentence—a good test is one that does what it is supposed to do. This thought can be further explained in the following manner:

1. A good test must actually measure what it is supposed to measure (validity).

2. It must do this accurately and consistently (reliability).

3. It must be fair to the students (objectivity).

4. It must pick out the good students from the poor (discrimination).

5. It must be long enough to do the job (comprehensiveness).

6. It must be easy to use (ease of administration and scoring).

All these factors should be present in a good test. They are interdependent. They affect each other. For purposes of discussion, each of the factors will be considered separately, but keep in mind that they are mutually causal and have a direct bearing on each other.

The Test Must Be Valid

A test is valid when it measures well what it is supposed to measure. Likewise, a single test item is valid when it does the job expected of it. This is the most important feature of a good examination.

Suppose that you, as a teacher of mathematics, had devised a test to measure the ability of your students to apply certain principles of mathematics in solving problems in their daily living. If the actual test measured only the students' ability to recall and write down certain facts on paper, it would not be valid. There is a significant difference between memorizing facts and being able to apply them in real situations. This point illustrates a common weakness in most teacher-made tests—too many of them are designed to measure memorization rather than application. In the words of Lindquist, "Good testing, as well as good teaching, should penalize rote learning rather than put a premium upon it. . . . It should be the teacher's objective in test construction so to phrase or present the questions and responses that only a genuine understanding of the concepts will enable the student to respond correctly."[1]

Consider another aspect of validity. A test designed to measure what a student has learned in an English course should measure his achievement in that course and nothing else. If the test is constructed so that a highly intelligent student can determine the correct answers without knowing the subject matter, the test measures general intelligence rather than achievement. Such a test is not valid. It does not measure what it is supposed to measure.

[1] Herbert E. Hawkes, E. F. Lindquist, and C. R. Mann, *The Construction and Use of Achievement Examinations.* Boston: Houghton Mifflin Company, 1936, p. 95.

In an achievement test you are presumably trying to measure achievement. Actually, a careful examination may show that you are measuring something in place of, or in addition to, achievement. In the example of the English course cited above it was stated that the test might be measuring intelligence primarily. The intelligent student would be credited with achievement he had not actually attained. There are other *constant* factors that affect the validity of an achievement test—factors that prevent the test from measuring what it is supposed to measure. A student may be a poor reader; he may have a limited vocabulary; he may have difficulty in memorizing; his reaction time may be slow. These and other, similar factors will tend to penalize certain students in many tests. The total score of such students will not be a valid indication of their real achievement.

Because of these many things which may affect a given test, it is a complex problem to determine validity in an accurate manner. In other words, it is difficult for a teacher to ascertain whether a test is measuring effectively what it is supposed to measure. When you, as a teacher, ask yourself how valid a particular test is, you will have to keep in mind that it may be measuring general intelligence, reaction time, memorizing ability, or some other factor in addition to actual achievement. As you look at the results on a given test with this thought in mind, you might be skeptical about its validity. Skepticism in the right degree is a good trait for any teacher to have, especially if it is followed by efforts toward improvement.

There is no simple formula to follow in determining the validity of a test. In fact, it is unwise to think about validity in terms of a single statement or expression. A test may be valid for one purpose but not another. A test may measure what it is supposed to measure with one group of students but not with another. For example, you may develop an arithmetic test that does very well in measuring the achievement of your students. This does not mean that it will measure equally well the students of your friend who is teaching in another town. You may have tried to measure various things that were not even included in his course of study. His students may be on a much higher or lower level than yours. The objectives of your course may be entirely different from his. All these factors affect validity. Thus in speaking of the validity of a test it must be in terms of definite, specified conditions or criteria.

Let's look at another example. Suppose that you wanted to select a standardized arithmetic test to use with these same students of yours. There are several such tests on the market. Because a certain test is being published and sold, you might possibly assume that it is a good examination and would be worth buying. The manual of directions may state that its validity is high. It may even include a coefficient expressing high validity. Many teachers have bought and used such tests without delving any deeper than this. After giving the test, these teachers may have been perplexed or confused because the test results did not tell them what they expected to find. After thinking it over a little more, they probably condemned the test as being worthless.

In reality, such teachers should reprimand themselves. They may have tried to use the test to measure something that it was not intended to measure. In this respect, they might be compared to the person who tries to use a voltmeter instead of an ohmmeter for measuring the resistance of an electrical circuit. In selecting a published test for your students, you would want to consider its validity from every possible angle. You would want to question it in terms of the level and range of your students, your objectives, plus any other criteria that may be pertinent. After reviewing the validity of various published tests with these questions in mind, you might find one that measures what you want it to measure, or you might give up the hunt and decide to try to construct a test of your own to do the job.

One logical method of determining the validity of a test would be to compare it with some predetermined criterion of validity. Let's consider this in terms of physical measurement. For example, suppose for some reason that you wanted to make a ruler that would measure accurately to within ½ inch. After constructing the scale you could find out easily and accurately whether it measured what you wanted it to measure. Ordinarily you would measure something with your ruler and then compare the results with those obtained on another ruler that you knew to be right. You could say with a high degree of certainty that your ruler was valid or was not valid. You could make the statement with precise figures to substantiate it.

The validity of your ruler might also be determined in a second way. Instead of using two rulers and comparing the results, you might use a standard unit of length (let's assume that it would be a bar of steel exactly ½ inch in length). You would find out how your ruler measures this standard unit in various combinations. In this instance, you would know ahead of time what the ruler should read. You could quickly find out whether or not it was valid. If necessary, you could make certain adjustments to make it valid.

Attempts to determine the validity of an achievement test might likewise follow either of these two methods (remembering that the measurement of such physical properties is more refined than the measurement of human achievement). In the first instance you would have to know ahead of time that a certain test was highly valid for the purpose you had in mind and the students you wanted to measure. Then you would try to develop a second test that was equally valid. As in the case of the ruler, you could give the second test to your students and then compare the results with those on the first test, which you knew to be doing a good job. It is easy to understand this approach and talk about the method, but the difficulty lies in finding a first test that you know is doing a good job. From a practical point of view, very few teachers are in a position to use this method in determining the validity of their examinations.

A variation of the second method is the one most often used, although in a much more subjective manner. What you try to do, in effect, is to get some standard of achievement approaching the ½-inch bar of steel mentioned above. There is no National Bureau of Achievement Standards; thus right away you recognize certain limitations. However, in a properly designed test, you are trying to measure certain specified objectives (as discussed in the previous chapter). They are known. They have been listed. In a crude manner they can be compared to the standard unit of length because they describe what you are trying to measure, just as the standard unit of length describes a much simpler property in exact terms. On the basis of these clearly stated objectives you can submit the test to several competent people who are thoroughly familiar with the content of the field being tested. After studying carefully the various parts of the test in terms of the objectives being measured, they give you their opinion on the validity of the test—they tell you whether they think it will measure what it is supposed to measure. As a result, you may make various changes, corrections, or additions.

To be sure, this is a crude and subjective method when you compare it with the measurement of length and weight, but if carried out thoroughly and conscientiously, it will result in a test much more valid than those ordinarily used in the classroom. In fact, your own, unaided critical inspection will result in improved validity.

One other aspect of validity should be considered in constructing any achievement test, namely, the validity of individual items. It is true that the validity of the total test will be dependent upon how well each item does what it is supposed to do. In many respects, it is more useful and desirable to give first attention to the validity of the individual items than to the validity of the test as a whole. Such reasoning would assume that, if the various items are in themselves highly valid, the total test should therefore be valid. For practical purposes, this assumption can be sustained, although the relationship between validity of individual test items and validity of the total test is more than a process of simple addition.

An important feature in considering the validity of individual items is that a useful determination can usually be made as each item is constructed. It is a process of self-questioning accompanied by a conscientious, critical attitude. In other words, you can determine very well the possible validity of an individual item by asking and answering this one question: Will this item really measure what it is supposed to measure? If teachers generally would make *effective* use of this question in constructing or reviewing their tests, this would lead to a significant improvement in the common run of examinations.

For example, suppose that you are a teacher of physics and are in the process of constructing an achievement test designed to measure the attainment of certain stated objectives. Suppose further that one or more of these objectives pertains to Ohm's law. At the moment you are working on an item or items to measure the student's understanding of the law and its applications. Being innately lazy, like most of us, you first think of a true-false item (or two) that bears on the subject. Perhaps you write something down:

T F Ohms Law is expressed by the equation $I = E/R$ (true)
$R = 1/E$ (false)

T-F Ohms Law is used in calculating the voltage and resistance of an electrical circuit

At this stage you have jotted down some statements with an addition or correction to make the items clearer. In the first item you have also included an alternative possibility in case you desire to make it a false statement. So far your efforts will add two more points to the test, and you feel that some progress is being made. Perhaps you begin to think that there ought to be a multiple-choice or completion item in this material, as you do not have quite enough of these types in the total test. For whatever reason, let's imagine that you look back over the two true-false items. You ask yourself, "Will these items really measure what they are supposed to measure? Are they valid?"

Of course the answer will be "no," for any student could mark them correctly without being able to apply Ohm's law. He would merely have to "parrot" something you mentioned in class or remember something he memorized out of the textbook. This begins to bother your conscience a little bit. You may get a little angry and start rationalizing that there just isn't time to do it right— you'll include the items anyway, even though they could be improved. After all, the students will not know the difference (you hope) , and who else is there to worry about?

This inner argument could go on for some time, but let's imagine that you finally decide that by including satisfactory items now a lot of time will be saved later on. So back to Ohm's law and its application. You are on the trail of one or more valid test items. Let's say your next effort looks like this (multiple-choice) :

_____ *If you wanted to calculate the resistance of an electrical circuit which one of the following formulas would you use?*

    A. $R = \Lambda D^2$
    B. $I = E/R$
    C. $R = VA$
    D. $E = 1/R$
    E. $R = V/A$

As you mull over this item you probably consider it to be better than the true-false efforts. But you still cannot answer the question conscientiously. Again, this item does not measure the student's ability to apply Ohm's law. It measures only the extent to which the student has memorized a formula that you gave him or that he read in a book. On you go in your quest for an item involving application. Imagine that your next efforts result in the following item:

Ohm's Law is expressed $I = E/R$. If, in an electrical circuit there is a pressure of 110 volts and a resistance of 2 ohms, what is the amperage?

                                                (answer)
                          (show your work)

This item does necessitate application, but it is somewhat artificial and requires primarily a resolving of the formula, along with an understanding of what the symbols mean. It is still not as valid as you would like. You make another attempt:

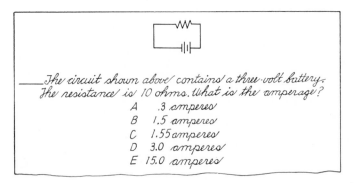

_____ *The circuit shown above contains a three-volt battery. The resistance is 10 ohms. What is the amperage?*

    A   .3 amperes
    B   1.5 amperes
    C   1.55 amperes
    D   3.0 amperes
    E   15.0 amperes

After careful study you decide that this item is the best yet. It presents a situation that calls for an application of Ohm's law. It is not nearly as artificial as the preceding example. The student is not given a formula. He has to deduce first that Ohm's law will apply to this situation, and after that he has to resolve the formula. He has only one chance in five of guessing the correct answer. If he makes a careless mistake, his answer will probably not match one of the choices, and so he must recheck his calculations. This is significant, for you are more interested in measuring application of the law than ability to do arithmetic.

If the above examples and descriptions are as clear as intended, you will now agree that the last item is more valid than those preceding it. If you are a teacher of electricity or physics, you may well be able to construct an item even more valid for the purpose. The point is that this same sequence of events can be followed through in any subject-matter field as such. This does not mean that you have to start out with a true-false type of item and then keep changing it. With very little practice, you can immediately make such items as the last example. It means developing a critical attitude. It means asking the question continuously, "Does this item measure what it is supposed to measure?"

As was stated at the beginning of this dicussion, the most important feature of any examination is its validity. The several other factors (reliability, objectivity, discrimination, comprehensiveness, ease of administration and scoring) might well be discussed as a part of validity, since they affect it either directly or indirectly. These features are treated under separate headings, however, in an attempt to clarify better what is meant in each case. (Other authors might discuss these concepts under slightly different headings.)

The Test Must Be Reliable

A reliable test is a "trustworthy" test. It is accurate. It is consistent. If the test measures in exactly the same manner each time it is administered, if the factors that affect the test scores affect them to the same extent every time the test is given, the test is said to be high in reliability. In other words, a highly reliable test should yield essentially the same score when administered twice to the same student, provided, of course, that no learning occurs while the test is being taken the first time or no learning or forgetting takes place between testings.

It can be seen immediately that reliability is closely connected with the validity of a test. If a test is valid, it must be reliable. That is, if a test measures effectively what it is supposed to measure, then presumably it does this accurately and consistently. At the same time it must be remembered that a test might be highly reliable and still not be valid.

Two examples will further illustrate these points. An ohmmeter is an electrical measuring instrument for determining the resistance (ohms) of a circuit. Like an achievement test, it must be valid and reliable to be of any use. If a particular ohmmeter measures the resistance of a circuit accurately and consistently, we could say that it is both valid and reliable because it measures accurately what it is supposed to measure. It can be depended upon. It has to be reliable before it can measure effectively what it is supposed to measure. Granted that a particular ohmmeter is highly reliable, it could not be used in measuring the voltage of a circuit —it would not measure what it is supposed to measure. In this instance it would be reliable but not valid.

A test in mathematics may be valid for a junior high school class in Arithmetic. In order to be valid it has to be reliable. This same test might also be highly reliable if given several times to an eighth-grade class in general metalwork. But no matter how reliable it might be in measuring the eighth-grade students, it would not be valid because it would not be measuring achievement in general metalwork. To repeat, a test must be reliable in order to be valid, but a test can be highly reliable without being valid.

In discussing validity, you were told that achievement tests very often measure things other than achievement (reading ability, intelligence, etc.). These *constant* factors must be excluded if the validity is to be trusted. Reliability, however, is often affected by *variable* factors—things that are different each time a test is given. Keep in mind that, if a test is reliable, you should get approximately the same score if you take the test a second time. Suppose that on a given test the various items are subjective in nature and the teacher has difficulty in scoring them. He may give credit on one student's paper and mark the same thing wrong on another.

In another instance a student may feel fine the first time a test is taken and get a high score. The second time he may be coming down with a cold and not care about a score. One time the room may be quiet; the next time it may be noisy. Perhaps the test is too short; perhaps the students guess differently each time. These are the types of variable factors that affect the reliability of a test. Symonds[2] lists twenty-five such factors that affect reliability.

One method for determining reliability is to prepare two equivalent forms of the test and administer them to the same group under the same conditions, with little or no time in between. Forms A and B of the test would measure the same objectives but would use different test items. After giving the tests, the scores would be compared to determine the reliability. If the test is high in reliability, the person who scored high on Form A would do likewise on Form B. The low scorer on one would be low on the other. A coefficient of correlation (relationship) would be obtained to indicate the extent of reliability.

While the above method might be satisfactory for determining reliability, most teachers will not have two equivalent forms of the same test. Another approach is to give the same test a second time. This method presumes that enough time has gone by so that the student will have forgotten the details. It also assumes that the achievement level is about the same. In this method the reliability is again determined by obtaining the coefficient of correlation between the two sets of results on the test.

Still another method is to divide the test into two parts (odd items 1, 3, 5, etc., vs. even items 2, 4, 6, etc.) and determine the correlation between them. Theoretically, this is assumed to be a correlation between two forms of the same test. Since each form is only one-half as long as the complete test, a step-up formula is used to indicate what the reliability would be if the length were increased.[3]

In the above paragraphs three methods of determining test reliability have been described as simply and briefly as possible. For the purposes of this text it has not seemed desirable to include a

[2] P. M. Symonds, "Factors Influencing Test Reliability," *Journal of Educational Psychology*, 19:73–87 (1928).

[3] Spearman-Brown Prophecy Formula.

more detailed outline of the various considerations and statistical procedures that must be understood and utilized in the determination of test reliability. This does not mean that such procedures are unimportant or ineffectual. On the contrary, they must be well understood by the competent test maker if he is to speak with any authority on the reliability of his examinations.

But the student or teacher who is just starting to develop a working understanding of test construction, and in this instance reliability, will be more confused than aided by a statistical treatment of the problem. This can and should come later.[4] Suffice it to say that an accurate *estimate* of reliability can be determined by a precise mathematical procedure—provided that a sufficient number of test scores is accumulated.[5]

The beginning test maker should keep in mind that the length of the test, the clarity and objectivity of the items, the simplicity of the directions, and the objectivity of scoring are factors that influence reliability. By concentrating on these considerations, the reliability of teacher-made tests can be improved, even though the test maker may not have a thorough understanding of the statistical determination of reliability.

In other words this means that the reliability of a test can generally be raised by increasing the length. The more responses required of the student, the more reliable the measurement of his achievement. The smaller the chances of guessing the correct answer to each item in the test, the greater the reliability. Clear and concise directions increase the reliability of the test. Confusing directions and complicated and ambiguous items decrease the reliability.

The Test Must Be Objective

Objectivity is an important factor that affects both the validity and reliability of an examination. There are two aspects of objectivity which should be considered in constructing a test. The first is concerned with the scoring of the test. The second pertains

[4] The bibliography at the end of this chapter contains numerous references for the person interested in further study.

[5] Chapter Sixteen contains a further method for determining reliability that may be more suited to the background of the average teacher.

to the interpretation of individual test items by the persons taking the test. Let us consider each of these separately.

The personal judgment of the individual who corrects the test should not be a factor affecting the score. Several people should be able to score the test and get the same results. After the key has been made, there should be no question as to whether an item is right or wrong or partly right or partly wrong.

It is obvious that the so-called old-type, or essay, tests, as usually constructed and scored, register poorly when measured by this standard. Instructors competent to judge rarely agree on the score that should be recorded for a given essay-test paper. They do not have a common *objective* basis for marking. Similar discrepancies result when several shop teachers are asked to "grade" shop projects or drawings on a subjective basis.

In scoring such test papers or projects, instructors often notice that students are making higher marks than usual. As a result, the scorer begins to grade "harder." That is, he begins to take off more points for errors. The reverse of this also happens when the students seem to be making low scores. Naturally, such a system is not objective and should not be tolerated in a testing program. In order to gauge the subjectivity of the ordinary essay, or discussion, type of test, one has only to select several competent instructors of the same subject and have each one score independently the same test paper covering materials that all of them teach. There will be considerable variation in the scores recorded for the single test paper. If the same instructors score the same test paper again one week later, the difference between the first and second set of scores is likely to be large enough to be significant. If you are in doubt about the point, try a simple experiment with some of your fellow teachers or fellow students. Give them an essay-type test paper or completed project, and have each person do his scoring independently with no other instructions than to give a letter mark (A,B,C, D,F) or a percentage mark. Suppose, after the marks are in, you carry the experiment one step further and ask each person to indicate how he arrived at his mark, or why he marked as he did. You will probably receive a variety of answers that will provide some interesting considerations to discuss or possibly argue about.

The above discussion is not meant to serve as a condemnation of the essay-type question as such. It is not to be assumed that such items should be eliminated altogether from tests. The fault lies in the construction and scoring of such items and is not inherent. When carefully constructed, an essay-type item measures well the ability of the student to organize and express his thoughts. Specific points on the construction and use of essay items are presented in Chapter Nine.

So far we have been talking about objectivity as it pertains to the scoring or marking of papers. The second aspect, equally important but more subtle and therefore more frequently neglected, has to do with the students' interpretation of the items in the test. Well-constructed test items should lend themselves to one and only one interpretation by students *who know the material involved.* That is, a given test item should mean essentially the same thing to students who know the point in question. This is a goal that is difficult to attain. Students are prone to read into test items meanings that were never intended by the test maker. In spite of how good a test item may appear at the start, there may be some students (good as well as poor) who interpret it wrongly. Obviously, this will affect the validity.[6]

As you consider this aspect of objectivity, stop for a moment and recall various tests that you have taken. How many times have you thought, "Just what is he trying to get at in this item?" In such instances you may have known well the subject matter being tested but may still have been unable to determine the answer that was "wanted." The item may have been ambiguous; it may have been inconsistent; the grammar may have been misleading; or there may have been some other subjective element that made it difficult to interpret the item. The point is that any person who has taken many tests has experienced this difficulty and should therefore strive to locate and remove or revise such items in the tests he makes or uses. Consider the following true-false item that is not objective from the student's point of view, an item taken from an actual test used in industrial-arts classes.

_____20. The claw hammer is designed especially for driving nails.

[6] This aspect of objectivity is often discussed directly as a factor in validity.

Would you mark this true or false? If you decided on your response hurriedly, go back over it and consider the item carefully. Of course the claw hammer is designed for driving nails. The hammer head is designed for this purpose. The balance of the hammer handle is related to the design and the purpose. But wait a minute. The words "claw" and "especially" must be in the item for a purpose. Your thinking might proceed along this line:

"Does he want me to consider the claw part of the hammer as being designed for pulling nails rather than driving them? It is conceivable that a hammer could be designed for driving nails and still not have a 'claw' on it. Therefore, that word 'especially' must mean that he wants the item marked 'false.' "

This line of reasoning might be carried further, but it is sufficient to indicate how a simple item, apparently obvious to the test maker, can cause consternation and difficulty to the person taking the test, even though he knows the subject matter being tested. The following items, again taken from teacher-made tests, are similarly lacking in objectivity, although possible interpretations are not included after each one. How would you answer these items?

_____ Wire is made from almost any kind of metal.
_____ The hack saw does for the metal worker what the back saw or panel crosscut saw does for the woodworker.
_____ A scratch awl can be used as a center punch.
_____ Benjamin Franklin was primarily an early American printer.
_____ Drill bits used in hand drills have a _____ shank.
_____ In order that an electrical wire will have a usable contact, it is necessary that it be (1) twined together (2) taped together (3) soldered (4) pasted.
_____ Mechanical drawings have (1) one view (2) two views (3) three views (4) four views (5) five views.
_____ The device used to hold different kinds of electric lamps is known as a _____ .

The above examples should be sufficient to indicate what is meant by objectivity from the student's point of view. Again, this aspect is closely related to the validity of individual items. It is a weakness that is found in most teacher-made tests. In constructing and using your tests, you must be constantly aware of student reactions and interpretations. With such an attitude, you will be much better able to detect and correct weaknesses of this type. You will learn to avoid ambiguous items. You will learn to design items that are clearly understood by the students. As a result, the validity and reliability of your tests will be increased.

To this point, we have discussed validity, reliability, and objectivity, as related to test construction. While each has been treated separately, it should be obvious by now that they are closely related and interdependent. There is no fine line of demarcation. Keeping this point well in mind, there are still other factors that enter into this relationship—factors that help to characterize a good test.

The Test Must Discriminate

A test discriminates when it is constructed in such a manner that it will detect or measure small differences in achievement or attainment—when it picks out the good from the poor. This is an absolute essential if the test is to be used reliably for ranking students on the basis of achievement or for assigning marks. Three things will be true of a test that meets this standard:

First, there will be a wide range of scores when the test is administered to students who have actually achieved amounts that are significantly different. If the *full range* of achievement is to be measured, scores are likely to vary from the lowest to the highest possible scores. However, for practical purposes, and for most subject-matter fields, scores should vary from near the highest possible score to a score that is less than half of the total number of points on the test.

Second, the test will include items at all levels of difficulty. That is, the items will vary uniformly in difficulty from the most difficult one, which will be answered correctly only by the best students, to an item so easy that practically all the students will answer it correctly.

Third, each item will discriminate between students who are high and those who are low in achievement. Each item will be missed more frequently by poor students than by good students. If the good students are just as likely to miss an item as the poor students, the item does not measure in a positive direction. It is often found that poor students will answer correctly certain items that the best students miss consistently. Such items discriminate negatively. An examination of these items usually reveals that they are ambiguous or technically weak in other respects. They are not objective from the students' point of view and therefore do not discriminate positively. Several of the examples cited in the previous section (page 117) are illustrative of this point. The good students are able to detect the second, hidden, unintended meaning, and as a result they often make a response different from the one intended by the test maker. In such instances the good students mark the item wrong, and the poor students select the right answer. Again, this is negative discrimination.

As is true with validity, reliability, and objectivity, the discriminating power of a test is increased by concentrating on and improving each individual item in the test. After a test has been administered, a simple item analysis can be made which will help to indicate the relative difficulty of each item and, of greater importance, the extent to which each discriminates between good and poor students. Although this technique is treated in more detail in Chapter Sixteen, a simple example will illustrate one procedure that can be used.

Suppose that you have given an achievement test to eighty students. After scoring the papers you select the twenty highest and the twenty lowest[7] and place them in separate piles. The next step would be to consider each item and compare the responses made on the two sets of papers. Suppose your tally looked something like that shown in Table 1 on page 120 (the items are hypothetical). Your deductions might read something like this:

"Item 1 discriminates positively because the best students answer it correctly more often than the poor students. Quite a few of the poor students answer it correctly; perhaps I should analyze the results of the poor students a little better.

"Item 2 shows perfect discrimination. I wonder why all the good students got that right and all the poor students got it wrong? I must ask some questions about this item. Perhaps my teaching is at fault.

"Item 3 is a puzzler. Actually the poor students answered it right more often than the good students. But only one more of them did this. Some people in both groups omitted the item. It covered an

[7] This is an arbitrary selection for purposes of illustration only. It might be adequate, although there are several things to consider in selecting the number of scores to be compared. These are described in Chapter Sixteen.

important bit of subject matter, too. They should have been able to answer that. Something must be wrong with the item. I don't want to throw it out, but it should be changed.

"Item 4 seems to be doing a pretty good job. Then again, nearly all of them got it right. If they all get it right, what's the use of including it in the test? But all of them didn't get it right. The two students that got it wrong had the lowest papers of all. I'll leave

Table 1. A Simple Item-analysis Chart Useful in Studying the Discriminating Power of Test Items

Item no.	20 papers with highest total score			20 papers with lowest total score		
	No. of correct responses	No. of incorrect	No. omitted	No. of correct responses	No. of incorrect	No. omitted
1	16	4	0	10	8	2
2	20	0	0	0	18	2
3	10	6	4	11	5	4
4	18	0	2	16	2	2
5	5	15	0	15	3	2
6	3	15	2	1	18	1

that question alone for the time being because it seems to be discriminating pretty well at the very low levels.

"Item 5 needs to be changed. It is discriminating negatively. Some of the good students got it right, but most of them got it wrong. At the same time, most of the poor students got it right. Probably the wording needs to be changed. I'll ask some of the good students why they marked it the way they did.

"Item 6 is a puzzler. Only three of the good students got it right. It must really discriminate. But then again, one of the poor students got it right too. Of course he could have guessed the right answer. But the three good students might have guessed too. That is an item that I didn't expect them all to know. The three good students that got it right were among the top five in the test. I don't think they were guessing. That looks like a pretty good item. I'il let it stand for the time being."

This imagined soliloquy is very subjective, to be sure, but it illustrates a first step that might be taken by teachers willing to spend the time and make the effort to improve the discriminating power of their tests. In so doing the validity, reliability, and objectivity are likely to be raised.

Certain cautions should be attached to this approach to discrimination. Because a test is improved to the point where each item discriminates positively, and without any question, does not mean that therefore it is a highly valid instrument. It only means that for a particular group the test has a high discriminating power in measuring whatever it does measure. This is no guarantee that it is measuring what it is supposed to measure. This caution is inserted to remind the reader again that the measurement of achievement is more complex than many teachers want to believe.

The Test Must Be Comprehensive

In considering comprehensiveness, an achievement test can be compared to sampling a layer cake or determining the contents of a carload of wheat or a carload of iron ore. Let's consider the layer cake first.

If you were asked to give an honest opinion on the goodness of a layer cake, you would want to do more than look at the cake and make your statement. Presumably you would want to taste it also. At the same time it would not be necessary to eat the entire cake before giving a verdict. A sample piece would do if you could be sure it was typical of the entire cake. In other words, if there were five different layers in the cake, you would want to sample all five before making a statement. If your sample contained only three of the layers, this might give you a pretty good idea about the cake, but you could not be sure about the other two layers without sampling them also. In this example we are not interested in how you determine whether the sample is good or poor. This is important in evaluating the cake or in constructing a test, but the illustration is concerned only with the importance of getting an adequate sample upon which to base your decision. It is not necessary to eat the whole cake. It is very necessary for the sample piece to include all the layers.

The same procedure is followed in testing the quality of a carload of wheat or a carload of iron ore. The tester does not attempt to measure each grain of wheat or each piece of ore in the cars. He takes samples from several levels at both ends of the car and the middle. On the basis of this sampling, he is able to give a highly reliable measure of what is contained in the entire car.[8]

In constructing an achievement test it is equally important to sample liberally all phases of instruction which are supposed to be covered by the test. It is not necessary and it would not be practical to test every point that is taught in the course. A natural question then is how long any test should therefore be. How much of a sampling should it include?[9] In other words, how comprehensive should it be?

A test should be comprehensive enough to be valid. It should include enough points so that it measures what it is supposed to measure. This is an easy statement to make but somewhat more difficult to put into practice. There is no specific formula which indicates when a test meets the criterion of comprehensiveness—it is a matter of judgment.[10] For the classroom teacher the best practice is a careful consideration of and answer to this question: Is this test comprehensive enough to measure accurately and well what I expect it to measure?

[8] An interesting side light in the case of iron ore is the procedure followed on the Iron Range of Minnesota. The samples referred to above are taken from each car as the ore train is assembled at the mines. The testing is done immediately, and the results are telephoned to the railroad classification yards at Proctor, just outside of Duluth. By the time the ore train reaches Proctor, the contents of all cars are known and classified. Before the train continues into Duluth, the cars are rearranged according to a carefully prepared plan based on the samples that have been taken. They then proceed to the loading docks at Duluth and are unloaded into the ore boats. As a result of this careful testing and classification procedure, a type of ore meeting exact specifications is delivered down the Lakes to the steel mills.

[9] The theory of sampling is somewhat more complex than might be indicated by this discussion. The student who is interested in pursuing this topic further is referred to the Encyclopedia of Educational Research, p. 908. This will provide a brief description of the several aspects of sampling, together with a bibliography for extended study.

[10] This is a good place to restate the fact that objective measurements are not intended as a substitute for judgment. Rather, their purpose is to provide objective data so that the judgments forthcoming will be made on a sound basis.

The Test Must Be Readily Administered and Scored

Consideration must be given to the features of the test which make it readily administered and scored. It should be so designed that a minimum of student time will be consumed in answering each item. The test items should also be constructed in such a manner that they can be scored quickly and efficiently.

This characteristic of a good test would seem to be logical and understandable without further elaboration at this point. (The later chapters on the actual construction of a test and specific types of items will contain various suggestions that will make for ease of administration and scoring.)

SUMMARY

Like a good tool or fine piece of machinery, a test must meet certain requirements before much faith can be placed in its use. The first requirement logically is that it must be able to do what is expected of it—it must be able to get the job done—it must be *valid*.

Validity is an inclusive term. Several factors may cause the validity of a test to be raised or lowered. These are reliability, objectivity, discrimination, comprehensiveness, and ease of administration and scoring. Reliability denotes accuracy or consistency. A valid test must be *reliable*. However, it is possible for a test to be reliable and still not valid. The validity of a test can be raised by eliminating all *constant* factors except achievement (native intelligence, reaction time, etc.). The reliability of a test may be improved by eliminating the *variable* factors that affect the total test score (provisions for guessing, subjectivity of items, length of test, etc.).

Objectivity is related closely to both validity and reliability. An objective test item is one about which there is no question as to how it should be scored. At the same time such an item will have a clear meaning to all the students who take the test (and who know the subject matter being tested). A test may be low in validity, because it is not reliable, because it is not objective.

Discrimination refers to the ability of a total test or individual test item to differentiate effectively between the good and poor students. An indication of discriminating power can be obtained by making a simple item analysis. A test must be *comprehensive* enough to be valid. It must sample liberally all the objectives that are being measured by the test. Finally, a good test will be easy to administer and easy to score.

Throughout this chapter you have been cautioned about making absolute statements concerning the attributes or *real* effectiveness of any test. The construction and interpretation of teacher-made tests are a relative matter. They do not approach perfection. This in no way lessens the importance of improving such tests for classroom use. It is hoped that these cautions will help you in developing a questioning attitude toward the *status quo* of test construction. With such an attitude, followed by conscientious efforts at improvement, you will be bound to add to the effectiveness of the tests you make and use. With such an attitude, plus a clear understanding of validity, reliability, and the other characteristics of a good test, the following chapters will become more meaningful and useful.

SOME THINGS TO DO AND QUESTIONS TO ANSWER

1. Explain your concept of validity by means of a tool with which you are familiar. Try carrying your thinking through several steps in the use of the tool and the use of an achievement test.

2. Without referring to the text, jot down how you will determine whether your tests are valid. If you have to refer to the text, do that now, but do not complete this assignment for a day or two. The point is, if you understand the meaning of validity, you should be able to express it in your own words and in a manner that will be useful to you on the job.

3. If you had only a piece of string at your disposal, how could you illustrate this fact: A valid test must be reliable, but a reliable test is not necessarily valid.

4. Imagine that you are in the process of constructing a single test item. What can you do to check on the validity or improve the validity of the item?

5. How is the term "reliability" related to the term "correlation"?

6. What method will you use to determine the reliability of your tests? Why?

7. What is the difference between a subjective test and an objective test?

8. Is a so-called objective test strictly objective? (This may appear to be a facetious question, but if it is considered carefully, it will make you think.)

9. How can test items be made objective as far as student interpretation is concerned?

10. Suppose you have just given a test containing fifty multiple-choice items. Now you want to determine whether each item is discriminating positively and whether any of the choices (possible answers) need to be changed. Show by means of a simple chart how you might obtain this information.

11. What relationship is there between the comprehensiveness of a test and the objectives being measured?

12. Why is it necessary to give some attention to the manner in which a test is to be scored?

13. Now that you have been considering validity, reliability, and the other characteristics of a good test, do you think it is necessary to have an understanding of the meaning of these terms? Why?

SELECTED REFERENCES FOR ADDITIONAL READING

Greene, Harry A., Albert Jorgensen, and J. Raymond Gerberich. *Measurement and Evaluation in the Secondary School.* New York: Longmans, Green & Co., Inc., 1943. Chap. IV.

Hawkes, Herbert E., E. F. Lindquist, and C. R. Mann. *The Construction and Use of Achievement Examinations.* Boston: Houghton Mifflin Company, 1936. Pp. 39–81.

Kuder, G. F., and M. W. Richardson. "The Theory of the Estimation of Test Reliability," *Psychometrika,* 2:151–160 (1937).

Lindquist, E. F., and W. W. Cook, "Experimental Procedures in Test Evaluation," *Journal of Experimental Education,* 1:163–185 (1933).

McCall, William A. *Measurement.* New York: The Macmillan Company, 1939. Chaps. II, III.

Remmers, H. H., and N. L. Gage. *Educational Measurement and Evaluation.* New York: Harper & Brothers, 1943. Chap. X.

Ross, C. C. *Measurement in Today's Schools.* New York: Prentice-Hall, Inc., 1947. Chap. III.

Smith, B. Othanel. *Logical Aspects of Educational Measurement.* New York: Columbia University Press, 1938.

CHAPTER

FIVE: GENERAL PRINCIPLES OF TEST CONSTRUCTION

I<small>F</small> a test is to be valid, reliable, and objective, if it is to be comprehensive, discriminating, and easily administered and scored, a definite, systematic procedure must be followed in its construction. This means more than paging through a textbook and picking out sentences or paragraphs from which to construct the test items. As has been stated previously, the making of a test is basically a twofold process: determining first what should be measured and then devising measuring instruments (items) that will best do the job. A simple elaboration of this process is given below in outline form. This step-by-step procedure is applicable both in constructing short unit tests and in devising comprehensive examinations. Following this outline a series of specific points is presented to serve as suggestions and reminders as the actual construction is carried out.

Steps to Follow in Building a Test[1]

1. List the Major Objectives for Which an Appraisal is Desired. Perhaps you will wish to put the objectives in question form (see page 94).

2. Examine the Course Content for Additional Objectives. This is a checking step. You want to make sure that all objectives are listed. Consult your course objectives, your course of study, the

---

[1] See Chapter Three for a more complete description of steps 1 through 4.

textbook, and other sources. If you have an analysis of the basic skills and knowledges, this will prove helpful.

3. Analyze and Define Each Objective in Terms of Expected Student Outcomes. This is the inventorying step. List the elements that are a part of each objective. Define each element in terms of student behavior. List items of subject matter related to each element. In certain instances a chart may be helpful (see page 96). This step will take time. It will involve considerable detail, but once accomplished it will contain information useful for a long time to come.

4. Establish a Table of Specifications. This is to be your blueprint for constructing individual test items. It will serve as a guide. It helps to indicate the emphasis that should be given to each objective. It can be simple or detailed. That will be up to you.

5. Construct One or More Test Items for Each Objective Listed. Determine which type(s) of test item will measure best the extent to which each specific objective has been attained. The number of items for any one objective will depend upon the nature of the objective. Naturally, this is a step that will take time. The following sections of this chapter contain numerous specific suggestions that will be helpful in carrying it out. One important point bears repetition here: The objective to be measured comes first; then you decide on the type of test item that will best do the job. You may say that this is only logical, but time after time you will find teachers who start out to make twenty-five true-false items, then fifteen multiple-choice, then twenty completion, and so on. They begin by selecting a type of test item and then try to find some subject matter to fit. This is common. It is wrong. It is an illogical approach to test construction.

(A variety of specific suggestions might have been included at this point to emphasize the numerous factors that should be considered in constructing individual items. Some of these suggestions are included in the latter part of this chapter, and others will be studied in connection with the several types of test items.)

Carrying out this step may result in several types of test items. If there are only a few items of certain types, these can be revised and adapted to the other types of items that are to be used. A general rule is to include no more than three or four types of items in a single test. There are exceptions to this rule, however, and additional types might be justified by the test maker.

6. Assemble the Items for the Test. After grouping the items by types, arrange them so that related items are together. For example, suppose that in a drawing test you have four multiple-choice items related to perspective drawings. These should be placed next to each other rather than scattered throughout the multiple-choice section. The reason for this is obvious—it saves student time as the test is taken. Following these groupings it is tempting to try to arrange the items according to difficulty. Item difficulty is a relative factor. Any item will be difficult if the student has not studied the material or if the instructor forgot to mention the point in class. At best the difficulty level of individual items in an informal teacher-made test can be determined only after a thorough tryout of the test. From a practical standpoint, then, little will be gained at the start by trying to arrange the items in the order of difficulty.

7. Write Clear and Concise Directions for Each Type of Question. The directions should tell the student *what* he is to do; *how* he is to do it; and *where* he is to place his response. They should also contain an example taken from the subject matter being tested. (Sample directions for the several types of test items are included in Chapters Six through Ten.)

8. Study Every Aspect of the Assembled Test. After the test is assembled and the directions are written, it is good policy to lay it aside for several days. Then pick it up again, and review each part critically. Consider each item from the point of view of the students who will take the test. Try to determine those items that may be ambiguous. Check on the grammar. Ask yourself questions such as the following:

1. Does each item *really* measure the students' attainment of the objective?

2. If not, how could it be revised to do so?

3. Is each set of directions clear? Do they apply to every item in the group, or do some items require specific directions?

4. Is there plenty of space to write the response?

You will think of other similar questions that will be helpful in checking the test.

9. Construct the Key. In constructing the key keep in mind the procedure to be followed in scoring the test. You may decide to revise certain items to make them easier to score.

10. Have Other Instructors Criticize and, If Possible, Actually Take the Test. This step, carried out conscientiously, will provide you with valuable suggestions for improving the validity of the test.

11. Make Any Necessary Revisions.

12. After the Test Has Been Administered to One or Two Groups of Students, Analyze and Improve It. Correct any weaknesses that are revealed. Continue to revise and improve the test from time to time.

At this point it should be reemphasized that these twelve steps have been presented briefly and almost in outline form. Do not let the brevity of the presentation detract from the importance of following a logical, step-by-step procedure in test construction. This suggested procedure has been inserted here in order that you might have a better understanding of the steps that are necessary in building a test. This will help to make the next few chapters more meaningful. At the same time it might be a good idea to make a mental note to come back and re-read this section after studying the several types of test items.

Card-file Test Building

A useful technique in the building of better tests is to develop a card file of effective test items. Such a file might be described as a kit of measuring tools. The test maker should strive to become a craftsman in using these tools. The competent mechanic knows from experience that it pays to buy good tools for his kit. He knows also that good tools require some care. They must be sharpened or adjusted from time to time. They must be kept clean. They must not be allowed to deteriorate. The test items in your kit must be chosen and cared for in like manner.

In building a card file of test items you assume that there are certain objectives that will be stable and therefore can be listed before any specific test is actually constructed. This is a valid assumption. For example, in the field of hand woodwork the teacher would want his students to become experienced and skillful in using the jack plane. There are numerous uses for the jack plane and a number of things that must be learned before it can be used effectively. The adjustment of the double plane iron, the application of pressure in planing a board, the adjustments of the plane iron in the plane, the planing of end grain—these are a few of the factors that enter into successful use of this plane.

The point here is that all these factors, and others, can be identified and listed. This can also be done for all the tools, materials, knowledges, and processes that relate to a study of hand woodwork. Likewise, many desirable attitudes, habits, appreciations, and the like, can be identified. After all these have been listed, it is possible to prepare a variety of test items that *might* be used in measuring each point. Each item is placed on a single card and filed under an appropriate heading. When it comes time to prepare a specific test, the objectives to be measured are listed. Then the card file is consulted to find all the possible items that can be used to measure the objectives. If the card file is complete, this process will result in many more items than are needed or wanted. It will be necessary to select the best ones. Perhaps some slight revisions will be needed. Perhaps some additional items will have to be constructed to measure an objective peculiar to a certain group. In spite of this, it is easy to understand how much time can be saved by means of a complete and well-prepared file of items.

A carefully prepared instructional analysis will provide one basis for constructing the test items. Other sources should also be used to ensure the inclusion of measurable traits other than skills and related information. The procedure is simple. Carrying it out takes time and effort. It cannot be done overnight, but in the long run it saves a great deal of time. In other words, it may take a year or two to build up a file that is relatively complete as well as effective. Improvements will always be in order, but once the system is well organized, a test can easily be assembled for any purpose and in a much shorter time than would otherwise be possible.

In building the file use one card for each item. Items such as the matching or cluster true-false, will, naturally, be put on one card, although there may be several points to the item. The best size of card is perhaps 5 by 8 inches, although this is relative and can be changed if desirable. A 3- by 5- or 4- by 6-inch card could be used for many of the items, but the larger size will make for uniformity and will provide plenty of space for most of the longer type items, and there will still be room to jot down figures and notes about the effectiveness of the items.

The accompanying illustrations will help to indicate the make-

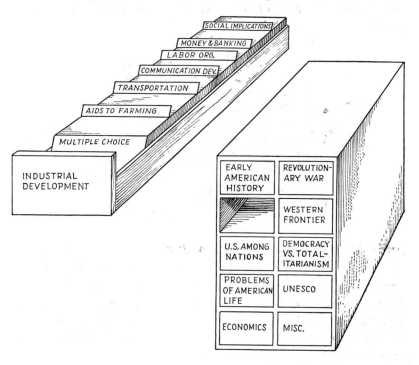

up of a typical card file of test items. The file headings shown are merely illustrative. The manner in which the items are grouped will be dependent upon the purposes of the test maker. Grouping the items under subject-matter headings would seem to be more logical and useful than to group them by types of items. A simple process will make the types of items readily identifiable. This is accomplished by selecting a standard color scheme and coloring the top edge of each card in accordance with the scheme. This is easy to do. For example, you would merely sort out all the multiple-choice items, hold them firmly together with a hand screw, and paint the tops of all with the desired colored ink, as shown in the accompanying illustration. Suppose the multiple-choice color is red. The several items would then be filed under the appropriate headings. It would be easy to select the multiple-choice items under a given subject merely by picking out the red-topped cards. This same process could be followed for any type of item.

If you are interested in an organized approach to test construction, you would do well to give careful consideration to the development of such a card file.

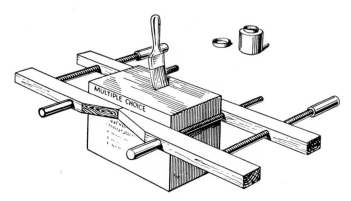

Specific Points to Observe in Test Construction

It should now be evident that there are many specific points to keep in mind in constructing an achievement examination. Some of these points have been mentioned already. Others will be emphasized later in the treatment of the various types of test items. Still others are grouped here to facilitate a consideration of the planning and construction of a test.

The following suggestions are not listed in the order of their importance, and you may note some repetition of points previously discussed. However, you will find the answers to some of the common questions asked by beginning test makers. By developing a working knowledge of the following suggestions you will have an effective check list that will be helpful in constructing your own tests.

Keep in Mind That It Is Not Possible to Measure All Outcomes of Instruction with One Type of Test. Be wary of trying to measure the development of manipulative skills with a written test. A good performance test is much more effective for such purposes. Careful and systematic observation will often provide a measure of the acquirement of certain traits that written tests can seldom, if ever, provide. This is not to condemn the preparation and use of written tests. On the contrary, such tests can be used even more frequently if, at the same time, they are used to advantage. The point is that written achievement tests will not do everything. They must be used wisely. Their results must be interpreted with a full knowledge of the limitations that exist.

Make the Test Comprehensive, but Exclude Insignificant and Trivial Items. This means sampling the whole range of instruction up to the time of the test. The next time you start to put an item in a test simply because it will add one more point to the total score, stop and reconsider. Remember this suggestion. The ordinary teacher-made test contains altogether too many items that have no real significance—items that are trivial and unimportant. The best they do is to provide a smoke screen through which it is difficult to ascertain real achievement. Keep in mind the example of the layer cake. Remember that you want a good sample of all the layers before passing final judgment. If you follow the steps suggested in the previous section, there should be little need for question about the comprehensiveness of your tests.

Devise Your Items so That They Require the Student Actually to Apply Things Learned Rather than Merely Recalling or Recognizing Facts. You have been told this several times already. It is one of the most important points to keep in mind. It should be uppermost in your thoughts as you begin to devise each new test item. In Chapter Four, while considering the validity of an item, this particular point was illustrated by several examples of items pertaining to Ohm's law. The importance of devising application items is again reiterated by using several additional items on Ohm's law, as reported by Lindquist.[2] Each of the following items appeared in a test given to 325 students. The percentage of students answering each item correctly is given beneath the item.

[2] Herbert E. Hawkes, E. F. Lindquist, and C. R. Mann, *The Construction and Use of Achievement Examinations.* Boston: Houghton Mifflin Company, 1936, pp. 93–94. Used by permission.

1. Write the formula for Ohm's law, using letters only.
   (Answered correctly by 87 per cent of the pupils.)
2. Which of the following is a correct formula for Ohm's
   law:
   (1) I = ER   (3) R = I over E
   (2) I = E over R   (4) E = R over I
   (Answered correctly by 80 per cent of the pupils.)
3. Which of the following is the correct formula for Ohm's
   law?
   (1) I = R over E   (3) I = R times E
   (2) R = E over I   (4) E = R over I
   (Answered correctly by 60 per cent of the pupils.)
4. Which of the following is a correct formula for Ohm's
   law?
   (1) I = R over E   (3) I = ER
   (2) E = IR   (4) E = R over I
   (Answered correctly by 56 per cent of the pupils.)
5. Is the expression .24 EIT equal to the expression
   .24 I^2RT?
   (1) Yes, because E = IR
   (2) Yes, because IR = EI
   (3) No, because the formulas do not contain the same
   letters.
   (4) No, because EI does not equal I^2R.
   (Answered correctly by 40 per cent of the pupils.)
6. What causes the fuse in a house lighting circuit to burn
   out if the two terminals in the light socket come into
   direct contact with each other?
   (1) The fuse is burned out by the sparks that form in
   the socket.
   (2) The closed circuit has a very low resistance.
   (3) Heat produced in the socket makes the fuse burn out.
   (4) The closed circuit gets hot because it has a very
   high resistance.
   (Answered correctly by 36 per cent of the pupils.)

Apparently a large number of the students had learned Ohm's
law by heart. They were able to answer items (1) and (2) with
little difficulty. When the form was changed somewhat in items
(3) and (4), some of the students fell by the wayside. Probably
they could not recognize the formula except as they had learned it.
Of course, the percentage of correct responses dropped significantly in the final items, which called for an application of the
law. Whereas 290 students were able to answer the first item correctly, only 18 per cent of them followed through on all the succeeding items.

One conclusion is worthy of quotation: "Certainly the ability to recall Ohm's Law in its familiar form is not acceptable evidence that the pupil can recognize the law in a less familiar form or use it in an interpretative situation. If an entire test consisted of questions similar to item 1, the results might appear to indicate excellent achievement, while, as a matter of fact, the understanding of the pupils might actually be superficial and inadequate."[3]

Make Certain That the Type of Test Item Used for Measuring Each Objective Is the One That Will Best Measure That Objective. Once again, this means that the objective comes first and the test item second. No one type of item is superior for all kinds of measurement. Certain types have advantages over others, but these are *specific* advantages in *specific* situations. In this respect test items can again be compared to a mechanic's tools. The woodworker, for example, uses different types of planes. Each type has been developed for specific situations—the jointer plane for joining long boards, the rabbet plane for cutting rabbets, the block plane for other purposes, the smooth plane for still other needs. Most of these planes can be used in performing more than one operation. They have a certain degree of flexibility. Conceivably you could plane the edge of a long board with a block plane, although it would take a longer time and the results might be questionable when compared with those obtained with the proper tool. At the same time, if the beginning craftsman in your class could afford only one plane in his kit, you would probably suggest a jack plane because it can be used in a variety of situations.

An almost exact line of reasoning can be used in discussing the selection of test items. Just as some amateurs will try to do all their planing with a block plane, so some amateur test makers try to measure all aspects of achievement with true-false test items. Just as the expert craftsman may have to design a special plane for a special job, so must the test maker sometimes devise special items to measure special outcomes. And just as the jack plane seems to be the best for general use, the multiple-choice test item is to be preferred when a single type of item is desired. This comparison could be extended further, but it should now be evident that the expert test maker, like other expert craftsmen, must know his

[3] *Ibid.*, p. 95.

tools, how to care for them, how to use them, and when to use them. Strive to make each test item the best one for that particular job.

Avoid Trick, or "Catch," Questions. Some teachers like to include puzzling items in which hidden meanings or subtle clues provide the correct responses. Such items are not fair to the students, nor are they valid measures of achievement. They will merely help to indicate the "brightness" of certain students in seeing through the smoke screen set up by the teacher.

This does not mean that all items must be easy to answer. It means that, if the student knows the point in question, he should be able to answer the item immediately without having to figure out what the test maker has in mind. Remember that you are trying to measure achievement, not general intelligence. Your purpose is to find out how much the student has achieved, not how easily you can trip him up.

Include a Large Number of Items in the Test. This tends to increase the reliability. Of course, one should not include more items just for the sake of adding points. The items must be good ones. The exact number to use will depend upon the purpose of the test and the types of items selected. A few carefully prepared multiple-choice items may be much more valid and reliable than a large number of true-false questions prepared in a hurry. With this qualification in mind the suggestion still holds—include a large number of items. Remember, each test must be comprehensive enough to be valid.

Do not "Lift" Statements Directly from Books and Use Them as Test Items. This is a common practice in many teacher-made tests. Sometimes an entire test will be constructed by paging through a book and selecting isolated sentences or paragraphs that seem appropriate. Perhaps the statements are to be used in a true-false test and are changed slightly to make them false. Very often one or two insignificant words will be replaced by a dash, and the statement then becomes a completion-type item. Such a practice should be avoided religiously.

The weakness of such items lies in the fact that students can provide the correct response without knowing what the response really means. This same point was illustrated in discussing the necessity of devising items that call for application rather than mere memorization (see page 133). Consider a further example. In answering the following items, taken directly from textbooks, what understanding does the student need?

```
T F   1. Cattle hides make the best grades of animal glue.
T F   2. Steel wool is made of finely shredded steel.
T F   3. A back saw is used to cut metal.
T F   4. Steel is refined pig iron.
T F   5. The attic of a frame house should be ventilated
         with screened louvres.
      6. When pounding with a mallet is necessary, a
         _____ chisel should be used.
      7. _____ is the natural color of shellac.
```

Without exception the above items could be answered correctly by a student who had little or no real understanding of the subject matter involved. Such items are not atypical. A simple perusal of various tests prepared by teachers in your particular field will reveal many similar items. The fault is a serious one. It may be indicative of a weakness not only in testing but in teaching as well. Many tests are made up entirely of items similar to those listed above. What does it mean when a student receives a high score on such a test? Perhaps the answer is contained in the statement of a father who said, "Johnny passed all his tests, completed all the exercises, and got an A in Electricity, but he didn't know where to start when I asked him to put a new cord in the electric fan." No doubt the teaching as well as the testing was at fault. They are closely related.

Whenever Possible, Avoid Items with Only Two Choices from Which the Student Selects One. This refers primarily to the true-false type of item, although others are sometimes constructed with no more choices. While adherence to this suggestion will result in items that are more difficult to guess, there is a more important reason to keep in mind—again, real understanding of the subject matter involved. Sometimes a modification of a two-choice item will make it possible to measure the understanding that has been acquired. The following true-false item pertains to information that was presented in Chapter Four of this book.

```
Yes   No    1. Is it possible for a test to be reliable
             without being valid?
```

Perhaps you can answer this item without hesitation. Perhaps you have a "hunch" as to the correct answer. Or perhaps you would be willing to take a fifty-fifty chance and guess. The right answer, achieved by any of these methods, would not indicate an understanding of this particular aspect of the relationship between validity and reliability. A simple modification, as follows, would make the two-response item much more valid.

Yes   No   1. Is it possible for a test to be reliable
                 without being valid?
                 Why? _____
                 _____

In this instance the response must be justified whether the student encircles "Yes" or "No." If the student guesses the right answer but gives the wrong reason, he gets no credit. If the student remembers the statement from the book but does not know why, he gets no credit. Such an item minimizes the guessing factor and, more important, provides a better indication of whether the student really understands the point in question. Other modifications of two-choice items will be presented later.

Check to Make Sure That No Item Can Be Answered Simply by Referring to Other Items. It is easy for this to happen unless a careful check is made. An illustration of this point is contained in the following examples taken from a teacher-made test on wood finishing. The total test contained 163 items. Items 83 and 98 read as follows:

_____ 83. Which one of the following characterizes spirit
          stain?
          A. Water
          B. Alcohol
          C. Oil
          D. Turpentine

_____ 98. Three kinds of stain are _____, _____,
          and _____.

In one instance where this test was used five students out of a class of twenty indicated that they had turned back to item 83 when answering item 98. Such a relationship is not always too obvious, especially when numerous items intervene. Nevertheless, the bright students will find such hints and weaknesses in tests that have not been checked carefully.

Make Each Item Independent of the Others. Do not have the correct answer to one item dependent upon the answer to another. The items may well be related to each other, but a right or wrong answer to one should not automatically result in a similar answer to the other. Consider two multiple-choice items that illustrate the advisability of this suggestion.

_____ 1. The number of board feet in 10 pieces of lumber 2" x 8" x 12' is
A. 96
B. 124
C. 160
D. 180
E. 248
_____ 2. At 11 cents per board foot the above lumber would cost
A. $10.56
B. $13.64
C. $17.60
D. $19.80
E. $30.00

If a student marked the wrong answer to item 1, he would almost automatically get the wrong answer for item 2. If he got the first item right, he would be almost certain to get the second right because the choices would provide a check on his arithmetic. The only point measured by the second item is the student's ability to multiply by 11 cents. Also, it is constructed in such a way that the student who knows how to multiply may get the item wrong because it is dependent on the previous item. If the multiplication is incidental, then the second item could well be combined as a part of the first. If the test maker really wants to measure the ability to multiply by 11 cents, then a separate problem should be outlined.

Include No Item for Which the Answer Is Obvious to a Person Who Does Not Know the Subject Matter. This suggestion refers to a common fault in test making. Many tests include items that could be answered easily by any intelligent person even though he knows nothing at all about the subject matter. Several examples will better explain this point.

T F The most important metal is copper.

This example, from a published teacher-made test, would be marked false by any intelligent person whether or not he knew anything about the importance of copper. The statement itself is absolute, but the word "important" is a relative term. This inconsistency would be apparent at once to most people, and the item could be marked correctly without any knowledge of copper and its relation to other metals. In many similar instances simple logic alone will provide the correct response. For example, the word "all" in the following item would make the statement obviously false to most people:

T F All drawing triangles have 45—degree angles.

In true-false items such words as "all," "never," "always," "none," "alone," "may," and "should" act as specific determiners. That is, the bright student will note such qualifying words immediately and will tend to mark his response accordingly. This tendency has been corroborated by Brinkmeier and Ruch,[4] who studied numerous teacher-made true-false tests. They reported that items containing the words "only" and "alone" were false nine out of ten times. With slightly less frequency the words "all," "no," "none," "never," "always" indicated false items. The words "should" and "may" served as good clues for marking items true. One out of five statements were usually obvious, and items containing more than twenty words were true three out of four times.

Unless the test maker corrects such deficiences in his true-false items, the intelligent student will be able to get a high mark without knowing much about the subject matter involved. This fault is not confined to true-false questions. Matching items often contain answers that are just as obvious. A common reason for this is the inclusion of heterogeneous bits of subject matter. The following sample from a matching test will illustrate this point:

[4] I. H. Brinkmeier and G. M. Ruch, "Minor Studies on Objective Examination Methods: III. Specific Determiners in True-False Statements," *Journal of Educational Research*, 22:110–118 (1930).

_____ The <u>number</u> of inches represented by   1. chuck
(3' – 9").
_____ The <u>part</u> of a drill press used to clamp   2. 45
the bit.
_____ The <u>measure</u> of the unit of resistance in   3. ohm
electricity.
_____ A <u>material</u> used to cover pitchy places   4. kerf
and knots before painting.
_____ The <u>groove</u> or <u>saw</u> <u>cut</u>.   5. shellac

There are several faults in this item selected from a teacher-made test. In this instance we are primarily interested in the obvious nature of the item. (The underlined words were not a part of the original item.) This item could be answered by a person possessing knowledge based only on vague generalities (which may have been obtained outside the shop). There is no question about the "number" item, and the level of reasoning required to ferret out the other correct responses is not very high.

Word the Items in the Simplest Manner Possible. Confine the terms used to the vocabulary level of the students. While this suggestion is applicable to any test item, particular attention should be paid to the wording of items containing information of a technical nature. How would you answer the following two items?

_____ The height of the bed charge of coke above the
tuyères in the cupola is dependent upon what?
A. the pressure at which air is supplied to the
cupola.
B. the amount of iron to be melted.
C. the percentage of ash in the coke.
D. the height of the tuyères.
E. none of the above.
_____ Blocking the head for a P.W. requires
A. 30 spacers.
B. 25 spacers.
C. a varying number of spacers.
D. the same number as you used before.

The chances are that if you understand the first item you will have difficulty with the second, and vice versa. The first refers to foundry work; the second is from the field of cosmetology. (P.W. is the abbreviation for permanent wave.) It is difficult to state whether or not the vocabulary level used in these items is too advanced. Certainly, a competent worker in either field should be able to understand these terms and expressions. A junior high school student on the other hand, might be confused, even though foundry work had been discussed in a General Metal Course or permanent waving in a Home-Economics class. The wording of items, then, and the selection of terms and expressions are a relative matter, requiring judgment on the part of the test maker. Nevertheless, the best general rule is to word each item as simply as possible.

State Questions Clearly. Eliminate Ambiguous Items. Though these suggestions have been made previously in discussing other factors, they are repeated here to give added emphasis. Sometimes an entire item is poorly constructed and needs to be entirely revised. Very often the clarity can be improved by changing a word or phrase. For the beginning test maker the important consideration is to keep in mind the students who will be reacting to the items. At best, it is a difficult process to construct a series of statements that will be interpreted with some degree of uniformity by a group of people.

Keep the Method of Recording Responses as Simple as Possible. The technique of answering test items can easily become more difficult for the student than recalling or recognizing the information needed to make the response. Involved methods of indicating responses tend to measure general intelligence rather than achievement. The controlled-completion type of item is usually confusing to students when they see it for the first time. As illustrated by the following example, it will be seen that at least four definite steps are necessary as the student responds to each point:

```
Directions: In the statements below certain key words have
been omitted.  The words or phrases that fit into the blank
spaces are included in the lettered list that follows the
statements.  Select the word that best fits in each blank
and place its letter in the appropriate blank at the left.
Use each letter only once.  In some cases it may be neces-
sary to choose the better of two possible answers.
____1. The generator is an automotive accessory usually
____2. driven by a belt.  It delivers (1) _____
____3. current and operates at all times when the engine
____4. is turning.  It is so designed that when the
____5. engine reaches a certain speed the (2) _____ of
```

___6. the generator will be greater than that of the
       (3) _____. Automobile generators usually have
       (4) _____ field poles. The third brush controls
       the generator (5) _____. Brushes are usually
       made of (6) _____.

       A. output   H. soft copper
       B. input   I. iron
       C. strength   J. battery
       D. carbon   K. alternating
       E. unit   L. two
       F. current   M. direct
       G. three   N. voltage
                                    O. resistance

In such an item the student must read the statement first. Then
he searches for an appropriate word for the first blank. Upon locating the proper word he notes the letter in front of it. He may
then place the letter in the proper space at the left of the item, or
he may make doubly sure and first transfer the letter to the blank
space in the item. It will still be necessary for him to record the
proper letter in the proper blank space at the left of the item. As
will be described later (Chapter Ten) the controlled-completion
item can be used to good advantage. However, it is often confusing to students the first time they see such an item, and there is
need for careful explanation on the part of the instructor. If such
explanation is not forthcoming, the item is apt to be answered in
an odd variety of ways.

Leave Sufficient Space for All Responses without Crowding.
No doubt you have taken tests where it was necessary to crowd
several words in a small space. This is hard on the student and
also makes the job of correcting more difficult. The easiest way to
avoid this fault is to make sure that a complete key is made before
the test is given. This will bring to light such faults.

*Arrange Blanks for Responses along One Side of the Page, if
Possible.* This facilitates scoring. The left side of the page is to be
preferred in most instances since the blanks will be next to the
item number and there will be less chance for errors on the part
of the student.

_____ 1. The unit of electrical resist-
                            ance is the _____.
_____ 2. Ripsaw teeth are shaped like
                            _____.

The above examples are sufficient to show that by placing the blanks at the left side of the page the test will be much easier to mark with a key. If the test maker feels that a certain type of item arranged in this manner will be confusing to the students, then a different arrangement should be employed. Of course, if an answer sheet is used, this suggestion need not be considered. An answer sheet is usually separate from the test and contains numbered blanks which the students fill in. There are numerous variations. The two major advantages of answer sheets are that (1) they make for easier and more rapid scoring and (2) the tests themselves can be used over and over. Two examples of typical answer sheets are shown in Figs. 1 and 2.

Arrange the Items so That Responses Will Not Form a Particular Pattern. This means that you should not have five true items, followed by five false items, followed by five true items, and so on. Likewise, in multiple-choice items you would not want the first two items answered by the fifth choice, the next two by the fourth choice, and the like. This fault is not common, although it is sometimes found. It can be corrected easily.

Arrange the Items in Such a Manner That It Will not Be Necessary for the Student to Refer to More than One Page in Answering a Given Item. Adherence to this suggestion will save student time and avoid confusion. It is much better to waste a sheet of paper than to have the students turning pages over and back while trying to determine what goes where. Most of the time a slight revision of the items will result in satisfactory page placement with no loss of space. Careful attention should be paid to this suggestion when you pass your test to the typist who will cut the stencil or do the duplicating.

Number the Responses Consecutively from the Beginning to the End of the Test. When each part of a test is numbered separately, it is more difficult to identify a particular item, especially as the test is analyzed for the purpose of improvement. The usual practice is to have only one set of consecutive numbers.

The Practice of Underlining Crucial Words, if Not Done Too Frequently and Indiscriminately, Tends to Increase the Objectivity of Test Items. By underlining certain words an otherwise ambiguous statement may become clear to the students.

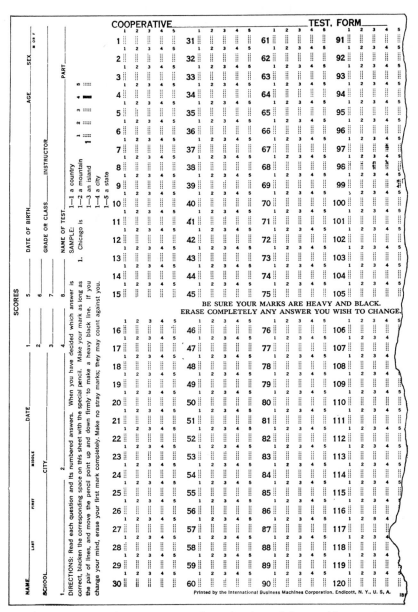

Fig. 1. An example of an answer sheet that is used for machine scoring.

FINAL EXAMINATION (FORM A)

Name	Code number	Date
Total points:	Number incorrect	Total score

```
      T  F              A  B  C  D         A  B  C  D        A  B  C  D
   1  □  □          22  □  □  □  □     44  □  □  □  □    66  □  □  □  □
   2  □  □          23  □  □  □  □     45  □  □  □  □    67  □  □  □  □
   3  □  □          24  □  □  □  □     46  □  □  □  □    68  □  □  □  □
   4  □  □          25  □  □  □  □     47  □  □  □  □    69  □  □  □  □
   5  □  □          26  □  □  □  □     48  □  □  □  □    70  □  □  □  □
   6  □  □          27  □  □  □  □     49  □  □  □  □    71  □  □  □  □
   7  □  □          28  □  □  □  □     50  □  □  □  □    72  □  □  □  □
   8  □  □          29  □  □  □  □     51  □  □  □  □    73  □  □  □  □
   9  □  □          30  □  □  □  □     52  □  □  □  □    74  □  □  □  □
  10  □  □          31  □  □  □  □     53  □  □  □  □    75  □  □  □  □
                    32  □  □  □  □     54  □  □  □  □    76  □  □  □  □
      A  B  C  D  E  33  □  □  □  □     55  □  □  □  □    77  □  □  □  □
  11  □  □  □  □  □  34  □  □  □  □     56  □  □  □  □    78  □  □  □  □
  12  □  □  □  □  □  35  □  □  □  □     57  □  □  □  □    79  □  □  □  □
  13  □  □  □  □  □  36  □  □  □  □     58  □  □  □  □    80  □  □  □  □
  14  □  □  □  □  □  37  □  □  □  □     59  □  □  □  □    81  □  □  □  □
  15  □  □  □  □  □  38  □  □  □  □     60  □  □  □  □    82  □  □  □  □
  16  □  □  □  □  □  39  □  □  □  □     61  □  □  □  □    83  □  □  □  □
  17  □  □  □  □  □  40  □  □  □  □     62  □  □  □  □    84  □  □  □  □
  18  □  □  □  □  □  41  □  □  □  □     63  □  □  □  □    85  □  □  □  □
  19  □  □  □  □  □  42  □  □  □  □     64  □  □  □  □    86  □  □  □  □
  20  □  □  □  □  □  43  □  □  □  □     65  □  □  □  □
  21  □  □  □  □  □
```

Fig. 2. An example of an answer sheet that can be used for hand scoring.

T F   In a transformer of <u>good</u> design the <u>best</u> efficiency
      obtainable is approximately fifty per cent.

As a result of emphasizing the words "good" and "best" in the above item, the student is not so likely to spend time thinking about the different grades of transformers and the varying degrees of efficiency that are attainable. If he has learned the amount of efficiency obtainable with a well-designed transformer, he will have little difficulty in answering this item. Hovland and Eberhart[5] studied this specific aspect of true-false items and reported a definite increase in reliability when underlining was carried out judiciously.

Avoid the Weighting of Items. Each single response should be numbered and should count one point. Almost invariably the beginning test maker will want to argue about this suggestion. He will say that some points of subject matter are more important than others and therefore should receive more credit when answered correctly in a test. It is true that certain objectives may be relatively more important than others. However, the numerous investigations that have been made on this subject indicate that little, if anything, is gained by taking the time to assign various weights to various items.[6] In either case the rank order of the students will be almost exactly the same. This means that it is not worth the effort for the typical classroom teacher to try to assign weights to his test items. If you feel that a certain objective is especially important, require the student to respond to several situations in which it is present. In other words, give one point for each item, but devise several items that bear on the particular objective.

If Certain Items Are to Be Corrected for Guessing, This Should Be Clearly Indicated in the Directions. When a correction formula is used, the students should be instructed not to guess and to omit those items which they are unable to answer.

5 C. E. Hovland and J. C. Eberhart, "New Method of Increasing the Reliability of the True-False Examination," *Journal of Educational Psychology,* 26:388–394 (1935).

6 E. A. Culler, "Studies in Psychometric Theory," *Journal of Experimental Psychology,* 9:271–298 (1926). See also "Educational Tests and Their Uses," *Review of Educational Research,* 3:1–80 (1933).

Correction formulas can be applied to all types of test items but are usually associated with the two-response items. The question of whether or not to correct for guessing is difficult to answer. Various investigations on this question have indicated that the validity of a standardized test tends to be raised slightly when a correction for guessing is carried out.[7] There does not seem to be much evidence to indicate that the informal type of test is significantly improved by correcting for guessing. From a statistical standpoint, the procedure can be logically justified, but in terms of the meaning of a single test score some doubts may be raised. The authors are of the opinion that little is to be gained in using correction formulas with teacher-made informal tests. In the words of Crawford and Burnham, "shrewd guessing can sometimes outwit statistical formulas designed to circumvent it."[8]

For certain standardized purposes a corrected score may well be justified, but at the same time it may be a poor indication of actual attainment. If the "right minus wrong" formula is used, it is possible for the student to mark one-half the items right and still obtain a score of zero. It is likewise possible for one student to have more correct responses than another, yet receive a lower total score. To be sure he may have guessed more items, but he also knew more items. The question is whether the corrected or uncorrected score is the best indication of achievement.

It has been the experience of the authors that very few students will conscientiously omit items they do not know. For this reason the total score will tend to be lower than actual attainment would warrant. Uncorrected scores would allow for guessing and thus make the total scores higher than they should be. Of the two faults it would seem best to err in the students' favor. The best solution is to avoid using the common true-false items and to let the laws of chance operate with the others.

Make Sure the Directions Are Clear and Complete. As has been

---

[7] "Educational Tests and Their Uses," *Review of Educational Research,* 5:482 (1935). See also W. W. Cook, *The Measurement of General Spelling Ability Involving Controlled Comparisons between Techniques.* University of Iowa, Studies in Education, Vol. 6, No. 6, 1932, p. 112.

[8] A. B. Crawford and P. S. Burnham, *Forecasting College Achievement,* Part I. New Haven: Yale University Press, 1946, p. 105.

stated previously, the directions should tell the student *what* to do, *how* to do it, and *where* to place his response. Include at least one example to show the student what is wanted. A large number of incorrect responses can be traced directly either to the student's failure to understand the directions or to his failure to read them carefully. In selecting examples take them from the subject matter of the test. Make them meaningful. Use the examples to teach certain points. (Sample directions for the various types of test items will be found in Chapters Six to Ten.)

Prepare a Proper Heading for the Test. The heading should provide an identification of the test, space for the student's name and total score, plus any other information that will be useful. A general rule is to make the heading as simple as possible while providing the needed data. Sometimes it will be desirable to include preliminary general directions indicating the time allowance, how the student is to proceed, and what he is to do when finished. For most teacher-made tests this will not be necessary.

A simple box heading for a test paper is shown in the following sample:

```
Johnson High School                  General Math. I
Mathematics Department               W. J. Williams

               FINAL TEST (Form A)
```

Name	Code Number	Date
Possible Score: 163	Number Wrong	Total Score

General Directions:

A Brief Review

To this point you have observed something about the purposes of informal achievement testing. You have become initially acquainted with the characteristics of a good test. You have just reviewed certain suggestions that should prove helpful in constructing your tests.

By now you are thoroughly familiar with the twofold nature of test construction: first determining or defining clearly what you want to measure, and second devising the type of test item that will best do the measuring. The next few chapters will be devoted to several aspects of the second step. You will become acquainted with various types of test items, their advantages, their limitations, points to observe in constructing, along with numerous samples to illustrate specific points.

Before proceeding to this discussion, however, this would seem to be a logical place to pause briefly and reflect on what has been covered thus far. By now you should have acquired some definite concepts on the place of measurement in teaching and, more specifically, some definite ideas of how *you* expect to make and use tests in your teaching.

If the authors have been successful to any degree, you will have begun the development of a critical attitude toward the construction, use, and interpretation of educational tests. You will have begun to appreciate the possibilities as well as the shortcomings of achievement tests used in the classroom. You will have realized that such terms as validity, reliability, objectivity, and the like, have numerous implications that cannot be summarized readily by means of a statistical formula or a given coefficient. You will be wary about using these terms loosely without precise facts to warrant your statements.

In short, you will have begun to appreciate the fact that achievement testing is much more than a process of writing out a number of questions and giving them to the students.

Perhaps you are one who does not need to be reminded of the limitations and qualifications mentioned in the above paragraphs. If so, you will understand that in testing, as in other fields of knowledge, the beginner is likely to arrive at conclusions and adopt generalizations that appear logical on the surface but will not bear the scrutiny of the experienced worker. A common example of this situation is the many teachers who talk glibly about intelligence quotients (I.Q.'s) without knowing what they really mean or how they are obtained. Your use and interpretation of achievement tests should be critical, analytical, and intelligent. That is why certain points have been stressed and reemphasized. That is why this digression has been inserted here. With this admonition in mind, we proceed to a discussion of the various types of test items.

Classification of Test Items

One means of classifying test items is to divide them into two general groups: recall items and recognition items. In answering a recall item the student is required to complete a statement, fill in a blank, or make a list. He must provide the missing words or phrases. Simple completion, listing, and essay items are examples of the recall type.

```
Columbus discovered America in the year _____.
```

In the recognition type of item the student chooses the correct or best response from the two or more possibilities that are listed. In such items the student *recognizes* the correct response. True-false, multiple-choice, and matching items are examples of the recognition type.

```
T F   An auger bit marked #8 will cut a hole one-quarter
      inch in diameter.
```

Sometimes the two types are used in combination, as in some forms of modified true-false items. The student may be required to recognize a true or false statement and then recall certain information to substantiate his choice.

```
T F   Three-phase current can be transmitted over a two-wire
      system.
      Explanation: _____
      _____
      _____
```

It might be argued that a certain amount of recalling and recognizing is necessary in responding to any well-constructed test item. Though this may be true, it will be largely a matter of degree. The classification will still be useful in determining the type of test item to use in a specific instance. For example, workers must be able to recall certain points of information taught in technical courses if they are to take full advantage of their training. It follows that test items designed to measure the extent to which students have mastered such points of information should be of the recall type.

Students often can recognize correct responses when listed among several choices and still not be able to recall outright the required answer.

If effective use of certain information being taught involves recall, then we must *teach* and *test* for recall and application of that information *in purposeful situations*. The phrase "in purposeful situations" is to be stressed in this instance and whenever a test item is constructed. Let's use our friend, Ohm's law, for an example. We are interested in determining whether a recognition or recall type of item should be used. In this case, imagine the course is for a vocational class in Electricity. We shall then assume that the students must be able to recall and apply Ohm's law when they get on the job. Would the following true-false items be satisfactory?

_____ The qualified electrical worker must be able to apply Ohm's law in his work.

_____ Ohm's law is expressed R = $\frac{E}{I}$.

_____ Ohm's law will be used in determining the resistance of electrical circuits.

With little scrutiny you would probably agree that such items would not do a good job. Remember, you want the students to be able to recall the law and be able to apply it. How would completion items do?

Ohm's law is expressed by the formula _____.
If you knew the current and voltage of a circuit, what law could you use to find the resistance? _____

In this instance the student would have to recall the formula and know something about when to use it. This would still be an inadequate measure of the student's ability at application. The problem is more than one of deciding whether to use a recall or recognition type of item. Even more important is the manner in which the item is constructed and the ability or trait it actually measures. In other words, while you may want the student to be able to recall certain information, the mere selection of a recall type of item is no proof that it will measure the ability to apply the information. Actually a well-prepared recognition type of item (multiple-choice) may be constructed in such a way that the student will have to do as much recalling as with a completion item, and he will have to recall the formula in order to solve an actual problem. The recalling will be but a step in the solution. It will not be the end in itself. Consider the following attempt at an item that measures application and demands some recall:

> Suppose that you were measuring the resistance of a particular wire to determine its suitability for use in a particular circuit. You find a voltage reading of 102 volts and a current of 6 amperes. Which of the following resistances would you record on your data sheet.
> A. .05+ ohms   D. 17   ohms
> B. .5   ohms   E. 61.2 ohms
> C. 6.12 ohms

Such an item would call for simple application in which Ohm's law would be used as a means of solving the problem. The student would have to recall the law even though the particular item is classed as a recognition type. Before the proper answer could be recognized, a certain amount of recalling would be required. With slight revision the recognition feature could be eliminated entirely; the item then becomes entirely recall in nature.

> _____ 6. Suppose that you were measuring the resistance of a particular wire to determine its suitability for use in a particular circuit. You find a voltage reading of 102 volts and a current of 6 amperes. What resistance would you record on your data sheet? (Show your work.)

In summarizing this brief discussion about recall and recognition items, the important consideration would be the type of application that is called for in the item. You may decide in a specific instance that a student should be able to recall a certain point of knowledge. In another situation it may be sufficient if he is able to recognize the desired answer. Too many test makers stop at this point without considering the most important factor, namely, how should the item be constructed so that it measures the student's grasp and real understanding of the point of knowledge. Expressing this thought in still another manner—avoid items that merely ask *what* or *who* or *when*. Stay away from items that require the student only to *define, name, list,* or *describe*. Make the student *interpret, explain, solve, state why, determine the significance, express his understanding,* or *show how*. You want to measure, not how much a student has superficially absorbed, but how well he can apply what he has absorbed. This is a challenge. It is with this thought in mind that you should examine critically the sample test items on the following pages.

Types of Test Items. For the purposes here intended test items have been classified under five main headings: (1) multiple-choice;[9] (2) alternate-response (true-false); (3) matching; (4) recall (completion and free-response[10]); (5) miscellaneous. There are many variations, adaptations, and combinations of these main types. In certain instances it is difficult to draw a fine line of demarcation to indicate where one type of item ends and another starts. This is of little import, however, since the exact name of an item is of minor concern if it does a good job of measuring what it is supposed to measure.

The next few chapters contain descriptions of these main types of items, together with variations of them. The explanations and examples will serve as guides to be used in designing individual items for various types of subject matter. Keep in mind that adaptations and variations can be devised to suit specific requirements that you may find in your teaching.

---

[9] Crawford and Burnham, *op. cit.,* p. 106, call "multiple-choice" a misnomer. They prefer the term "restricted-answer" as being more descriptive of this type of item.

[10] This type of item is sometimes called "simple-recall" or "short-answer." It is difficult to differentiate between this type and the completion type. There is little agreement in the literature as to the difference. Perhaps the best way to describe the free-response item is to characterize it with a blank space at the end of a statement calling for a written expression by the student. A completion item will consist of a sentence or paragraph in which significant words are missing and must be provided by the student. A free-response item may be answered by a word or phrase, but it may also require a paragraph. In this sense, the essay-type item would thus be classified as a free-response item.

SUMMARY

Test construction requires a systematic, organized approach if positive results are to be forthcoming. The following steps will serve as a guide to the test maker who would strive to make his examinations as valid as possible:

1. List the major objectives for which an appraisal is desired.
2. Examine the course content for additional objectives.
3. Analyze and define each objective in terms of expected student outcomes.
4. Establish a table of specifications.
5. Construct one or more test items for each objective listed.
6. Assemble the items for the test.
7. Write clear and concise directions for each type of question.
8. Study every aspect of the assembled test.
9. Construct the key.
10. Have other instructors criticize and, if possible, actually take the test.
11. Make any necessary revisions.
12. After the test has been administered to one or two groups of students, analyze and improve it.

A helpful means for constructing tests is a card file of effective test items. Such a file can be developed over a period of time, and the busy instructor will find it has various uses. There are several ways in which such a file can be organized, but the important point is for the instructor to get in the habit of systematically contributing items to his file.

There are numerous points to be observed in constructing a test. Some of the more important are listed below. Others will be included in the discussion of specific types of test items.

1. It is not possible to measure all outcomes of instruction with one type of test.
2. Make the test comprehensive, but exclude insignificant and trivial items.
3. Devise your items so that they require the student actually to apply things learned rather than merely recall or recognize facts.

4. Make certain that the type of item used for measuring each objective is the one that will measure best that objective.

5. Avoid trick or "catch" questions.

6. Include a large number of items in the test.

7. Do not "lift" statements directly from books and use them as test items.

8. Whenever possible, avoid items with only two choices from which the student selects one.

9. Check to make sure that no item can be answered simply by referring to other items.

10. Make each item independent of the others.

11. Include no item for which the response is obvious to a person who does not know the subject matter.

12. Word the items in the simplest possible manner.

13. State questions clearly. Eliminate ambiguous items.

14. Keep the method of recording responses as simple as possible. (Keep the student in mind.)

15. Leave sufficient space for all responses without crowding.

16. Arrange blanks for responses along one side of the page, if possible.

17. Arrange the items so that responses will not form a particular pattern.

18. Arrange the items in such a manner that it will not be necessary for the student to refer to more than one page in answering a given item.

19. Number the responses consecutively from the beginning to the end of the test.

20. The practice of underlining crucial words, if not done too frequently and indiscriminately, tends to increase the objectivity of test items.

21. Avoid the weighting of items.

22. If certain items are to be corrected for guessing, this should be clearly indicated in the directions.

23. Make sure the directions are clear and complete.

24. Prepare a proper heading for the test.

Test items can be classified in several ways. One method is to divide them into two groups: those which demand recall (completion, listing, etc.), and those which call only for recognition of the correct answer (multiple-choice, true-false, etc.). It is difficult to draw a fine line of demarcation between the two. Either type can be a good item if it is designed to measure application of things learned. This is the important criterion to keep in mind.

For the purpose of this discussion test items have been classified under five main headings: (1) multiple-choice; (2) true-false; (3) matching; (4) recall; (5) miscellaneous. There are many adaptations, modifications, and combinations of these main types.

SOME THINGS TO DO AND QUESTIONS TO ANSWER

1. Do you think it is really necessary to list the objectives to be measured before listing the bits of subject matter that help in realizing the objectives? Why?

2. If you were to make a card file of test items for a particular field, how would you proceed? Select a particular field. What are some of the headings under which you would file the items? How did you arrive at these headings?

3. Think of yourself in a teaching situation. What are some instances in which you will not be able to use pencil-and-paper tests? How will your evaluation proceed in those instances?

4. How will you decide whether a particular test item is trivial or insignificant? Give an example.

5. Consider the following statement: "To every action there is an opposite and equal reaction." Now, construct two test items, one that measures the ability to apply the fact as well as one that measures only the retention of the fact. Be prepared to discuss the procedure you followed and some of your conclusions after having made these two types of items.

6. What is the significance of saying that the objective comes first and the test item second?

7. Shown at right are the top and front views of an object. Can you draw a correct right end view? Do you consider this to be a trick or catch question? Why?

8. When is a trick question not a trick question?

9. What do you think about "lifting" statements and using them as test items?

10. Why is it a poor policy to have the correct answer to one item dependent upon the correct answer to another item?

11. Have you ever tried to look for "specific determiners" in a test

that you have taken? Do you think such words as "all," "never," "always," and the like, should be left out of test items entirely? Why?

12. Is it possible to word a test item so that it is too simple?

13. Some persons might not agree with the authors that the blanks for responses should be placed at the left of the page. What do you think?

14. Do you agree that little is to be gained by having some items count more than others? Why?

15. What do you think about correcting for guessing? How do you react when told not to guess?

16. Do you think it is necessary to include an example along with the directions for a particular set of test items?

17. Prepare a sample heading for a test, using your name and a subject in which you are interested. See if you can devise a better heading than that included in the text.

18. Prepare two sample recall and recognition items from your special field of interest. Using these two items as examples, discuss the phrase "application of information in purposeful situations."

19. What do you think about using the "who, what, when" types of test item?

20. Consider the following cliché: "What a man is depends upon what he does when he has nothing to do." Construct a recall item and a recognition item that measure an understanding of this statement.

21. By means of an original example can you show how a recognition item can call for recall on the part of the student?

SELECTED REFERENCES FOR ADDITIONAL READING

Adkins, Dorothy C., and associates. *Construction and Analysis of Achievement Tests.* Washington, D.C.: Government Printing Office, 1947. Chap. II.

Greene, Harry A., Albert N. Jorgensen, and J. Raymond Gerberich. *Measurement and Evaluation in the Secondary School.* New York: Longmans, Green & Co., Inc., 1943. Chap. VIII.

Hawkes, Herbert E., E. F. Lindquist, and C. R. Mann. *The Construction and Use of Achievement Examinations.* Boston: Houghton Mifflin Company, 1936. Pp. 107–118.

Lee, J. Murray. *A Guide to Measurement in Secondary Schools.* New York: Appleton-Century-Crofts, Inc., 1936. Chap. X.

Loevinger, Jane. *Systematic Approach to the Construction and Evaluation of Tests of Ability.* Psychological Monographs, Vol. 61, No. 4,

Whole No. 285. Washington, D.C.: American Psychological Association, 1947. Pp. 49.

McCall, William A. *Measurement,* Part Two. New York: The Macmillan Company, 1939.

Ross, C. C. *Measurement in Today's Schools.* New York: Prentice-Hall, Inc., 1947. Chap. IV.

CHAPTER

SIX: MULTIPLE–CHOICE ITEMS

A MULTIPLE-CHOICE item consists of a question or incomplete statement followed by several possible answers. The student must select the best or correct answer in accordance with the directions given. The preliminary problem can usually be stated either as a question or as an incomplete statement as shown in the following example:

```
Question:  A hexagon has how many sides?
A. 3 ⎫
B. 4 ⎪ Possible
C. 5 ⎬ answers
D. 6 ⎪
E. 7 ⎭
```

```
Incomplete statement:  The number of sides contained in a
                       hexagon is
A. 3 ⎫
B. 4 ⎪ Possible
C. 5 ⎬ answers
D. 6 ⎪
E. 7 ⎭
```

The multiple-choice item, in its several forms, is one of the most valuable types that can be incorporated in a written test. Before discussing the uses, limitations, and points to observe in constructing multiple-choice items, several examples of common variations will be presented.[1]

[1] The individual items contained in these examples and those in the following chapters are not necessarily from related subject-matter fields. The first item may be from one field. the second from another. and so on.

One Right Answer

This is the simplest kind of multiple-choice item. The student is required to identify the one correct response listed among several that are totally wrong but not obviously wrong.[2]

Directions: Each of the questions or incomplete statements
listed below is followed by several words, phrases, or
series of numbers. From these, you are to choose the one
which answers the question or completes the statement correctly. Place the letter of that word or phrase (A,B,C,D,
or E) in the numbered blank space at the left of the item.
The first item is answered as an example to follow.
(D)x. An auger bit that bores a 1/2" hole is stamped with
     what number?
     A. 2
     B. 4
     C. 6
     D. 8
     E. 10
____1. A line with a true length of 84' is represented on
     paper by a line 10 1/2" long. What scale was used?
     A. 1/32
     B. 1/16
     C. 1/8
     D. 3/16
     E. 1/4

____22. The central theme of The Citadel by A. J. Cronin
     is
     A. warfare in the Middle Ages.
     B. Japanese aggression in China.
     C. the growth of the Oxford group.
     D. corruption in the medical profession.

____16. If a blue dish is stared at for a few minutes and
     then quickly taken away, the color of the after-
     image will be
     A. red
     B. green
     C. dark purple
     D. orange

[2] Directions will not be repeated for individual test items except as a new type of item requires different directions.

____32. The specific heat of ice is .5 and that of water
is 1. Yet it takes 80 calories of heat to change
one gram of ice into water at zero degrees Centigrade. This is because
A. ice is colder than water.
B. the specific heat of water is greater than
that of ice.
C. water expands from zero degrees Centigrade to
4 degrees C.
D. it takes work to overcome the forces holding
the molecules in ice together.
E. water radiates heat faster than ice.

____1. A ship is moving north at 20 miles per hour. The
pennant flying at the top points exactly southeast.
The wind, whose velocity is 20 miles per hour, is
blowing toward the
A. southwest
B. south
C. west
D. east
E. southeast

____13. Extra legal organ-   ____14. Plebiscite means
ization means
A. unlawful   A. diplomatic com-
                                      promise
B. law-enforcing   B. use of arbitra-
                                      tion
C. law-making   C. vote of the
                                      people
D. outside the law   D. military conquest
E. unnecessary   E. use of propaganda

____7. In 1935 the index of cost of living had fallen to
82.6 relative to 1929. That is,
A. $82.60 would buy as much in 1929 as $100 did in
1935.
B. Prices had decreased 17.4% in 1935.
C. $82.60 would buy as much in 1935 as $100 did in
1929.
D. The appropriate expenditure required for various
American standards of living would be more in
1935 than in 1929.

____41. Although the father of a large family, many of
whom became famous as musicians, his traditions
and teachings were forgotten for almost a hundred
years. His name was
A. Palestrina
B. Bach
C. Mozart
D. Liszt
E. Weber

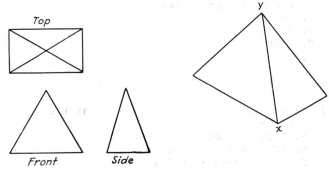

____13. Consider the line XY in the isometric drawing
above. In which of the orthographic views, if
any, is this line shown in its true length?
A. Front
B. Side
C. Top
D. In none of the views

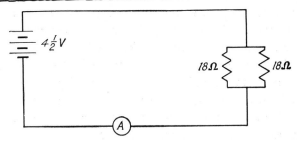

____25. In the circuit shown above the current reading on
the ammeter will be
A. 5 amperes
B. 500 microamperes
C. 2 amperes
D. 2 milliamperes
E. 500 milliamperes

_____16. The national coarse thread corresponds most
       closely to which of the following?
       A. S.A.E.
       B. U.S.S.
       C. N.S.
       D. N.F.T.

_____3. When using the left—hand rule the fore finger points
      in the direction of the
      A. current
      B. force
      C. flux
      D. torque

_____12. An exposure made at 1/100 second at f/8 is equiva-
       lent to
       A. 1/200 second at f/16
       B. 1/25 second at f/16
       C. 1/40 second at f/4.5
       D. 1/25 second at f/4.5

Best Answer

This variation requires the student to select the correct answer or best response from a series of several responses. It is perhaps the most valuable of the several forms of multiple-choice items. It has often been criticized, however, because the selection of the best response involves judgment. This is not a valid criticism. The fact that it does require judgment or inferential reasoning or complete understanding to select the best response is the most important feature of the item. A major responsibility of good teaching is to get the students to the point where they can form judgments, draw conclusions, make close discriminations, and arrive at decisions. You must teach and test for these abilities.

This type of multiple-choice item may be varied to require the student to: (1) Select the *two* best responses from a series of possible answers, (2) indicate the *worst* response or the least desirable solution, (3) indicate both the *best* and the *worst* responses. All of these variations can be employed to measure the student's ability to use logical reasoning and make application of things learned.

Directions: Each of the questions or incomplete statements listed below is followed by several possible answers. Choose the answer that best answers the question or completes the statement. Place the identifying letter of that answer (A,B,C,D, or E) in the numbered blank space at the left of the item. The first item is answered as an example.

(B) (x) You are finishing a fine piece of furniture, and notice a bad spot in the wood. Which of the following methods would be the best to use in repairing the surface?
  A. Fill the hole with stick shellac.
  B. Inlay with the same kind of wood.
  C. Fill with glue and sawdust from the same kind of wood.
  D. Drill out the bad spot.

_____ A man is found unconscious on the floor beside a gas stove from which gas is issuing. The most important thing to do is
  A. call a doctor
  B. take the man to a hospital
  C. throw cold water on the man
  D. get the man into fresh air and start artificial respiration
  E. rub the man's arms and legs

__13. The Law of Effect is an expression of the relationship between success and pleasant feelings. Which of the following is an application of this principle in the teaching of Industrial Arts?
  A. The beginning projects for a new class should be relatively simple.
  B. The first efforts of the pupil should result in a completed project with little attention paid to the proper skills.
  C. The teacher should do most of the operations for the beginning student in order that the first project may be successful.
  D. Students will do little work if they do not experience pleasant feelings.
  E. Students will not learn if they experience unpleasant feelings in the first activities of the class.

____1. The most _important_ _difference_ between a standard-
ized achievement test and the informal, classroom-
teacher type is:
(A) The standardized test has been constructed by
    experts in test construction and subject
    matter.
(B) The standardized test has a far more adequate
    sampling of the subject matter to the course.
(C) Every item in the standardized test has been
    proven.
(D) Norms are furnished for the standardized test
    that fit the classroom situation.
(E) The standardized test is generally more valid
    in the classroom situation.

____91. The most tangible result of granting women the
right to vote has been to
A. bring about a higher moral tone in politics.
B. prevent poorly qualified candidates from becom-
   ing elected to public office.
C. increase the amount of social legislation.
D. increase the number of votes.
E. increase expenditures for educational purposes.

____92. Which of the following circumstances best explains
the fact that Federal regulation of motorbus and
truck transportation did not come until 1936?
A. attempts at Federal regulation had been declared
   unconstitutional.
B. such transportation was not of great interstate
   significance until that decade.
C. public opinion was opposed to such regulation.
D. Federal regulation of other means of transportation had been ineffective.
E. Federal regulation of railroads had been too
   arbitrary.

____29. If you had a job in the printing industry and did a
lot of work with stereotypes, you would likely be
working in a
A. newspaper printing plant.
B. photoengraving shop.
C. small job shop.
D. lithographing establishment.
E. paper supply company.

_____1. It is more economical to buy medium-sized prunes in
       preference to large prunes because
       A. there is more pulp per prune.
       B. large prunes provide fewer stones per unit of
          weight.
       C. large prunes provide more pulp per prune.
       D. medium-sized prunes provide more pulp per pound
          as purchased.

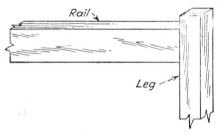

_____19. Imagine that the table rail and leg shown above are
        to be part of a <u>fine</u> piece of furniture. Of the
        following, what are the <u>two</u> best methods for
_____20. fastening the rail to the leg?
        A. screws and glue
        B. mortise and tenon
        C. end lap
        D. dado
        E. dowels and glue
        F. bolts

_____2. A university student had recurring sinus infections.
       He was told at the health service that he might
       build up his resistance to colds by
       A. eating more carbohydrates.
       B. taking an iron tonic.
       C. taking cod-liver oil.
       D. eating yeast.
       E. taking regular exercise.

_____6. With respect to the paintings by Picasso one might
       say the main force is
       A. the idea that the form expresses.
       B. the form rather than the idea.
       C. the relationship of parts.
       D. the distortion.
       E. the placement of emphasis.

____76. Mrs. Jones' first child walked when he was 15
months old, so when her second child was that age,
she gave him walking exercises. In spite of this
exercise, however, the second child did not walk
until he was 17 months old. This may be accounted
for by the fact that
A. maturation depends upon learning ability.
B. the child was mentally retarded.
C. conditioning depends upon learning ability.
D. learning depends upon maturation.
E. the first child was advanced in its development.

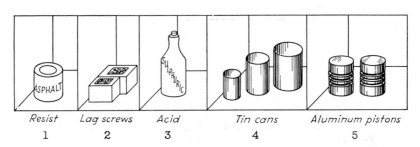

Resist	Lag screws	Acid	Tin cans	Aluminum pistons
1	2	3	4	5

____32. The illustrations above represent compartments of a
storage cabinet for <u>art</u> <u>metal</u> equipment and
supplies. Which one of the compartments contains
materials that would <u>not</u> be useful to an ordinary
class in art metal work?
A. 1
B. 2
C. 3
D. 4
E. 5

____35. The difference between demand and desire of con-
sumers is that
A. demand applies to strictly necessary wants.
B. desire becomes demand if no purchase has been
made.
C. people do not demand all they desire because of
lack of purchasing power.
D. consumers' desires are often not in agreement
with social welfare.
E. demand applies only to goods that can be
measured in physical units.

_____3. In the past strong third parties of American
national politics have existed for only a short time
because
A. they were too radical.
B. the reforms they advocated were usually absorbed
into the major party programs.
C. the issues they raised disappeared with changing
conditions.
D. Congress legislated them out of existence.
E. they became popular.

_____5. What is your reaction to the chimneys on Folwell
Hall?
A. They are an example of art for art's sake.
B. They show a functional use of materials.
C. They are not related to the style of the build-
ing.
D. They contribute to a unified impression.
E. They are necessary ornamentations.

_____23. The fame of Pearl S. Buck rests primarily on her
A. interesting development of the "stream-of-con-
sciousness" technique.
B. witty portrayal of diplomatic society.
C. clarification of the class struggle in fictional
form.
D. masterly portrayal of the life of the Chinese
peasant.

Association Items

The association type of multiple-choice item includes a word,
phrase, or illustrations, followed by several choices, one of which
is most closely associated with the first part. It might be considered as another variation of the best-answer type.[3] When properly
constructed this type of item can measure well the inferential
reasoning ability of the students.

[3] It is also referred to as a matching-type item by some persons. In reality
there is very little difference between the matching type of item and the
multiple-choice type of item.

<u>Directions</u>: The following groups of words refer to gas welding. The first word is closely related to another word in the group. Select the word to which the first word is most closely related. Place the identifying letter of the word in the blank space at the left. The first item is answered as an example.

(C)x. Gauge: (A) hose, (B) torch, (C) pressure, (D) tip

_____1. Neutral: (A) tempering, (B) pressure, (C) flame, (D) annealing

_____2. Carbon: (A) brass, (B) steel, (C) aluminum, (D) copper

_____3. Annealing: (A) plunging, (B) hardening, (C) tempering, (D) softening

---

_____16. calculate (A. marvel, B. administer, C. plaster, D. reckon, E. convene)

_____17. ignite (A. ignorant, B. congest, C. shoot, D. kindle, E. swindle)

_____18. craftsman (A. redeemer, B. deceiver, C. boatman, D. sentinel, E. workman)

_____19. barter (A. trundle, B. exchange, C. landlord, D. joke, E. boatman)

_____16. 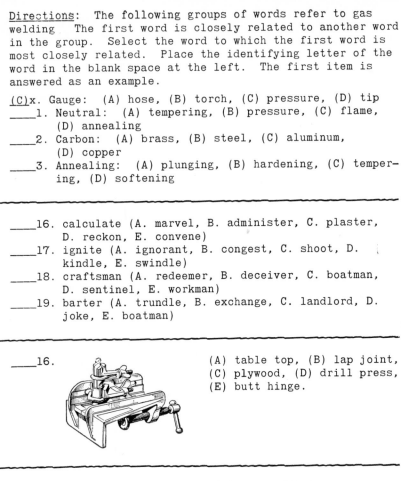 (A) table top, (B) lap joint, (C) plywood, (D) drill press, (E) butt hinge.

_____27.  (A) dado, (B) try square, (C) end lap, (D) rabbet plane, (E) cross lap

Analogy-type Items

The analogy item is an adaptation of a mathematical type of abbreviation (4:2::10:?). The student is required to discover the relationship that exists between the first two parts of the item. He then applies this relationship to the third and fourth parts. The third part is given, but the fourth must be selected from the

several choices on the basis of the relationship existing between
the first two parts. This type of item has been used more often in
intelligence testing than in achievement tests.

Directions: In the following items determine the relationship between the first two parts of the item. Then apply
this relationship to the third and fourth parts by selecting the proper choice (A,B,C,D, or E) to go with the third
part. Place the letter of your choice in the blank space
at the left. The first two items are answered as examples:
(D) (x) 4:2::10:?   (A) 20, (B) 16, (C) 8, (D) 5, (E) 3
           (is to)   (as)   (is to)
(B) (x) Hack saw : saw blade :: jack plane : ?   (A) chisel,
         (B) plane iron, (C) cap screw, (D) block plane,
         (E) jointer plane

____6. Carpentry : hammer and saw :: foundry work : ?
       (A) expansion and contraction, (B) tap and die,
       (C) cope and drag, (D) flange and fuse, (E) hollow
       mandrel and blowhorn.

____18. Sampling is to comprehensiveness as item analysis
        is to
        (A) Reliability
        (B) Ease of administration
        (C) Subjectivity
        (D) Discrimination
        (E) Objectivity

____11.
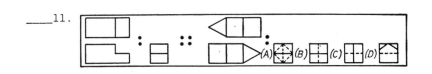

____17. Electricity : Edison :: Printing : ?   (A) Franklin,
        (B) Goudy, (C) Caslon, (D) Gutenberg, (E) Chelten-
        ham.

Reverse Multiple-choice

The reverse multiple-choice item differs from other forms in
that the student is required to choose the poorest or wrong re-

sponse from among several correct responses. This variation is especially adapted for that type of material in which there are several correct or best responses. It has two features. First it is usually easier to construct three or four responses that are true about a general fact than to make several that are plausible but still wrong. Second, in deciding on their response, students seem to consider more of the choices listed after such items. If this is true, then such items might be said to demand more interpretation and discrimination on the part of the student. Experience has shown that a section of reverse multiple-choice items should not be placed immediately after regular multiple-choice items in a test. The students are apt to be confused when, after selecting the best response in one set of items, they are confronted immediately with a similar set of items requiring the opposite type of response.

Directions: Each of the questions or incomplete statements listed below is followed by several answers. All but one of the answers are correct. One is wrong. You are to pick out the one that is wrong or false. Place the letter of that choice (A,B,C,D, or E) in the numbered blank space at the left of the item. The first item is answered as an example.

(C)(x) Saws are set to
    A. keep them from binding
    B. make them cut faster
    C. straighten the teeth
    D. keep the teeth sharp longer
    E. keep the saw from becoming too hot

____52. If the corner grocer is prosperous
    A. the laborer is prosperous
    B. the manufacturer is prosperous
    C. the excess reserves of the banks are decreasing
    D. production is decreasing

____39. The chief functions of the Federal Reserve banks are to
    A. invest in business enterprises
    B. influence interest rates
    C. carry on open-market operations
    D. provide elastic currency

____22. Authors who are particularly successful in re-
producing the rhythms and idioms of everyday speech
are
A. James M. Cain
B. Edith Wharton
C. Ernest Hemingway
D. John Steinbeck

____23. To read imaginatively is to
A. meet experience vicariously
B. associate material read with one's own
experiences.
C. read primarily for facts
D. read constructively

____32. The United States Congress has a check over the
executive departments through its
A. control of appropriations
B. right to assign duties and powers
C. right to create departments, bureaus, and
divisions
D. power to pass a vote of no confidence
E. power of impeachment

____33. The duties of the Federal government to the states
include
A. protection from foreign invasion
B. guaranty of republican form of government
C. approval of interstate compacts
D. protection from domestic uprising
E. guaranty of their territorial integrity

____1. In an electric circuit with capacitance
A. there is an opposition to any change in voltage
B. the current phase is affected by voltage lagging
current
C. the current flowing varies with the frequency of
the supply voltage
D. after initial charging, direct current will flow
in the circuit
E. after initial charging, alternating current will
flow in the circuit

____62. The square knot is a good knot for
    A. tying two ropes together
    B. tying packages
    C. making a large loop that will not slip
    D. shortening a rope
    E. securing several boxes together

____2. Nichrome wire is used in making electric
    A. toasters
    B. heaters
    C. stoves
    D. light bulbs
    E. heating pads

____47. The flutes of a hand tap are made to
    A. give the tap its cutting edge
    B. reduce friction
    C. reduce the weight of the tap
    D. allow the chips to pass out
    E. allow oil to reach the threads

____16. Some of the more common papers used in the printing
       industry are
    A. pulp
    B. graphic
    C. calendered
    D. sulphite
    E. coated

____31. The following are examples of a simple machine:
    A. wedge
    B. crowbar
    C. wheelbarrow
    D. pulley
    E. try square

Uses and Advantages of Multiple-choice Items

1. The multiple-choice item can be designed to measure effectively the student's ability to interpret, discriminate, select, and make application of things learned. It can be used to measure understanding, judgment, and inferential reasoning ability. For these

purposes it is generally the most valuable of the several types of objective test items.

2. It can be used to measure what one can recognize, which represents a much wider field than what one can recall.

3. Its scoring can be made entirely objective. It is well adapted to machine scoring.

4. The guessing factor does not present as much of a problem in multiple-choice items as in several other types.

5. Students are generally well acquainted with this type of item. They understand what is to be done. There is not likely to be confusion as to how to proceed (unless one of the variations is used without proper explanation).

Mosier, Myers, and Price[4] have set forth fourteen types of questions that can be measured by multiple-choice items. Their list with illustrative examples is included below in slightly modified form. Note that each of the items is measuring some aspect of the person's understanding of the concept of central tendency as used in statistics (in each instance the correct choice is A).

1. Questions relating to definition.
   a. What means the same as . . . ?
   b. Which of the following statements expresses this concept in different terms?

```
The value which is determined by adding all the scores and
dividing by the number of cases is known in statistics as
the
A. arithmetic mean
B. median
C. mode
D. harmonic mean
E. average deviation
```

2. Questions relating to purpose.
   a. What purpose is served by . . . ?
   b. What principle is exemplified by . . . ?
   c. Why is this done . . . ?
   d. What is the most important reason for . . . ?

[4] Charles I. Mosier, M. C. Myers, and Helen G. Price, "Suggestions for the Construction of Multiple Choice Test Items," *Educational and Psychological Measurement,* 5:267–269 (Autumn, 1945). Used by permission.

The mean is obtained for the purpose of providing
A. a single number to represent a whole series of numbers.
B. the central point in a series.
C. a measure of group variability.
D. an indication of the most frequent response given.
E. an estimate of the relationship between two variables.

3. Questions relating to cause.
   a. What is the cause of . . . ?
   b. Under which of the following conditions is this true . . . ?

From which of the following measures of central tendency
will the sum of the deviations equal zero?
A. the mean
B. the mode
C. the median
D. an arbitrary origin
E. any measure of central tendency

4. Questions relating to effect.
   a. What is the effect of . . . ?
   b. If this is done, what will happen?
   c. Which of the following should be done [to achieve a given
      purpose]?

The arithmetic mean of 55 cases is 83.00. If three of the
cases with values of 82, 115, and 130 are deleted from the
data, the mean of the remaining 52 cases will be
A. 81.50
B. 77.05
C. 83.00
D. 84.50
E. 94.08

5. Questions relating to association.
   What tends to occur in connection with . . . ? [Temporal,
   causal, or concomitant association.]

If the distribution of scores is skewed positively, the
mean will be
A. lower than the median
B. the same as the median
C. higher than the median
D. relatively unaffected
E. the same as the mode

6. Questions relating to recognition of error.
   Which of the following constitutes an error [with respect to a given situation]?

The mean should not be used as the measure of central tendency when
A. the distribution of scores is significantly skewed
B. there are a large number of cases
C. a nontechnical report is to be prepared
D. the data are continuous
E. other statistical formulas are to be computed

7. Questions relating to identification of error.
   a. What kind of error is this?
   b. What is the name of this error?
   c. What recognized principle is violated?

In computation of the mean of a distribution from grouped data, the sums of the deviations above and below the arbitrary origin were found to be 127 and 189, respectively. The final value for the mean was in error. Of the following possibilities, that one which is most likely to have caused the error is that the computer
A. failed to note the correct sign in adding the mean of the deviations to the assumed origin
B. used an assumed mean higher than the true mean
C. omitted some of the cases in tabulating the data
D. divided by the wrong number of cases
E. multiplied by the wrong class-interval value

8. Questions relating to evaluation.
   What is the best evaluation of . . . [for a given purpose] and for what reason?

When the number of cases is small, e.g., less than 20, and the magnitude of the values is likewise small, the use of an assumed mean in the computation of the mean can best be evaluated as
A. less efficient than computation from actual values
B. likely to distort the value obtained by the introduction of a constant error
C. more accurate than the use of actual values
D. neither better nor worse than computation by other methods
E. applicable only if the distribution is reasonably symmetrical

9. Questions relating to difference.

What is the [an] important difference between . . . ?

Of the following statements, the one which best characterizes the essential difference between the mean and the median as measures of the central tendency of a distribution
is that
A. the magnitude of each score does not contribute propor-
   tionately to the computation of the median but does for
   the mean
B. the median is a point whereas the mean is a distance
C. the mean is less affected by extreme values than is the
   median
D. the median is easier to compute than the mean
E. the median is more generally used than the mean

10. Questions relating to similarity.

What is the [an] important similarity between . . . ?

The mean and median are both measures of
A. central tendency
B. distance
C. position
D. variation
E. relationship

11. Questions relating to arrangement.

In the proper order [to achieve a given purpose or to follow
a given rule], which of the following comes first [or last or
follows a given item]?

In the computation of the mean for data already grouped in
class intervals, the most efficient first step is to
A. determine the arbitrary origin and enter the deviation
   values
B. find the midpoints of the class intervals
C. multiply the frequency in each interval by the midpoint
   of the interval
D. add the column of scores
E. find the reciprocal of the total number of cases

12. Questions relating to incomplete arrangement.

In the proper order, which of the following should be inserted here to complete the series?

In the derivation of the formula for computing the mean
from grouped data using an arbitrary origin, the following
steps were taken:

(a) $X' = \dfrac{X - A}{i}$

(b) $\Sigma x = i\Sigma X' + NA$

(c) $\dfrac{\Sigma X}{N} = A + \dfrac{i\Sigma X'}{N}$

The step which is implied between steps (a) and (b) is

A. solving (a) for X
B. summing (a) over the N cases
C. multiplying by i
D. adding A to both terms of (a)
E. dividing by N

13. Questions relating to common principle.

All the following items except one are retarded by a common principle:

a. What is the principle?

b. Which item does not belong?

c. Which of the following items should be substituted?

All except one of the following items (arithmetic mean,
median, mode, and quartile) are measures of central tendency. Of the following statistics, that one which could be
substituted in the series for the item improperly included
is

A. harmonic mean for quartile
B. average deviation for mode
C. range for quartile
D. standard deviation for quartile
E. 50th percentile for median

14. Questions relating to controversial subjects.

Although not everyone agrees on the desirability of . . . ,
those who support its desirability do so primarily for the reason that:

Although not everyone agrees that the mean is the best
measure of central tendency, those who advocate its general
use base their recommendation primarily on the fact that
the mean

A. has the smallest sampling error
B. is the easiest to compute
C. is most readily understood
D. is the most typical score
E. is not affected by extreme scores

Limitations

1. Many test makers do not know how or do not take the time to utilize multiple-choice items properly. In too many instances the item is constructed to measure memorization only, rather than application.

2. It is difficult to devise items so that the several "decoy"[5] choices are plausible though not correct or most desirable. The decoy statements are often obviously wrong. In other instances they provide clues that make the correct response obvious.

3. It is easy to include more than one response that can be marked correctly. In other words, it is sometimes difficult to construct a good item so that one and only one response is the correct one.

4. The multiple-choice test is space consuming and time consuming.[6]

Points to Be Observed in Constructing Multiple-choice Items

1. The Stem[7] of the Item Should Contain a Central Problem. It should not be merely an incomplete statement followed by four or five true-false statements only one of which is true.

Poor

```
_____ Pine knots
         A. should be covered with shellac before paint-
            ing.
         B. will stop giving off pitch if they are treated
            with raw linseed oil.
         C. can sometimes be sealed with turpentine.
         D. should be cut out before the board is used.
         E. do not need any protective coating.
```

[5] The term "decoy" refers to wrong answers among the several alternative or possible answers.

[6] It should be emphasized that these two points are presented as limitations and not criticisms of multiple-choice items.

[7] The word "stem" in this instance refers to the first part of the item—the introductory statement or question. It is sometimes called the "problem" or the "lead." The remainder of the item may be referred to as "choices," "alternatives," "answers," "options," or "possible responses."

Better

_____ You are about to paint a new garage that has been
constructed from pine boards containing numerous
knots. In order to avoid paint discoloration
which of the following would you use to cover the
knots?
A. shellac
B. raw linseed oil
C. turpentine
D. varnish
E. lacquer

In the first example above the five choices are merely a collec-
tion of true-false statements that start with the same words, "Pine
knots." There is no central problem. The several choices are not
plausible answers to a single problem or introductory question.

In the second item a central problem is described. It is followed
by several brief choices each of which might be plausible to a person not knowing the subject matter. While the second example is
considerably better because of a central problem, it, too, might be
improved to measure more than the ability to recognize the material used in covering knots.

_____ You are about to construct a garage from pine
lumber containing numerous tight knots. When
looking at the lumber you begin to wonder if the
presence of so many knots will affect the painting of the garage. Which of the following statements would best express a solution to your
problem?
A. In most instances it will not be necessary to
   worry about the knots.
B. Cover the knots with shellac before painting.
C. Cut out the knots before construction starts.
D. Be sure that the priming coat contains a sufficient amount of linseed oil.

In this instance the central problem is followed by choices that
call for more discrimination on the part of the student. It would be
a better measure of the student's real understanding of the point
in question. It helps to illustrate an important point: A central

problem is necessary in a well-constructed multiple-choice item, but it is only the first part of the item. Having a central problem does not of itself guarantee that the item will measure application of the material being tested.

The central problem may be in the form of a direct question, or it may be an incomplete statement. The direct question will usually require more words, although it is likely to be less ambiguous. In using a direct question the choices tend to be more homogeneous, and irrelevant clues are less likely to occur in the problem. Most items will lend themselves to either approach. For beginning test makers, it is suggested that the central problem first be stated in the form of a direct question. It may later be changed to an incomplete statement, but in most instances the direct question will suffice.

2. The Item Should Be Practical and Realistic. It should not be academic and artificial (as so many items are). It should demand knowledge and understanding that the student must have or use as a part of his everyday living or on the job. It should not be designed to measure innate intelligence (unless it is to be used in an intelligence test).

Poor—Academic

    ____1. Which of the following is the formula to use in determining board feet?

    A. $\dfrac{T'' \times W' \times L''}{144}$

    B. $\dfrac{T'' \times W'' \times L''}{12}$

    C. $\dfrac{T'' \times W'' \times L'}{144}$

    D. $\dfrac{T'' \times W'' \times L'}{12}$

Better—Practical

    ____2. In order to construct a window box you need <u>two</u> pieces of cypress 3/4" thick, 8" wide, and 6' long (2 pieces 3/4" x 8" x 6'). If the lumberyard charges 16 cents per board foot for cypress, what will be the cost of the lumber?

    A. $ .64
    B. $ .96
    C. $1.08
    D. $1.28
    E. $1.46

In the item asking for the correct board-foot formula the student is very apt to say, "So what?" He would be justified in this. It is doubtful that he would ever need the ability to recite the formula for finding board feet. That is all the item would measure. It is unrealistic. It is artificial. If the test maker were interested in measuring the ability of the student to use the formula, this could be accomplished much better with a practical problem, as in the second example.

Poor

_____3. An oblique drawing may be defined as being
   A. the same as an isometric drawing.
   B. similar to an isometric drawing.
   C. closely related to a perspective drawing.
   D. similar to a cabinet drawing.
   E. similar to an orthographic projection.

Better

    I   2   3   4   5

_____4. Which of the above drawings of a cube is known as an oblique drawing?
   A. 1
   B. 2
   C. 3
   D. 4
   E. 5

The first example concerning an oblique drawing is also academic. If it is necessary for a student to be able to identify an oblique drawing, it would be much more practical to use illustrations, as in the second example. If it is essential for the student to know and understand an oblique drawing, a still better measure would be to have him actually construct a drawing.

Closely allied to academic and unreal items are those which are trivial or almost useless when viewed in the light of practicality. As an example of this point, consider two examples from the field of printing:

Poor—No Central Problem

    ____1. The primary colors are
        A. Red, green, yellow.
        B. Orange, blue, green.
        C. Yellow, blue, green.
        D. Red, yellow, blue.
        E. Red, blue, orange.

Better

    ____2. Suppose that you are about to run a platen press job
        that requires <u>green</u> ink. It is necessary to mix the
        ink. Which of the following statements best expres-
        ses the procedure to follow?
        A. Apply blue ink first, then yellow
        B. Apply red ink, then yellow
        C. Apply yellow ink, then blue
        D. Apply yellow ink, then red
        E. Apply red ink, then blue

A student could memorize the primary colors and answer the first item correctly without having a practical understanding of what to do with the information. In the second example it is necessary for the student to apply an understanding of primary and secondary colors in solving a practical problem. It measures also an understanding of the procedure to follow in actually mixing the inks. Such an item measuring more than one point of knowledge is not undesirable in an achievement test.[8]

3. The Stated Problem Should Be Specific, Clear, and as Brief as Possible. There should be no question in the student's mind as to what the problem is. It should be as simple as possible. It should be readily understandable. It should not contain irrelevant information.

Poor

    ____1. You happen to pick up a threaded bolt. After look-
        ing at it for a while, you ask yourself if the prin-
        ciple used in the bolt is an example of any of the
        simple machines. If your understanding is correct
        you would conclude
        A. that the threaded bolt illustrates the principle
          of the lever.
        B. that the threaded bolt illustrates the principle
          of the wheel and axle.

[8] In a diagnostic test, however, each item should measure one specific point.

    C. that the threaded bolt illustrates the principle
       of the wedge.
    D. that the threaded bolt illustrates the principle
       of the inclined plane.
    E. that the threaded bolt illustrates the principle
       of the pulley.

Better

    ____2. A threaded bolt illustrates the principle of the
       A. lever
       B. wheel and axle
       C. wedge
       D. inclined plane
       E. pulley

The first example above can be criticized in several ways. It is not as simple as it might be. The preliminary statement contains irrelevant information that does not add to the effectiveness of the problem. There is needless repetition in each of the choices. An unnecessary amount of time would be consumed in answering the item. In this particular instance the objective could be measured more effectively and in shorter time by revising the item to read as in the second example.

It will not always be possible or desirable to make each item as brief as the second example above. The items must be considered in terms of all the suggestions presented here. Brevity and simplicity are two of these suggestions, but in making the items brief and simple you must be sure not to exclude the other features. In some instances there will be information in the central problem that appears irrelevant to the casual reader but in reality may be very important in the selection of the right choice.

4. Illustrations Are Sometimes Useful in Presenting the Central Problem. This is especially true in devising items concerning technical processes, tools, machines, understanding of drawings, and the like. A good general rule is to use an illustration whenever possible. In most cases this will help to make the item more practical and realistic and therefore more effective. In the first example the central problem would be confusing to say the least. Most students would have to stop and consider the several word meanings in an effort to obtain a mental picture of the piece of board in

Poor

_____1. A slanting cut on a board that intersects two per-
pendicular surfaces but not two parallel surfaces is
properly called
   A. a bevel
   B. an angle
   C. a slant
   D. a chamfer
   E. none of the above

Better

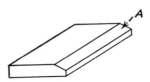

_____2. In the drawing above, the part of the board marked
"A" is properly called
   A. a bevel
   B. an angle
   C. a slant
   D. a chamfer
   E. none of the above

question. The example would take unnecessary time. The student
might mark the wrong response while knowing the point being
tested. This example would tend to measure intelligence as well
as achievement. All these criticisms disappear in the case of the
second example.

Sometimes a single illustration will provide material for several
items, as in the following example:

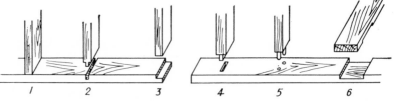

_____1. Which of the above joints would be the best to use
in attaching the shelves of a bookcase to the sides?
   A. 1   D. 4
   B. 2   E. 5
   C. 3   F. 6

```
____2. Which of the above joints would be the best to use
       in attaching a drawer front to the sides?
       A. 1
       B. 2
       C. 3
       D. 4
       E. 5
       F. 6
```

These two examples might be augmented by many other sample items that show the advantage of using illustrations in describing the central problem. In selecting or preparing illustrations for your multiple-choice items, two important points should be kept in mind. Keep the illustrations as simple as possible, and make them clear.

5. *Have at Least Four and Preferably Five Possible Answers* (*Choices*). When there are fewer than four choices, the item is little better than a true-false question. It is much easier to guess the correct response. In answering this item any intelligent student

```
____1. When fastening boards with nails, the nails should
       be driven
       A. in line with the grain.
       B. staggered.
       C. the handiest way.
```

would discard choice C immediately. That would leave only two choices, with a fifty-fifty chance of guessing the correct response. If it is possible to prepare only two or three good choices, then the test maker should use another type of item to do the measuring.

In certain instances it may be desirable to include six or even a greater number of choices (see page 186). These occasions will be rare, however.

6. *Include No Responses[9] That Are Obviously Wrong.* If a response is obviously wrong, it might as well be left out. There should not be one correct response listed among four obviously wrong ones, for an intelligent student can answer such an item by a process of elimination. All the possible answers should be worded

---

[9] The terms "responses," "answers," "choices," "alternatives" are used interchangeably to indicate the A,B,C,D,E parts of the items.

in such a manner that the student must know the subject matter in order to select the correct response.

The listing of obviously wrong responses is a common fault exhibited by beginning test makers. The example in the previous section includes one response (*C*) that is illustrative of this point. Because of the obviously wrong answer the guessing factor becomes very prominent. Consider the following item taken from a teacher-made test in the field of printing. Whether or not you are acquainted with the field of printing, you will probably be able to choose the correct response[10] by a simple process of elimination.

```
____9. A dirty proof has (1) two errors, (2) no errors,
              (3) many errors, (4) one error
```

In the next example, from the field of drafting, at least two of the choices (4 and 5) could be eliminated immediately because of

```
____16. Every circle shown on a drawing should have (1) one
         center line;  (2) two center lines;  (3) three
         center lines;  (4) no center lines;  (5) an odd
         number of center lines.
```

their obviously wrong nature. It is quite likely also that the correct answer could be determined through logical reasoning by an intelligent person who knows nothing at all about center lines or how they are used. The point to be emphasized here, however, is to check each item to make sure that none of the choices is obviously wrong.

7. *Avoid the Inclusion of Irrelevant Clues.* One common fault in this respect is to have the correct response consistently longer or consistently shorter than the "decoys." Very often the correct response must be an expanded statement in order to make it correct. The better students become aware of such defects and mark the

```
____ The electrons in a current flow
     A. from positive to negative.
     B. from negative to positive.
     C. actually from negative to positive, but due to an
        early error we say they flow from positive to neg-
        ative.
     D. whichever way the circuit is connected.
     E. along lines of least resistance.
```
[10] Choice (3).

correct answer by looking at the structure of the choices rather than the meaning. In this example the student may or may not be aware of the teacher's habits as to length of choices. However, he may remember vaguely something said in class about an "error," and because of the long explanation required in choice C he would tend to choose that response without knowing what the error really referred to. In the following example, from the field of auto mechanics, the correct answer is, again, significantly longer than the rest. In this instance the several choices could be lengthened

```
____ One of the most common causes of piston trouble is
     A. warped piston
     B. piston slap
     C. deposit of carbon on the piston
     D. scored pistons
```

without much difficulty, but the best procedure would be to revise the entire item by providing a central problem that is more realistic and practical.

In making multiple-choice items, then, be sure to keep the several choices about the same length. At the same time, check the grammatical construction of each item. Faulty grammar is another common weakness. Certain choices may be automatically discarded because of the grammar, as in the following example:

```
____6. A boring tool has a tendency to spring
       1. up
       2. down
       3. toward the top
       4. not to spring at all
```

In this item choices 1 and 3 mean the same thing. This reduces the possible answers to three. Many students would note the grammatical inconsistency of choice 4, simply because it does not "read right" with the incomplete statement. This would narrow the choices to two, "up" or "down," and the item would be no more reliable than a true-false question.

```
____ The power hack-saw blade may be
     1.  6 in. long
     2.  8 in. long
     3. 10 in. long
     4. 14 in. long
```

The preceding is an absurd item in several ways, but here we are concerned only with the grammatical construction. Consider the word "may" in the introductory statement. An intelligent student could argue logically that any one of the responses would be correct because of the use of "may." In the following example you will be able to detect at least two of the "decoys" by merely reading the introductory statement before each of the choices:

　　____ Greater sensitivity can be obtained
　　　　　(a) by a detector tube followed by two stages of
　　　　　　　audio-free amplification
　　　　　(b) by a detector tube preceded by two stages of R.F.
　　　　　　　amplification
　　　　　(c) by T.R.F.
　　　　　(d) superheterodyne
　　　　　(e) class-A type

Probably the maker of the above item worked diligently on the first choice, which was to serve as a decoy. Then the correct response was added. After that things must have begun to get difficult, or it was time to go home, for the last two choices do not even begin to be grammatically consistent.

These examples are sufficient to indicate what is meant by irrelevant clues. There are many variations of this weakness, and the bright students detect such clues almost immediately. Such faults can be corrected if you are careful in checking each item.

8. *Place the Choices at the End of the Incomplete Statement.* This makes for continuity of reading. It is less confusing for the student. A simple example will illustrate the desirability of adhering to this suggestion. In this example the several choices consist

　　____ We use a (1) hack saw, (2) crosscut saw, (3) coping
　　　　　saw, (4) rip saw, (5) back saw, when cutting
　　　　　curves in thin pieces of wood.

of no more than three words each. Nevertheless, the student must read part way, then skip over the choices to see what he is supposed to do, and finally come back to the several choices to determine the correct answer. With very little effort, this item could be revised to include the choices at the end. (It should also contain a realistic central problem.)

9. List Each Choice on a Separate Line. This takes more paper, but it is much easier for the student. For informal classroom tests the authors have also found it best to identify each response with a capital letter (A,B,C,D,E). When figures (1,2,3, etc.) or lower-case letters (a,b,c,d, etc.) are used, it is sometimes difficult to determine just what the student has placed in the blank space. This is because several of the characters are similar in appearance, and the student who is vague about the correct response may deliberately write a five that looks something like a three or a (c) that somewhat resembles an (e). This is somewhat avoided by using capital letters.

____39. Suppose that you have wound a coil of insulated
wire around a soft iron core. Next you attach the
coil to several dry cells in series. You then have
an example of
A. a simple generator.
B. a simple motor.
C. a circuit breaker.
D. an electromagnet.
E. a simple dynamo.

10. When the Choices Include a Series of Figures, Put Them in Order. The figures (or dates) may be in an ascending or descending order. This makes it easier for the student in selecting his response.

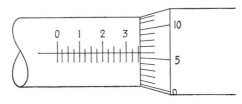

____2. What is the correct reading on the one-inch microm-
eter shown above?

A. .315	A. .3165
B. .3165	B. .516
C. .3215	C. .356
D. .356	D. .3215
E. .516	E. .315
(This)	*(Not this)*

11. Scatter the Correct Responses. Make sure that the correct responses do not follow any particular pattern. It is easy to comply with this suggestion when the items are checked prior to duplication.

12. When a Negative Response Is Desired, Be Sure to Make This Clear. Perhaps the easiest way to emphasize the negative choice is to capitalize or underline the words that characterize the item (poorest, not, no, least, etc.). The following examples illustrate this procedure:

```
____ If you were teaching a class the correct marks to use
     in reading proof, which one of the following would not
     be included?
     A. X
     B. #
     C. cr
     D. stet
     E. wf


____ Which one of the following IS NOT an example of a
     simple machine?
     A. wedge
     B. crowbar
     C. wheelbarrow
     D. pulley
     E. try square
```

13. Do Not Use a Multiple-choice Item if a Simpler Type Will Be Sufficient. This suggestion is made with respect to classroom tests and for that type of information where there is only one correct response that can be written down with one word or a figure. As one illustration of this point, the multiple-choice sample test item on page 188 might be rewritten as a simple recall and be much more effective.

```
____16. Every circle shown on a drawing should have how
        many center lines?
```

SUMMARY

Multiple-choice items consist of a question or incomplete statement followed by several possible answers, from which the testee selects the correct one. The item may take several forms. The student may be required to select the one correct answer; he may be asked to choose the best answer, the worst, or both. The item may be constructed in the form of an analogy, or it may call for association. When well constructed, the multiple-choice item is one of the best, if not *the* best, of the objective tests. Some suggestions follow for use in constructing multiple-choice items:

1. The stem of the item should contain a central problem.

2. The item should be practical and realistic.

3. The stated problem should be specific, clear, and as brief as possible.

4. Illustrations are sometimes useful in presenting the central problem.

5. Have at least four and preferably five answers (choices) .

6. Include no responses that are obviously wrong.

7. Avoid the inclusion of irrelevant clues.

8. Place the choices at the end of the incomplete statement.

9. List each choice on a separate line.

10. When the choices include a series of figures, put these in order.

11. Scatter the correct responses.

12. When a negative response is desired, be sure to make this clear.

13. Do not use a multiple-choice item if a simpler type will be sufficient.

SOME THINGS TO DO AND QUESTIONS TO ANSWER

1. Can you think of some other names that might be more descriptive of the multiple-choice type of item?

2. What do you think about the best-answer type of item that calls for discrimination on the part of the student? In other words, what has been your reaction when you have taken this type of test? Should this have any bearing on the type of items you make in your tests?

3. Why is it a good idea to think in terms of a central problem when starting out to construct a multiple-choice item?

4. At this point it would be a good idea to construct several types of multiple-choice items, following closely the suggestions contained in this chapter. Start out by first listing or describing the specific objective

you wish to measure. If time and facilities are available, it would be interesting to have the various class members try to answer your items. Their comments might contain some useful suggestions for later consideration. While you are completing this assignment, make plans to start a file of good test items. You will find it a great convenience on many occasions. The secret, of course, is to organize your efforts and then keep at it.

5. What do you think about including a section of reverse multiple-choice items in your tests?

6. How can regular multiple-choice items be constructed to measure in the same manner as reverse multiple-choice items?

7. Make a list of the faults to be avoided in constructing multiple-choice items.

SELECTED REFERENCES FOR ADDITIONAL READING

Adkins, Dorothy C., and associates. *Construction and Analysis of Achievement Tests.* Washington, D.C.: Government Printing Office, 1947. Chap. II.

Hawkes, Herbert E., E. F. Lindquist, and C. R. Mann. *The Construction and Use of Achievement Examinations.* Boston: Houghton Mifflin Company, 1936. Pp. 136–147, 175–178, 368–372.

McNamara, Walter J., and Ellis Weitzman. "The Effect of Choice Placement on the Difficulty of Multiple-choice Questions," *Journal of Educational Psychology,* 36:103–113 (February, 1945).

Mosier, Charles I., M. C. Myers, and Helen G. Price. "Suggestions for the Construction of Multiple-choice Test Items," *Educational and Psychological Measurement,* 5:261–271 (Autumn, 1945).

Rinsland, Henry Daniel. *Constructing Tests and Grading in Elementary and High School Subjects.* New York: Prentice-Hall, Inc., 1938. Chap. II.

Ross, C. C. *Measurement in Today's Schools.* New York: Prentice-Hall, Inc., 1947. Pp. 145–151.

CHAPTER

SEVEN: TRUE–FALSE ITEMS

THE true-false (alternate response) item is probably the best known of the various types of objective test items. It is the easiest to construct. At the same time it is the most abused.

Fundamentally, the true-false item consists of a declaratory statement or a situation that is either true or false (right or wrong). The student decides which of the two possible choices is the correct one and places his answer accordingly. There are numerous variations and modifications that have been developed in an effort to correct certain of the weaknesses inherent in this type of item. Samples of several varieties of true-false items are presented on the next few pages. Keep in mind that still other adaptations can be constructed by the resourceful test maker.

Regular True-False

As stated above, the unmodified type of true-false item usually consists of a simple statement that may be either true or false. The student is required to indicate whether or not the statement is true. This type of item has been used extensively. It has often been used indiscriminately. The following sample items illustrate several of the methods that are used in constructing the item and indicating the response:

Directions: Some of the following statements are true and
some are false. If the statement is true place a plus (+)
in the blank space at the left. If the statement is false
place a zero (0) in the space. The first item is answered
as an example.
(+) (x) A jack plane is longer than a block plane.
____(1) There are two board feet in a piece of lumber
        1" x 6" x 24".
____(2) Shellac is thinned with alcohol.
____(3) To bore a 1/2" hole in a piece of stock, use a
        No. 6 auger bit.

Directions: Listed below are a number of statements. Some
are true and some are false. If the statement is true encircle the "T" at the left of the statement. If the statement is false, encircle the "F." The first item is answered as an example.
(x)   T (F) The ohm is the unit of current.
(1)   T   F   The law of magnets states that like poles repel
              and unlike poles attract.
(2)   T   F   An electric current can be measured by using an
              ammeter connected in series with the circuit.
(3)   T   F   Dry cells connected in series will give less
              voltage than dry cells connected in parallel.

Directions: A series of questions is listed below. Each
of them can be answered by "yes" or "no." Encircle the
correct answer at the left of the question. The first
question is answered as an example.
Yes (No) (x) Is a 2H pencil harder than a 4H pencil?
Yes No   (1) Are hidden lines shown in sectional views?
Yes No   (2) Does a working drawing give the necessary
              information for assembling a project?
Yes No   (3) When a sphere is projected on a plane, will
              it show on that plane as a line?

Directions: Listed below are several true and false statements. You are to check (X) only those items that are
false. Do nothing if the statement is true.
( ) 1. The purpose of a condenser in a distributer is to
        prevent the spark from burning the breaker points.
( ) 2. An internal-combustion engine is more efficient
        than an external-combustion engine.
( ) 3. The Prony Test is one method that can be used in
        measuring brake horsepower.

Correction for Guessing

<u>Directions</u>: Some of the following statements are true and
some are false. If the statement is true, place a "+" in
the blank space at the left. If the statement is false,
place a "0" in the blank space. <u>DO</u> <u>NOT</u> <u>GUESS</u>. Your score
for this section will be found by subtracting the number
wrong from the number right. The first item is answered as
an example.

<u>+</u> (x) A No. 6 jeweler's file is finer than a No. 00.

____(1) Brass is annealed by heating it to a dull red and
        cooling it in air.

____(2) A hack-saw blade having 20 teeth per inch is the
        proper one to use in sawing 28 gauge material.

____(3) A cape chisel is used for chipping filleted corners
        and concave surfaces.

<u>Directions</u>: Below are listed a series of words used in
machine-shop practice. Some are spelled correctly. Some
are misspelled. If the word is spelled correctly, place a
(+) in the blank space preceding the word. If the word is
misspelled, place a (0) in the blank space. DO NOT GUESS.
Each wrong answer will subtract two points. Each omitted
answer will subtract one point. The first word "thread" is
spelled correctly so a plus (+) has been placed in the
blank space as an example.

<u>+</u> x. thread   ____5. alinment
____1. mikrometer   ____6. caleper
____2. pitch   ____7. spindle
____3. hermaphrodite   ____8. knurl
____4. verneir

<u>Directions</u>: Listed below are various common formulas used
in machine-shop work. Some are stated correctly. Some
are incorrect. If the formula is stated correctly place a
"C" in the blank space at the left. If the formula is incorrect place an "I" in the blank space. The first formula
is incorrect. Therefore an "I" is placed in the blank
space.

<u>(I)</u> (x) $CS = \dfrac{3.14 \times D \times RPM}{120}$

____(1) $RPM = \dfrac{12 \times CS}{3.14 \times D}$

____(2) Approximate $RPM = \dfrac{8 \times CS}{D}$

____(3) Offset = tangent of 1/2 included angle x L

Directions: The following items are a test of your ability
to recognize proper proof marks.   There are nine mistakes
in the printed matter.   A numbered proof mark refers to
each of the mistakes.   If the proof mark is the correct one
for the particular error, place a (+) in the numbered column at the left.   If the proof mark is incorrect place a
(0) in the space.   In the first item the proof mark "X" is
the correct way to indicate a broken letter.   Therefore, a
(+) is placed in the blank space.

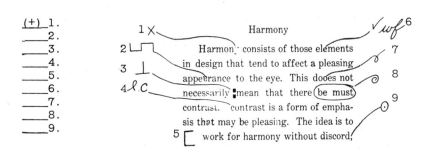

(+) 1.
____2.
____3.
____4.
____5.
____6.
____7.
____8.
____9.

____1. When men under the age of 45 are compared with women
       under the age of 45 we find a smaller proportion of
       men married.
____2. The divorce rate for marriages made in the teens is
       low.
____3. A characteristic of a poorly adjusted individual is
       a sense of humor.
____4. A child is regarded as a mental defective if his
       I.Q. is below 70.
____5. To say that an adult is egocentric is saying that he
       is emotionally mature.

T F   5. Gothic architecture differs from Greek architecture
         in that it shows a greater interest in pure form
         rather than construction.
T F   6. Until about 1820 painting in America was almost en-
         tirely portraiture.
T F   7. Polyphonic music means pompous, stately, grand
         music.
T F   8. The terms "partials," "overtones," "harmonics," are
         synonyms — they all refer to the same acoustical
         phenomenon.

True-False Items Related to Each Other

____1. Real prosperity must be based upon increased pro-
       duction.
____2. The real wages will increase even though the money
       wages remain constant.
____3. The standard of living is based upon the rate of pay
       per hour.
____4. If, during this period of generally increased pro-
       duction, the production of farm products does not
       increase, the farmers' prosperity will decrease.

Cluster True-False

The cluster true-false item is very similar to the regular type. It usually consists of an incomplete statement followed by several phrases or clauses, each of which will complete the statement. The student is required to indicate those phrases or clauses which form true and those which form false statements. Sometimes the cluster of statements will be related to a drawing or photograph preceding the items. This type has not been used extensively, but in certain instances it may be more effective than the simple true-false item. It has sometimes been called a multiple-response type of item. In such instances the student may be required to pick out only those items which are true or those items which are false. This begins to approach the multiple-choice type of item.

Directions: Each of the incomplete statements below is
followed by several items, each of which will complete the
statement and make it either true or false. Place a plus
(+) in the blank space at the left of each item that makes
a true statement. Place a zero (0) in the blank space at
the left of each item that makes a false statement. The
first item is answered as an example.
The Browne & Sharpe gauge is used to measure
(x) (+) copper
(1)____ steel wire
(2)____ brass
(3)____ aluminum
(4)____ sheet steel
Crocus cloth is finer than
(5)____ rouge
(6)____ tripoli
(7)____ #000 steel wool
(8)____ aluminum oxide cloth #160
(9)____ rotten stone

Directions: Each of the incomplete statements below is
followed by several phrases, each of which completes the
statement, and makes it true or false. If the completed
statement is true encircle the "T" before the item. If
false, encircle the "F." The first item is answered as an
example.

        A transformer
T Ⓕ (x) is normally used with direct current.
T F (1) consists of a primary and secondary coil.
T F (2) steps down the voltage and current together.
T F (3) has a power output that is theoretically the same
        as its power input.

        A series-type electric motor is characterized by
T F (4) its constant speed under varying loads.
T F (5) high starting torque.
T F (6) universal operation on either A.C. or D.C.

        Spar varnish
____1. is darker than cabinet rubbing varnish.
____2. is especially adapted to outside use.
____3. is thinned with denatured alcohol.
____4. contains more oil than ordinary varnish.

If a person with good technical training had been appointed
to lay out a city plan when Minneapolis was incorporated as
a city, we should today have:
____41. all land used to good advantage.
____42. all streets laid out in parallel lines.
____43. all houses harmonious.
____44. definite provision for open spaces and interesting
        views.
____45. fewer buildings of poor architectural design.

Major adjustments of adolescence are
____56. achieving freedom from family.
____57. deciding upon vocation.
____58. understanding to a greater extent the relation of
        parents to each other.
____59. achieving some unity in own personality.
____60. establishing a satisfactory relationship with the
        opposite sex.
____61. understanding to a greater degree the problems in
        community relations.

Factors which determine how people use their resources are
____52. ability to recognize values.
____53. ability to face situations honestly.
____54. ability to recognize assets and limitations.
____55. extent to which they wish for and dream of things
       they desire.

Democracy holds that
____42. there shall be a system of "one man, one vote."
____43. the press shall be censored.
____44. in the eyes of law all men are born free and equal.
____45. there shall be a rule of the majority.
____46. the Era of Liberalism has passed.
____47. there shall be a government "by the people."
____48. there shall be only one political faction in the
       state.

Directions: The following questions pertain to the diagram
at the top of the set of questions. Each question can be
answered by "Yes" or "No." If the correct answer is "Yes"
encircle that word at the left of the item. If the correct
answer is "No" encircle that word. DO NOT GUESS. There
will be a correction for guessing.

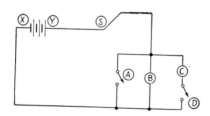

Yes   No   1. If switch D is closed will it cause a short
              circuit?
Yes   No   2. If switch S is open will there be a flow of
              current?
Yes   No   3. If switches S and A were closed would this
              create a short circuit?
Yes   No   4. Can light B be controlled by switch D?
Yes   No   5. Does the current in this circuit flow from
              X to Y?

Directions: The lettered squares immediately below contain
several pictorial sketches. The numbered squares contain
three views of each of these representations. (Front, top,
and right side). If a particular view is shown correctly,
place a plus (+) in the numbered blank space at the left.
If the view is shown incorrectly place a zero (0) in the
space. The first view is incorrect; therefore a "0" has
been placed in the blank space as an example.

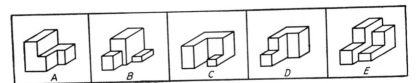

1. (0)

2. ____

3. ____

4. ____

5. ____

6. ____

7. ____

8. ____

9. ____

10. ____

11. ____

12. ____

13. ____

14. ____

15. ____

① Front A	② Top A	③ Side A
④ Front B	⑤ Top B	⑥ Side B
⑦ Front C	⑧ Top C	⑨ Side C
⑩ Front D	⑪ Top D	⑫ Side D
⑬ Front E	⑭ Top E	⑮ Side E

Directions: In the statements below a number of answers
are given after each question. Put the letter of the right
answer, or answers, in the blank space at the left of the
question.

_____1. Which of the following are correct expressions of
Ohm's law?
   A. Watts times volts equals KWH.
   B. Current times resistance equals force.
   C. I equals E over R.
   D. Watts equals amperes times volts.
   E. E equals I over R.

Modified True-False

There are many variations and modifications of the true-false
test item. These modifications correct certain of the weaknesses
and have much greater testing value than the plain true-false item.
They compare favorably with other types.

Modified true-false items may be designed to require the student
to mark the items that are true but to *modify* the false items
by (1) crossing out the word that makes the statement false or
(2) identifying the word that makes the statement false and listing
another word that would make it true. Another variation requires
the student to justify his response, whether true or false. Still another modification has the student choose the correct word from a
list of words given.

The variations and modified forms should be substituted for the
plain true-false item whenever possible.

Directions: Some of the following statements are true and
some are false. If the statement is true, encircle the
"T" at the left and do no more. If the statement is false,
encircle the "F" and do two more things:
   1. In blank "A" insert the word that makes the statement
      false.
   2. In blank "B" insert the word that would make it true.
DO NOT USE WORDS THAT ARE UNDERLINED. The first item is
answered as an example.
(x) T (F) Large city newspapers are printed on cylinder
         presses.
          A. (cylinder)   B. (rotary)

(1) T F The optical center of a page lies just below the
         true center.
          A._____   B._____

(2) T F Some antique papers are finished with a <u>deckle</u>
         <u>edge</u>.
         A._____   B._____
(3) T F The better grades of paper contain a high rag con-
         tent.
         A._____   B._____

T F 51. For most subject fields, a range between the high
         and the low grades of approximately 1/4 the total
         number of possible points is an indication of
         good discrimination.
         <u>a</u>. _____   b. _____
T F 52. When a teacher wonders if the instruction has
         been weak in certain areas, he can determine the
         location of any weak points through the use of a
         general achievement test.
         <u>a</u>. _____   <u>b</u>. _____

---

(14) T F <u>A straight line touching a circle</u> at but one
          point is a segment.
          A._____   B._____
(15) T F The distance a screw travels along its axis, in
          one complete revolution, is called the lead.
          A._____   B._____
(16) T F The <u>Ozalid</u> <u>method</u> of making prints is a liquid
          process.
          A._____   B._____

---

(1) T F When <u>cutting a 1/2" hole in sheet tin,</u> use a
         hollow punch.
         A._____   B._____
(2) T F <u>Fir plywood</u> is sold by the board foot.
         A._____   B._____
(3) T F When using spirit stain be sure to sponge the wood
         with water in order to raise the grain.
         A._____   B._____

<u>Directions</u>: Some of the following statements are true,
some are false. If a statement is true encircle the "T" at
the left and do no more. If the statement is false, encircle the "F" <u>and</u> <u>underline</u> the one word that makes it
false. The first two items are answered as examples.
(x) T(F) The contact points of the breaker points are made
          of <u>copper</u>.

(x) Ⓣ F   Spark plugs should be inserted with approximately
forty foot-pounds tightening torque.
(1) T F   Heavy-duty, high-compression engines operate best
with hot-running spark plugs.
(2) T F   An automobile engine-starting motor may require as
much as 200 amperes of current.

Directions: Some of the following statements are true,
some are false. If the statement is true, encircle the "T"
at the left and explain why it is true in the blank spaces
below the item. If the statement is false, encircle the
"F" at the left and explain why it is false. The first
item is answered as an example.

(x) T Ⓕ   Lard oil is a satisfactory lubricant to use while
drilling cast iron.
Explanation: (No lubricant should be used when
drilling cast iron.)
(1) T F   If you were to make a wood pattern for a gray iron
casting, 8 ft long, the pattern would have a
length of 8 ft, 2 inches.
Explanation:_____

(2) T F   The etching solution for copper consists of 2
parts of water to one part of sulphuric acid.
Explanation:_____

Directions: In the following statements certain conclusions are drawn which may or may not be true. If you
think the statement is true encircle the (T) at the left.
If you think it false encircle the (F). THEN, encircle one
or more of the five reasons (A, B, C, D, E) which support
the judgment you have made. In some cases there will be
only one correct reason, in others more than one. The
first item is answered as an example to follow.
T Ⓕ
A B CⒹE   A new instrument has been devised which fits
over the head and enables the psychologist,
after some practice, to estimate the memory
ability of the individual being tested.
A. Phrenology has been shown to be an accurate
method of forecasting mental abilities.
B. This may be regarded as a form of mental
testing.
C. Memory cannot be regarded as a unitary trait.
D. The shape of the skull reveals nothing regarding mental abilities.
E. We cannot put any faith in mental telepathy.

T F
A B C D E 1. In schools which are supported by the people,
              all children should be given the same educa-
              tion.
              A. In America "all men are created equal."
              B. Children are apt to develop inferiority
                 complexes if they are not treated alike.
              C. Training should take account of individual
                 differences.
              D. In a democracy an attempt should be made
                 to equalize people by giving them the same
                 education.
T F
A B C D E 2. If a student dreams that she has been elected
              president of her sorority, the probability is
              that she has a desire to be president.
              A. Dreams are often expressions of hidden
                 thoughts and motives.
              B. To believe that is to believe in mental
                 telepathy.
              C. It is impossible to tell anything about a
                 person's motives from his dreams.
              D. A dream may be the expression of an un-
                 conscious desire.
              E. Dream analysis may be regarded as a form
                 of pseudo psychology.

Directions: In the first blank to the left of each item
write the letter (G) if you think the suggestion is a good
one, (P) if it is a poor suggestion. In the second blank
space place the letter (A, B, C, D, or E) of the statement
that best explains why it is a good or poor suggestion.
____73. Use contrasting color for walls and woodwork when
        there is much woodwork.
____74. A. Woodwork would serve as desirable emphasis in a
           room.
        B. This would be a means of introducing color at
           structural points.
        C. A feeling of restlessness is likely to be cre-
           ated.
        D. Desirable emphasis is created.
        E. Woodwork should not be contrasted with walls.
____75. Use silk taffeta draperies in a Cape Cod house.
____76. A. Silk taffeta draperies are in good taste.
        B. The simplicity of a Cape Cod house needs enrich-
           ment.
        C. Silk taffeta is domestic in spirit as is a Cape
           Cod house.

    D. Less fine textures are more harmonious with the
       spirit of a Cape Cod house.
    E. If silk taffeta is fashionable, it may be used
       in any house.

<u>Directions</u>: If the following items are true encircle the
"T" and do no more. If the item is false encircle the "F"
and explain in the blank why it is false. The first item
is answered as an example.

(x) T (F) In the drawing below the arrows indicate the true
       direction of electron flow.
       Explanation: <u>(According to electron principle,</u>
       <u>current flow is electron flow and is from negative</u>
       <u>to positive.)</u>

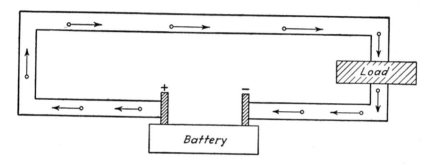

(x) T F For a given current the voltage drop across "A"
       (below) is higher than that across "B".
       Explanation:_____

_____

_____

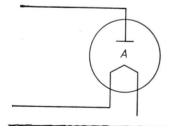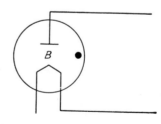

Controlled-correction Type

<u>Directions</u>: The true and false statements below refer to
the uses of different woods. If the statement describes a
true use encircle the "T" at the start of the item and do
no more. If the statement is false encircle the "F" and
also underline the correct word in the list just below the
item. The first item is answered as an example.

(x) T (F) Basswood is commonly used for house flooring.
            (walnut, beech, <u>oak,</u> cherry)
(1) T F Cypress would be a good wood to use in making a
          window box.
            (walnut, oak, pine, red cedar)
(2) T F Flying airplane models are usually made from
          balsam.
            (beech, balsa, basswood, butternut)
(3) T F Pine is considered one of the best woods to use in
          constructing fine furniture.
            (walnut, red cedar, fir, hickory)

<u>Directions</u>: Some of the following statements are true,
some are false. If the statement is true encircle the "T"
preceding the item and do no more. If the statement is
false encircle the "F" and do two things:
1. Underline the word that makes the statement false.
2. From the list just below select the word that would
   make the item true and place the letter preceding that
   word in the blank space before the item.
The first item is answered as an example.

A. 10	F. ampere	K. direct	P. steel
B. 15	G. attract	L. ohm	Q. voltage
C. 25	H. cell	M. parallel	R. watt
D. alternating	I. copper	N. repel	
E. aluminum	J. current	O. series	

(x) T (F) <u>(L)</u> The <u>volt</u> is the unit of resistance.
(1) T F ____ If a D.C. circuit has a pressure of 20 volts
                and a current of 5 amperes the resistance
                would be 4 ohms.
(2) T F ____ The elements of a telegraph circuit are con-
                nected in parallel.

Uses and Advantages of True-False Items

1. The true-false item is used by most teachers and therefore is
known to the students. This is perhaps an advantage as far as
knowing how to answer the item is concerned, but there is also a

negative aspect to consider. The students learn the weaknesses that are inherent in many such items and are able to obtain high scores by noting the grammatical construction, the choice of words, or other clues.

2. It is relatively easy to construct. For this reason it is used extensively. However, while it is easy to construct true-false items, the quality is often doubtful.

3. It can be used to sample a wide range of subject matter. Because the items can be answered in a short time a large number can be included in a single test. A general rule is that the average student is able to answer between three and five true-false items a minute. Naturally, the rate of answering will vary with the type of student and the type of material being tested.

4. It can be scored readily in an objective manner.

5. It can be used effectively as an instructional test to promote interest and introduce points for discussion. This is perhaps the most important use for the plain true-false item. Few teachers take advantage of this use. Because the item is relatively easy to construct and because it can be answered in a short time, it is a valuable type of item to use in giving short daily tests that may be used to motivate the students for a new assignment, to review a previous lesson, to locate points to be retaught, or to introduce controversial points for class discussion.

6. It can be constructed as a simple factual question or as a thought question that requires reasoning. The type of item calling for discrimination and reasoning is, understandably, the more difficult to prepare. The modified types lend themselves more readily to this latter approach.

7. It is especially useful when there are only two choices governing a particular point. For example, the law of magnets states that like poles repel and unlike poles attract. In developing a test item to measure an understanding of this law, a multiple-choice item could not be used effectively since there are only two plausible answers, "attract" or "repel." A similar situation would arise in devising an item to measure a student's understanding of whether a ripsaw cuts with the grain or across the grain.

8. Cluster true-false items can be used to check several points concerning a particular concept, principle, or mechanical unit.

When well constructed, they tend to reveal more accurately the student's complete understanding.

9. Modified true-false items can be designed to correct many of the weaknesses noted below. They can require the student to exercise judgment and utilize his knowledge in situations that call for understanding rather than mere memorization. As stated previously, the modified form should be substituted for the plain true-false item whenever possible.

Limitations

1. The plain true-false item is of doubtful value for measuring achievement.

2. It encourages guessing. While correction formulas are sometimes employed to counteract this weakness, many students will continue to guess. In most true-false tests many of the items can be answered correctly without any knowledge of the subject matter involved.

3. Difficulty is encountered in constructing items that are either completely true or completely false without making the correct response obvious. Several examples of this point are presented, with the suggestions for constructing the items.

4. It is difficult to avoid ambiguities, unimportant details, and irrelevant clues. A common weakness is items taken directly from a textbook.

5. A true-false test is likely to be low in reliability unless it includes a large number of items.

6. Minor details tend to receive as much credit as significant points.

7. A true-false test is difficult to construct if the material is in any way controversial.

Points to Consider in Constructing True-False Items

1. Make Approximately Half of the Items True and Half False. If you are in the habit of having significantly more true statements than false statements, the students soon become aware of this. Whenever they are in doubt about a certain item, the "smart thing" will be to mark it true. They then have a better than even chance of guessing the correct response. There should be no set pattern in distributing the true and false items throughout the test. In other words, make sure that the students will not be able to mark an item false simply because a certain number of true statements precede it and therefore it is time for a different response. This is avoided by a random distribution.

   2. *Make the Method of Indicating Responses as Simple as Possible.* Do not make the student write out "true" or "false" or "yes" or "no." This takes unnecessary time. Do not employ a system in which there is any question as to whether the student's response is true or false. If the student is to write his response in a blank space, it is better to use "+" and "0" than "+" and "—." Have the students encircle "T" or "F" rather than write in these letters. These simple suggestions will make for easier scoring and more objective scoring. The logic underlying the suggestions is indicated in viewing the responses in the following examples. How would you mark these items?

```
   ┬    6. The standard size of a business letterhead is
             8½" x 11".  (+ or -)
          7. The etching solution for copper consists of 2
             parts of water to 1 part of sulphuric acid.
             (T or F)
```

Such responses are sometimes planned and sometimes the result of carelessness. Of course, you might be arbitrary and state that, unless the answer is clearly indicated, the item will be marked wrong. However, this situation would be corrected to a large degree by using one of the following preferred methods for indicating responses to true-false items:

```
   T (F)  1. Varnish is thinned with alcohol.
   (T) F  2. Shellac is thinned with alcohol.
```

```
    0  3. Varnish is thinned with alcohol.
    +  4. Shellac is thinned with alcohol.
```

```
   Yes (No)  1. Is varnish thinned with alcohol?
   (Yes) No  2. Is shellac thinned with alcohol?
```

Directions to use with each of these methods of responses are included with the sample items at the beginning of this chapter.

3. Wherever Possible, Construct the Items to Make Application of Things Learned. This point is applicable to any type of test item, but especially so to true-false items, in which the invariable tendency is to test for acquisition of facts alone. This is one of the important factors that makes it inadvisable to use plain true-false items in measuring *real* achievement.

The following example, which measures memorization only, is typical of most of the true-false items found in teacher-made tests:

```
T F   16. The dimensions of a board foot are 1" x 12" x 12".
```

In order to answer this item correctly, the student has only to remember a definition from his textbook or a statement given in class by the instructor. He may know the definition without having any idea as to its application in a practical situation. By a slight revision this deficiency could be corrected, at least partially.

```
T F   16. A piece of lumber 2" x 6" x 24" would contain four
          board feet.
```

In this instance the student must know what a board foot is, but he must also be able to determine the number of board feet in a piece of lumber with given dimensions. He would have to apply his knowledge of board feet. Of course the guessing element could enter the picture, so that the student could get the item right without being able to apply the definition of a board foot. This could be eliminated to a large degree by making a modified item, as follows:

```
T F   16. A piece of lumber 2" x 6" x 24" would contain four
          board feet.
          A._____   B._____
```

It is sometimes difficult to revise a true-false item so that it calls for application rather than mere memorization. In such instances other types of items should be considered.

4. Do Not "Lift" Statements Directly from Books. This is another common fault in constructing true-false items. When such a practice is carried out, it encourages students to memorize statements without understanding what the statements mean. Such "knowledge" is invariably temporary in nature. Lifted statements in a test, like lifted statements from a talk or magazine article, are often ambiguous and do not convey the true meaning intended. As a result the students are puzzled and may mark the item wrong even though knowing the point being tested.

5. *Use Direct Statements. Avoid Words with General Meanings.* In comparing things the comparison should be direct. Whenever possible, use a quantitative statement rather than a qualitative statement.

Words with general meanings, such as "large," "great," "many," and "few," tend to make an item ambiguous to the student and should be avoided.

Poor

____1. Many screwdrivers have sharp points.

Better

____2. A properly dressed screwdriver has a sharp point.

In the first example the word "many" would immediately cause the student to wonder what the item is supposed to measure. The entire statement is vague and indecisive, for many screwdrivers do have sharp points when they are improperly dressed. From that point of view the item would be marked true. But the student may interpret the item as meaning that many types of screwdrivers should have sharp points. In this light, the item would be marked false. The second example is an improvement in that a direct statement is used, thus making the meaning much clearer. Consider another example, where a single word makes the item highly ambiguous. The test maker intended that this item should be cor-

____1. Electricity travels at about the same rate as light.

rectly marked as a true statement. The word "about" is used in a comparative sense and would make the intended meaning vague, especially to the better students. In this instance the item would be improved by dropping "about."

6. *Do Not Make the True Statements Consistently Longer than*

the False Statements. In studying a large number of true-false tests Brinkmeier and Ruch found that items containing more than twenty words were true three out of four times.[1]

7. *Avoid Negative Statements.* Negative statements tend to be confusing to students. With little effort they can be revised into positive statements. As you read the example given below, note how you pause in determining whether to mark it true or false.

Poor

    ____1. Walnut is not a good wood for furniture construction.

Better

    ____2. Walnut is a poor wood for furniture construction.

8. *Be Careful with Specific Determiners.* Mention has already been made of the fact that many true-false items can be answered correctly by locating qualifying words that become specific determiners (see page 140). Whenever you use such words as "no," "never," "always," "may," "should," "all," "only," be sure that they do not make the correct answers obvious, as in the following selected examples:

    ____ 1. A block plane is <u>always</u> used to plane end grain.
    ____ 2. When making a piece of furniture it <u>may</u> sometimes be desirable to use a soft wood.
    ____ 3. Copper wire is the <u>only</u> wire used for conducting electricity.
    ____ 4. The <u>most</u> important metal is copper.
    ____ 5. Display work and important books are <u>never</u> hand set.
    ____ 6. The slope of a roof should <u>always</u> be 45 degrees.
    ____ 7. <u>All</u> drawing triangles have 45-degree angles.
    ____ 8. A left-side view <u>never</u> describes an object as clearly as the right-side view.
    ____ 9. A board is <u>always</u> longer than it is wide.
    ____10. Stereotypers make curved plates <u>only.</u>

Teacher-made tests will provide many examples similar to the above. The important point is not to omit such words entirely but

[1] I. H. Brinkmeier and G. M. Ruch, "Minor Studies on Objective Examination Methods: III. Specific Determiners in True-False Statements," *Journal of Educational Research*, 22:110–118 (September, 1930).

to be careful in using them and to make sure that such words do not make the correct answer obvious. It is the test maker who determines whether or not particular words become specific determiners.

9. Make the Point of the Item Obvious. There should be no question about what you are trying to measure. This does not mean that the correct answer should be obvious, but rather that the student who knows the subject matter should understand immediately what is being tested. A good practice is to have the significant part (crucial element) of the item come at the end of the statement. Sometimes this can be achieved by underlining the significant part of the item. In the following example it is not clear what the test maker is trying to measure:

Poor

_____1. The electric furnace besides producing a poor grade of steel is expensive to operate.

Better

_____2. The electric furnace besides being expensive to operate produces a poor grade of steel.

Better

_____3. The electric furnace produces a <u>poor</u> grade of steel.

The student will tend to accept the first part of the statement as a fact ("besides producing a poor grade of steel"). That is a natural reaction. Then he considers the last part of the statement as being the significant part (crucial element). If he follows this procedure, his answer will be wrong. In the second example, this fault is corrected by placing the crucial element at the end of the statement. Perhaps the best procedure would be to eliminate the "expense" clause altogether, as in the third example. This would make the item simpler without detracting from the point being measured. By underlining the word "poor" it becomes obvious that the point being measured is whether the electric furnace produces a good or poor grade of steel.

10. Avoid Catch Questions. Do not devise items that endeavor to catch the student unawares. Such questions are poor measures of achievement. A student may know the point being measured but still not be able to detect the "joker" that really determines the correct response. In other words such items measure general intelligence and alertness rather than achievement and are not fair to the student.

Several examples of catch questions follow. In student terminology they would probably be defined as being "dirty." They are good examples of how *not* to construct true-false items.

T F   48. The head of the thumbtack should be rounded and rather thick to allow the T square and triangle to slide over it easily.

_____20. The plane iron should be dipped in water frequently when it is being sharpened to remove the feather edge.

_____24. One can bore a hole without splitting the stock even if one bores all the way through.

_____ 1. The term slug usually means a lead six points in thickness.

_____15. The amperage flowing in a series circuit is additive.

_____ 3. It is possible to buy a 10-inch bastard second-cut file.

11. If You Plan to Correct for Guessing, Be Sure to Emphasize This in the Directions. The authors have previously stated their opinion that informal teacher-made tests are not significantly improved by using a correction formula (see page 147). The reader should keep in mind, however, that the statement of an opinion does not establish a fact. Lindquist states that the chance factor is "perhaps too large to be disregarded, even in the informal classroom testing situation."[2]

[2] Herbert E. Hawkes, E. F. Lindquist, and C. R. Mann, *The Construction and Use of Achievement Examinations.* Boston: Houghton Mifflin Company, 1936, p. 158.

In the absence of convincing experimental evidence on either side, it is necessary for the test maker to use his best judgment in determining whether to correct for guessing in using plain true-false items. The best solution is to avoid using plain true-false items entirely.

If a correction formula is to be used, this should be clearly indicated in the directions and the method of correction explained. Various formulas have been devised, but the one most widely used is to subtract the number wrong from the number right (right — wrong). The net result of this formula is to subtract two points for each item marked incorrectly and one point for each item omitted.

12. Wherever Possible, Use Modified True-False Items Rather than the Plain Type. This suggestion is especially applicable for comprehensive achievement tests. As explained previously, the plain true-false item can be used to advantage in certain types of instructional tests, but the inherent weaknesses and common abuses of the item make it a poor measure of real achievement. It may be easier to construct simple true-false items, but the other types will usually do a better job of measuring.

SUMMARY

The true-false item consists of a declaratory statement that is either true or false (right or wrong). It is used widely and often abused. There are numerous variations and modifications that help to correct certain of the inherent weaknesses.

This type of item is relatively easy to construct, although the quality is often doubtful. It can be used to sample a wide range of subject matter. Students can usually answer three to five true-false items per minute. The item can be scored readily in an objective manner. It is especially useful when there are only two choices governing a particular point.

The true-false item is of doubtful value for measuring achievement. It encourages guessing. Difficulty is encountered in constructing items that are completely true or false without being obvious. Ambiguities, unimportant details, irrelevant clues—these are added weaknesses of the typical true-false item.

The following points will prove helpful in constructing true-false items:

1. Make approximately half the items true and half false.

2. Make the method of indicating responses as simple as possible.

3. Whenever possible, construct the items to make application of things learned.

4. Do not "lift" statements directly from books.

5. Use direct statements. Avoid words with general meanings.

6. Do not make the true statements consistently longer than the false statements.

7. Avoid negative statements.

8. Be careful with specific determiners.

9. Make the point of the item obvious.

10. Avoid catch questions.

11. If you plan to correct for guessing, be sure to emphasize this in the directions.

12. Wherever possible, use modified true-false items rather than the plain type.

SOME THINGS TO DO AND QUESTIONS TO ANSWER

1. Why do you like or dislike true-false items in the tests that you are called upon to take?

2. Do you think there should be a correction for guessing when true-false items are included in a test? Why?

3. Consider the example of a spelling item on page 197. Where could such an item be used to advantage? What are its weaknesses?

4. Consider the relationship between test validity and reliability. Construct two true-false items (any type) that measure an understanding of this relationship.

5. In constructing true-false items in which the student has to explain or justify his response (see page 205) what difficulty is apt to be encountered?

6. Construct a sample true-false item that calls for reasoning on the part of the student.

7. Why is it a poor policy to "lift" statements directly from books?

8. If possible, secure a true-false test that has been prepared for a subject-matter field foreign to your own. See how many items you can answer because they are obvious or because there is some weakness in

the construction. Such an activity will be enjoyable as well as instructive.

9. What is your reaction to the following item?

```
T F   Many of the words on this page start with the letter
      "e."
```

10. What is your description of a catch question?

SELECTED REFERENCES FOR ADDITIONAL READING

Brinkmeier, I. H. and G. M. Ruch. "Minor Studies on Objective Examination Methods: III. Specific Determiners in True-False Statements," *Journal of Educational Research,* 22:110–118 (September, 1930).

Curtis, F. D., W. C. Darling, and N. H. Sherman. "A Study of the Relative Values of Two Modifications of the True-False Test," *Journal of Educational Research,* 36:517–527 (March, 1943).

Greene, Harry A., Albert N. Jorgensen, and J. Raymond Gerberich. *Measurement and Evaluation in the Secondary School.* New York: Longmans, Green & Co., Inc., 1943. Chap. VIII.

Hawkes, Herbert E., E. F. Lindquist, and C. R. Mann. *The Construction and Use of Achievement Examinations.* Boston: Houghton Mifflin Company, 1936. Pp. 152–159.

Rinsland, Henry Daniel. *Constructing Tests and Grading in Elementary and High School Subjects.* New York: Prentice-Hall, Inc., 1938. Chap. VI.

Ross, C. C. *Measurement in Today's Schools.* New York: Prentice-Hall, Inc., 1947. Pp. 114–115, 139–144.

Weidemann, Charles C. *How to Construct the True-False Examination.* New York: Bureau of Publications, Teachers College, Columbia University, 1926. Pp. 126.

CHAPTER

EIGHT: MATCHING ITEMS

As the name implies, this type of item requires the matching of two or more sets of material in accordance with given directions. The common matching item consists of two columns of words or phrases. The student is required to match each item in one list with the item in the other list to which it is most closely related. Strictly speaking, a matching item is a variation of the multiple-choice type in which the same choices are applicable in answering each of the items. This can be illustrated with a simple example, presented first as a matching-type item.

Directions: The two columns below contain related words and phrases pertaining to hand saws. Select the type of saw in the right-hand column that is most closely related to the descriptive phrase in the left-hand column and place the identifying letter in the blank space provided. The first item is answered as an example.

(D) x. Used in making rough cuts across the grain.

____1. Used in cutting curves in thin stock.

____2. Is inserted in a rigid frame to insure accurate work.

____3. Designed to cut parallel to the grain of the wood.

____4. Used with a bench hook.

A. back saw
B. coping saw
C. compass saw
D. crosscut saw
E. mitre saw
F. rip saw

With slight revision four multiple-choice items could be made from this material, as shown by the following two examples:

____1. Which of the following saws is used in cutting
curves in thin stock?
A. back saw
B. coping saw
C. compass saw
D. crosscut saw
E. mitre saw
F. rip saw

____2. Which of the following saws is inserted in a rigid
frame to insure accurate work?
A. back saw
B. coping saw
C. compass saw
D. crosscut saw
E. mitre saw
F. rip saw

____3. Etc.

Almost any matching item could similarly be made into multiple-choice items, cumbersome and space consuming though they might be.

There are numerous variations of the matching-type item. Several varieties will be illustrated in the following examples, but keep in mind that still other adaptations can be made to suit individual purposes.

Directions: Listed in the two columns below are common
layout and measuring tools and their uses in bench metalwork. Place in the blank space at the left the letter
which identifies the tool used to perform each operation.
Use each letter only once. The first item is answered as
an example.

x. (E)	locating centers of round objects	A. caliper rule
18. ____	locating center for drawing circles	B. center punch
		C. combination square
19. ____	locating center for drilling	D. dividers
		E. hermaphrodite calipers
20. ____	drawing arcs of circles	F. outside calipers
21. ____	drawing lines at 45° angles	G. prick punch
		H. scale
22. ____	measuring outside diameters	I. sheet-metal gauge
		J. surface gauge
23. ____	measuring diameter of wire	

Terms and Their Definitions

Directions: The two columns below contain terms and
definitions pertaining to screw threads. Match each
definition in the left-hand column with the proper term in
the right-hand column. Place the identifying letter of the
term in the blank space provided.

____38. The smallest diameter of the   A. crest
        screw thread.   B. depth
____39. The diameter of an imaginary   C. "flat"
        cylinder that would cut equally   D. lead
        the width and depth of the   E. major diameter
        thread.   F. minor diameter
____40. The width of the thread at the   G. pitch
        top surface.   H. pitch diameter
____41. The width of the thread at the   I. root
        bottom surface.   J. taper
____42. The term sometimes used to
        designate either the top or the
        bottom of the thread.
____43. The vertical distance from the
        bottom of the thread to the out-
        side.
____44. The distance a screw advances in
        one turn.

Same Item as Identification

Directions: You are to match the parts of the screw
thread illustrated below. Each part is numbered. Select
the proper name for each numbered part and place the
identifying letter in the numbered blank space at the left.
The first item is answered as an example.

(A) 1.(Example)   A. crest
                                               B. depth
____2.   C. lead
                                               D. linear pitch
____3.   E. major diameter
                                               F. minor diameter
____4.   G. pitch
                                               H. pitch diameter
____5.   I. root
                                               J. thread angle
____6.

____7.

Problem and Solution

Directions: The left-hand column below contains several
common household jobs that require fasteners before they
can be completed. In the right-hand column are several
types of fasteners that might be used. You are to select
the best fastener for each job and place the identifying
letter in the blank space provided. Use any fastener more
than once if necessary.

____1. The edge of a carpet needs fasten- A. brad
       ing   B. box nail
____2. A small ornament ($\frac{1}{4}$" plywood) is   C. casing nail
       loose on the front of a kitchen   D. common nail
       cabinet   E. finishing nail
____3. You are laying oak flooring   F. spike
____4. A medicine cabinet must be crated G. tack
       for shipping
____5. You are fastening the drawer sides
       to the drawer front
____6. You are building forms for a
       cement sidewalk

Identification

Directions: The columns below contain illustrations of
geometric figures and their names. You are to match the
names in the left-hand column with the proper illustration
in the right-hand columns. Place the identifying letter
in the blank space provided. The first item is answered
as an example.

(A) x. square

____13. obtuse angle

____14. acute angle

____15. isosceles triangle

____16. equilateral triangle

____17. right triangle

____18. rhombus

____1. A condition in which the lens   A. astigmatism
of the eye becomes clouded or   B. cataract
opaque   C. hyperopia
____2. Severe inflammation of the eye   D. myopia
or of the conjunctiva   E. ophthalmia
____3. Color blindness   F. strabismus
____4. Farsightedness   G. none of the above
____5. A condition in which both eyes
cannot be focused on the same
object

____1. Lends money to home owners   A. A.A.A.
____2. Insures bank depositors   B. A.F.L.
____3. A labor organization made up of in- C. C.I.O.
dustrial unions   D. F.C.C.
____4. A labor organization made up primarily E. F.E.R.A.
of craft unions   F. F.D.I.C.
____5. Federal corporation lending money to G. N.L.R.B.
state for relief purposes prior to the H. N.R.A.
Roosevelt Administration   I. H.O.L.C.
____6. Attempts to safeguard the issuance of J. S.E.C.
securities in the United States   K. R.F.C.
____7. Authorized to determine which labor
group should be the bargaining agent
for the employees of a given factory

Directions: On the left listed below are several types of
matching items. On the right are several types of learning. For each type of matching item on the left put the
number which corresponds to that type of learning which the
matching item will best measure. The first item is
answered as an example.

               Matching Item   Type of Learning
X. (B) Dates with events   A. Computation skill
66. ____ Cause with effect   B. Association
67. ____ Familiar problems with   C. Understanding
solutions   D. Following directions
68. ____ Theoretical problems with E. Judgment
solutions   F. Application
69. ____ Fractions with decimal   G. Social skill
equivalents   H. Mechanical skill
70. ____ Terms with definitions

____23. The Easy Chair   A. Atlantic
____24. Issues and Men   B. Current History
____25. The Bookshelf — A Guide   C. Fortune
     to Good Books   D. Harper's
____26. To the Ladies   E. Nation
____27. Life in the United States   F. Liberty
____28. Quarterly Survey   G. New Republic
     H. Saturday Evening Post
     I. Scribner's

Directions: Each of the illustrations on the right below represents a type of drawing. You are to match each drawing with its proper name on the left. The proper name may not be included in the left-hand column. It is not necessary to have a letter in each blank. You may also use a letter more than once if necessary.

____1. isometric

____2. perspective

____3. dimetric

____4. orthographic

____5. orthographic section

____6. cabinet

____7. auxiliary

Key List

A. black
B. blue, dull, light value
C. blue-green, bright, medium value
D. gray
E. green, dull, dark value
F. orange, dull, medium value
G. red-orange, bright, medium value
H. yellow, light
I. yellow-orange, dull, light value

____54.
____55.
____56. Three warm colors which would make the most pleasing combination in a figured drapery material (54, 55, 56).
____57. The color for a vase which would be most effective in bringing out the color in a rust (red-orange) wall hanging.
____58. Color for a ceiling which would give the maximum light to a room.

____59. Suitable complementary color for a chair which is
       to be used with a dark—blue rug.
____60. A color for curtains which will make a small room
       with light-tan walls seem larger.
____61. Color which would be good for the walls of a south-
       west bedroom.

Symbols and Their Names

Directions: The two columns below contain illustrations
of electrical symbols and their proper names. You are to
match each name in the left—hand column with the proper
symbol in the right—hand column. Use each symbol only
once. The first item is correctly answered as an example.
(H) x. battery

____63. inductance

____64. resistance

____65. capacitance

____66. antenna

____67. fuse

____68. S.P. switch

____69. potentiometer

<u>Directions</u>: Which factors of a good test, found at the top
of the page, are implied or referred to in the statements
below? In the blank before each statement place the letter
of the term which you believe is implied or referred to by
the speaker. The first item is answered as an example.

A. Reliability
B. Validity
C. Objectivity
D. Comprehensiveness
E. Discrimination

<u>(D)</u>   (example) "When you plan to make a test remember
       you should sample the course of study the way you
       would sample a cake."

77. ____   "Well, I've finally finished making this test and
       it contains questions from all levels of dif-
       ficulty."

78. ____   "Mr. Tinkham, if you are going to correct this
       test be sure that you follow the key I made out,
       for the key is the only fair judge to all the
       students."

79. ____   "Bill, you have taken this test three times and
       you have missed the same questions every time."

80. ____   "I wonder if this test will really tell me what
       the students know about the subject."

81. ____   "What is wrong with these students? I gave them a
       test yesterday and they did fine; today by mis-
       take, I gave them the same test and they did
       poorly."

82. ____   "Although I gave the students many tests in this
       course and they all did very well, they still
       don't really know the subject matter of the
       course."

83. ____   "This is the tenth time I've had to explain what
       the word 'uranology' means during this test. I'd
       better think of a better word to use in that ques-
       tion."

84. ____   "I want each item in this test to tell me exactly
       which students know the material and which ones
       don't."

85. ____   "I have gone through the subject matter of this
       unit and found that 30 questions cover the unit
       completely."

86. ____   "I have made each item in this test simple, con-
       cise, and to the point so anyone who knows the
       subject shouldn't have any trouble understanding
       the questions."

Joints and Their Identification

<u>Directions</u>: Match the joints with their proper names. Put
the identifying letter in the blank space, as in the example.

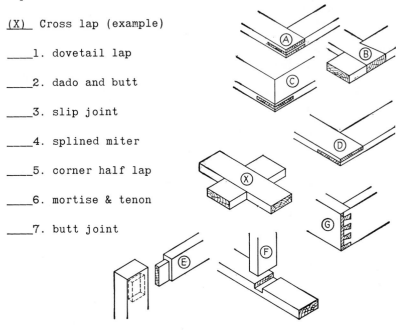

<u>(X)</u> Cross lap (example)

_____1. dovetail lap

_____2. dado and butt

_____3. slip joint

_____4. splined miter

_____5. corner half lap

_____6. mortise & tenon

_____7. butt joint

<u>Directions</u>: The columns below contain the names of men
identified with the printing industry and the types of work
with which they are associated. Before each man's name
place the identifying letter of the appropriate field with
which he's primarily identified. Use each letter as often
as is necessary. The first item is answered as an example.

(E) 1. Bodoni	_____ 9. Gutenberg	A. Casting machine
_____2. Caxton	_____10. Jensen	B. Machine composi-
_____3. Pi Sheng	_____11. Ludlow	tion
_____4. Franklin	_____12. Mergenthaler	C. Presses
_____5. Garamond		D. General printer
_____6. Harris		E. Type design
_____7. Goudy		F. Type foundry
_____8. Gordon		

Classification

Directions: You are to classify each of the following
tools, machines, and materials according to the five classifications listed just below. The first item, "carriage
bolt," would be classified as a fastening device. Therefore, you would put a "B" in the blank space before the
item. Follow a similar procedure for each item.

A. Cutting device   D. Holding device
B. Fastening device   E. Laying-out tool
C. Forming or shaping device

(B) x. carriage bolt   ____10. end nippers
____1. hollow punch   ____11. burring machine
____2. toolmaker's clamp   ____12. scriber
____3. cold chisel   ____13. pipe vise
____4. surface gauge   ____14. lag screw
____5. sandbag   ____15. dividers
____6. cap screw   ____16. roundnose pliers
____7. stock   ____17. solid punch
____8. center punch   ____18. drill chuck
____9. hand seamer   ____19. rivet

Directions: Read each of the descriptions below and select
the word or phrase in the key list which best describes the
adjustment made by the individual. Place the letter of
that word or phrase in the blank space preceding the description. Use each letter as often as is necessary. In
the example, the adjustment has been a good one, based upon
reasoned choice, so an (A) has been placed in the blank
space.

Key List

A. Good adjustment, action based upon reasoned choice
B. Withdrawal or flight from the situation
C. Logic-tight compartments
D. Projection
E. Rationalization
F. Identification
G. Neurotic manifestations
H. Futile efforts to reach unattainable goals

(A) (Example) Mrs. Jones, although a very unattractive
     woman, was one of the most popular and well-liked
     people in town. She never failed to say something
     flattering and pleasing to the people she met. She
     admits that she has made deliberate attempts to de-
     velop an attractive personality.
____1. Sally had always admired movie actresses. She fre-
     quently imagined herself playing one of Ann Harding's
     roles.
____2. Mr. Nelson was admired in the business world for his

strict honesty, but his friends disliked playing
bridge with him because they frequently found him
looking at his neighbor's hand.

_____3. A woman novelist who had always wanted to be a
physician wrote a novel in which the heroine was a
successful surgeon.

Directions: Place an A, B or C before each of the following statements and in terms of the following classification:
A. a fact supported by scientific evidence
B. a controversial issue upon which evidence is lacking or
   not in agreement
C. a statement which evidence shows is not a fact

_____52. The regular use of nasal sprays or drops will
        prevent colds.
_____53. The use of tobacco lowers mental efficiency.
_____54. Most severe mental illness comes on suddenly.
_____55. Chips from granite or enamel kettles are a frequent
        cause of appendicitis.
_____56. A boil is due to "bad" blood.

Directions: In the blank space before each of the following advertising statements write the letter of the description (A, B, or C) which best fits the statement.
Descriptions: A. Informative
               B. Extravagant, false, or misleading
               C. Planned to stimulate desire for glamour
                  or prestige

_____1. Three-piece with gorgeous full-fluffed wolf.
       Beige — so pale, so delicate, so utterly delicious.
_____2. Bemberg Rayon Triple-sheer.
_____3. Hop-sacking — Fabric contains: 84% rayon, 8% wool,
       8% silk.
_____4. Ginger Rogers' Dresses — selected and approved by
       this great Hollywood star. You'll be thrilled —
       the dresses are ever so simple, neat, and smart.
_____5. 26.3% warmer, 61% longer wearing, 1½ lb. lighter in
       weight.
_____6. The finest thing in hosiery — Crustal Crepes.
_____7. Announces Elf Crepe — light and charming as the
       name implies.
_____8. Momme imported all-silk pongee — 15¢ yd. Genuine
       Japanese pongee.
_____9. Shorts, vat-dyed, with cloth-covered elastic sides.

Modified Matching

<u>Directions</u>: In the table below, three aluminum alloys are
listed across the top with four properties listed on the
left side. Check the properties that apply to each alloy.
For example, the alloy "250" can be annealed so a check (x)
has been placed in that square. Follow a similar procedure for each of the properties and each of the alloys.

Properties	Alloys		
	250	350	1750
Can be torch-welded			
Can be hardened by heat-treating			
Can be work-hardened			
Can be annealed	(x)		

<u>Directions</u>: Below is a list of reference books followed by
a series of questions. You are to choose the <u>best</u> reference book to use in answering each question and place
the letter of that book in the blank space provided.
<u>Reference Books</u>:   A. American government textbook
                     B. Atlas
                     C. Dictionary of the English language
                     D. Economics textbook
                     E. Encyclopaedia Britannica
                     F. History textbooks on Europe since 1914
                     G. Newspaper files
                     H. Reader's Guide to Periodical
                        Literature
                     I. Who's Who in America
                     J. World Almanac
____13. What educational institutions did President
        Roosevelt attend?
____14. How does inflation affect the real income of the
        wage earners?
____15. How many people are employed in the major manu-
        facturing industries of the U.S.?
____16. How far is it from Moscow to London?
____17. What were the effects of the World War I inflation
        in Germany?
____18. Where and when was Philip LaFollette born?
____19. What do we mean by a system of checks and balances?
____20. Where did Abraham Lincoln get his education and
        legal training?

Classification

<u>Directions</u>:   Listed below are various sheet–metal articles
that require three different types of layout work. You are
to identify the type of layout required for each article,
by using the identifying letter. In the first item, an
oval funnel would require triangulation so a "T" is placed
in the blank space at the left.

P –– Parallel line development
R –– Radial development
T –– Triangulation

<u>(T)</u> x. An oval funnel
_____ 1. 90° pipe intersection of like diameters
_____ 2. 45° pipe intersection of unlike diameters
_____ 3. A funnel with an offset spout
_____ 4. A large frustum of a cone (24" diam.)
_____ 5. A small conical roof collar (8" diam.)
_____ 6. A small round pan with flaring sides (6" diam.)
_____ 7. A multiple–piece elbow
_____ 8. A funnel with a tap 4" diam.
_____ 9. A 90° elbow
_____10. An adapter from square to round
_____11. A combination measure and funnel
_____12. A compound offset

A. Cape
B. Chamois
C. Doeskin
D. <u>Glacé</u>
E. Kid
F. Mocha
G. Pigskin
H. Suede

<u>Situations</u>
_____19. John wants a pair of durable leather gloves he
        could wear for golf in early spring and late fall.
_____20. Sue wants a fine pair of dress gloves, strong and
        yet thin, that will conform to her hand.
_____21. Ruth is looking for a pair of brown leather gloves,
        velvet finished, for street wear, that will be
        washable, soft, and supple.
_____22. Mary is desirous of finding a navy–blue glove that
        she can use for general business and street wear,
        and she would like it heavy enough that she might
        also wear it for sport. It should be washable.

Classification

Directions: Listed below are several types of lubricants
followed by automotive units that require one of these
lubricants. You are to match each unit with the correct
type of lubricant and place the identifying letter in the
blank space provided. Use each letter (A, B, etc.) as many
times as is necessary. The first item is answered as an
example.

A. engine oil	D. lubricant impregnated
B. fibrous grease	E. penetrating dripless lubricant
C. gear oil	F. pressure-gun lubricant

(C) x. transmission	____ 8. front-wheel bearings
____1. distributor	____ 9. drag-link ends
____2. striker plate	____10. spring pens
____3. universal joint	____11. steering gear
____4. dovetail	____12. carburetor air cleaner
____5. differential	____13. spindle pin
____6. door hinges	____14. drive-shaft center bearing
____7. generator	

Uses and Advantages of Matching Items

1. The matching exercise may require the student to match such things as:

   a. Terms or words with their definitions.

   b. Characteristics with the mechanical units to which they apply.

   c. Short questions with their answers.

   d. Symbols with their proper names.

   e. Descriptive phrases with other phrases.

   f. Causes with effects.

   g. Principles with situations in which the principles apply.

   h. Parts or mechanical units with their proper names.

   i. Parts with the unit to which they belong.

   j. Problems with their solutions.

2. As may be seen from the above list, the matching item can be used for testing various outcomes. It is especially applicable for measuring the student's ability to recognize relationships and make associations and for naming and identifying things learned (the *who, what, where, when* type of subject matter).

3. It is relatively easy to construct. A large number of responses can be included in a small space and with one group of directions.

4. It can be made totally objective and can be scored quickly.

5. When it is properly constructed, the guessing factor is practically eliminated.

6. The classification type of matching item is sometimes given separate treatment. This is unnecessary, for it is fundamentally a matching process with similar uses, advantages, and limitations.

Limitations of the Matching Item

1. Since the phrases or clauses must necessarily be short, the matching exercise provides a poor measure of complete understandings and interpretations.

2. It is inferior to the multiple-choice item in measuring judgment and application of things taught.

3. It is likely to overemphasize the memorization of facts. Because they are easy to construct, matching items tend to be used when another type would provide a more valid measurement.

4. It is likely to contain irrelevant clues to the correct response. Such clues are usually subtle and unintentional and therefore difficult for the test maker to detect.

Points to Be Observed in Constructing Matching Items

1. Have at Least Five and Not More than Twelve Responses in Each Matching Exercise. This is somewhat of an arbitrary rule based on common sense and experience. (Some writers state that five to seven responses are preferable.[1]) When there are less than five responses, the material can usually be measured more effectively by another type of item (multiple-choice, preferably). When there are more than twelve responses, the matching item tends to become confusing and the student wastes time by having to review too many possible choices.

If the test maker constructs a matching item that has fifteen or twenty responses, he can do two things. First he may well decide that eight or ten of the responses are adequate to sample the points in question, and hence he shortens the item. By cutting out the

[1] Herbert E. Hawkes, E. F. Lindquist, and C. R. Mann, *The Construction and Use of Achievement Examinations.* Boston: Houghton Mifflin Company, 1936, p. 150.

obvious and weak response the item is usually improved. Second he can make two separate items with eight or ten responses in each. Usually the same directions can be used for both sets. As a result of this approach the student is able to complete the two short sets in a shorter time than it takes to finish one long set.

For certain types of classification items more than twelve responses may be justified. If the student has to keep in mind only three or four categories each time, he will be able to answer fifteen or twenty responses without too much difficulty. *But, before adding long items of this type to your tests, ask yourself whether they will increase or decrease the validity of the test.* Exceptional items can be justified if you can prove to yourself that they are really measuring what you want to measure. This is a sobering and useful criterion that should be uppermost in your mind at all times.

2. Include at Least Three Extra Choices from Which Responses Must Be Chosen. This tends to reduce the possibility of guessing or answering by a process of elimination. The several examples at the beginning of the chapter illustrate this suggestion. The same results are obtained if the several choices can be used more than once, as in the classification type.

As an example of this point consider the following item from the wood-finishing field:

```
Directions:  Place the letters from Column II in the blank
of Column I which best describes it.  Think in terms of oil
paint.
46. ____ pigment          A. boiled linseed oil
47. ____ drier            B. iron oxide
48. ____ solvent          C. turpentine
49. ____ vehicle          D. terebene
50. ____ remover          E. lye
```

In this instance we are primarily interested in the number of possible responses. Suppose you know that boiled linseed oil is a "vehicle," turpentine a "solvent," and lye a "remover." Without knowing anything about terebene or iron oxide, you would have a fifty-fifty chance of marking them correctly. And if you happened to know or rationalize that iron oxide is a "pigment," you could mark the "drier" correctly without any idea whatsoever as to the nature of terebene.

While this item might be improved in several ways, a first requirement would be to reduce the possibility of correct guessing by adding more choices in the right column. Or the choices in the right column might remain the same, with additional responses called for in the left column, as follows:

Directions: The two columns below refer to several finishing materials and their uses. You are to match each material with the primary use to which it is put. Place the identifying letter of the proper use in the blank space preceding each material. Use each letter more than once when necessary.

_____46. boiled linseed oil   A. drier
_____47. iron oxide   B. pigment
_____48. turpentine   C. remover
_____49. lye   D. solvent
_____50. alcohol   E. vehicle
_____51. amyl acetate
_____52. terebene
_____53. ocher

By revising the item in the above manner, the student will not be able to cross off each letter as it is used. There will be a tendency to review all the five uses in considering each of the materials. Such an arrangement calls for more discrimination.

3. Use Only Homogeneous or Related Materials in Any One Exercise. This suggestion should be adhered to strictly. It will help in correcting a common weakness found in matching items. When unrelated materials are included, the correct responses can usually be determined by rationalization or a process of elimination. Consider an example that illustrates this point.

Directions: Match the two columns below. Use each letter only once and place it in the blank space at the left of the column.

_____1. material used for making   A. 1/2
        window boxes   B. orthographic
_____2. a type of drawing   C. T x W x L
_____3. a grade of sandpaper   D. finishing nails
_____4. formula for board feet   E. cast iron
_____5. used in laying floors   F. mortise and tenon
_____6. table legs and rails   G. redwood
                                   H. $\dfrac{T'' \times W'' \times L'}{12}$
                                   I. cross lap
                                   J. photograph
                                   K. casing nail

Each of the above responses is generally related to the field of woodwork. *But—for testing purposes this is definitely unrelated material.* This becomes obvious as each response is considered. The first item pertains to the construction of window boxes. The only applicable materials listed are cast iron and redwood. That would narrow the choices to two, and since this is a woodworking test, there would be little doubt as to which choice should be selected. The second response, "a type of drawing," could be narrowed down to two choices immediately (orthographic, photograph). Simple rationalization would result in choosing the word "orthographic." In considering the third item a process of elimination would result in the discarding of every choice except the first, ($\frac{1}{2}$). Similar reasoning could be used for each response, and in no case would the student have to choose between more than two possible answers, the correct choice usually being obvious. It would be easier to guess the right answers in this particular item than in a series of true-false statements used to cover the same material.

Whenever you prepare a matching item, confine it to one area of instruction. All the responses should be applicable to that area. If this suggestion is followed, there should be little doubt about the homogeneity of the material.

4. Include at Least Three Plausible Choices from Which the Correct Response Must Be Selected. This suggestion is closely related to the one just preceding. It is a further check on the homogeneity of the material tested. If, in order to carry out this suggestion, it becomes necessary to include three times as many items in one column as in the other, use some other type of test item. In the following example there are at least three plausible choices for each response. Of course, the person who knows the subject matter can and should be able to select the correct responses immediately.

Directions: Listed in the two columns below are related words or phrases pertaining to fundamentals of radio. Place in the blank space in front of the word or phrase in the left-hand column the identifying letter of the word in the right-hand column which is most closely related in meaning. Use each letter only once. The first item is answered as an example. "A" is placed in the blank space because the "B" battery is the source of plate current.

(A) x. source of plate current	A. "B" battery
____62. changing in alternating current to pulsating direct current	(do not use)
	B. cathode
____63. controls the flow of electrons in a vacuum tube	C. choke
	D. coupling
____64. steps up weak radio-frequency waves	E. filtering
	F. grid
____65. source of electron emission in a vacuum tube	G. inductance
	H. impedance
____66. controls voltage drop	I. plate
____67. strengthens the resistance property of coils	J. reactance
	K. rectification
	L. resistor
	M. transformer

5. *Place the Column Containing the Longer Statements on the Left Side of the Page.* Require the students to record their responses at the left of this column. This saves time and makes the process of selection easier. The reasoning behind this suggestion can be illustrated by a simple example wherein the suggestion *is not* carried out.

____1. Sill	A. Timbers making up the body of the floor frame
____2. Girder	
____3. Bridging	B. The first part of the frame structure to be set
____4. Etc.	
	C. A beam delivering a concentrated load to a wall or piers
	D. A system of bracing
	E. Etc.

In order to select the correct response for the word "sill," it is necessary to start reading the possible choices on the right. This takes time. It may be confusing. By following the suggestion given above these difficulties would be corrected. The item would appear as follows:

____1. Timbers making up the body of the floor frame	A. Bridging
	B. Girder
____2. The first part of the frame structure to be set	C. Joist
	D. Plate
____3. A beam delivering a concentrated load to a wall or piers	E. Sill
	F. Stud
____4. A system of bracing	
____5. Etc.	

The procedure is now simplified. As the several responses are selected, it is necessary only to glance over the single words at the right, rather than reading through the longer statements, as in the first instance.

6. Use Illustrations Whenever Possible. This suggestion is especially applicable to matching items pertaining to tools, parts, mechanical units, and the like. Descriptions and definitions of such things are often confusing to the students, even though they may know the points being tested. Simple drawings will usually correct the confusion and save time in answering.

The following example contains definitions of several types of rafters. The apparent objective of the item is to measure the extent of the students' ability to tell one type of rafter from another. The authors cannot help wondering how many experienced carpenters would be able to answer this item without difficulty.

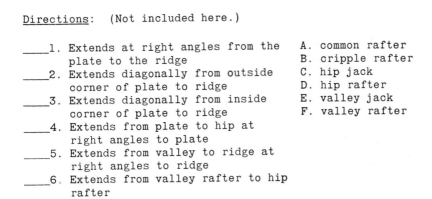

Directions: (Not included here.)

_____1. Extends at right angles from the   A. common rafter
         plate to the ridge   B. cripple rafter
_____2. Extends diagonally from outside   C. hip jack
         corner of plate to ridge   D. hip rafter
_____3. Extends diagonally from inside   E. valley jack
         corner of plate to ridge   F. valley rafter
_____4. Extends from plate to hip at
         right angles to plate
_____5. Extends from valley to ridge at
         right angles to ridge
_____6. Extends from valley rafter to hip
         rafter

Inspection of the item will reveal that it does not follow the suggestion of having extra choices, but in this instance we are primarily concerned with the definitions. It would be interesting to watch a group of students attempting to answer this item. It is likely that arms and hands would be placed in many positions in trying to determine the meanings associated with "diagonal," "right angles," "plate," "ridge," "valley," and "hip." Perhaps neophytes in the carpentry trade should know these definitions, but it would be so much simpler to use an illustration as in the following example:

____1. hip rafter
____2. common rafter
____3. valley jack rafter
____4. hip jack
____5. valley rafter

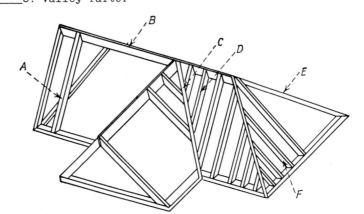

7. Arrange the Selection Column in a Logical Order. The purpose of this suggestion is to make it easier for the student to locate
the correct responses. The selection column will usually be on the
right side, although in classification items and other modifications
it may be in another place.

When the column consists of a series of words, these should be
placed in alphabetical order (note examples given here). A series
of figures should be placed in ascending or descending order. The
logic of this suggestion is illustrated by the poor arrangement of
the following example, in which you are required to match several
fractions with their decimal equivalents set up in a haphazard list.
(This item is merely illustrative; it has not been taken from a
test.)

____1. 17/64	A. .125	
____2. 1/16	B. .015625	
____3. 3/8	C. .4375	
____4. 3/64	D. .046875	
____5. 7/16	E. .046875	
____6. 11/32	F. .0625	
	G. .34375	
	H. .625	
	I. .3625	
	J. .375	
	K. .265625	

The typical reader would probably be confused, at least as he started out to try to answer this item. It would be a process of looking back and forth and up and down. This is an extreme example, but it illustrates the value of putting the choices in some logical order if student time is to be saved. A similar practice should be followed when the item pertains to a series of dates.

____1. Smith–Hughes Act	A. 1862
____2. George–Barden Act	B. 1886
____3. George–Deen Act	C. 1911
____4. Morrill Act	D. 1917
____5. George–Ellzey Act	E. 1920
____6. Smith–Lever Act	F. 1927
	G. 1933
	H. 1937
	I. 1941
	J. 1946

8. Keep the Student in Mind as the Item Is Prepared. Try to determine the lines of reasoning the students will follow as they look at the item. Think of all the possible ways each response might be answered. This will usually result in some changes and improvements. It is a helpful means for locating irrelevant clues and ambiguous choices.

9. Make Sure the Entire Exercise Appears on One Page. It is disconcerting, to say the least, when some of the choices are on one side of a sheet and the remainder on the other side. The test maker should check carefully to make certain that this does not happen when the test is reproduced.

10. Make the Directions Specific. State the area of instructions to which the things listed apply. Tell how the matching is to proceed. Be sure to emphasize that the choices may be used only once, or more than once, as the case may be. (The directions accompanying the examples at the beginning of this chapter will serve as useful guides.)

11. Use Capital Letters to Label the Parts in the Column from Which Responses Are to Be Selected. As was stated in a previous chapter, this suggestion will result in more legible responses since the differences between capital letters are more pronounced than between lower-case letters or figures.

SUMMARY

Matching items require the matching of two sets of materials in accordance with given directions. In a sense they are a variation of the multiple-choice item. They are especially applicable for measuring the "who," "what," "where," "when" type of subject matter. They are relatively easy to construct, can be made objective, and can be scored quickly.

The typical matching item provides a poor indication of complete understanding and is inferior to the multiple-choice item for measuring judgment and application. It is apt to stress the memorization of facts and will often contain subtle, irrelevant clues to the correct response.

The following suggestions will prove helpful in constructing matching items:

1. Have at least five and not more than twelve responses in each matching exercise.

2. Include at least three extra choices from which responses must be chosen.

3. Use only homogeneous or related materials in any one exercise.

4. Include at least three plausible choices from which the correct response must be selected.

5. Place the column containing the longer statements on the left side of the page.

6. Use illustrations whenever possible.

7. Arrange the selection column in a logical order.

8. Keep the student in mind as the item is prepared.

9. Make sure the entire exercise appears on one page.

10. Make the directions specific.

11. Use capital letters to label the parts in the column from which the responses are to be selected.

SOME THINGS TO DO AND QUESTIONS TO ANSWER

1. It was stated that a matching item is a variation of a multiple-choice item. When should each type be used? What is the advantage of each?

2. What is the difference between the classification type and a regular matching item?

3. Prepare a matching item made up of short questions and their answers.

4. Many matching items can easily be made into recall items. Prepare a simple example of this process.

5. Why is it a poor policy to include more than twelve responses in a single matching exercise?

6. It was said that a classification item might include more than twelve responses. Why?

7. Explain why the length of responses makes a difference as to the placement of columns.

8. Explain what is meant by homogeneous materials. Use examples from your particular field of interest.

9. Why should there be at least three plausible choices for each response?

10. Why should one column contain more items than the other?

SELECTED REFERENCES FOR ADDITIONAL READING

Greene, Harry A., Albert N. Jorgensen, and J. Raymond Gerberich. *Measurement and Evaluation in the Secondary School.* New York: Longmans, Green & Co., Inc., 1943. Chap. VIII.

Hawkes, Herbert E., E. F. Lindquist, and C. R. Mann. *The Construction and Use of Achievement Examinations.* Boston: Houghton Mifflin Company, 1936. Pp. 147–152.

Lee, J. Murray. *A Guide to Measurement in Secondary Schools.* New York: Appleton-Century-Crofts, Inc., 1936. Chap. XI.

Remmers, H. H., and N. L. Gage. *Educational Measurement and Evaluation.* New York: Harper & Brothers, 1943. Chap. IX.

Rinsland, Henry Daniel. *Constructing Tests and Grading in Elementary and High School Subjects.* New York: Prentice-Hall, Inc., 1938. Chap. V.

Ross, C. C. *Measurement in Today's Schools.* New York: Prentice-Hall, Inc., 1947. Pp. 151–156.

CHAPTER

NINE: RECALL ITEMS

For the purposes here the recall item is considered as that type where the student supplies the answer. There are several forms and numerous adaptations. The student may be required merely to supply a single word missing from a statement. He may answer a direct question by writing in a single word, figure, or date. There may be a problem to complete, a list to enumerate, a sketch to fill in, or a paragraph to write.

Recall items are sometimes classified under two main headings: (1) completion or simple recall; (2) free response.[1] Because of the close similarity and because students are sometimes confused in trying to differentiate between the types, the authors have endeavored to group them together for a single consideration. Strictly speaking, the essay-type item should also be included under this heading. This is logical and desirable. Essay-type items can be made objective in nature and are the best kind for measuring certain outcomes. The final section of this chapter is devoted to such items.

The reader may wonder at the slight difference between certain of the types illustrated below. Do not let this be confusing. These

[1] See W. W. Cook, "Achievement Tests," *Encyclopedia of Educational Research*, pp. 1289–1293. See also Herbert E. Hawkes, E. F. Lindquist, and C. R. Mann, *The Construction and Use of Achievement Examinations* (Boston: Houghton Mifflin Company, 1936), pp. 125–136.

are recall-type items, and there is little to gain by trying to establish criteria that differentiate any more finely than this.

Simple Recall

The simple recall item is usually considered as requiring the student to supply a word, figure, or date. The word (sometimes more than one) may come at the end of a statement, it may be an answer to a direct question, or it may be associated with another word or phrase. The first example below illustrates these three approaches, using the same subject matter.

```
_____1. The unit of electrical current is the
             ____.
_____1. What is the unit of electrical current?
_____1. Current
```

```
Directions:  Each of the men listed below has made an im-
portant contribution to the field of printing.  Identify
each of them by writing a few descriptive words in the
blank space provided.  The first item is answered as an
example.
(x) Gutenberg ____(invented movable type)_____
(1) Stanhope _____
(2) Bodoni _____
(3) Mergenthaler _____
(4) Ludlow _____
(5) Didot _____
```

```
Directions:  Each of the statements below contains a blank
at or near the end of the statement.  You are to supply the
missing word.  Write your word in the large blank space at
the left of the item.  The first item is correctly answered
as an example.
(galvanized)(x) Sheet steel—coated with zinc is called ____
             iron.
_____(1) Core solders are of two main types, acid
             and ____.
_____(2) Bronze is composed of copper and ____.
_____(3) The operation that changes the shape or
             size of a hole by means of a tool pressed
             or drawn through it is known as ____.
```

Directions: Answer each of the following questions by
writing in the correct answer in the blank space at the
left.   The first question is answered as an example.
__(Edison)__ (x) Who invented the electric light?
_____(1) What is a variable resistor called?
_____(2) What is the unit of capacitance?
_____(3) What formula is used to find the circumfer-
                 ence of a circle?
_____(4) What instrument is used to measure the
                 charge of a storage battery?

Directions: Listed below are several inventions.   In the
blank space before each invention write in the name of the
inventor commonly associated with the invention.   The first
item is answered as an example.
__(Edison)__ 1. Electric light
_____2. Air brakes
_____3. Telephone
_____4. Telegraph

Sentence-completion

There is practically no difference between the sentence-completion and the simple recall type. The former usually requires the
student to recall and supply one or more key words that have been
omitted from statements. The words, when inserted in the appropriate blanks, make the statements complete, meaningful, and true.
The statements may be isolated and unrelated, or they may be
combined to form short paragraphs that carry a continuous line
of thought.

Directions: Each of the blank spaces in the following
statements indicates the place of an omitted word.   Complete the meaning of each statement by writing the correct
word in the corresponding numbered blank at the left.   The
first item is answered as an example.
__(block)__ (x) The best plane for planing end grain is the
                (x) ____ plane.
_____(1) Spirit stains are made by mixing (1) ____
                 with (2) ____.
_____(2)
_____(3) Casein glue is a (3) ____ product.
_____(4) To prepare casein glue mix it with (4)____.

_____4. Electromagnetic radiation was discussed by
_____.
_____5. The "father of modern radio" is ____.
_____6. To every force there is an opposite and
equal reaction. This is a statement of one
of ____ laws.
_____7. Who was the first person to demonstrate that
air exerts a pressure?

_____1. The leading competitor of the United States
in the world corn market is ____.
_____2. The basis of our country's wealth lies in
its ____.
_____3. The art of forest land and resource manage-
ment is called ____.
_____4. The leading agricultural crop in the United
States is ____.

_____1. Ghon is a term used in relation to the dis-
ease ____.
_____2. The green coloring substance of plants is
called ____.
_____3. The term applied to energy use when the body
is at complete rest is ____.

_____52. In the event that no candidate for the
Presidency secures a majority of the
electoral vote, the duty of electing the
President belongs to ____.
_____53. The states were the first to attempt to
regulate railroads. These laws were
popularly known as the ____ laws.
_____54. The first ten amendments to the Constitu-
tion are generally known as ____.

Directions:[2] Complete the following exercise by filling in
the proper word (or words) in the several blank spaces.
    Saws are one of the most important tool groups used by
the woodworker. To saw curves in thin stock a _____
saw is used. If the stock is thicker than 3/8 inch it is
best to cut the curves with a _____ saw. If you

[2] This item would be much easier to score if the student were required to
write his answers at the left, as in the preceding example.

wished to cut across the grain in a straight line, you
could use either a _____ or _____ saw. The
most accurate saw for cutting across grain is the _____
saw. For rough-cutting with the grain we use a _____
saw.

<hr>

Directions: In the following sentences certain key words
are omitted. The omissions are indicated by the small
blank spaces. Write the words that complete the meaning of
the sentences in the numbered blank spaces at the left.
___(six)___x. In one inch there are (x) ____ picas.
_____1. The standard letterhead size is ____.
_____2. Type set by hand is assembled in a ____
                 stick.
_____3. Most papers are sold in reams of ____
                 sheets.
_____4. The unit of measure in printing is the ____.
_____5. The proportion generally accepted as the
                 most pleasing to the eye is ____.

Problems or Situations

The ordinary arithmetic problem is a recall-type item. Variations can be devised to require the student to do such things as
complete a formula, fill in missing parts, or use the formula in
solving a specified problem. The situation type may require the
student to indicate his response by making a simple sketch, by
completing a sketch, by completing an outline, or by writing out
a response in narrative form. Basically, these items are very similar
to the simple recall or sentence-completion type.

Directions: Follow the directions given with each of the
problems listed below. Write each answer in the blank
space at the left. You may use your handbook to locate any
formulas that might be needed.
_____(1) A gear blank is 10.5" in diameter. The
                  diametral pitch is 4. Calculate the number
                  of teeth in the blank.
_____(2) You have a piece of steel 16" long, 2" in
                  diameter. The work is revolving at 150
                  rpm. What is the cutting speed in feet per
                  minute?
_____(3) For a piece of round stock (16" x 2")
                  calculate the tailstock set over for turn-
                  ing a taper of 7/8" per foot for a distance
                  of 8" on the stock.

<u>Directions</u>:   A toaster marked 1,000 watts, 120 volts, is
brought into the shop in which you are working.   The
customer's complaint is that it insists on blowing fuses.
With this knowledge answer the following questions.
_____(1) How much current should the toaster draw
when working properly?
_____(2) How much resistance would you expect to
find in the element, <u>if</u> <u>it</u> <u>is</u> <u>not</u> <u>defec-</u>
<u>tive</u>?
_____(3) The cord and plug can be separated from the
toaster itself.   How much resistance would
you expect to find between the two wires in
the cord?

<u>Directions</u>:   Shown below are various lines.   Using the
scale shown after each line you are to determine the proper
length of each line and write your answer in the blank
space at the left.   Use your architect's scale to do the
measuring.
_____1. _____
($\frac{1}{4}$" = 1' − 0")
_____2. _____(3" = 1' − 0")
_____3. _____
(3/8" = 1' − 0")
_____4. _____(3/4" = 1' − 0")

<u>Directions</u>:   Complete the following formulas by writing in
the missing words, figures, terms or symbols.
73. Circumference of a circle = _____
74. Board foot = <u>T</u>" x _____
75. RPM = <u>CS</u> x _____

Assume that polydactylism (the occurrence of more than the
usual number of fingers and toes) is a dominant inherited
characteristic.   If both the husband and wife are polydactyl and the germ plasm for each is <u>PN</u> (P − polydactyl gene;
N − normal gene) we can predict the following for their
eight (8) children:
_____ are polydactyl with genes PP.
_____ are polydactyl with genes PN.
_____ are normal with genes NN.

_____1. At what rpm should a milling cutter operate when its diameter is 6" and the cutting speed is specified as 35 feet per minute?

$$(\text{rpm} = \frac{CS \times 12}{3.1416 \times D})$$

_____2. What is the cutting speed of a milling cutter 3" in diameter rotating at 200 rpm? $(CS = \frac{3.1416 \times D \times rpm}{12})$

_____3. Find C when D = 2.347. (C = πD)

Directions: In the following situations you are to determine the proper rake, lubricant, and type of tool to use. The tool will be one of the four standard types. The material and speed are given. The first item is answered as an example.

Cast iron is to be turned at 150 FPM.
Rake (positive) Lubricant (dry) Tool (tungsten carbide)
Aluminum is to be turned at 300 FPM.
Rake(1)_____ Lubricant(2)___ Tool(3)_____
Brass is to be turned at 150 FPM.
Rake(4)_____ Lubricant(5)___ Tool(6)_____

Directions: In the topographic sketch at the right below, the horizontal distance from A to B is 740 feet. The difference in elevation is 59 feet. The slope from point A to B is uniform. The difference in elevation of contour 300 and point A is 9 feet.

_____1. What is the horizontal distance from point A to the 300 contour line?

_____2. What is the horizontal distance from point A to the 290 contour?

_____3. What is the horizontal distance from the 280 to the 290 contour?

<u>Directions</u>: It is desired to control the hall light in a
house from three different places. Complete the diagram
below to perform that task. You will receive one point for
each switch wired correctly.

115-volt
___supply___

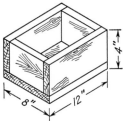

Hall light

<u>Directions</u>: Pictured below is a box to be made of 3/4"
pine. You are to figure the cost of building ten (10) such
boxes at 11¢ per bd. ft.

Answer

<u>Directions</u>: In each set of drawings below the top view is
incorrect because one line is missing. You are to draw in
the line that is missing.

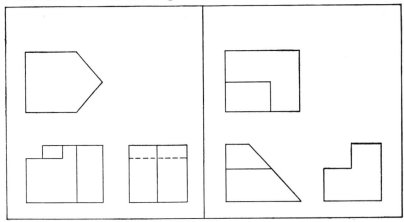

<u>Directions</u>: What type of photographic developer would you use in each of the following situations?

    _____1. A picture made with a pinhole camera on direct positive paper.

    _____2. A picture made with a 35-mm. camera on Panatomic X film.

    _____3. To produce warm tones on such papers as Opal G.

    _____4. To produce cold tones on such papers as Velox.

<u>Directions</u>: Shown below are three views of a block. You are to sketch in the necessary dimensions. <u>Use</u> <u>letters</u> <u>instead</u> <u>of</u> <u>figures</u> as in the example shown on the right. Ten dimensions are necessary. You will receive one point for each one correctly placed.

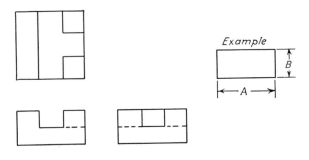

<u>Directions</u>: In each of the squares below the front and top views are given. You are to sketch in the correct end view.

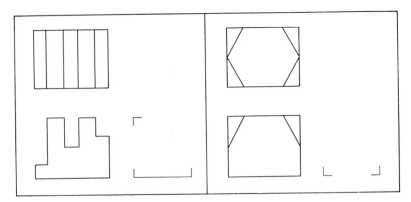

Identification

A recall-type item may be used to measure the student's ability to indicate the proper names of such things as tools, mechanical units, symbols, instruments, or specific parts. This type may also be used to measure the ability of the student to analyze special difficulties or identify the errors in a drawing.

Directions: Listed below are several abbreviations used in woodworking. You are to write the proper meaning in the blank space at the left. The first item is answered as an example.

(good one side)	x. G1S
	1. S2S
	2. RHB
	3. per
	4. FHB
	5. 8d

Directions: Shown below are various symbols used in radio and electricity. Write the proper name for each symbol in the numbered blank space at the left of the symbol.

1.
2.
3.
4.
5.
6.
7.
8.

<u>Directions</u>: You are to identify each of the parts in-
dicated in the drawing below. Write the correct name in
the blank space provided at the left. The first item is
answered as an example.

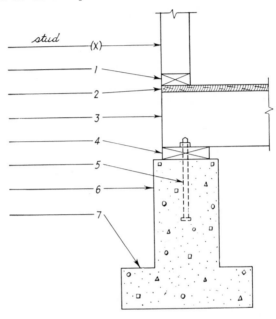

_____ _stud_ ____(X)_____→
_____ 1
_____ 2
_____ 3
_____ 4
_____ 5
_____ 6
_____ 7

<u>Directions</u>: In the space provided write in the names of
the standard moldings shown below. Use abbreviations where
possible.

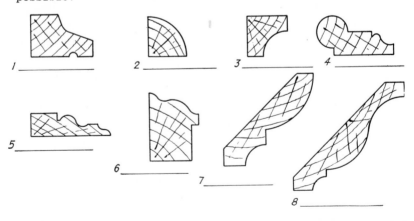

1 _____   2 _____   3 _____   4 _____

5 _____   6 _____   7 _____   8 _____

<u>Directions:</u> Pictured below are six common types of files.
Write the correct name for each file in the corresponding
numbered blank at the left.

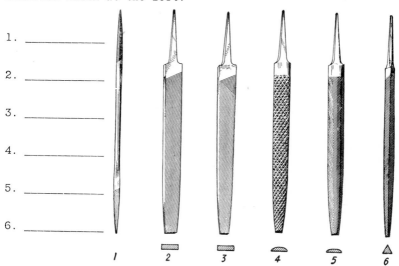

1. _____

2. _____

3. _____

4. _____

5. _____

6. _____

1   *2*   *3*   *4*   *5*   *6*

Listing, or Enumeration

The listing, or enumeration, type of item requires the student
to supply a list of terms, rules, factors, steps, and the like, that
have been taught and emphasized in a given course. It is used frequently and is often abused. The student may or may not be required to list in a particular order the things called for.

List <u>in the order that they occur</u> the four strokes of the
Otto cycle.
1. _____
2. _____
3. _____
4. _____

List <u>in correct order</u> the five (5) steps to be taken in
tempering the tip of a screwdriver.
32. _____
33. _____
34. _____
35. _____
36. _____

What are the four <u>essential</u> parts of a simple alternating-current generator?

11. _____   13. _____
12. _____   14. _____

List four types of reamers in the sequence that you would use them to finish a blind hole which is .003" oversize.

1. _____   3. _____
2. _____   4. _____

What are the three primary colors?

72. _____
73. _____
74. _____

What are the four major classifications of scaffolds?

1. _____   3. _____
2. _____   4. _____

Other Variations

The recall-type item can be modified or adapted in a variety of other ways. Cause-and-effect items can be devised so that the student supplies one or the other. Generalizations can be given, with the student required to supply examples. Suggestions and associations, comparisons, tabulations, completion analyses—these are a few of the variations that might be useful in certain situations. Brief examples are given of three different variations. This should be sufficient to indicate the variety of possibilities inherent in the recall-type item.

Analogies

<u>Directions</u>: This exercise consists of incomplete analogies. Insert the proper word in the blank space provided. An analogy of this type, A:B::C:D, means that A has the same relation to B that C has to D (2:4::10: ____).

1. Flow of water: flow of electricity:: gallons per minute: _____.
2. Ampere: current:: _____: resistance.
3. Purple: red and blue:: green: _____.

Cause and Effect

Directions: Each of the printed lines below contains some
fault or imperfection. In the blank space at the right you
are to state the cause of the fault. The first item is
answered as an example.

The dog is cold.   x.____(Letter "e" upside down)_____

The dog is good.   1._____

The dog is happy, 2._____

The dog is sad.   3._____

Generalization and Justification

Directions: Accept each of the statements below as a fact.
In the blank space give an example or reason that justifies
the statement.
1. Some wood products are stronger than similar metal products.
   Example _____
2. Inferior softwoods can now be made stronger than the
   strongest hardwood of 25 years ago.
   Reason _____

Uses and Advantages of Recall-type Items

1. The recall-type item can be used to measure the retention of specific points. It demands accurate information. It is relatively easy to construct and is applicable to any field in which achievement is being measured.

2. The common types are used primarily in measuring the *who, what, when, where* type of information.

3. Recall items can be substituted for recognition items when it is desired to have the student recall outright the information being tested. For example, the identification-type item can often be used in place of matching exercises, with only a slight revision necessary, as shown in the illustration on the next page.

4. The several variations can be used effectively to sample a wide range of subject matter.

5. Recall items can be made to measure well the application of certain knowledges, as in detecting the errors in a drawing.

6. They tend to have a high discriminating value. The guessing factor is minimized in well-prepared items.

7. The problem and situation type of item is especially valuable for measuring certain types of subject matter involving arithmetic computations, use of formulas, use of measuring instruments, and similar abilities.

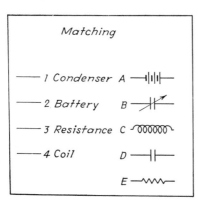

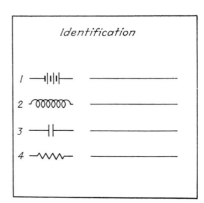

Limitations

1. Because the simple types of recall items are easy to construct, they tend to be used excessively. As a result there is an overemphasis on verbal facility and the memorization of facts. Because of the nature and construction of many items, they often provide a better measure of native intelligence than of achievement in a given course.

2. Unless care is exercised in constructing recall items, the scoring is apt to become subjective. In some of the types it is extremely difficult to avoid subjectivity in the scoring.

3. It is difficult to measure complete understandings with the simple types (simple recall and completion).

4. From the student's point of view the items may be time consuming. The student may know the material being tested but have difficulty in recalling the exact word needed to fill in a certain blank.

Points to Be Observed in Construction

1. Use Direct Questions Whenever Possible. Direct questions will help in avoiding ambiguous statements. They are not so likely to contain irrelevant clues. As a general rule the question form will result in an item that is easier to score.

2. *Make Sentence-completion Items as Specific as Possible.* State the problem or describe the situation clearly and concisely. Omit only key words. Do not omit long phrases. In a given sentence do not omit more than three words. A short statement with one key word omitted is preferable. Consider the following examples of poor recall items that *do not* follow this suggestion:

_____9-11. In woodworking a ____, ____, and ____ are used to mark measurements.

_____
_____

_____20. In starting a saw cut the strokes should be ____ and _____.

16. Proper kiln drying involves _____, _____, _____, and sometimes _____.

1. Safety as applied to a school shop resolves into one's using _____, _____, and _____.

8. Machine screws are ordered according to _____ _____, _____, _____.
9. When making a cut with a shaper the _____ should be in the _____ of the _____ whenever possible.
10. A router is essentially an _____.

These examples of poor construction could be augmented by many others. They should be sufficient to indicate the necessity for making each item specific, for omitting only key words, and for avoiding the omission of too many words. It would be difficult to revise the above examples to make them more effective as simple completion items. The best practice would be to omit them altogether from the test and use a different type of item to do the measuring.

The several items that follow have been selected to illustrate what is meant by statements that are specific and have only key words omitted:

```
_____1. An electric motor which runs on either D.C.
                   or A.C. is called (a-an) ____ motor.
_____2. Core solders are of two types, (2)____ and
                   (3)____.
_____3.
_____4. Ottmar Mergenthaler invented the ____.
_____5. The henry is the unit of ____.
_____6. In the symbol SAE 2335 the type of steel
                   indicated by the figure "2" would be ____.
_____7. When the rise of a roof is 8 feet and the
                   span is 24 feet the pitch would be ____.
```

3. Do Not Copy Statements Directly from Textbooks. Copying statements directly from textbooks is a common fault. It results in an artificial type of learning by the students. It places undue emphasis upon rote memorization. When statements are copied verbatim, they are very likely to be ambiguous or to contain clues that give the item away. In an effort to get rid of such clues the test maker is likely to leave too many blanks, with the result that the value of the item is lost entirely. This is clearly illustrated by the items just below, selected from a test in machine woodworking:

```
2. _____ are made by combining an
   _____ of desired kind and degree of coarseness
   and hardness with an appropriate _____.
3. A _____ _____ is a piece of natural
   _____ of special quality mounted on a shaft and
   _____ to the thickness and diameter desired.
```

There is little need to point out the weaknesses of these items. There can be little question about their ambiguity and the need for rote memorization in order to provide the correct answers. Such items should be avoided religiously in a real achievement test.

4. In Simple Recall and Sentence-completion Items Place the Blanks near or at the End of the Statement. This makes for continuity in reading the statement. It becomes more functional and logical. If the blanks come at the beginning of the item, the student must begin with a blank, read the item, and then mentally retrace his steps to decide or record what should be in the blanks. Most items of this type can be revised so that the blanks come at or near the end.

Several examples will show the logic of this suggestion. These examples have been selected from teacher-made tests. Some are better items than others. The only purpose here is to show how the items are improved when the blanks come at or near the end of the statement.

Poor

```
4. _____ is the natural color of shellac.
```

Better

```
4. The natural color of shellac is _____ .
```

Poor

```
12. _____ is put on wood screws to make them enter
    the wood more easily.
```

Better

```
12. Wood screws will enter the wood easier if they are
    given a coating of _____ .
```

Poor

```
1. A _____ is a collection of all sizes and styles
   of one design of type.
```

Better

```
1. A collection of all sizes and styles of one design of
   type is called a (an) _____ .
```

5. Avoid the Inclusion of Irrelevant Clues. Be careful that the item does not provide so much information that it can be answered solely on the basis of general intelligence. It is a poor practice to omit verbs. Watch out for words such as "a" and "an" when they come just before the omitted word. They might provide a clue to the correct response.

Consider the following two items from a printing test:

```
2. Men's social cards should carry the courtesy title
   "_____ ."
```

21. It is customary to _____ every noun and important word in a menu.

In each instance nothing more than general intelligence is required to write in the correct answer. The second item also illustrates the inadvisability of omitting verbs. Almost invariably this
makes the correct answer obvious. In the next example a verb is
again omitted. The correct response is obvious. The item is also

7. A dry cell should be _____ when purchased by
means of an ammeter.

humorous when read literally. (How does an ammeter purchase
a dry cell?) Some recall items are little better than true-false questions from the point of view of guessing. In the following example there are only two possible answers, and this is immediately
apparent:

10. Sheet metal 10 gauge is _____ than sheet metal
28 gauge.

6. Construct the Item so There Is Only One Correct Response.
If synonyms are to be accepted, this should be indicated in the
key. This suggestion pertains primarily to the simple recall and
the sentence-completion type of items. Listing and free-response
items may sometimes have more than one correct response. However, the suggestion should be considered carefully even for these
types, for if there are several possible answers, it may be best to use
another type of item in order to obtain objectivity in the scoring.

7. Design Enumeration Items to Call for Specific Facts. Each
thing to be listed should involve only a few words. Because of the
subjective scoring factor the student should not be required to
list long, involved statements. The subjectivity inherent in many
enumeration items is illustrated by the examples which follow:

5. List at least four (4) reasons why safety practices are
important.
a. _____
b. _____
c. _____
d. _____

There is almost no end of possible responses that could be used in answering this. From the point of view of specificity compare the above with the following item calling for definite information:

```
In the following spaces list the four common electrical
frequencies that have been used for light and power in the
United States.
37. _____
38. _____
39. _____
40. _____
```

8. Rarely Should One Question Call for More than Six or Eight Things to Be Listed. Allow one point for each thing to be listed. Do not try to use a listing item if the student can choose from a great variety of possible answers to supply the responses. That is, do not call for five things out of a list of fifteen taught in the course. To do so would place in the same category all students who listed five things and would indicate that each had achieved equally with respect to the fifteen points in question. A student who had learned all fifteen things would receive on this listing exercise the same score as the student who had learned only five of the fifteen. Such a listing item would be very low in discriminating power. Every effort should be made to design items that will detect small differences in achievement.

9. If the Student Is Required to List Things in a Given Order, Determine, before the Test Is Given, How the Responses Are to Be Scored. Use a system of scoring that will take off points in accordance with the number of errors made. The logic of this suggestion can be shown by considering an oversimplified listing item requiring the testee to list the first six letters of the alphabet in correct order. Suppose that this had been done as in the figure on page 264, and you had placed your scoring key next to the item. How would you score the item? Would you allow no credit, or would you take off one point or two points? Note that the scoring key does not agree with any of the letters listed; yet, except for A, they follow each other in the correct order. This same situation could exist in listing the coarseness of files or the steps to follow in squaring a piece of stock, or in any similar situation.

Many instructors are inclined to give the student no credit if a single error is made. With respect to the alphabet this might be justified, but in doing so all students who make errors, regardless of their number, are placed in the same category. The student who gets one item out of order receives no more credit than the student who gets six out of order. There are several ways in which this might be corrected. One method is to allow one point for placing the first item first. Then allow one additional point for each item that is placed immediately after the item that it should

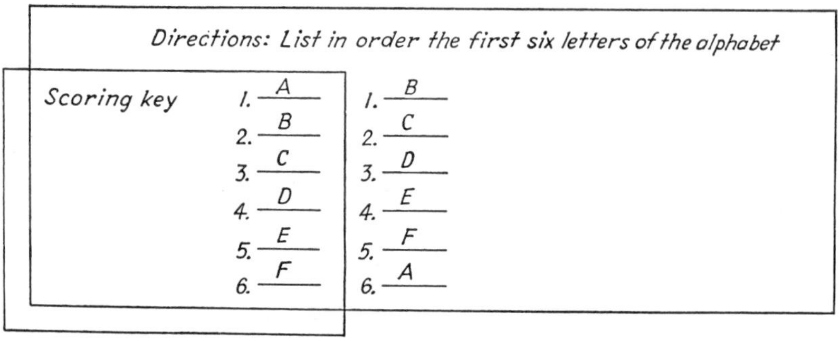

Fig. 1. Illustrating one difficulty in marking correct-order items.

follow. In the above example this would mean that the student would receive four points for the item. The nature of the subject matter and the objective being measured should determine the method of scoring that is followed. This is a matter to be decided by the test maker but it should be determined before the test is given.

10. Make All Sketches or Illustrations Clear and of Sufficient Size. For certain types of items in such fields as drafting it is especially necessary to have illustrations that are clear and of sufficient size.

11. Whenever Possible, Require the Student to Solve Problems or Use Previous Learning. If this suggestion is followed conscientiously, it may mean that many simple recall and sentence-completion items will be discarded. In most tests this would result in improvement. It does not mean that the common completion types should be discarded entirely. Rather they should be used prudently and should not be overemphasized. Recall items can be devised so that they require the student to make application of things learned. The typical teacher-made test can accommodate many more such items.

12. Be Sure There Is Plenty of Room to Indicate Responses. As the items are being constructed, keep in mind the method that is to be used in scoring the items. Wherever possible arrange the space for responses on one side of the page, preferably the left. This makes for ease of scoring. Most of the examples at the beginning of this chapter are arranged in this manner.

Essay Items

The essay-type test item requires the student to make a comparison, write a description, or explain certain points on which instruction has been given. It is usually considered in contrast to the so-called objective-type items. In reality, a well-constructed essay item can be made objective in nature and is another type of recall item. It is difficult to state explicitly where the simple recall or free-response items stop and essay items begin. From a literal viewpoint a descriptive paragraph is certainly a type of free response. At the same time a one-word answer to a direct question is not an essay in the usual sense of the word.

Little is to be gained by trying to draw a fine line of demarcation. For the purpose here intended the essay item is considered as that type in which the student is allowed freedom of expression in describing, explaining, comparing, or reasoning. This is in contrast to the items that require the student merely to list, enumerate, or name something. From this point of view, essay items are considered as another one of the various types of test items used to measure certain outcomes of learning. This consideration is somewhat at variance with the usual treatment of essay items. With the advent of the so-called "objective-testing" movement it became popular to criticize and ridicule the "write all you know" type of test that had been used by most teachers. The subjectivity of the scoring, the poor sampling of what had been learned, the amount of time necessary to answer only a few questions, the opportunity for bluffing on the part of the student—these were the major points of condemnation of the "traditional" examination, which was another name for a group of *poor* essay items. These criticisms were usually valid and justified—there is no question about that. The unfortunate point is that essay items, as such, were condemned rather than the method by which they were constructed, used, and scored, as should have been the case. In other words, essay items are not inherently inferior. They should be considered carefully along with other types of items when the test maker is endeavoring to ascertain the best method for measuring a certain objective.

It might be wise to suggest that the designations "traditional" and "old-type" no longer be used synonymously with essay items. In the first place the terms as used in testing carry a negative implication. This is not justified with respect to well-constructed essay items. In the second place the typical item has, by tradition it seems, become the true-false item with its several glaring weaknesses. Would it not be better to think of "old-type" tests as those consisting solely of "who," "what," "where" items, the "new-type" tests being the kinds that measure understanding and application of things learned?

The purpose of this brief digression has not been to add some new terms and words in an effort to confuse you, but rather to emphasize the point that essay items can be used effectively and should be used. They have value in measuring the ability of the student to organize his thoughts and express himself clearly. They can be devised to measure complete understanding. It should be emphasized, however, that these values are found only in carefully prepared essay items.

The question is sometimes asked whether essay items should be used with other types in a single test. This question cannot be answered by "yes" or "no." It is a matter of judgment. There will be instances where essay items can be used effectively right along with multiple-choice, matching, and other types of items. In such cases they will be of the short-answer variety and hard to distinguish from certain other free-response recall items, thus:

14. In the space below describe how a door bell works by tracing the action that takes place. Use a drawing if necessary.

At other times essay items will be much more comprehensive in nature and will not be readily fitted into a typical achievement test. In other words, it is not always possible or desirable to have the student organize his thoughts and express himself completely in 1 or 2 or 5 or 10 minutes, as is necessary in the ordinary test. The ability to work independently, to locate sources of material, to organize a presentation, and to express ideas clearly—these are highly important outcomes of effective learning. They cannot be measured by true-false and similar items. They cannot be measured readily by requiring the student to close his books and react to a group of stereotyped questions. They can be measured, at least partially, by well-conceived and carefully constructed essay items that allow the student to look at a quantity of materials before organizing and expressing his thought. The student might be given a week or more to prepare his reply.

This concept begins to approach the term-paper assignment except that it is more restricted and is based on the various suggestions given below for the construction and correction of essay items. The paper would be prepared and scored in accordance with careful, predetermined specifications. Essay items of this type would, naturally, be used very sparingly because of the time factor involved.

Points to Consider in Constructing Essay Items

1. Decide upon the Objective to Be Measured. It will be a good idea to write down exactly what you want to measure. For example, "whether the student understands how a doorbell actually works." Conceivably this could be measured by using other types of items (cluster true-false or several multiple-choice). In this instance, the objective is to find out how well the student can use his own words to describe what happens and a short essay item would work better than the other types.

2. Call for Specific Answers. Do not be vague. Do not use items such as the following:

```
Write all you know about the history of the metal lathe.
```

State the item in a simple, direct manner. Word the statement in such a manner as to provide the student with an outline that he can follow in formulating his response.

Poor

What is the difference between an engineer and a draftsman?

Better

Compare an engineer with a draftsman in terms of the duties
that each performs.

Poor

Prepare a two-page report on the tool- and die-making
trade.
This is to be handed in on May 23.

Better

You are to prepare a report on the work of the tool and die
maker. The major headings will be as follows: (1) typical
duties (with examples); (2) hours of work; (3) pay;
(4) advantages; (5) disadvantages. The headings need not
be in this order. Use any reference books you desire. If
possible, talk with a tool and die maker and get his reactions. In preparing your report imagine that you are
giving advice to a friend who is thinking about entering
this occupation. The report is due on May 23.

*3. Require the Student to "Compare," "Explain Why," "De-
scribe," or "Tell How," Not to "List" or "Enumerate."* The purpose of this suggestion is to ensure a type of item that calls for
application of things learned. This is more than a process of using
the words mentioned above, but they should prove helpful in devising a type of item that is desirable. This point is easily illustrated by the following item:

Briefly describe the three types of D.C. motors.

In this instance the test maker used the word "describe" when
he might just as well have asked the student to "define the three
types of D.C. motors." In other words, this item could be answered
by the student who had done nothing more than memorize some
statements from the textbook. If the student had been asked to
describe why there are three types of D.C. motors or when each
should be used, he would need more than an abstract understanding of the material being tested. In the above example another
type of item would measure this objective more easily and quickly.

4. Determine Definite Specifications for Marking. Allow one point for each significant point expected in the response. This, rather than the assumed importance of the item, should form the basis for weighting or assigning a value to it. The best practice is to write out the points that are to be covered in the item. This serves as a check list to be used in marking. The item on the working of a doorbell can be used as a simple example of this procedure. There are five significant points to look for in the response of the student. There are different words in which he may express

```
14. In the space below describe how a doorbell works by
    tracing the action that takes place.
    MARKING KEY (1 point each)
    1. Current magnetizes core of electromagnet
    2. Attracts armature
    3. As armature moves contact is broken
    4. Spring pulls armature back
    5. Operation keeps repeating
```

these ideas, but it would be easy to determine the extent to which he understands the action. In this instance there need be little question about the objectivity of the scoring, and it should be easy to see why this item would count five points in the total possible score on the test.

Some essay items, such as the one on the tool- and diemaker, cannot be scored as readily as this. The specific points to be covered are not always so apparent. Sometimes there is a wide variety of possible answers. These conditions should be noted carefully as the item is constructed. Often a few changes in directions will make possible more objective scoring. In the question relating to the tool- and diemaker, a step was made in this direction when the student was directed to group his comments under five headings. The test maker might be able to list the significant points to be included under each of the headings, but let us assume that in this instance it would be difficult to do. The item could then be marked by giving separate consideration to each of the five main headings and by checking all papers for the comments under one heading before proceeding to the next. Each heading might be marked on a scale of three points—poor, acceptable, good. This is somewhat subjective, to be sure, but much better than trying to

assign marks to a group of papers on a general topic with no specified order of presentation.

5. *Follow a Definite Procedure in Marking.* It should be readily
apparent by now that the method of scoring essay items is an important factor affecting their validity. The following four points
sum up the statements that have been made in this respect:

 a. Write out the answer expected for each item. Include every
 point that is to be accepted. Only in rare instances will it be
 impractical to do this.

 b. Score one essay item on all test papers before proceeding to
 the next.

 c. Give value to an item by allowing one point for each point
 covered in the answer.

 d. Conceal the students' names on the test papers, or in some
 manner make sure their identity is not revealed as the item
 is being scored.

SUMMARY

In a recall item the student supplies the answer. There are various kinds and types of recall item, including simple recall, sentence-completion, problems or situations, identification, listing
or enumeration, and the like. The essay-type item might also be
considered a recall item.

The recall item is useful in measuring the retention of specific
points. It is relatively easy to construct. The several variations can
be used effectively in obtaining a wide sampling, and they tend
to have a high discriminating value.

Because the simple types are easy to construct, they tend to be
used excessively. This results in an overemphasis on memorization
and verbal facility. Care must be exercised if subjectivity in scoring is to be avoided. Some points follow that will be helpful in constructing recall items:

1. Use direct questions whenever possible.

2. Make sentence-completion items as specific as possible.

3. Do not copy statements directly from textbooks.

4. In simple recall and sentence-completion items place the
blanks at or near the end of the statement.

5. Avoid the inclusion of irrelevant clues.

6. Construct the item so there is only one correct response.

7. Design enumeration items to call for specific facts.

8. Rarely should one question call for more than six or eight things to be listed.

9. If the student is required to list things in a given order, determine, before the test is given, how the responses are to be scored.

10. Make all sketches or illustrations clear and of sufficient size.

11. Whenever possible, require the student to solve problems or use previous learning.

12. Be sure there is plenty of room to indicate responses.

The essay-type item requires the student to make a comparison, write a description, or explain certain points. The student is allowed freedom of expression in analyzing, comparing, describing, explaining, or reasoning.

Essay items have been criticized severely and usually justifiably. The fault, however, has been in the construction and scoring. They are not inherently inferior. When carefully constructed and scored, they can provide very useful information about a student's development or achievement. Five points that will be helpful in constructing essay items are as follows:

1. Decide upon the objective to be measured. Be specific.

2. Call for specific answers.

3. Require the student to "compare," "explain why," "describe," or "tell how," not to "list," or "enumerate."

4. Determine definite specifications for marking.

5. Follow a definite procedure in marking.

SOME THINGS TO DO AND QUESTIONS TO ANSWER

1. What have you liked or disliked about the recall items that you have been called upon to answer?

2. Jot down some specific examples of subject matter that should be measured by recall items.

3. The primary colors are red, blue, and yellow. Using this fact as a basis, construct as many different types of recall items as you can. Keep in mind some of the basic points about the usefulness of test items. If necessary, use this additional fact: The secondary colors are purple, green, and orange.

4. This time use the following cliché as a basis for building various recall items: What a man is depends upon what he does when he has nothing to do. Once again, construct as many different kinds of recall items as you can.

5. On the basis of these two activities (questions 3 and 4) what generalizations can you make about recall items?

6. What are the advantages, if any, of the problem type of recall item?

7. Jot down some examples in your area of interest where good illustrations will help to make recall items more effective.

8. What are some points that must be kept in mind in using or developing illustrations for this type of item?

9. Prepare a sample item of the generalization and justification type (see page 257). What is the value of this type of item?

10. Do you prefer a matching or identification-type item (see page 258)? Why?

11. In your opinion what is the best method for scoring recall items of the correct-order type?

12. Design an essay item that is valid and can be scored objectively.

SELECTED REFERENCES FOR ADDITIONAL READING

Hawkes, Herbert E., E. F. Lindquist, and C. R. Mann. *The Construction and Use of Achievement Examinations*. Boston: Houghton Mifflin Company, 1936. Pp. 125–136.

Monroe, Walter S., and Ralph E. Carter. *The Use of Different Types of Thought Questions in Secondary Schools and Their Relative Difficulty for Students*. Urbana: University of Illinois Press, Bureau of Educational Research, *Bull.* 14, 1923. P. 26.

Remmers, H. H., and N. L. Gage. *Educational Measurement and Evaluation*. New York: Harper & Brothers, 1943. Chap. VIII, XII.

Rinsland, Henry Daniel. *Constructing Tests and Grading in Elementary and High School Subjects*. New York: Prentice-Hall, Inc., 1938. Chaps. III, IV.

Ross, C. C. *Measurement in Today's Schools*. New York: Prentice-Hall, Inc., 1947. Pp. 131–139; also Chap. VI.

Weidemann, C. C. "Review of Essay Test Studies," *Journal of Higher Education*, 12:41–44 (January, 1941).

CHAPTER

TEN: MODIFIED, ADAPTED, AND COMBINED ITEMS

THE several standard types of test items have now been presented. In each instance the common modifications and adaptations have also been described and illustrated. During this discussion it has been repeated that still other adaptations or modifications could be developed to fit particular situations in special subject-matter areas. The important point is not that teachers should make new or novel test items just to produce something different. This will accomplish little. The point is that sometimes a common test item will not measure effectively what the instructor wishes to measure. In such instances he should not forget about the material but should endeavor to construct an item that does a good job of measuring.

Such items will usually be adaptations, modifications, or combinations of the several types that have been described in preceding chapters. The uses, limitations, and suggestions for construction will, for the most part, be similar to those already stated. With this in mind the next few pages are devoted to a presentation of such items that have been developed by teachers and students. The first section pertains to controlled completion items, which are being used more and more by some makers of informal tests. Because of this increase in use some specific suggestions are included to aid the person who is interested in constructing such items.

Following the first section, a variety of other items is included. These are merely sample items to illustrate some possible variations. A great many others could be constructed. Suggestions for construction and the uses and limitations of each type are not included, since this would be mainly a repetition of various points already mentioned. As you study each sample, relate it to the specific subject matter in which you are interested. Try to determine whether or not it would be applicable. Jot down your ideas in the margin. The major purpose of this chapter is to have you think in terms of constructing special items for your special field to be used on special occasions.

Controlled Completion Items

The controlled completion item is a variation that requires the student to recognize and select from a list of possible responses the correct answer for each blank. It is fundamentally of the recognition type. It is similar to multiple-choice and matching items. It can be used effectively to measure the student's ability to make close discriminations. It is well suited to measurement along a continuous line of thought. From the standpoint of scoring, it is totally objective.

On the basis of these few statements, it would seem that the controlled completion item should be used much more than it is. On the surface the item appears relatively easy to construct. In reality it is very difficult to construct so that it is valid and reliable. Too often, controlled completion items can be answered by the student who knows nothing more than the simple rules pertaining to grammatical construction and English usage.

> Directions: Several incomplete statements are listed below. Each blank space indicates that a word or group of words has been left out. From the list given below the statements you are to select the word or group of words that will make each statement correct. Write these words in the blank space provided. Use each word or group only once. The first blank is filled in as an example.
> x. A broken grease seal in a transfer case may be caused by a (clogged vent).
> 1. The transmission countershaft main-drive gear is driven by _____.
> 2. On a propeller shaft the yokes are mounted _____.

3. The yokes are mounted in this manner to prevent
   _____.
4. Steering stops are used to protect the _____.
5. Bearings that are adjustable are usually _____.

speed fluctuation	differential
tapered roller bearings	constant—velocity joints
a clogged vent (example)	oscillation
in the same plane	the propeller shaft from
two—row ball bearings	moving
transmission main—drive	reverse—idler gear
gear	opposite each other
slip joint	

<u>Directions</u>: In the statements below certain key words have
been omitted. The words or phrases that fit into the blank
spaces are included in the lettered list that follows the
statements. Select the word that best fits in each blank
and place its letter in the appropriate blank at the left.
Use each letter only <u>once.</u> In some cases it may be necessary to choose the better of two possible answers. The
first blank is filled in as an example to follow.

     The size of a gear is given in terms of its diameter
x.<u>(A)</u> at the pitch line. This is called the (x)____.
1.____ This term is not to be confused with the diametral
2.____ pitch which refers to the number of teeth per inch
3.____ of (1)____. The outside diameter of a gear varies
4.____ with the (2)____. In formula, the outside diameter
5.____ is designated by the letter (3)____. The distance
6.____ on the pitch line from the center of one tooth to
7.____ the center of the next is called (4)____. In
8.____ formula it is represented by the letter (5) ____.
     The part of a tooth above the pitch line is called
the (6)____. The part of the tooth below the pitch
line not including the clearance is called the
(7)_____ and is also known as the (8)____ of the
tooth.

A. pitch diameter	J. number of teeth
B. circular pitch	K. diameter
C. outside diameter	L. D
D. diameter of the pitch	M. D'
circle	N. D"
E. thickness of the tooth	O. P'
F. addendum	P. dedendum
G. clearance	Q. extension
H. working face	R. submersion
I. flank	

Key List

A. At about the same level   K. In a series of heights
B. At very different levels   L. Informal
C. Balance   M. Largest number of objects
D. Broken   N. Related
E. Center of interest   O. Rhythm
F. Continuous   P. Shapes
G. Emphasis   Q. Sizes
H. Ends of the grouping   R. Tones
I. Formal   S. Unrelated
J. Harmony

____30.
____31.
____32.
____33.
____34.
____35.

____36.

The name given to the principle which has to do
with movement in design is (30). The problem in
its use is to be certain that it is (31) movement.
It can be obtained through a repetition of (32),
through a progression of (33), and (34) line movement. We see it applied in the placement of pictures when they lead the eye around the room (35).
The successful use of this principle is evidenced
in the grouping of objects when the eye is easily
carried to the (36).

Directions:[1] Below is a series of drawings consisting of
one pictorial and two orthographic views each. The right
side views are missing. They have been placed in a column
at the left, along with some views that do not fit. You
are to select the proper side view and place the letter
(A,B, etc.) of the drawing to which it belongs in the blank
space at the left. There should not be a letter in every
blank.

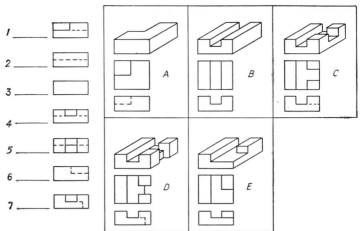

[1] It will be seen from studying this example that controlled completion
items of this type are very similar to matching items.

A few suggestions follow for the person who is interested in constructing such items:

1. Observe the same suggestions pertaining to the number and selection of words to be omitted that were given for simple recall-type items.

2. The list of words or phrases from which choices are to be made should include several extra words or phrases.

3. For each blank there should be at least three plausible responses, but only one that is correct. If, in order to have three plausible responses, it is necessary to include three times as many choices as there are blanks, it will probably be better to use another type of test item for this particular subject matter.

4. All subject matter included in a given item should be related.

5. Include not fewer than five or six or more than fifteen blanks in any one series.

6. Make sure that the selection of the correct response for each blank depends upon knowledge of the subject matter in question. The best way to check this factor is to have the item answered by a person who is not familiar with the subject matter.

Samples of Other Variations

Some of the following samples will be easily identified as modifications of types already described. Others will be a combination of several types. Still others will not lend themselves readily to classification as to type. No attempt has been made to attach a name to each of the examples presented, although this could be done. But at best the process would be an artificial one that might be more confusing than helpful. The important consideration is for the reader to review these several examples while keeping in mind the various instructional situations which he will experience. Some of the following items might not have much use in a typical survey achievement test. On the other hand, they might be very effective in supplementing the day-to-day instruction of the teacher. For example, the crossword-puzzle type of item on page 281 might be considered a bit cumbersome to be included in a typical achievement test at the end of a course. Whether or not this is true, such an item might be very useful in motivating the students, in reviewing terms or expressions, or in engendering some healthy competition to see who can complete the puzzle in the shortest time. Perhaps the students might be encouraged to construct some crossword puzzles, or other items, of their own. Going a step fur ther, one part of the course might be a simulated "quiz program" in which the students submit their own items and conduct their own examination. The instructor might let himself be "put on the spot." If organized and carried out properly, such an undertaking might be educational as well as entertaining. This would be one approach of the instructor who wishes to make testing and evalu- ation an integral part of his teaching efforts.

Directions: The circuit illustrated in the following diagram will allow an operator to send messages from station
A to station B. Sketch in an addition to the circuit that
will enable an operator at station B to send messages back
to station A. Make your addition as simple as possible.

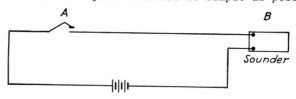

Directions: Below are described some situations that often
arise in dealing with young children. Following that are
three possible solutions. You are to rank each solution in
order of preference -- 1 for the best, 2 for the next best,
and 3 for the poorest solution.

Willie was never allowed to touch the scissors. One day he
slipped in while his mother was busy, got the scissors, and
cut up a deck of cards belonging to his older brother.
What should be done?
____35. Get some scissors and material and let him cut.
____36. Have him paste some of the cards together.
____37. Have the older brother cut up some of Willie's
        things.

Louise, three years old, is very jealous of her little
brother. She scratches him and tears his clothes beyond
repair. What should be done?
____38. Keep the baby entirely away from Louise.
____39. Isolate her when she is caught worrying the baby.
____40. Explain to her how he must be cared for and let her
        help.

Directions: In the following the items marked 1 and 5 are the first and last respectively. You are to indicate the proper order of events by placing the numbers 2, 3, and 4 in the proper blank space.

1. Food is chewed
36. ____ a reflex is initiated.
37. ____ sensory nerves are stimulated.
38. ____ The salivary glands are activated.
5. Saliva is secreted.

1. An athlete runs the 100-yard dash.
39. ____ Exercise brings about an increased production of the by-products of metabolism.
40. ____ Carbon dioxide stimulates the breathing center.
41. ____ Carbon dioxide accumulates in the blood.
5. The rate and depth of his breathing increases.

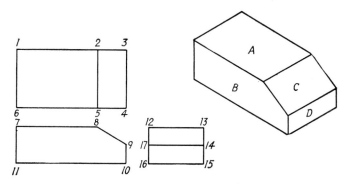

Directions: In the above drawings the visible surfaces of the isometric drawing are lettered. All points on the orthographic drawings are numbered. In the table below you are to relate the lettered surfaces to the numbered points in each view. For example, the top view of surface A is bounded by the points 1, 2, 5, 6, so you would write these numbers in the charts after A and under the top view as shown below. Complete the chart in this manner.

Isometric Surface	Top View	Front View	Side View
A	(1-2-5-6)		
B			
C			
D			

Directions: The following sentences have errors of order. Encircle words or phrases out of order and show by arrows where they should go. The first item is answered as an example.

(Example) He brought a (hot) cup of coffee.
1. He must either be incompetent or lazy.
2. He put his money in the bank, which was in five-dollar bills.
3. Drivers who hurry in nine cases out of ten have no real occasion for hurrying.
4. The coroner investigating the death today brought in a verdict of suicide.

Directions: Read the following quotation carefully. Then read each statement following the quotation and fill in the blank in one of three ways.
S – if the item is actually stated
I – if the item is implied
N – if the item is neither stated nor implied
The first item is answered as an example to follow. The item is implied so an (I) is placed in the blank space.

"Every red–blooded American citizen resents any attack upon our American school system. Our public schools are supported by public funds, and they are open to every ambitious boy or girl who wishes an education. Truly, our great land is a place of equal educational opportunity for all."

(I) (Example) Americans who attack our school system are not red–blooded citizens.
____1. An ambitious Negro boy in America can get as good an education as a white boy.
____2. Persons who have an inadequate education have themselves to blame.
____3. The American schools are open to every ambitious boy who wishes an education.
____4. In a democracy everybody should support our public institutions.
____5. No attack should be made on schools which are open to every ambitious student.
____6. In America there is equal educational opportunity for all.
____7. The term, educational opportunity, means the presence of schools open to all.

Directions: Now, in terms of the above question, check (X) each of the following statements that you think are true.
____8. The author proves his point beyond a doubt.
____9. He does not prove his point but gives some evidence for it.

____10. He asserts his position without any evidence whatever.

____11. He avoids expressions that would tend to prejudice the reader.

____12. He explains clearly what he means by equal educational opportunity.

Directions:[2] The following crossword puzzle uses terms and expressions pertaining to radio work. Complete the exercise as you would a regular crossword puzzle.

Horizontal

1. the pressure that causes current to flow.
8. the symbol for inductance
9. metric measure used for lengths of small antenna
11. symbol for mutual conductance
12. smallest unit for sizes of condensers
16. number of vibrations per second
17. abbreviation for unit of capacity
18. what does a good radio repairman do with his head? (facetious)
22. very small unit of time in electronic work
24. unit of reluctance
27. formula for power
29. means voltage
31. denotes inductive reactance
33. symbol for ohms
34. abbreviation for term used in measuring the electrolyte in a storage battery

Vertical

2. the unit of resistance
4. the length of time for a condenser to take a certain amount of charge
5. unit of measurement of current flow
7. another name for potential difference
12. one-millionth of a farad
14. weak spots in circuits for protection purposes
21. abbreviation for signal voltage
22. one-thousandth part of a whole unit
26. the phase of the current in relation to voltage when flowing through an inductance

---

[2] If the test maker desired, this item could be marked on the basis of twenty-four points, the number of responses.

Directions: Pictured below are several simple operations
involving cutting tools. You are to decide if the picture
illustrates a correct or incorrect procedure. If the procedure is correct, write the word "correct" in the blank
space provided. If the procedure is incorrect write the
word "incorrect" in the blank space and write a brief description of what is wrong.

<u>Directions</u>: Number (1, 2, 3) the items of each group in chronological order by placing the proper number in the blank space at the left.[3] For example,

<u>(2)</u> Presidency of Coolidge
<u>(1)</u> Presidency of Wilson
<u>(3)</u> Presidency of Franklin Roosevelt

____62. Matteotti murder
____63. March on Rome
____64. Abolition of the Chamber of Deputies in Italy

____65. Dictatorship of Lenin
____66. Kerenski regime
____67. Exile of Trotsky

____68. Congress of Vienna
____69. Treaty of Versailles
____70. Treaty of San Stefano

<u>Directions</u>: In the items below you are to read the argu-
ment which is incomplete since something has to be assumed
in order to make the argument good. Then you are to place
in the blank space the letter of the assumption that must
be accepted if the argument is to stand. The first item is
answered as an example to follow.

<u>Argument</u>: Lizards must be mammals, for they have back-
           bones. This argument assumes that
<u>(B)</u> (Example) A. Some mammals have backbones.
              B. All animals with backbones are mammals.
              C. A few animals with backbones are lizards.
              D. All mammals are lizards.
              E. A few animals without backbones are liz-
                 ards, but this is not true as a rule.

<u>Argument</u>: Mr. X must be a Democrat because he voted for
           Roosevelt. This argument assumes that
____2. A. All Democrats voted for Roosevelt.
       B. Some Republicans voted for Roosevelt.
       C. Anyone who voted for Roosevelt is a Democrat.
       D. Some Democrats voted for the Republican candi-
          date.
       E. Many communists voted for Roosevelt.

---

[3] Some test makers prefer to give only one point for each group of three. In
other words, each item is all right or all wrong.

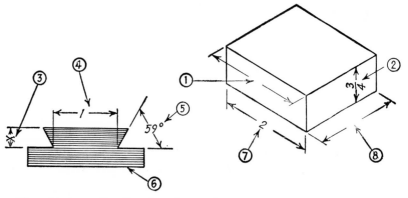

Directions: In the drawings above the numbered leaders indicate parts of the drawing that are either correct, incorrect, or poor practice. In column A below list the numbers of those leaders that point to incorrect or poor practices. In the space that follows indicate briefly why it is incorrect or poor practice. The first item is answered as an example to follow.

(A) Reason

(4) (extension lines and dimensions should lie outside the object)

_____ _____
_____ _____
_____ _____
_____ _____
_____ _____
_____ _____
_____ _____
_____ _____

Directions: The following exercise pertains to terms used in printing. In each group four of the terms are very closely related. One of the terms is not as closely related as the others. You are to cross out this term. In the first item below four of the terms relate to the part of a piece of type. The word "ampersand" is not the name of a part; therefore it is crossed out.

(Example) — foot, shoulder, ~~ampersand~~, nick, serif

1. em quad, 5-em space, 3-en space, en quad, 2-em quad
2. quad, chase, furniture, quoin, reglet
3. underlay, tympan, pin, platen, draw sheet
4. pulp, graphic, coated, calendered, sulphite

Directions: Imagine that in starting to drill a hole in mild steel, the drill has drifted away from center. Figure 1 below shows the original center mark and diameter of the hole being drilled. In the remaining figures, do the following:
1. In figure 2 draw the hole as it will appear when the drill has drifted.
2. In figure 3 indicate with a mark the direction in which the drill will have to be drifted back.
3. In figure 4, complete the sketch of the tip of the tool used to drift the drill back to center.
4. In the blank space provided write the name of this tool.

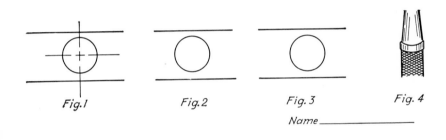

Fig.1   Fig.2   Fig. 3   Fig. 4

Name _____

Directions: Complete the wiring diagram below so that Lamp No. 1 is controlled by a double-pole snap switch; Lamp No. 2 is controlled by two three-way switches; and the bell is controlled by the push button.

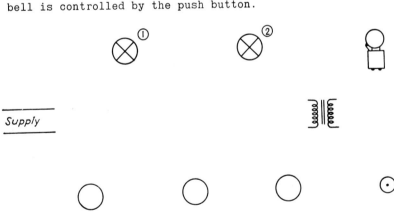

Supply

<u>Directions</u>: Following each generalization given below is a
group of statements which you may assume to be true. You
are to decide whether the statement <u>supports</u> the given
generalization. If it does, encircle the (Yes) at the
left. If it does not support the generalization encircle
the (No).

<u>Generalization</u>: The major dictatorships arose in Europe
when the existing governments had shown
themselves unwilling or unable to solve
the nations' problems.
(Assume each of the following statements
to be true.)

Yes No   1. In 1917 the Czarist regime was unable to
furnish the Russian soldiers with sufficient
ammunition and food.

Yes No   2. The Italian government added to the economic
distress of postwar Italy by depreciating the
currency to meet the government deficits.

Yes No   3. Most of the Bolshevik leaders, including
Lenin, have been exiled by the Czarist government.

Yes No   4. The democratic government of the Weimar Republic permitted both Lutherans and Catholics
to maintain churches in Germany.

Yes No   5. Hitler attracted followers to National Social-
ism by promising jobs to the six million unemployed.

Yes No   6. Illiteracy in Czarist Russia was well over
50%.

Yes No   7. In pre-Hitler Germany, the percentage of university graduates unable to secure work was
gradually increasing.

Yes No   8. The Bolsheviks were unable to win support with
the slogan, "Land for the peasants and bread
for the workers."

<u>Directions</u>: In the blank space at the left of each item
place the letter of the word(s) whose meaning is closest to
that of the first word.

____32. Producer ── A.buyer;   B.maker;   C.consumer;
                        D.owner;   E.receiver

____33. Orthographic ── A.picture drawing;   B.one view;
                            C.perspective;   D.working drawing;
                            E.isometric

____34. Skiving ── A.cutting;   B.shaving;   C.trimming;
                       D.smoothing

Directions: Shown below is the top view of a cube. You
are to convert this into an angular perspective drawing by
using a straight edge (and compass if necessary). Several
parts of the drawing are already given. Use these in your
construction. Leave all of your construction lines, but
darken the lines of the finished perspective.

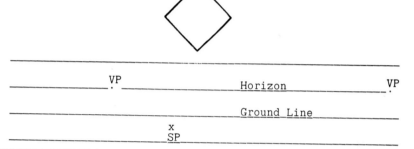

Directions: First, read the following quotation. Then,
mark each of the succeeding statements in one of three
ways:
R — if the statement is a reasonable interpretation of the
    material in the quotation.
I — if the interpretation might be true but insufficient
    facts are given to justify it.
C — if the interpretation is contradicted by the material
    in the quotation.
"In Germany, with a totalitarian government, no one was
unemployed. Furthermore, strikes were prohibited by law so
industry could proceed in peace. Americans should stop
criticising the government of this people who were econom-
ically better off than we."
_____1. A country in which strikes are prohibited is econom-
       ically better off than one where strikes occur.
_____2. German workers were so well satisfied that they did
       not wish to strike.
_____3. Before the war unemployment was greater in the U.S.
       than in Germany.
_____4. America could copy Germany's economic methods to
       advantage.
_____5. Governments should be criticised if they are dic-
       tatorial.
_____6. Some unemployment is necessary for the working of
       any economic system.
_____7. The munitions industry absorbed all of Germany's
       unemployed.
_____8. Where there are no strikes industry can proceed in
       peace.

<u>Directions</u>: The several illustrations just below represent
the grouping of printed matter on single pages. You are to
determine whether or not the grouping on each page represents <u>good</u> <u>balance</u>. In the numbered blank spaces state
whether the balance is good or poor and briefly state the
reasons for your decision.

Page 1 _____

Page 2 _____

Page 3 _____

Page 4 _____

Page 5 _____

Page 1   *Page 2*   *Page 3*   *Page 4*   *Page 5*

<u>Directions</u>: Each of the following items contains five sets
of words, phrases, terms, or names. <u>One</u> of the five <u>is</u> <u>not</u>
closely related to the other four. Select the one that <u>is</u>
<u>not</u> related to the other four and write the letter of that
choice (A,B,C,D,E) in the blank space provided. The first
item is answered as an example to follow.

x. <u>(B)</u> A. Questioning
        B. Lecturing
        C. Observation
        D. Written test
        E. Performance test

1. ____ A. Primary mass
         B. Vertical and hori-
            zontal space divi-
            sion
         C. Contour development
         D. Oblique projection
         E. Surface enrichment

2. ____ A. Matching
         B. Multiple-choice
         C. True-false
         D. Cluster true-false
         E. Listing

3. ____ A. Spencer
         B. Froebel
         C. Woodward
         D. Comenius
         E. Pestalozzi

4. ____ A. Investigate
         B. Tell
         C. Check
         D. Motivate
         E. Show

5. ____ A. Printing
         B. Art metalwork
         C. Water-color
            painting
         D. Leather work
         E. Model airplanes

<u>Directions</u>[4]: Read the following story. Then answer the
questions by placing the letter of what you consider to be
the best answer in the blank space before each question.
You may refer back to the story as often as you wish.

Story

Two boys, Bill and Tom, were playing with a small
horse-shoe magnet when one of them suggested that they try
to make a compass.

Tom said, "I'll get the stuff if you tell me what to
get."

Bill said that they needed a needle, a cork and a pan
of water. Tom got the needle and Bill started stroking it
on the magnet. He stroked in only one direction.

"Why do you rub it that way?" asked Tom.

"The needle won't be a good magnet unless you rub it
this way," was Bill's reply.

Tom had not been able to find a pan, but Bill said
that a big bucket would be all right. Bill thrust the
needle through the top of a flat cork and carefully placed
it on the water in the iron bucket Tom brought. The cork
immediately started toward one side of the bucket. When
the needle reached the side it seemed to stick there. Bill
picked up the cork with the needle in it and put it in the
center of the bucket again, but once more it went to the
side and stuck. This time it did not stick in the same
place as on the first trial.

Finally Bill said, "I don't know what's wrong. It certainly isn't acting like a compass."

"Perhaps you should have rubbed the needle both ways on
the magnet," offered Tom. "Let's try that."

"O.K.," said Bill, and he started stroking the needle
on the magnet again.

Questions

____1. Do you think the needle worked as a compass after
    the boys had stroked both ways on the magnet?
    A. Yes
    B. No
    C. Cannot be sure
____2. What part of Bill's plan for making a compass was
    most likely to cause trouble?
    A. Using a cork
    B. Using a needle
    C. Using a pan or bucket made of iron
____3. Which of these things was probably responsible for
    the boys' failure?

[4] Adapted from *The Measurement of Understanding* (Chicago: The National Society for the Study of Education, 45th Yearbook, Part I, 1946), pp.
115-116. Used by permission.

A. Stroking the needle only one way
B. Using a bucket made of iron
C. Using a bucket that was permanently magnetized
D. Using a cork to float the needle
____4. Do you think the needle was magnetized?
A. Yes
B. No
C. The story did not give any clue
____5. The usual compass has a magnetized needle which is balanced on a pivot so that the ends are free to swing in any direction. What in the boys' plan took the place of the pivot?
A. The water
B. The needle
C. The bucket
____6. Why might stroking the magnet only one way make it a stronger magnet?
A. It drives the magnetism deeper
B. It arranges the particles that make the needle a magnet
C. It gives every part of the needle a chance to be touched the same amount of time
____7. Which of these changes in the boys' plan would be most likely to bring success?
A. Using a nail instead of a needle
B. Stroking or rubbing in all directions
C. Using oil instead of water
D. Using a glass bowl instead of an iron bucket
____8. Why do you think the needle moved toward the side of the bucket?
A. The needle, being a magnet, exerted a pull on the iron in the bucket
B. The needle, being free to move, started moving toward the north magnetic pole
C. The boys probably left their magnet on that side of the bucket
____9. If the compass the boys made had worked would the needle have pointed directly north and south?
A. Yes
B. No
C. The story does not give enough information to answer

Directions: In the blank space at the left place the letter of the one word or term that does not belong with the other four.
____1. A. copper   D. nickel
       B. brass   E. silver
       C. iron

_____2. A. mountain
       B. hill
       C. plain
       D. plateau
       E. isthmus
_____3. A. capacitance
       B. volt
       C. henry
       D. ohm
       E. ampere

Directions[5]: One characteristic of a scientist is that he
believes that every effect has a cause and he tries to dis-
cover these cause-and-effect relationships. For example,
  When a piece of iron is heated, it expands.
  Heating the iron is the cause.
  Expansion of the iron is the effect.
Listed below are several statements similar to the above.
On the line at the left of each statement place the capital
letter corresponding to one of the following relationships:
  A. The first part of the statement is the cause of the
     second part.
  B. The first part of the statement is the result of the
     second part.
  C. The two parts have no cause-and-effect relationship.
  D. One part of the statement contradicts the other.
The first item is answered as an example.
(B)   1. Plants make food when the sun shines.
_____ 2. Air contains oxygen and also nitrogen.
_____ 3. A bulging forehead indicates a brilliant mind.
_____ 4. John walked under a ladder and he failed in
         science.
_____ 5. The draft is open; the fire burns more rapidly.
_____ 6. When the moon passes between the earth and sun, the
         sun is not visible.
_____ 7. When a dish full of cold water is heated, the water
         overflows.
_____ 8. When cold air is heated, the relative humidity in-
         creases.
_____ 9. Growing yeast plants give off CO_2; therefore there
         are holes in the bread.
_____10. Wiley Post wore an oxygen helmet; his plane worked
         perfectly.

[5] Adapted from *Ninth Grade Science Examination*, 1935 (Rochester, N.Y.:
Board of Education).

Directions[6]:   An experiment is described below. Assume
that the facts given and the results obtained are correct.
Following the description are several statements suggested
as interpretations of the experiment. You are to mark an
A, B, or C in the blank space preceding each statement.
A. The statement is a reasonable interpretation of the
   results obtained.
B. The statement might possibly be true but insufficient
   facts are given to justify the interpretation.
C. The statement cannot be true because it is contradicted
   by the results obtained in the experiment.

The Experiment: Some white starch was treated with a brown
iodine solution. This was done ten times and each time a
blue color was formed.
      Later some white starch was mixed with saliva. The
mixture was left for a time and then it was treated with
brown iodine solution. This was done ten times and each
time no blue color was formed.

      Place an A, B, or C before each of the following state-
ments. The first item is answered as an example to follow.
 (B) x. The starch was changed to sugar by the action of
         saliva.
____28. Saliva digested the starch.
____29. Starch acted upon the iodine.
____30. Saliva produced a change in the starch.
____31. Starch mixed with iodine solution did not turn
         blue.

Directions[7]: Listed below are certain facts followed by
several statements. You are to determine whether each
statement is
A. a cause of the fact.
B. a result of the fact.
C. not related to the fact.
Place the proper letter (A, B, or C) in the blank space
preceding each statement.
Fact: A flash of lightning occurs.
Statements:
____3. A roar of thunder can be heard.
____4. Electricity passed between clouds and the earth.
____5. It is dangerous to stand under a tree during a
        rainstorm.

[6] Adapted from *The Measurement of Understanding*, p. 125.
[7] Adapted from *Eighth Grade General Science Examination*, 1936 (Rochester, N.Y.: Board of Education).

Fact: Metals expand when heated.
Statements:
_____12. The molecules of metal become farther apart when heated.
_____13. When the temperature increases, the mercury in the thermometer rises.
_____14. Telephone wires are slack in summer and tighter in winter.

Directions[8]: Answer the following questions by writing in the blank at the left of each question the number of each item in the right-hand list that you think fits. Any item may be used in more than one blank and some may not fit any blank. As an example, cabbage, potatoes, and tomatoes are cheap sources of vitamin C; hence 3, 18, and 24 are written in blank (A).

Which of the foods listed   FOODS

(3, 18, 24) A. are inexpensive sources   1. apple (baked)
               of vitamin C?   2. butter
                                             3. cabbage (raw)
                                             4. chocolate
                                             5. cream of wheat
_____ B. help build resistance to   6. dates
               respiratory infections?   7. egg white
                                             8. egg yolk
                                             9. halibut
                                            10. lake trout
_____ C. aid in formation of   11. liver
               strong teeth and bones?   12. mayonnaise
                                            13. Mazola
                                            14. milk (whole)
                                            15. navy beans
_____ D. contain appreciable   16. oatmeal
               amounts of vitamin C   17. oranges
               after cooking?   18. potatoes
                                            19. round steak
                                            20. sauerkraut
_____ E. are valuable only for the 21. spinach
               energy they provide?   22. starch
                                            23. sugar
                                            24. tomatoes
                                            25. watermelon

[8] Taken from *Studies in College Examinations,* 1934 (Minneapolis, Minn.: University of Minnesota. Committee on Educational Research), p. 178.

Directions[9]: Each of the following is the statement of a
supposed fact. In the first blank write an important probable consequence of the fact. In the second blank indicate an historical event which served as the basis of
your judgment.
1. Strict censorship of the press is established.
   Consequence:_____

   _____

   Basis:_____
2. A new disarmament conference is called.
   Consequence:_____

   _____

   Basis:_____
3. A two-camp alliance system is built up.
   Consequence:_____

   _____

   Basis:_____

Directions[9]: A number of generalizations follow. Cite a
specific historical event to illustrate the truth of the
generalization.
   1. Peace treaties have often created fresh sources of
friction.

   _____

   _____

Directions[9]: Give an historical example to prove the truth
of each assertion.
1. Conservatives of the Metternich type are to be found in
   our country today.
   Example:_____

Before leaving this consideration of modified and adapted items,
it will be well to turn back to Chapter Two and study some of the
examples presented there, especially those relating to scholastic-
aptitude testing. It should be apparent by now that there is an almost infinite number of variations by means of which test items
can be adapted to fit a specific purpose. As you undertake the development of a test, now or in the future, it will be helpful to page
through these various examples in search of ideas for items that
can be fitted to your purpose. It will be one means for helping to
make sure that you measure other things than the memorization
of facts.

[9] *Ibid.,* pp. 185–186.

SOME THINGS TO DO AND QUESTIONS TO ANSWER

1. In what ways do you think the crossword-puzzle type of item (see page 281) might be useful in your teaching area?

2. Select a word or term in your area of interest that needs to be understood by a student. Now devise a test item that will measure a *real understanding* of the term or word.

3. What is the value of an item in which the student reacts to cause-and-effect situations? Where will such items be useful in your area of teaching?

4. How does the master-list item (page 291) differ from a matching item? Does it have any advantages or disadvantages in relation to a matching item?

5. Just for fun, develop a test item that is not exactly the same as any you have observed thus far. Let your imagination enter the picture. Novelty *in the right degree* is very useful in certain testing situations. Start out by listing what you wish to measure, and then develop a *different* item. If you are in a class, it will be interesting to pool your accomplishments. It may help to keep in mind that somebody, not very different from you, developed the items you have observed thus far in this book.

6. Where would the controlled completion type of item be useful in your area of teaching?

7. What is the purpose of controlling the responses to an item?

8. Study the examples from the field of history (pages 283, 294). Of what use will such items be in your teaching? If time is available, it might be well to prepare some similar items for your area of interest.

SELECTED REFERENCES FOR ADDITIONAL READING

Adkins, Dorothy C., and associates. *Construction and Analysis of Achievement Tests.* Washington, D.C.: Government Printing Office, 1947. Chap. II.

Henry, Nelson B. (ed.) *The Measurement of Understanding.* 45th Yearbook, National Society for the Study of Education, Part I. Chicago: University of Chicago Press, 1946. Sec. II.

Rinsland, Henry Daniel. *Constructing Tests and Grading in Elementary and High School Subjects.* New York: Prentice-Hall, Inc., 1938. Chap. VII.

CHAPTER
ELEVEN: OBJECT TESTS

You have observed that numerous pictures, drawings, and sketches have been included in the sample test items which appear in the preceding chapters. These illustrations have been used to clarify and simplify the problems and ideas presented. Their use in testing situations replaces many word descriptions. This partially removes the handicap frequently placed upon the poor reader or the so-called "nonacademic" student. Good illustrations also help provide practical situations for measuring the student's ability to solve problems which are similar to those frequently encountered in the shop.

Why not carry this idea a step further by using the actual objects (tools, materials, etc.) instead of their word descriptions and pictorial representations? This would enable you to measure in a more direct manner the ability to apply things learned. Instead of referring the student to pictorial or word descriptions of objects, you would have him examine the actual objects and then respond to certain questions about them. Such measuring devices are called object tests. For purpose of definition we can say that an object test is one that utilizes concrete, tangible things rather than simulated situations.

Perhaps you have administered or have taken tests in which students were required to identify actual tools and materials or specimens and to write the name of and answer a specific question about each as it was shown to the class by the instructor. This is one acceptable method of administering an object test. In other instances the tools and materials may have been displayed at numbered stations on workbenches or laboratory cabinets and the students directed to move in an orderly manner from one station to another. At each station they would write the name and/or the principal use of the specimen, tool, or material displayed there. Perhaps they were directed to answer specific questions about each object. The following set of directions taken from the answer sheet to be completed by students provides a brief description of how the object test can be administered:

Directions to Students: For each of the numbered items on this answer sheet there is a corresponding station in the shop. When your instructor gives the order, go directly to the station bearing the number which he has assigned you. When, and not before, he gives the signal, observe what has been displayed at your station and then answer the question which bears the same number as the station. As each succeeding signal is given, advance promptly to the next numbered station in order and answer the question bearing its number. At stations bearing two numbers, 16 and 17 for example, you are to remain one extra time interval or until the second signal to advance is given. If the station bears three numbers, you are to remain there until the third signal to advance is sounded.

An object test can be designed and used primarily as an instructional device, or it can be made sufficiently comprehensive to serve as an instrument for the measurement of achievement. It may be administered as a separate test or as a section in such comprehensive tests as mid-term or final examinations.

Items Appropriate for Object Tests

By exercising imagination and initiative, one can set up specimens, tools, materials, and equipment in realistic situations which will measure in a very practical and effective manner many specific knowledges related to the major outcomes of the course. The following examples are merely illustrative of the numerous types of situations which may be incorporated in object tests. The pictures show displays as they might appear at numbered stations. Items at the right are as they would appear on answer sheets.

The testing situations which require that students be able to identify the various kinds and sizes of tools and kinds and grades of materials are most readily adapted to the object test. Figure 1 shows a station which has been set up to measure the student's ability to identify woods commonly used in the shop. In addition to the identification of the kinds of woods, the student might be required to identify specific features of the material. For example,

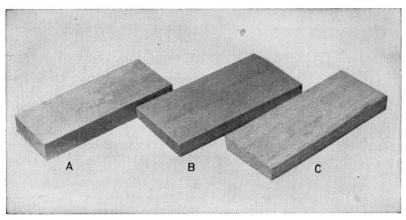

Fig. 1. Station set up to measure ability to identify woods. In a comprehensive test for a woodworking course, several stations with three or four samples of wood at each might be used.

3. Name of each wood?

A. _____

B. _____

C. _____

at the station shown in Figure 2 the student is required to name each kind of wood and in addition indicate whether it has open or close grain. Other stations might be designed to require the student to identify certain woods displayed and to tell whether each is considered a hard- or softwood. Further, he might be required to indicate whether each of the particular samples shown is plain- or quartersawed.

In the preceding examples, identification can be made by merely observing the materials as they are. Other situations can be set up which require the utilization of additional senses or which provide for the making of simple checks or tests. The identification of five samples of finishing materials displayed in lettered containers, for example, would remain dependent upon the sense of both sight and smell. To identify samples of iron and steels, provisions might be made for utilization of the spark test as shown in Figure 3. Another example of a simple check made to determine identity is the burning test frequently used in clothing courses in the area of home economics to determine the materials from which each of several samples of fabrics is made.

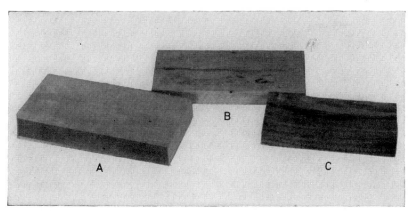

Fig. 2. Measures ability to identify woods by name and to distinguish between open and close grain.

17. Name woods and indicate whether each is open or close grain.
A. Name_____Grain_____
B. Name_____Grain_____
C. Name_____Grain_____

In addition to determining the kind or classification of certain items, as in Figure 4, students may also be required to indicate, within certain predetermined tolerances, the size or grade of specific items. Figure 5, for example, pictures a test situation which requires that the student identify the nails and screws displayed, both by type and by size.

Tools, as well as materials, may be displayed at numbered stations for the purpose of requiring that students identify them. Figure 6 shows examples. The instructor may require that the student also give the primary use of each tool, displayed as shown in Figure 7. Or he may require the student to give the names of certain parts of a tool or piece of equipment. The parts to be named can be removed from the tool as shown in Figure 8. Perhaps the

Fig. 3. Station set up to permit the
utilization of the spark test to determine identity of iron and steels.

32. Use spark test to iden-
    tify each specimen.
    I_____
    II_____
    III_____
    IIII_____
    IIIII_____

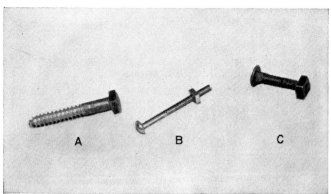

Fig. 4. Measures ability to identify
kinds of bolts and screws.

28. Type of bolt or screw?
    A._____
    B._____
    C._____

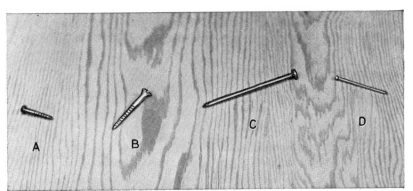

Fig. 5. Measures ability to identify kinds and sizes of nails and screws. Tolerances to be permitted with respect to sizes should be specified in the key to the test.

27. Kinds of nails and screws <u>and</u> size of each.
A. Kind_____Size_____
B. Kind_____Size_____
C. Kind_____Size_____
D. Kind_____Size_____

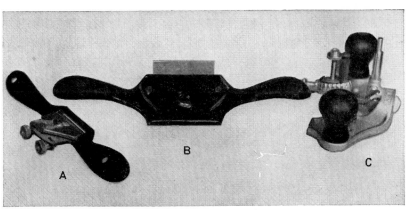

Fig. 6. Station designed to measure ability to identify tools by proper name.

17. Name of each?
A._____
B._____
C._____

parts to be named might be indicated by writing letters directly on them with chalk, by tagging them, by placing identifying letters at the ends of arrows pointing to the parts to be named, or by taping one end of a string to each part and the other to a card bearing its identifying letter.

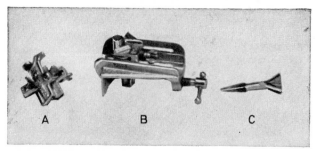

*Fig. 7. Station prepared to measure
ability to identify tools and give the
major use of each.*

3. Name and primary use of
   each?
   A. Name_____
      Use_____
   B. Name_____
      Use_____
   C. Name_____
      Use_____

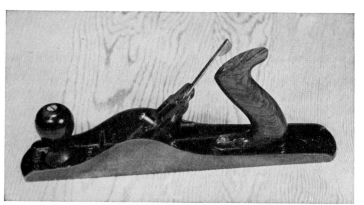

*Fig. 8. Measures ability to identify
names of parts of tools by proper
name.*

4. Name each missing part.
   A._____
   B._____
   C._____

Another example of responses, other than or in addition to identification, which might be obtained is shown in Figure 9. In this
case the student is required to give the proper name of each bit
displayed and to indicate how each is sized. This same item may
be altered to require the student to examine the marking which

appears on each bit and then indicate the next largest or next smallest bit in the set as normally sold.

Other examples are as follows: Four files may be displayed, with the requirement that the student indicate the type of each file as to shape. At another station the requirement may be to classify the files displayed with respect to coarseness. Here again tolerances may be permitted and, if so, should be specified in the key. Such

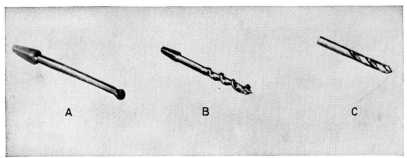

Fig. 9. Measures ability to identify kinds of bits and knowledge of how each is sized.

16. Name each bit and indicate how it is sized (by eighths, sixteenths, and so on).
   A. Name_____
      How sized_____
   B. Name_____
      How sized_____
   C. Name_____
      How sized_____

abrasive materials as sandpaper, steel wool, and emery cloth may be displayed, with the requirement that the grade of each, within specified tolerances, be given.

The two pieces of stock shown in Figure 10 have been dimensioned, with the intent of measuring the student's knowledge of the order in which dimensions should be written. Observe that one piece is wider than it is long.

The examples shown in Figures 11 and 12 are illustrative of the items which can be prepared to measure knowledge of processes or operations performed on stock. Types of joints, connections, and seams are other possibilities.

Items can be incorporated in an object test which measures ability to read and measure with selected measuring instruments. Fig-

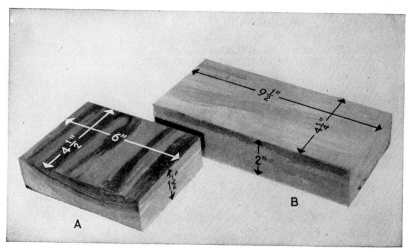

Fig. 10. Station designed to measure knowledge of the order in which dimensions should be listed.

7. Write the three dimensions of each piece of stock in the correct order.
A._____
B._____

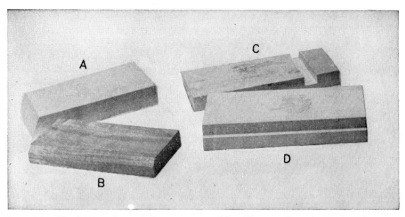

Fig. 11. Measures knowledge of names of cuts made in woodworking. If all four cuts are to be placed on one piece of stock, each must be clearly marked.

10. Name of cut on each piece of stock?
A._____
B._____
C._____
D._____

A   B

Fig. 12. Station designed to test abil-   27. Type or series of
ity to identify types of threads.   thread?
                                                    A._____
                                                    B._____

Fig. 13. Tests ability to measure   27. Give the following meas-
with and read a rule.   urements to the nearest
                                                    sixty-fourth.
                                                    A. Length of long sec-
                                                       tion_____
                                                    B. Diameter of short
                                                       section_____

ure 13, for example, shows a station designed to test the ability
to measure with and read a rule. The problem of *reading* a micrometer has been isolated in the station shown in Figure 14,
while the ability to make a measurement *and* the ability to read
the instrument are incorporated in the item shown in Figure 15.

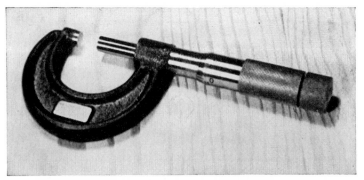

Fig. 14. Measures ability to read a micrometer.

28. What is the reading set on the micrometer (to the nearest .0005")?

_____

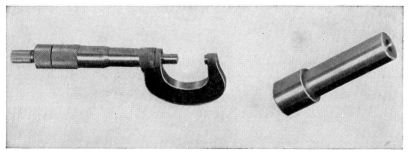

Fig. 15. Tests ability to measure with and read a micrometer. If this station consumes too much time, the second measurement might be omitted. If only one measurement still requires more time than the other stations, two or more numbers might be assigned to the station (see page 320).

25. Give the following measurements to the nearest .0005":

A. Diam. of long section
_____

B. Diam. of short section_____

Understanding of the manner in which tools should be adjusted and machines set up and the ability to recognize proper and improper adjustments and setups can be readily measured with the object test. The instructor may display five double plane irons and ask the student to indicate which is set properly for planing hardwoods and which is set properly for planing softwoods, or the student may be asked to indicate what is wrong with the plane irons which are improperly set. Figure 16 shows another example. In this case the student is required to indicate the number of threads per inch for which the quick-change gearbox on a lathe has been set.

The drill press may be set up to revolve the spindle at a given

Fig. 16. *Measures knowledge of proper setting of a machine tool.*

7. Gear box is set to cut how many threads per inch?_____

r.p.m. and the student required to indicate by referring to a table of cutting speeds whether the press is set too fast, properly, or too slow for drilling a specified material with a twist drill of given size and type. The milling machine may be set up in a similar manner.

Adaptation of Recognition-type Items for Use in Object Tests

The examples presented thus far require the student to recall the proper responses and write them in the spaces provided. These items generally require more knowledge on the part of the student, become more discriminating, and permit less guessing and "bluffing" than do the recognition-type items. However, the test maker may wish to decrease the time for administering the object test and increase its objectivity by using adaptations of such items as multiple-choice, matching, and controlled completion.

Figures 17 to 20 show stations which illustrate how the controlled-response principle can be utilized in object tests.

Fig. 17. Multiple-choice item adapted for use in an object test to measure knowledge of cuts. Response controlled to save time and to increase objectivity.

```
12. What is the name of the
    cut on this piece of
    stock?
    (Check one.)
    _____A. Groove
    _____B. Dado
    _____C. Rabbet
    _____D. Plow
```

Uses of the Object Test

The preceding examples are illustrative of the types of items which can be incorporated in an object test to measure such outcomes as:

1. The ability to identify various kinds, sizes, and grades of tools and materials.

2. Knowledge of specific uses of materials and tools and the ability to select those which are appropriate for specific purposes.

3. The ability to identify and name specific joints, shapes, and cuts which are made and used in the shop.

4. Knowledge and understanding of proper tool adjustments and machine setups.

5. The ability to perform simple operations or specific steps in complex operations. (The operations which can be included in

the object test as described in this chapter are much simpler and shorter than the ones appropriate for the construction of the rigidly controlled and carefully administered manipulative-performance tests presented in Chapter Twelve.)

Fig. 18. Adaptation of multiple-choice item to measure ability to check machine setup—setting of quick-change gearbox on lathe.

11. Quick-change gearbox set to cut (check one):
____A. $2\frac{1}{4}$ threads per in.
____B. 18 threads per in.
____C. 36 threads per in.
____D. 72 threads per in.

Advantages of the Object Test

Experience in administering and studying the results obtained with the object test will reveal that it has definite advantages over the written test as a means of measuring certain aspects of achievement in shop and laboratory courses. The authors strongly recommend that you try the object test in your program. This recommendation is based upon the following advantages:

1. It Provides a Direct and Valid Measure. From the standpoint of the validity of individual items, the object-test items seem to be

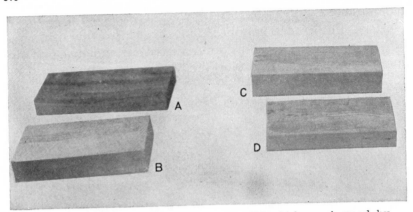

Fig. 19. Adaptation of matching item. In this case guessing has been minimized by adding two extra possible responses.

33. Identify each wood by writing its letter in the space to the left of its name.

____Sycamore ____Cherry
____Walnut   ____Red gum
____Birch   ____Maple

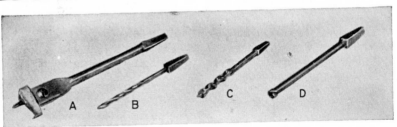

Fig. 20. Adaptation of matching item with four extra possible responses.

22. Identify each bit by writing its letter in the space to the left of its name.

____Bitstock twist drill
____Gimlet
____Drill point
____Foerstner bit
____Fly cutter
____Dowel bit
____High-speed twist drill
____Expansive bit

far superior to most items which appear in written tests. With a written test we may attempt to measure the ability to apply things learned, but our measure is frequently indirect at best. There is a distinct difference between being able to tell *how* to identify, select, make a decision, or do a piece of work and being able to perform the act — actually identifying, selecting, making the decision, or doing the job in a realistic shop situation. If our objective is to teach students to apply certain knowledges and principles, then we must measure their ability to make the application. This measurement requires a situation which will cause the student to apply the subject matter in order to arrive at the correct responses.

The items in an object test are designed to minimize the effects of reading and writing ability and language facility upon the student's score. As the influence of these factors is diminished, the validity of the test as a measure of certain aspects of achievement is increased.

2. Students' Reactions Are Favorable. The authors have been especially impressed and influenced by the reactions of students to object tests. Ordinarily, students are not particularly delighted at the thought of taking tests. The majority, however, generally find the object test to be interesting, stimulating, and challenging. Although it does require some writing, students are inclined to look upon it as an escape from written examinations. They are impressed with and respond favorably to the practical nature of a test which makes use of actual objects in realistic shop situations.

3. It Has Important Instructional Values. Any achievement test, if properly administered, has some instructional value. The object test is especially effective as a means of getting students to observe closely and make a study of the tools and materials with which they work. In preparing for the test and after having completed it, they begin to observe more critically than formerly; they become more responsive to the distinguishing features of tools and materials and grow in ability to identify at sight and to call by their proper names the different types, sizes, and grades of items in the shop. They begin to select more intelligently than formerly the appropriate tools and materials.

4. It Can Be Made Highly Discriminative. The object test can be designed to measure small differences in achievement. There is very little opportunity for guessing or "bluffing," especially when the test consists of items which require the student to recall and write specific responses.

5. *It Can Be Adapted to Measure Numerous Outcomes.* The examples in this chapter indicate the extent to which the object test can be adapted to measure many types of outcomes (see list on page 308). The usefulness and adaptability of the test depend upon the initiative and resourcefulness of the test maker.

Constructing the Object Test

The general procedure for constructing object tests is much the same as that for constructing written examinations. We start with objectives and the specific points of subject matter which contribute to their realization. After completing the selection of subject-matter points to be included in the test, the test maker incorporates each in one or more test items of the type which will measure best the command of the subject matter in question.

There are several considerations which apply specifically to the construction of object-test items. Some have to do with the physical setup of the various stations, others with the construction of the answer sheet. They are as follows:

1. Stations should be spaced far enough apart to eliminate interference and prevent cheating.

2. Stations should be numbered in accordance with some simple system which will enable the student to find his way from one station to another without confusion. Since no two students begin the test at the same station and since each advances until he returns to the station at which he began the test, the series of stations should form a closed circuit.

From any station in the circuit the number of the next succeeding station should be clearly visible. Arrows made on the floor or on bench tops can be used to advantage in directing students to succeeding stations. Methods of numbering which have been used are (1) large numbers made with chalk on bench tops, (2) numbered cards lying on workbenches or machines, (3) numbers on cards attached to standards, and (4) numbered tags fastened to machines or at work stations.

3. When two or more items are displayed at one station, they

should bear letters rather than numbers to prevent their becoming confused with station numbers. The letters should be placed on or near or be fastened to the objects to eliminate the possibility of their becoming disarranged.

4. Stations in the test should be set up to require about the same amount of the student's time at each. This means that all stations will usually call either for a single response or for the same number of responses, if more than one. Some time can be saved by designing the setup at each station to require two to four responses. Experience in administering object tests reveals that the signals to advance will need to be given about 20 to 25 seconds apart if stations require only one short response. The time should be increased 10 to 15 seconds for each additional short response required. Stations set up for longer time intervals permit the inclusion of a few stations where measurements are to be made, machine setups evaluated, or one or two steps of an operation performed.

Each time an object test is administered, the instructor should check for errors in time allotments. Only through experience in administering tests of this type can he determine the appropriate time intervals which should be established.

5. Make extensive use of machines and other items of equipment, as well as hand tools and samples of materials which can be displayed on benches.

6. Keep questions short but complete enough so that the observation of the station combined with the reading of the question will leave no doubt as to what is required.

7. Make the key to allow one point for each correct response. Do not attempt to weight responses. Number the responses consecutively in the key to facilitate the making of item analyses.

8. Do not make one response dependent upon another. To avoid having one answer dependent upon another, the test maker may find it necessary to measure only one type of outcome at a station. For purposes of illustration, let us assume that at one station in a general shop test there are displayed two containers, marked "A" and "B," containing finishing materials. The student is to identify each *and* give its proper thinner. At first glance one might conclude that this is a very good item. Apparently it measures two

things: (1) the ability to identify certain finishing materials; (2) knowledge of the proper thinner to use with each. But does it? True there are two problems, but can we with reasonable effort isolate them to the extent that we can determine, by checking the student's responses, what he knows and what he does not? Let us assume that in container A there is varnish and in container B shellac and that we expect students to list turpentine and alcohol as their respective thinners. The key has been constructed accordingly. Now let us examine the answers submitted by two students. How would you score their responses?

George's responses:	John's responses:	Responses as listed in key:
A. (orange shellac) (turpentine)	A. (linseed oil) (turpentine)	A. (varnish) (turpentine)
B. (lacquer) (alcohol)	B. (lacquer) (banana oil)	B. (shellac) (alcohol)

If we follow the key blindly, George would get credit for two correct responses out of four and John would get credit for one out of four. Neither student has been able to identify the materials. George reveals complete ignorance of what should be used as thinners for the materials that he does list. John apparently knows that linseed oil may be thinned with turpentine if the application of an oil finish demands it and that the term "banana oil" is sometimes used to designate the proper thinner for lacquer. Perhaps George should receive no credit and John two points. Then, too, George may know that turpentine is used as a thinner for varnish but simply cannot identify varnish. Perhaps he should have one point on this basis. But what was our initial purpose in setting up this item? We were trying to measure the ability to identify varnish and shellac and the knowledge of the proper thinner to use in each. At best it would be difficult to determine whether either student submitted a single satisfactory response.

The preceding discussion is sufficient to show the difficulty encountered in trying to measure two different types of outcomes with one item in which responses become dependent upon each other.

9. In constructing matching or controlled completion items for use in an object test, always include at least two extra choices or

have displayed at least two items more than the number of responses required. This is necessary to minimize guessing.

10. Make certain that the mechanics of the object test will not aid students, through assistance in the process of elimination or otherwise, in the selection of correct responses. For instance, instead of placing three lines on the answer sheet on which students are directed to write the letters used to designate the three close-grain woods that are to be displayed along with four open-grain woods, the letters of each of the seven should be listed on the answer sheet and the student required to check the letters which represent close-grain woods. Leaving three spaces for answers simply serves as a clue to the number of woods which are close-grain.

An item submitted by a student teacher who came under the supervision of one of the authors illustrates another common mechanical error which occurs in constructing object tests. In an effort to increase the number of responses required of students, this student teacher asked the students to indicate which of three double plane irons was set too close for planing softwoods, which was set correctly, and which had the plane-iron cap set too far back from the cutting edge. Without any knowledge at all of the manner in which a double plane iron should be set for planing softwoods, an observant student could readily select the double plane iron which fell between the two extremes as the one properly set. As was true in this case, advantages which result from mechanical errors in constructing test items usually favor the students of superior intelligence.

11. Prepare specifications for the physical setup for each numbered test station. This brief description will serve as a useful guide in making preparations for administering the test. It will also enable the instructor to save considerable time when he administers the test again at a later date.

12. Prepare an answer sheet with complete directions. This should be duplicated for student use during the test.

13. Prepare the key for scoring the papers. This should be done *before* the test is administered. After the tools and equipment have been removed from test stations, the chances are that the instructor will not be able to construct the key.

Following are a set of specifications, the answer sheet, and the key for a typical object test in the area of woodwork.

OBJECT TEST: BENCH WOODWORK
SPECIFICATIONS
Station
Number
1. Three pieces of stock, each approximately 3/4" x 4"
   x 8"; A – walnut; B – cherry; C – chestnut.
2. Three pieces of sandpaper of different grades, each
   piece approximately 1/4 sheet cut so as not to include
   grade designation; A – No. 1; B – No. 1/0; C – No.
   4/0.
3. Two sizes and kinds of wood screws: A – No. 6, flathead bright; B – No. 10, roundhead blue.
4. Three pieces of stock approximately 3/4" x 4" x 8",
   each bearing one cut as follows: A – stop chamfer;
   B – dado; C – bevel.
5. One piece of hardwood 27/32" x 2 19/64" x 6 43/64".
6. Three nails: A – 6d box; B – 8d common; C – 4d
   finish.
7. Three pieces of stock, each approximately 3/4" x 4"
   x 8"; A – Honduras mahogany; B – maple; C – red gum.
8. Three 1/2–pint jars containing samples of finishing
   materials: A – lacquer thinner; B – clear gloss
   varnish; C – alcohol.
9. One auger bit, No. 7, solid–center single twist, double
   cutter, medium screw.
10. One each: A – countersink; B – doweling jig.
11. Three bits: A – No. 13 auger bit; B – No. 7 bitstock
    drill; C – 3/8" twist drill.
12. Three 1/2 pint jars containing:
    A – clear lacquer; B – turpentine; C – paste wood
    filler.
13. Two pieces of stock: A – 1 1/2" x 3 1/2" x 7 1/4";
    B – 2" x 7 1/2" x 5 1/2". All dimensions to be clearly
    marked with pencil or chalk.
14. Two planes: A – jack plane; B – rabbet plane.
15. Two saws: A – 10–point crosscut saw: B – 6–point rip
    saw.
16. Two pieces of stock approximately 3/4" x 4" x 8":
    A – white oak; B – yellow poplar.
17. Three pieces of stock approximately 3/4" x 4" x 8",
    each bearing one cut as follows: A – groove; B –
    bead; C – rabbet.
18. Five planes as follows: A – rabbet plane; B –
    jointer; C – universal plow plane; D – block plane;
    E – jack plane; F – fore plane.
19. Screw chart and one No. 10, 1 1/2" flathead bright
    wood screw.
20. Three jack planes with frogs set as follows:
    A – frog too far to rear; B – frog too far forward;
    C – frog properly set for planing hard woods.

Station
Number

21. Jack plane with following parts missing: A – plane-iron cap; B – adjusting nut; C – lever cap.

22. Piece of stock approximately 3/4" x 4" x 8" with all six surfaces clearly designated A, B, C, etc. The best face, edge, and end to be designated B, C, and F, respectively, and the other face, edge, and end, A, E, and D, respectively.

23. One rule and two pieces of stock of each of following dimensions: A – 2 pieces 3/4" x 4" x 8"; B – 2 pieces 1" x 4" x 8"; C – 2 pieces 1/2" x 4" x 8".

24. Six pieces of stock each approximately 3/4" x 2" x 6" as follows: A – chestnut; B – walnut; C – red gum; D – cherry; E – white oak; F – maple.

25. Samples of stain of same color as follows: A – oil stain; B – spirit stain; C – water stain. (Kind of stain clearly written on each container.)

26. Six double plane irons set as follows: A – plane-iron cap set 3/16" from cutting edge; B – cap set 1/32" from cutting edge; C – cap on bevel side of plane iron, 1/32" from heel of bevel; D – cap on bevel side, 1/16" from heel of bevel; E – cap set 1/16" from cutting edge; F – cap set flush with cutting edge.

27. A piece of stock approximately 3/4" x 3" x 8" with one end laid off for cutting a tenon with all lines for shoulder cuts marked "A" and lines for cheek cuts marked "B".

28. Two pieces of stock approximately 3/4" x 4" x 8": A – quarter-sawed black walnut; B – plain-sawed red birch.

29. Two planes: A – smoothing plane; B – jointer.

30. Three 1/2-pint jars containing: A – clear lacquer; B – oil stain; C – white shellac.

OBJECT TEST: BENCH WORKWORK
ANSWER SHEET[1]

Name _____ Code no. _____ Date _____
Total points ___ No. wrong _____ No. correct _____
Directions: 1. For each of the numbered items on this answer sheet there is a corresponding station in the shop. When your instructor gives the order, go directly to the station bearing the number which he has assigned you. When, and not before, he gives you the signal, observe

[1] Answers have been inserted and numbered consecutively on this answer sheet to make of it a key to be used for scoring the test. Numbers to the right of blanks left for responses would not appear on copies to be distributed to students.

carefully what has been displayed at your station and then
answer the question which bears the same number as the
station. As each succeeding signal is given advance
promptly to the next numbered station in order and answer
the question bearing its number. Do not advance until the
signal is given.
  2. Where two or more objects are displayed at one
station, they will be lettered "A", "B," etc. Be sure to
write your response to the question about each object on
the line bearing its letter.
  3. Move a tool or piece of material only when this is
necessary to obtain the answer to a question. Be sure to
leave the objects at each station just as you found them.

Station
Number

1. Name of each wood?
   A.___(walnut)____(1)
   B.___(cherry)____(2)
   C.___(chestnut)___(3)
2. Grade of each piece of
   sandpaper?
   A.___(No. 1)_____(4)
   B.___(No. 1/0)___(5)
   C.___(No. 4/0)___(6)
   (Tolerance: one grade)
3. Kind and size of each
   screw?
   A. Kind__(flathead
            bright)____(7)
      Size__(No. 6)____(8)
   B. Kind__(roundhead
            blue)_____(9)
      Size__(No. 10)___(10)
   (Tolerance: one size)
4. Name of cut on each
   piece?
   A.___(Stop chamfer)_(11)
   B.___(dado)_____(12)
   C.___(bevel)_____(13)
5. Width and length to
   nearest 1/64"?
   A. Thickness
        (2 19/64)_____(14)
   B. Length
        (6 43/64)_____(15)
6. Kind and size of each
   nail?
   A. Kind__(box)_____(16)
      Size__(6d)_____(17)
   B. Kind__(common)___(18)
      Size__(8d)_____(19)
   C. Kind__(finish)___(20)
      Size__(4d)_____(21)
7. Name of each wood?
   A.___(Honduras ma-
        hogany)_____(22)
   B.___(maple)_____(23)
   C.___(red gum)_____(24)

Station
Number

8. Name of each finishing
   material?
   A.___(lacquer thin-
        ner)_____(25)
   B.___(clear lacquer)(26)
   C.___(alcohol)_____(27)
9. Write complete specifications for this bit,
   including four specific
   items.
   A.___(solid-center
        single twist)__(28)
   B.___(double cutter)(29)
   C.___(medium screw)_(30)
   D.___(No. 7-7/16")__(31)
10. Name a major use of each
    tool.
    A. Name(countersink)(32)
       Use_(countersink
            screws)_____(33)
    B. Name__(doweling
             jig)_____(34)
       Use__(align auger
             bit)_____(35)
11. How is each bit gener-
    ally sized? (Six-
    teenths, eighths, _etc.)
    A.___(by six-
         teenths)_____(36)
    B.___(by thirty-
         seconds)_____(37)
    C.___(by sixty-
         fourths)_____(38)
12. Names of finishing
    materials?
    A.___(clear lacquer)(39)
    B.___(turpentine)___(40)
    C.___(paste wood
         filler)_____(41)

Station
Number
13. Write dimensions of each
    piece of stock in proper
    order.
    A.__(1 1/2" X 3 1/2"__
           X 7 1/4")____(42)
    B.__(2" X 7 1/2"__
           X 5 1/2")____(43)
14. Name and major use of
    each?
    A. Name__(jack__
              plane)____(44)
       Use__(general-__
             purpose__
             plane)____(45)
    B. Name__(rabbet__
              plane)____(46)
       Use__(cutting__
             rabbets)____(47)
15. Kind of saw and number
    of points per inch?
    A. Kind__(crosscut)_(48)
       No. points__(10)_(49)
    B. Kind__(rip saw)__(50)
       No. points__(6)__(51)
16. Name of each wood and
    type of grain?
    A. Name__(white oak)(52)
       Grain__(open)____(53)
    B. Name__(yellow__
              poplar)____(54)
       Grain__(close)____(55)
17. Name of cut on each?
    A.__(groove)____(56)
    B.__(bead)____(57)
    C.__(rabbet)____(58)
18. If you could purchase
    only one of these planes
    for general use in the
    home workshop, which
    would be your:
    A. First choice_(E)_(59)
    B. Last choice_(C)_(60)
19. Size of bit to use for:
    A. Counterboring for
       head of screw____
       (3/8")____(61)
    B. Pilot hole(3/16")(62)
    C. Anchor hole(1/8")(63)
20. Which plane has frog
    properly set?
    Check one.
    A.____
    B.____
    C.__(√)____(64)
21. Names of missing parts?
    A.__(plane iron cap)(65)
    B.__(adjusting nut)_(66)
    C.__(lever cap)____(67)

Station
Number
22. Examine stock carefully
    and write letters which
    appear on the six sur-
    faces to indicate the
    order in which you
    would plane surfaces in
    squaring stock to
    dimensions.
    First__(B)____(68)
    Second__(C)____(69)
    Third__(F)____(70)
    Fourth__(D)____(71)
    Fifth__(E)____(72)
    Sixth__(A)____(73)
23. Proper size (diameter)
    of dowel to use in mak-
    ing dowel glue joint
    with each pair of pieces
    of stock?
    A.__(3/8")____(74)
    B.__(1/2")____(75)
    C.__(1/4")____(76)
24. Place check to left of
    letters representing
    woods which normally re-
    quire paste wood filler
    in finishing.
    (√)A. (77)____D.
    (√)B. (78)_(√)_E.(79)
    ____C.____F.
25. Place check to left of
    letter designating stain
    which is best for refin-
    ishing purposes.
    ____A.
    __(√)__B.(80)
    ____C.
26. Place one check to left
    of letter designating
    double plane iron which
    is properly set for
    planing hard woods and
    two checks to indicate
    plane iron properly set
    for soft woods.
    ____A.____D.
    (√)_B. (81)_(√√)_E.(82)
    ____C.____F.
27. Check letter represent-
    ing lines which should
    be cut first in making
    tenon by hand.
    ____A.
    __(√)__B.(83)
28. Name of each wood and
    how each is sawed, plain
    or quartered?
    A. Name__(walnut)____(84)
       How sawed__
       quartered)____(85)
    B. Name__(red birch)(86)
       How sawed_(plain)(87)

Station   Station
Number   Number
  29. Name and major use of   30. Name of each finishing
      each?   material.
      A. Name (smoothing)(88)   A. (clear lacquer) (92)
         Use (surfacing   B. (oil stain)   (93)
              stock)   (89)   C. (white shellac) (94)
      B. Name (jointer)   (90)
         Use (jointing
              long pieces)(91)

Administering the Object Test

The validity and general effectiveness of the object test are de
pendent upon the manner in which it is administered. Timing
and the control of students as they move from one station to another are the major problems. Detailed instructions must be given.
Students must understand and follow them to the letter.

The following suggestions will prove helpful in administering
this type of test:

1. Prepare detailed written instructions for the test. Explain
these carefully and completely to the students before starting the
test. You will find it advisable to prepare one or two sample stations in the classroom for purposes of illustrating and explaining
directions for taking the test. A previously prepared blackboard
sketch showing the relative location of each station in the shop
will prove helpful in orienting students.

2. Assign each student a number. This is done to eliminate confusion in getting students evenly distributed about the circuit of
stations. Direct each student to report, upon your signal, to the
station bearing his assigned number.

3. Leave the maximum number of stations between each two
students when assigning them to stations. For example, let us assume that there are to be 45 stations in the test and 15 students in
the class. In this case, place the first student at station 1, the second student at station 4, the third student at station 7, and so on.

It has been recommended (see page 313) that all stations be designed to consume about the same amount of the student's time.
In the event that you desire to include two or three stations requiring twice as much time as the others, each of these two or three
stations should be given two numbers (three numbers if they require three times as much time, and so on). Be sure that you plan
the assignment of stations ahead of time and have a sufficient num-

ber of stations vacant just in front of the stations bearing multiple numbers so that you will never have two students at or near one station at the same time (see Figure 21).

4. If the object test is included as one section of a comprehensive examination, there is an advantage in administering the object test before the written part of the examination, in that all students necessarily finish the object test at the same time.

8	7-6 X	5	4 ←———	3 X	2	1 X

(Initial location of students)

9. X·	10	11	———→ 12-13 X	14	15 X	16

8	7-6 X	5 ←———	4 X	3	2 X	1

(Students advanced one station)

9	10 X	11 ———→	12-13 X	14	15	16 X

Fig. 21. Initial position of students and their location after they receive the first signal to advance. Stations 6–7 and 12–13 require twice as much time as the others and for this reason have been given two numbers. Observe that students were not assigned to the two stations preceding these.

5. If the class is large and the number of stations small, the class may be divided into two or more groups for purposes of taking the object test, one group completing the object test while the others continue with the written part of the examination or with some other assignment.

6. Although the instructor may administer an object test by displaying individually the various tools and materials while the students remain seated, this practice definitely limits the scope of the practical test. Even if the test is employed only to measure ability to identify and give the major use of items in the shop, the authors recommend that these items be displayed at numbered stations and that the students be directed to move in an orderly manner from one station to another.

7. Students have a tendency to lag behind at stations which give them difficulty and to rush on through the easy ones. Supervise the class carefully. Permit no infraction of the directions. Insist that all students wait for the signal and that all advance promptly when the signal is given. This signal to advance may be given orally, or a bell or gong may be used.

8. Carefully observe the timing. Give the signals to advance at regular intervals. Note any adjustments which should be made in timing when a similar test is to be given again.

9. Collect the answer sheets immediately after students reach the point at which they began the test. Permit no student to return to stations which gave him difficulty.

10. In order to take full advantage of the instructional value of the object test, as soon as answer sheets have been collected the instructor should move the entire class from one station to another in order to explain the correct responses, answer students' questions, and clarify misunderstandings.

SUMMARY

The object test utilizes concrete, tangible things—tools, materials, equipment, specimens, and so on—in test situations designed to measure understandings. An object is displayed. The student is asked to identify it, indicate its use, or answer some other specific question about it. Students may be required to detect errors in work situations which have been prepared for test purposes. Some manipulative performance may be involved in certain object-test situations, but usually the test is limited to the measurement of understanding.

There are two principal ways of administering an object test. The instructor may display at a central point in the classroom a series of numbered objects while students remain at their seats. As each object is displayed, the students respond to the question on the answer sheet which bears the same number as the object. A procedure which is somewhat more satisfactory, and one which permits the use of a greater variety of test situations, requires that the instructor display the objects at a series of numbered stations throughout the classroom, shop, or laboratory. Students then pass in order from one numbered station to the next, pausing long enough at each to enter on a prepared answer sheet the required response.

The object test may be used to measure the student's

1. Ability to identify the various kinds, sizes, and grades of tools and materials.

2. Knowledge of specific uses of materials and tools, and ability to select those which are appropriate for the specific purposes.

3. Ability to identify certain processes which have been performed on materials and to indicate their application.

4. Knowledge and understanding of proper tool adjustments and setups required to utilize equipment for specific purposes.

5. Ability to perform simple operations or elementary steps of complex operations.

Among the advantages of the object test are the fact that it provides a somewhat more direct measure of understanding than do certain other tests, that it is acceptable to students, and that it has high instructional value.

SOME THINGS TO DO AND QUESTIONS TO ANSWER

1. What are the advantages of using the actual objects in test situations, as contrasted with the use of sketches, symbols, or word descriptions? The disadvantages?

2. Give specific examples from such fields as home economics, agriculture, the sciences, and the industrial arts to show the various uses which may be made of object tests.

3. Under what circumstances would you administer the object test by displaying the various objects at a central place while students remain seated? Under what conditions would you display the objects at numbered stations and have students pass in order from one station to the next?

4. What arrangements may be made in administering an object test to permit students to spend extra time at stations which require more time than the others?

5. When an object test is administered for the first time, what observations should the instructor make which will enable him to revise the test or to improve the manner in which it is administered?

6. Plan and describe specific object-test situations which will meas-

ure the student's ability to detect errors in machine or equipment setups and adjustments.

7. How would you score object-test items which require students to
rank, on the basis of given criteria, the four objects at a particular
station?

SELECTED REFERENCES FOR ADDITIONAL READING

Bloom, Samuel L. "Identification Test," *Industrial Arts and Vocational
Education,* 34:65–66 (February, 1945).

Hawkes, Herbert E., E. F. Lindquist, and C. R. Mann. *The Construction and Use of Achievement Examinations.* Boston: Houghton Mifflin Company, 1936. Chap. V.

Newkirk, Louis V., and Harry A. Greene. *Tests and Measurements in
Industrial Education.* New York: John Wiley & Sons, Inc., 1935. Pp.
118–120.

CHAPTER

TWELVE: MANIPULATIVE–
PERFORMANCE TESTS

REPEATEDLY, emphasis has been placed upon the importance of evaluating achievement in terms of objectives. The necessity of sampling liberally all aspects of achievement has also been stressed. The development of skill in the performance of certain manipulative operations is one of the stated and acceptable objectives for almost every practical arts and vocational course and for certain phases of other courses in the curriculum. This means that the measurement of ability to perform manipulative operations should become an important phase of the total program of evaluation for such courses.

Written tests generally are not valid for the measurement of *manipulative skills*. The fact that a student can supply flawless answers to questions about how to cut a mortise and tenon joint does not constitute positive proof that he can actually cut the joint with any acceptable degree of skill. His failure to answer questions satisfactorily would not prove his inability to cut the joint.

In spite of the general agreement with and acceptance of this point of view, far too many instructors state as one of their important objectives the development of certain manipulative skills and spend the greater portion of class time in developing these skills but then administer a few written tests as the main, if not the only, means of measuring achievement. Perhaps a progress chart is constructed in good faith, but all too frequently entries on it are discontinued after the first few weeks of school. Certainly the hasty awarding of marks to finished projects at the end of the term does not provide an adequate measure and evaluation of manipulative skill.

The instructor has at his disposal three basic means of measuring and evaluating the student's skill in the performance of manipulative operations. One method is through careful, systematic, objective observation of the student's daily work and the recording of the results at frequent intervals on some form of progress chart or record. The careful checking, testing, and evaluation of finished projects provide a second method. The administration of manipulative-performance tests is a third possibility. In a comprehensive program of measurement and evaluation all three methods are used to measure manipulative skill. This and succeeding chapters are devoted to these three means of measurement. It is with the performance test that this chapter is concerned.

Precisely what is a manipulative-performance test? It is a test designed to analyze and measure the student's skill in the performance of selected operations under *rigidly controlled conditions*. As the student completes specific operations, the instructor carefully observes the performance and records on a previously prepared check list the extent to which the student meets the standards. The time required to perform the various phases of the operation is recorded; a record is made of the precision and accuracy with which the student works; errors in procedure are noted and checked; the application and observation of specific points and safety precautions are recorded; and the completed work is carefully measured and checked. The performance test provides the basis for a thorough analysis of the entire performance and an evaluation of each element in that performance.

The well-constructed performance test usually includes:

1. A set of directions to be followed by persons who are to administer the test, together with instructions for scoring the test.

2. A drawing and specifications or a detailed description of the job to be performed by the student.

3. Directions to be followed by the student in taking the test. These directions may or may not include a detailed plan of pro-

cedure which lists the steps to be followed in the order that they are to be performed in completing the task.

4. Provisions for recording time consumed and a means of indicating credit or points earned on the basis of time.

5. A check list to be used by the observer in checking the details of the method or procedure followed by the student.

6. A check list to be used by the examiner in scoring the completed job. This may include detailed provisions for recording slight variations in accuracy and quality of work and a description of instruments and devices to be used in measuring the completed job. Quality scales may also be included as a part of the test. These are especially desirable if the test involves several elements whose evaluation must remain dependent upon the judgment of the examiner.

The type of performance test presented in this chapter is not to be confused with the object test of Chapter Eleven, with the aptitude test involving manipulative performance, or with the trade test in which the performance of certain operations is required. The object test makes use of actual tools, materials, and equipment in measuring the student's understanding of these items. There may be some performance incorporated in test situations set up at certain stations in the object test, but the performance must necessarily be limited to the completion of only one or two steps of an operation or the execution of a very simple, short procedure. The object test may involve specific elements closely related to performance, but in the main this test measures knowledge and understanding. The performance test, on the other hand, requires the student to complete one or more significant operations under rigidly controlled conditions. Each operation involves several steps, and completion of the test by the student generally requires 10 to 50 minutes. The student is observed carefully as he performs, and a detailed record is made of everything he does. There may be as many as thirty or forty or more items against which his performance is checked.

The aptitude test involving manual performance is an instrument ". . . designed to predict the subject's *potential skill*. The function of the test in this case is to judge either how quickly the subject can develop the skills required for performance of particu lar job duties or the level of such skills that he can develop."[1] The trade test involving performance is designed to measure efficiency in a trade. It is used for the purpose of selection and placement of workers. Its administration may consume several hours to two or three days. The person being tested may remain under the direct observation of the examiner during the entire period, or, as is the case with some trade tests, the examiner may merely check the completed work to determine the score on the test. Neither the aptitude nor the trade test would provide an adequate measure of achievement in the school shop. The aptitude test would certainly be invalid for this purpose. There would be very few cases in which a trade test, even if there were time to administer it to all students in the class, would measure manipulative achievement in a particular course as well as a series of performance tests designed for that course by the instructor.

Measurable Aspects of Performance

Conscious manipulative performance of the type with which we are concerned here is a highly complex process. Its accurate measurement is likewise complicated. Before the test maker can design instruments for measuring accurately the student's ability to perform manipulative operations, he must thoroughly understand the various measurable aspects of performance.

What is manipulative performance? How is it related to mental or intellectual processes? Manipulative performance is not merely a matter of physical "doing." There is considerable "knowing" involved. The manipulative operations to be performed constitute problems to be solved. Their solution requires physical work of a skilled order accompanied and directed by the conscious application of previously acquired knowledges and understandings. The performer is continually analyzing the problem and evaluating his progress. At practically every turn he weighs certain technical knowledges and understandings and makes certain choices and decisions which affect his work. In fact, the technical knowledge which he applies in completing the performance overshadows, in many cases, the actual "doing" in importance.

[1] Dorothy C. Adkins, and associates, *Construction and Analysis of Achievement Tests*. Washington, D.C.: Government Printing Office, 1947, p. 211.

What are the essential features of manipulative performance which should be considered in evaluating this important outcome of instruction? What are the measurable aspects of performance? The following are important elements of skill which should be considered in evaluating a student's ability to perform a given operation or series of related operations:

1. *Speed*—the student's rate of work as compared with a predetermined standard.

2. *Quality*—the precision with which the student works and the extent to which the completed job conforms to prescribed dimensions and specifications.

3. *Procedure*—the extent to which the student follows the detailed steps of the accepted method for completing the prescribed job; the extent to which he demonstrates his ability to select, care for, and use properly the tools, materials, and equipment required to complete the job; his observance of safety precautions; his application of essential information in making decisions affecting his performance; and the confidence, deliberation, and self-assurance with which the work is performed.

The well-constructed manipulative-performance test provides for the measurement of each of these important elements of skill. A test designed to measure only one of these, rate of work, or the observance of safety precautions, for instance, is of questionable value, even though such tests are frequently given in an effort to analyze a student's specific strengths and weaknesses. A test administered to measure rate of performance without regard to the other elements of skill will cause the student to sacrifice for speed such items as accuracy, proper procedure, and proper use and care of tools. A high level of achievement in any one aspect of skill when measured by itself is of no particular consequence. The student's skill in the performance of manipulative operations must be measured and analyzed by use of testing situations in which *both examiner and the student place appropriate emphasis upon each aspect of performance*—speed, quality, and procedure.

Certain of these various aspects of performance can be measured directly and rather objectively either while the student works or by checking and testing the completed job, whereas other elements lend themselves to evaluation only through the observer. For instance, the time required to complete the various operations in-cluded in the job and the total time consumed by the entire performance can be accurately measured with a stop watch and re-corded by an observer. As far as many of the elements which have to do with procedure or method of work are concerned, the ob-server can determine definitely that the student either did or did not do certain things and can record in an objective manner his observations. The extent to which the completed work conforms to specifications can be accurately determined by the use of preci-sion measuring instruments. However, such items as the confidence and assurance with which the student tackled the job, the general appearance of the finished product, the smoothness of the finished surfaces, and the extent to which tool marks, scratches, and other blemishes mar the work do not lend themselves readily to precise and objective measurement but are left to the considered judgment of the observer as a practicable means of evaluation.

Uses and Advantages

The uses and advantages of manipulative-performance tests can be summarized as follows:

1. The performance test can be designed and administered to provide a more objective, reliable, and valid measure of the stu-dent's ability to perform *certain operations* than can be obtained by any other practicable means.

2. It provides a careful analysis and measurement of the extent to which the student has mastered the various elements of skill. This is especially important from the standpoint of diagnosis and reteaching. The results obtained by administering carefully pre-pared performance tests provide the instructor with an analysis of the effectiveness of his own demonstrations and reveal to him points upon which greater emphasis should be placed. Taking a performance test and studying its results enable the student to analyze his own strengths and weaknesses. This experience focuses his attention upon the details which make for effective perform-ance.

3. The performance test measures the results of instruction in their direct application.

Limitations

The major limitations and difficulties in constructing and administering manipulative-performance tests are as follows:

1. The administration of the performance test consumes considerable time. One instructor can administer a performance test to from only two to perhaps six students at a time. In some cases only one student can take the test at a given time with satisfactory results.

2. Its administration presents the problem of planning profitable activities for students who are waiting to take the test and for those who have already completed it.

3. It involves an element of the "exercise," which most instructors prefer to keep to a minimum in their teaching.

4. The performance test is difficult to construct.

5. It is difficult to administer. Even though the performance test be carefully constructed to yield objective and reliable measurements, the instructor who administers it must have considerable training and experience in order to acquire the skill necessary to obtain objective and reliable results.

6. The performance test, while it contains a great amount of detail and is apparently objective, can be misleading. *The fact that it requires actual performance on the part of the student does not necessarily make it a good test.*

7. The formality and control which characterize the administration of the performance test tend to penalize the student who experiences difficulty in working under pressure.

Constructing Manipulative-performance Tests

The construction of a satisfactory performance test is not an easy task. If the instructor is to succeed in constructing a performance test of high quality, he must be able to make a careful, detailed analysis of operations to be incorporated in the test. He must necessarily exercise considerable initiative and imagination in order to devise means of measuring all the important aspects of the student's performance.

There is no rigid, mechanical procedure which can be followed to ensure the construction of an objective, reliable, and valid, yet practical, performance test. The following general procedure, together with some specific suggestions, should prove helpful, however.

1. Select Operations to Be Incorporated in the Performance Test. The difficulties involved in their construction, the time required to administer performance tests, and the basic necessity of providing valid measures of achievement make it mandatory that operations to be included in the performance test be selected with care. A random selection certainly will not suffice. When the instructor compiles the list of items which must be mastered by students if the course objective pertaining to manipulative skill is to be realized, he will have listed numerous operations. The degree of efficiency achieved in certain of these operations will lend itself to measurement by performance tests. For practical reasons, the use of performance tests to measure proficiency in others of these operations should not be attempted. The following suggestions should prove helpful in selecting operations which may be satisfactorily incorporated in performance tests:

   a. Select operations which are typical and representative of those which have been taught.
   b. Select operations which, by the time the test is to be administered, will have been demonstrated to and practiced by all students to be tested.
   c. If the performance of each student is to be compared with that of the other students in the class, restrict the selection to basic operations with which all students to be tested will have had about the same amount of experience.
   d. For each performance test select an operation, or a group of related operations, which can be completed in 15 to 50 minutes. It is impractical to design a performance test which a given student cannot complete in one class period.
   e. Select operations which are sufficiently difficult to reveal any real and significant differences in achievement. Operations which can be performed equally well by all students are not suitable for testing purposes. The test maker should deliberately choose those operations which, in performance, either result in perceptible errors or provide opportunities for

variation in one or more of the measurable aspects of performance.

f. Select operations which involve the tools, materials, and equipment commonly used in the course.

g. Select operations for which there are sufficient sets of necessary tools and equipment to permit the preparation of the number of work stations required to complete the administration of the test to the class in a reasonable length of time.

h. Select operations involving definite steps of procedure and which require the application of specific knowledges and understandings along with the manipulative work.

Let us assume that we are teaching a general course in woodwork in which are enrolled ninth- and tenth-grade students. One of the stated objectives of the course is to develop a measure of skill in the performance of certain basic operations. There is a list of basic operations which we expect each student to learn. "Core" projects have been designed which include these basic operations. Students are permitted some freedom in the selection of projects in that there are alternate projects including about the same operations. A student may select or design other projects with the understanding that they include predetermined operations and meet other practical requirements as to size, amounts, and types of material, and the like.

In order to obtain an accurate measure of the extent to which the objective pertaining to manipulative skill has been achieved, we have decided to construct and administer performance tests for each of the four areas of work. Since eight of the twenty-four students have performed the basic, required operations in woodworking, we shall construct and administer to these eight boys a performance test in that area.

We examine the list of operations taught. Keeping in mind the criteria for selecting operations to include in a performance test (page 332), we make a selection which includes the following operations from the list of forty-three included in the woodworking area:

1. Square stock.
2. Lay out and cut a dado.
3. Locate and bore a hole.

4. Lay out, saw, and pare a circular cut.

5. Lay out and cut a chamfer.

Each operation selected is typical and representative of those which have been taught. Each has been demonstrated to all students to be tested and has been performed and practiced to approximately the same extent by all students. Each seems to be sufficiently difficult to reveal significant and measurable differences in student performance. Each requires the use of readily available tools and materials commonly used in the course. The performance of each operation involves definite steps of procedure, along with application of specific knowledges and understandings.

2. *Make a Preliminary Analysis of Each Operation Selected.* Until this preliminary analysis has been made, the selection of operations to include in the test must necessarily remain tentative. The analysis of each operation should reveal (1) the approved step-by-step procedure to be followed in performing the operation, together with the specific safety precautions to be observed and the more important points of information which the student must consider and apply to complete satisfactorily the operation, and (2) the tools and equipment required to perform the operation. Table 1 shows a preliminary analysis of each of the five operations which have been tentatively selected for a performance test in woodworking.

If the instructor makes extensive use of analysis procedures in organizing subject matter for instructional purposes, this second step in the construction of a performance test will probably become one of making a careful study of the analyses already available in the shop.

3. *Select or Design an Appropriate Job.* After the operations to be incorporated in the performance test have been analyzed, the next step is to design a simple job or exercise in which these operations, but no others, are involved. This job should be definite, specific, and one that can be completed in an acceptable length of time.

For a performance test incorporating the five operations previously selected from the area of woodwork, a test block seems to be logical and adequate. A single piece of stock to be finished to dimensions and a dado cut to be made across one face, one corner to

Table 1. Analysis of Operations Tentatively Selected for Inclusion in Performance Test

Operation	Steps of procedure and specific points to apply	Tools required

1. Square stock	1. Select best face; plane true; mark
	  a. Shearing cuts; plane with grain
	  b. Tests: flat, straight, free of wind
	2. Select best edge; plane straight and square with face; test; mark
	3. Select best end; plane straight
	  a. Precautions against splitting edge
	  b. Care in setting plane for finish cut
	4. With gauge lay off width; rip off surplus stock; plane to dimensions; test
	  a. Allowance for finish cut
	5. Lay off length; mark; saw off surplus; plane to dimensions; test
	  a. Allowance for finish cut
	  b. Precautions against splitting
	6. Gauge thickness; plane to dimension; test
		1. Jack plane
		2. Marking gauge
		3. Hard lead pencil or knife
		4. Ripsaw
		5. Crosscut or back saw
		6. Try square
		7. Rule

2. Lay out and cut dado	1. Locate dado on stock; square lines across face and 90° to edge 2. Gauge depth of cut on both edges 3. Drop perpendiculars to depth lines on both edges 4. Saw kerfs; cut to center of lines 5. Rough chisel cuts from both faces; complete rough cuts 6. Pare to depth lines	1. Rule 2. Try square 3. Knife or pencil 4. Back saw 5. Chisel
3. Locate and bore hole	1. Locate hole; rule or marking gauge 2. Bore from face side; start bit; test for perpendicular 3. Stop when screw pierces reverse side; turn stock and bore from reverse side	1. Brace and bit 2. Pencil 3. Try square
4. Lay out and cut curve	1. Locate center of curve 2. Scribe arc 3. Draw lines through center and parallel to end and edge 4. Drop perpendiculars across end and edge in line with lines drawn in 3 above 5. Remove surplus stock with coping saw 6. Pare to center of curved line; test	1. Rule 2. Try square 3. Pencil 4. Compass or dividers 5. 1″ paring chisel 6. Coping saw
5. Lay out and cut chamfer	1. Lay off chamfer; gauge with pencil and square or rule 2. Plane to gauged line; test 3. Take finish cut; one continuous cut to center of gauged lines.	1. Pencil 2. Rule or try square 3. Jack plane

be rounded, three holes to be bored through the stock, and a chamfer to be planed along one edge and across one end should form
the basis for an effective test.

The selection of a single piece of stock on which all five operations can be performed will result in a test far less complicated
than a test involving a separate piece of material for each operation.

In determining the dimensions and characteristics of the test

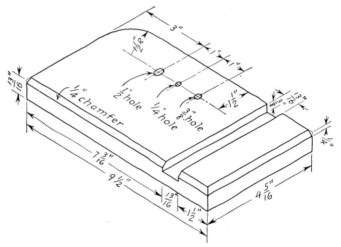

Fig. 1. Tentative design for test block to be used in performance test.

block, at least two factors should be considered. (1) If we make the
block either too small or too large, we place certain handicaps
upon the student and extend the time necessary to complete the
test without adding anything to its validity. (2) In the interest of
saving time, a soft, easily worked wood should be used. With these
factors in mind, let us proceed to design a test block around which
the performance test can be constructed. The sketch shown in
Figure 1 seems to incorporate the specific details in accordance
with our requirements.

As a part of the process of selecting or designing an appropriate
job around which to construct the performance test, a rough
check should be made of each tentative design to determine (1)
whether it can be executed by the students in an acceptable length

of time and (2) whether each major element included in the job lends itself to variation in performance or is of sufficient difficulty to reveal significant and readily measurable differences in ability to perform.

To make this check on the design as shown in the sketch in Figure 1, one of the authors asked thirty tenth-grade students— ten of low, ten of average, and ten of high ability—to make the test block from the sketch. Results of this rough check revealed that the students differed significantly in their ability to perform each operation involved but that the block as designed will consume too much time. By having one face, one edge, and one end finished before the stock is issued to the students, considerable time can be saved. Except for knowledge of the order of the first three steps involved in squaring stock, the elimination of these steps will not detract too much from the value of the test. Additional time can be saved by decreasing the depth of the dado and the size of the chamfer and by eliminating two of the three holes.

4. *Prepare Drawing and/or Specifications for the Job.* If the job involves construction, a working drawing, preferably of the pictorial type, should be prepared. The drawing and specifications should leave no doubt as to what is required of the student. Further, they serve as a guide to the examiner in preparing the physical setup for the performance test and thus become essential to the standardization of testing procedure.

From the preliminary sketch of a test block for the performance test in woodwork, as adapted to incorporate changes suggested by the result of the check on the design, the drawing has been executed and the specifications added to complete this step. They have been incorporated in the completed performance test included in the latter part of this chapter (see page 354).

5. *List All Specific Points Feasible for Testing Purposes.* The fifth step calls for a careful study of the preliminary analysis completed in Step 2 and of the drawing and specifications for the job to be performed by the student in order to arrive at a comprehensive list of the specific points from which those to be included in the test may be selected. A consideration of the means of measurement at our disposal not only will aid in the completion of this list but will result in a classification or grouping of the points

which will in turn facilitate the construction of the mechanical aspects of the test. While the objectives of the course, together with a consideration of the several factors listed on page 332, led to the selection of the major elements to be included in the test, it is not until the test job has been designed and adequately described that the detailed points which may be included in the test can be listed and a means of measuring each systematically prescribed.

As has been pointed out, there are certain aspects of the performance which must necessarily be checked by an observer as the student executes the job requirement, while other qualities can best be measured by checking the student's completed work. Under each of these classifications of points to be evaluated, there will appear (1) certain items which can be measured objectively, either by observing that specific acts were or were not performed or by making use of precision measuring tools to determine the degree or extent of variation from a specified standard, and (2) qualities whose measurement becomes a matter of the judgment of the examiner. In the majority of instances the measurement of qualities of the latter type will require provisions for distinguishing among varying degrees of compliance.

As an example of a quality which is either met completely or not met at all consider the following: The drawing calls for a $\frac{3}{8}$ inch hole to be bored. Auger bits are made in fixed diameters varying by sixteenths of an inch. Boring a $\frac{5}{8}$ or $\frac{3}{4}$ inch hole or any size other than $\frac{3}{8}$ inch would not constitute partial fulfillment of the requirement of selecting the bit of proper size, and thus would not merit partial credit. If, however, the student cuts a piece of red oak $\frac{1}{64}$ inch longer than the $13\frac{5}{8}$ inches specified on the drawing, his error is one of degree and thus merits partial credit.

Ordinarily, the qualities listed should be expressed in terms of effective or correct performance; however, in the case of errors commonly made, evidence of guarding against a given difficulty or avoiding a common error may be included as a point for which credit may be given.

Returning again to the problem of constructing the performance test in the area of woodwork, let us consider the matter of classification of each of the points which may be incorporated in the test, the possible means of measuring each, and the objectivity with which each can be measured. Included in Table 2 are the specific points for the test classified as to the objectivity with which they can be measured as well as to whether they must be observed during the performance or can best be measured in the completed job. Items with respect to which students vary in competence have been checked. Possibilities for their measurement have also been listed.

6. Select the Specific Points to Be Included in the Test. From the list of items included in the analysis, the test maker selects the points against which the student's performance should be checked. Obviously, he cannot and should not always make provisions for the inclusion of every specific item listed in the analysis. After considering such factors as (1) the relative importance and relationship of each item to competence in the performance of the operation of which it is a part, (2) the objectivity and reliability with which it can be measured, (3) its discriminating power, and (4) the availability of means for its measurement, the instructor may choose the items for the test. Only after he has completed the test, administered it to several students, and made analyses of the results obtained does he have any better basis than his own judgment or the combined judgments of several instructors in his field for the selection of specific items for the test.

7. Construct the Check List. The specific items to be included in the performance test are incorporated in the check list to be used in administering the test.

Usually the check list will include two distinct sections: one to be executed by the examiner either during or immediately following the student's performance, the second to be used to record the results of a careful analysis of the student's completed work.

The following are suggestions which should be considered in constructing the check list for the performance test:

a. Remember that the examiner must concentrate upon the observation of the performer or performers to whom the test is to be administered. For this reason the check list must be designed to require a minimum amount of writing. Make it truly a *check list,* not merely a form to receive miscellaneous comments.

Table 2. Analysis and Classification of Measurable Qualities to Be Included in Woodwork Performance Test

Qualities	Directly and objectively measurable	Involving varying and measurable degrees of compliance	Measurable during performance	Measurable in completed work	Means of measurement
Time required to:					
1. Complete squaring stock...........	x	x	x	....	Time measured by observer with stop watch
2. Lay out and cut dado...........	x	x	x	....	
3. Locate and bore hole............	x	x	x	....	
4. Lay out and cut curve...........	x	x	x	....	
5. Lay out and cut chamfer.........	x	x	x	....	
6. Complete the job.	x	x	x	....	Total time recorded for 1 to 5
Other indications of rate of work:					
1. Did not spend excessive amount of time studying drawing.........	....	x	x	....	
2. Lost no time pondering problem; worked continuously...........	....	x	x	....	
3. Did not spend excessive time checking measurements.	...	x	x	....	Observed and recorded by examiner
4. No lost motion or meaningless activity with tools....	....	x	x	....	
5. Lost no time hunting for tools.....	....	x	x	....	
Procedure for completion of squaring of stock:					
1. Completes squaring of stock by working to length, width, and thickness in that order.	x	....	x	....	

Table 2. Analysis and Classification of Measurable Qualities to Be Included in Woodwork Performance Test (Continued)

Qualities	Directly and objectively measurable	Involving varying and measurable degrees of compliance	Measurable during performance	Measurable in completed work	Means of measurement
2. Lays off length:					
a. Stands rule on edge.........	x	....	x	....	
b. Places rule parallel to edge of stock.........	x	x	x	....	
c. Measures from 1″ mark.......	x	....	x	....	
d. From edge 2 squares line across face....	x	....	x	....	
e. From face 1 squares lines across edges 2 and 5.........	x	....	x	....	
f. Connects lines across face 6...	x	....	x	....	
g. Makes all lines with knife or hard pencil....	x	....	x	....	Observed and recorded by examiner
h. Does not retrace lines.........	x	....	x	....	
3. Saws off surplus stock:					
a. Places stock in vise with face up and parallel to bench top...	x	x	x	....	
b. Saws from edge 2.............	x	x	x	....	
c. Starts saw smoothly......	x	x	x	....	
d. Checks alignment of saw...	x	....	x	....	
e. Takes long, free strokes........	x	x	x	....	
f. Holds surplus stock to maintain alignment.	x	....	x	....	

Table 2. Analysis and Classification of Measurable Qualities to Be Included in Woodwork Performance Test (*Continued*)

Qualities	Directly and objectively measurable	Involving varying and measurable degrees of compliance	Measurable during performance	Measurable in completed work	Means of measurement
g. Holds surplus stock and lightens stroke at end of cut.....	x	....	x	....	
h. Saws outside of line...........	x	....	x	....	
i. Leaves no more than 1/16″ for planing........	x	....	x	....	
4. Planes to center of layout line:					
a. Places stock low in vise with end horizontal.....	x	x	x	....	
b. Checks or adjusts plane....	x	....	x	....	
c. Takes light shearing cuts..	x	x	x	....	
d. Guards against splitting edge..	x	x	x	....	Observed and recorded by examiner
5. Lays off width:					
a. Selects marking gauge.........	x	....	x	....	
b. Checks setting with rule......	x	....	x	....	
c. Makes light, uniform, continuous lines...	x	x	x	....	
d. Does not retrace lines.....	x	....	x	....	
e. Marks both surfaces..........	x	....	x	....	
6. Planes stock to width:					
a. Places stock low in vise with edge horizontal.....	x	x	x	....	
b. Takes heavy cuts to remove surplus stock..	x	....	x	....	

Table 2. Analysis and Classification of Measurable Qualities to Be Included in Woodwork Performance Test (Continued)

Qualities	Directly and objectively measurable	Involving varying and measurable degrees of compliance	Measurable during performance	Measurable in completed work	Means of measurement
c. Reduces cut to finish.........	x	....	x	....	
d. Checks frequently.......	x	x	x	....	
e. Last cut removes full shaving..........	x	....	x	....	
f. All cuts taken with the grain..	x	....	x	....	
7. Lays off thickness:					
a. Uses marking gauge.........	x	....	x	....	
b. Checks setting with rule......	x	....	x	....	
c. Marks both edges and ends.	x	....	x	....	
d. Makes light, continuous, uniform lines.....	x	x	x	....	Observed and recorded by examiner
e. Does not retrace lines..........	x	....	x	....	
8. Planes stock to thickness:					
a. Places stock between vise dog and bench stop or horizontal in vise..........	x	x	x	....	
b. Removes excess stock with heavy cuts....	x	....	x	....	
c. Reduces cut to finish.........	x	....	x	....	
d. Checks frequently as lines are approached	x	x	x	....	
e. All cuts taken with grain.....	x	....	x	....	

Table 2. Analysis and Classification of Measurable Qualities to Be Included in Woodwork Performance Test (Continued)

Qualities	Directly and objectively measurable	Involving varying and measurable degrees of compliance	Measurable during performance	Measurable in completed work	Means of measurement
Procedure for laying out and cutting dado:					
1. Locates dado:					
a. Measures from end of stock with rule on edge..........	x	....	x	....	
b. Places rule parallel to edge...	x	x	x	....	
c. Measures from 1″ mark.......	x	....	x	....	
d. Locates both sides of dado without moving rule..........	x	....	x	....	
e. Makes light marks with knife or hard pencil.........	x	....	x	....	
2. Lays out dado:					Observed and recorded by examiner
a. From edge 2 squares lines across face 1...	x	....	x	....	
b. From face 1 drops lines across edges 2 and 5.........	x	....	x	....	
c. Makes light knife or pencil lines..........	x	....	x	....	
d. Checks setting of marking gauge with rule	x	....	x	....	
e. Gauges depth lines on edges 2 and 5.........	x	....	x	....	
3. Cuts dado:					
a. Places stock in vise horizontally..........	x	....	x	....	

Table 2. Analysis and Classification of Measurable Qualities to Be Included in Woodwork Performance Test (*Continued*)

Qualities	Directly and objectively measurable	Involving varying and measurable degrees of compliance	Measurable during performance	Measurable in completed work	Means of measurement
b. Starts saw smoothly......	x	x	....	....	
c. Saws inside of lines across face	x	....	x	....	
d. Saw kerfs made uniform in depth and to center of depth lines on edges 2 and 5........	x	x	x	....	
e. Removes surplus stock with chisel, bevel up	x	....	x	....	
f. Places chisel slightly above depth lines....	x	....	x	....	
g. Makes rough cuts from edges 2 and 5.......	x	....	x	....	Observed and recorded by examiner
h. Pares to center of lines........	x	....	x	....	
i. Does not need to pare sides...	x	....	x	....	
Procedure for locating and boring hole:					
1. Locates hole:					
a. With square or rule on edge measures distances from end and edge......	x	....	x	....	
b. Gauges or draws light lines whose intersection locates hole.....	x	....	x	....	
2. Bores hole:					
a. Places stock in vise horizontally..........	x	....	x	....	

Table 2. Analysis and Classification of Measurable Qualities to Be Included in Woodwork Performance Test (*Continued*)

Qualities	Directly and objectively measurable	Involving varying and measurable degrees of compliance	Measurable during performance	Measurable in completed work	Means of measurement
b. Locates stock to avoid striking metal when bit clears stock....	x	....	x	....	
c. Starts bit, and checks alignment.........	x	....	x	....	
d. Stops bit when screw breaks through.......	x	....	x	....	
e. Changes stock in vise, and bores from reverse side.....	x	....	x	....	
f. Exercises caution to prevent splitting as hole is finished.....	x	x	x	....	
Procedure for laying out and cutting curve:					Observed and recorded by examiner
1. Lays out curve:					
a. Locates center with rule or square........	x	....	x	....	
b. Draws light lines whose intersection locates center....	x	....	x	....	
c. Sets and checks dividers or compass..........	x	....	x	....	
d. Scribes arc lightly and uniformly	x	x	x	....	
e. Measures to determine exact points of tangency........	x	....	x	....	

Table 2. Analysis and Classification of Measurable Qualities to Be Included in Woodwork Performance Test (Continued)

Qualities	Directly and objectively measurable	Involving varying and measurable degrees of compliance	Measurable during performance	Measurable in completed work	Means of measurement
f. Drops lines across end and edge at point of tangency......	x	....	x	....	
2. Cuts curve:					
a. Removes excess stock with saw.	x	....	x	....	
b. With 1″ chisel pares stock to center of arc...	x	....	x	....	
c. Keeps bevel up or away from stock.........	x	....	x	....	
d. Checks frequently for squareness.....	x	x	x	....	
e. All cuts taken with the grain.	x	....	x	....	
Procedure for laying out and cutting chamfer:					Observed and recorded by examiner
1. Lays out chamfer:					
a. Measures distance from arris to edge of chamfer.......	x	....	x	....	
b. Gauges lines for chamfer.......	x	....	x	....	
c. Marks with pencil, not knife or marking gauge.	x	....	x	....	
2. Cuts chamfer along edge:					
a. Planes chamfer along edge first	x	....	x	....	
b. Takes deep continuous cuts to remove surplus	x	....	x	....	
c. Planes with the grain.........	x	....	x	....	

Table 2. Analysis and Classification of Measurable Qualities to Be Included
in Woodwork Performance Test (*Continued*)

Qualities	Directly and objectively measurable	Involving varying and measurable degrees of compliance	Measurable during performance	Measurable in completed work	Means of measurement
d. Lightens cut to finish.........	x	....	x	....	
e. Checks frequently as lines are approached	x	....	x	....	
f. Removes full shaving on last cut...........	x	....	x	....	
3. Cuts chamfer along end:					
a. Planes toward chamfered edge	x	....	x	....	
b. Takes shearing cuts..........	x	....	....	....	
c. Checks frequently as lines are approached	x	x	x	....	
d. Takes light, continuous cut to finish.......	x	x	x	....	Observed and recorded by examiner
Additional evidence of effective procedure:					
1. Approached problem deliberately and with confidence..........	....	x	x	....	
2. Shows evidence at all times of knowing what to do and how to do it...	....	x	x	....	
3. Keeps tools orderly, arranged...	....	....	....	....	
4. Does not abuse tools...........	....	x	x	....	
5. Exercises safety precautions:					
a. Keeps cutting-edge tools away from work.....	....	x	x	....	

Table 2. Analysis and Classification of Measurable Qualities to Be Included in Woodwork Performance Test (*Continued*)

Qualities	Directly and objectively measurable	Involving varying and measurable degrees of compliance	Measurable during performance	Measurable in completed work	Means of measurement
b. Does not drop tools.........	x	x	x	....	Observed and recorded by examiner
c. Keeps hands behind cutting edge when using chisel.........	x	x	x	....	
Accuracy of work:					
1. Dimensions:					
a. Variations in thickness, width, and length........	x	x	....	x	
b. Location and variations in width and depth of dado.......	....	....	....	....	
c. Location of center of hole as indicated by layout lines....	x	x	....	x	Measured with precision instruments
d. Size of hole....	x	....	....	x	
e. Variation of center of hole from intersection of layout lines.........	x	x	....	x	
f. Location of center of arc......	x	x	....	x	
g. Radius of arc as laid out.......	x	x	....	x	
h. Variations in radius of curve as cut..........	x	x	....	x	
i. Depth of irregularities....	x	x	....	x	Jig made to check irregularities; small numbered drill or feeler gauges

Table 2. Analysis and Classification of Measurable Qualities to Be Included in Woodwork Performance Test (Continued)

Qualities	Directly and objectively measurable	Involving varying and measurable degrees of compliance	Measurable during performance	Measurable in completed work	Means of measurement
j. Variations in distances of arrises of chamfer from surfaces 1, 2, and 3.......	x	x	....	x	Rule
k. Variations in face 6 from true plane.........	x	x	....	x	Straight edge, machined surface, and feeler gauges
2. Angles—variations from specified angle of:					
a. Surface 4 with 1	x	x	....	x	Protractor or instrument constructed to magnify error
b. Surface 4 with 2	x	x	....	x	Protractor or instrument constructed to magnify error
c. Surface 5 with 1	x	x	....	x	Protractor or instrument constructed to magnify error
d. Sides of dado with surface 2..	x	x	....	x	Protractor or instrument constructed to magnify error
e. Sides of dado with surface 1..	x	x	....	x	Protractor or instrument constructed to magnify error
f. Curve with surface 1.........	x	x	....	x	Protractor or instrument constructed to magnify error
g. Chamfer with surface 1......	x	x	....	x	Protractor or instrument constructed to magnify error
h. Hole with surface 1.........	x	x	....	x	Dowel and protractor or instrument constructed to magnify error

Table 2. Analysis and Classification of Measurable Qualities to Be Included
in Woodwork Performance Test (Concluded)

Qualities	Directly and objectively measurable	Involving varying and measurable degrees of compliance	Measurable during performance	Measurable in completed work	Means of measurement
Additional evidence of quality of work:					
1. General appearance of work.....	....	x	....	x	Observed and recorded by examiner
2. Smoothness of surfaces 4, 5, 6......	....	x	....	x	Observed and recorded by examiner
3. Extent to which all layout lines are fine and distinct......	....	x	....	x	Observed and recorded by examiner
4. Extent to which stock has been chipped, split, and dented..........	x	x	....	x	Number of blemishes counted and recorded
5. Extent to which all angles are sharp and distinct......	....	x	....	x	Observed and recorded by examiner

b. Make sure that provisions are made for checking the important measurable aspects of effective performance and for reporting on the specific points which are indicative of efficiency with respect to each.

c. Place related items together under appropriate headings, and make provisions for subtotals in the score column to facilitate use of the test for diagnostic purposes. In the section of the check list to be executed during or immediately following the student's performance, items should occur on the check list in the same order in which they would normally receive the student's attention as he completes the work.

d. To minimize the problem of weighting, select and group items in the check list in such a manner as to make each of

about the same relative importance as any other in the list.
Trivial and insignificant points should be excluded. Avoid
complicated procedures for determining the relative point
values to be assigned each item in the check list. Your considered judgment as the instructor, or the combined judgments of other instructors of the school system who teach in
your field and who thoroughly understand your objectives,
will probably be as valid as any other criterion for assigning
values to the various items in the check list.

e. For all items with respect to which students normally vary
significantly in efficiency, make provisions for giving appropriate credit for the various discernible degrees of efficiency or quality. Generally, distinctions should be attempted
on the basis of not less than three or more than five levels of
proficiency. In a woodworking test, for example, four points
might be given for working to within a tolerance of $\frac{1}{64}$ inch,
three points for $\frac{1}{32}$ inch, two points for $\frac{3}{64}$ inch, one point
for $\frac{1}{16}$ inch, and no credit for an error of greater than $\frac{1}{16}$
inch. Some elements, however, might involve only two possibilities with respect to the awarding or withholding of
credit. In checking upon the selection of the proper tool for
laying off the chamfer as the student takes the woodworking
test, full credit would probably be given if he selects the
pencil and chamfer stick furnished him for that purpose and
no credit at all if he chooses to use the marking gauge.

8. *Prepare Set of Directions and Instructions to Be Followed
by the Student.* This set of directions should include:

a. The purpose of the test.

b. Exactly what the student is to do. In some cases the instructor may wish to include in these directions the detailed step-
by-step procedure to be followed by the student. If, however,
the test is designed to measure knowledge of the correct procedure as well as the ability to follow that procedure, the
instructor should include only sufficient details to ensure an
understanding of the job requirement.

c. The major factors to be considered in evaluating the student's performance. The student should know, for instance,
the relative importance to be attached to the time element

and to such factors as accuracy, following the procedure taught, etc.

9. Prepare Set of Directions for Administering the Test. Even if the instructor is to administer the test without the aid of assistants, this is a desirable step. First, preparation of the directions will ensure his thinking through the details involved in administering the test. Second, it is of the utmost importance that the same procedure be followed in administering the test to all students. If assistants are to be used or if the test is to be used by several instructors in the school system, directions to the examiner become a "must."

10. Select or Construct Devices for Testing Student's Completed Work. Many performance tests are so designed and administered that the student's completed work must be tested or measured and evaluated in order to arrive at his total score on the test. Generally the ordinary measuring tools—calipers, micrometers, rules, protractors, etc.—will serve adequately to obtain measures of accuracy. Special but easily constructed gauges can be designed to magnify errors and make closer distinctions between degrees of accuracy. (See Chapter Fourteen for a more complete description of means of testing and evaluating completed projects.)

11. Try Test, and Subject It to Criticism of Others. Rarely does one individual construct a performance test which is free of flaws the first time it is administered. If you are in a position to subject your performance tests to the criticisms of other teachers in your field, you can obtain many helpful suggestions. Make an analysis of the results obtained the first few times each test is administered. Experience in administering a test will enable you to make intelligent adjustments in such items as time limitations, tolerances, and the specific aspects of the student's performance which should be noted and checked.

To illustrate the procedures presented in the preceding paragraphs, the woodwork performance test proposed in the first part of this chapter has been completed and included at this point.

PERFORMANCE TEST: BENCH WOODWORK
Name _____ Date _____
Class _____ Section _____ Instructor _____
Possible Score:
Time <u>100</u> Procedure <u>236</u> Quality of work <u>498</u>   Total <u>834</u>
Student's Score:
Time ____ Procedure ____ Quality of Work ____ Total ____
                    Directions
A. To the Student:
    1. Read these directions carefully. Study the drawing
and specifications for the job you are to perform. Obtain
from your instructor an explanation of all directions which
are not clear to you. Your instructor will tell you when
to start to work.
    2. The purpose of this test is to measure how well you
can perform the basic operations included in the job described below. In completing these operations you are to
follow the procedures demonstrated and taught by your instructor.
    3. The amount of time required, the procedures fol-
lowed, and the quality of the finished work will be considered in evaluating your performance. By completing the
job in 30 minutes or less, you can earn a total of 100
points for time. Five points will be deducted for each
minute required beyond 30. You must stop if you have not
finished by the end of 50 minutes. You can earn 236 points
by following the correct procedure in every detail. You
will receive an additional 498 points if your finished work
meets all standards of accuracy and quality. To obtain the
highest possible score, follow the proper procedures and
work as accurately and rapidly as you can. Plan to finish
the test.
    4. When the instructor tells you to start, proceed as
    follows:
        a. Leave the surfaces marked, "1," "2," and "3" as
           they are. Finish working the stock to dimen-
           sions. Finish surfaces 4, 5, and 6 by planing,
           and number them in the order finished.
        b. Lay out and cut the dado.
        c. Locate and bore the hole.
        d. Lay out, cut, and pare the curve.
        e. Lay out and cut the chamfer.
        f. Turn in your work to your instructor when you
           have finished.
Note: These directions and the drawing and specifications
will be available to you while you take the test.

Specifications: To be made of straight-grain, plain-sawed
yellow poplar, basswood, or white pine. Stock to be
issued: 7/8" x 5 1/16" x 9 15/16", with surfaces 1, 2, and

3 accurately planed true, straight, free of wind, and 90°
to each other. Saw, chisel, and plane cuts to be made to
center of layout lines. No sanding permitted.

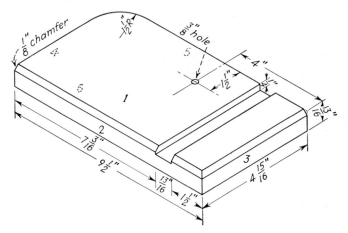

Working drawing and specifications for the test block.

B. <u>To the Examiner</u>:
   1. Prepare the work stations prior to the arrival of
the students. At each station arrange the following in a
uniform and orderly manner:

a. Back saw
b. Set of chisels
c. Set of auger bits
d. Try or combination square
e. Brace
f. Marking gauge
g. Rule
h. Dividers or compass
i. Bench hook
j. Jack plane
k. Knife

l. Hard and soft pencils
m. Chamfer stick
n. T bevel
o. Hammer
p. Mallet
q. A set of directions to
   the student, drawing, and
   specifications
r. A piece of stock as
   required
s. A scrap of the same stock

   2. Instruct the student to study the directions carefully. Ask appropriate questions to make sure that he
understands what to do.
   3. Direct the student to begin work and record the
time. Also record the time at the start and completion of
each major phase of the performance.
   4. As the student works, execute, with as little interference as possible, the appropriate check list.
   5. If the student at any point clearly makes, or is
about to make, an error which will prevent his completing
the test, or a major phase of it, instruct him as to the
proper procedure at that point but allow him no credit, on
the procedure check list, for the specific steps which required your assistance.

RECORD OF TIME CONSUMED AND CREDIT EARNED FOR TIME

Operation	Time Started	Time Completed	Minutes Required
1. Complete squaring of stock			
2. Lay out and cut dado			
3. Locate and bore hole			
4. Lay out, cut, and pare curve			
5. Lay out and cut chamfer			

Total time to the nearest minute _____
Points earned for time _____
(Allow 100 points if work is completed in 30 minutes or
less. Deduct 5 points for each minute over 30.)

PROCEDURE CHECK LIST
(To be executed while student performs.)

Item of Work	Maximum Credit	Credit Earned
I. Completes squaring of stock		
A. Works stock to length as first step . .	5	
1. Stands rule on edge to measure length; keeps rule parallel to edge of stock	2	
2. Measures from 1" mark	2	
3. From edge 2 squares line across face 1.	2	
4. From face 1 squares lines across edges 2 and 5	2	
5. Connects lines across face 6. . . .	2	
6. Makes all lines with knife or hard pencil.	2	
7. Makes light lines and does not retrace	2	
8. To cut, places stock in vise or bench hook with face 1 up	2	
9. Saws from edge 2.	2	
10. Starts saw smoothly	2	

Item of Work	Maximum Credit	Credit Earned
11. Checks alignment of saw	2	
12. Takes long, free strokes.	2	
13. Holds surplus stock and lightens stroke to prevent splitting at finish of cut	2	
14. Saws outside of line but leaves no more than 1/16" for planing	2	
15. To plane end, places stock low in vise with end parallel to bench top	2	
16. Checks and/or adjusts plane, using scrap	2	
17. Takes light, shearing cuts.	2	
18. Exercises proper precautions against splitting edges	2	
19. Planes to center of layout lines; checks.	2	
B. Works stock to width immediately after getting length.	5	
1. Checks setting of marking gauge with rule	2	
2. Gauges light, uniform, continuous lines	2	
3. Gauges lines on both 1 and 6. . . .	2	
4. Places stock low in vise with edge horizontal.	2	
5. Takes heavy cuts to remove surplus.	2	
6. Checks frequently	2	
7. All cuts taken with grain	2	
8. Removes full shaving with last cut.	2	
9. Planes to center of gauged lines. .	2	
C. Works stock to thickness immediately after width	5	
1. Checks setting of marking gauge with rule	2	
2. Lays off thickness on both edges and ends.	2	
3. Places stock either flat on bench between vise dog and bench stop or horizontal in vise.	2	
4. Takes heavy cuts to remove excess stock	2	
5. Reduces cut and planes to center of gauged lines.	2	
6. Checks frequently	2	
7. All cuts taken with grain	2	
Total points for squaring stock	85	

Item of Work	Maximum Credit	Credit Earned
II. Lays out and cuts dado		
1. Measures from <u>end</u> <u>3</u> to locate dado . .	2	
2. Rule on edge parallel to edge of stock. . . . . :	2	
3. Measures from 1" mark.	2	
4. Locates both sides of dado without moving rule.	2	
5. From <u>edge</u> <u>2</u> squares lines across <u>face</u> <u>1</u>.	2	
6. From face 1 squares lines across edges 2 and 5 at each side of dado	2	
7. Uses knife or hard pencil for layout, except for depth lines	2	
8. Gauges depth lines with marking gauge.	2	
9. Checks setting of gauge with rule. . .	2	
10. Locates stock in vise with face 1 horizontal	2	
11. Located dado so as to prevent striking metal with saw	2	
12. Saws inside and to center of lines across face.	2	
13. Saw kerfs made uniform in depth and to center of depth lines.	2	
14. Selects chisel of proper width	2	
15. Chisels with bevel <u>up</u>.	2	
16. Places edge of chisel slightly above depth lines to remove surplus stock. .	2	
17. Chisels from both edges to prevent splitting.	2	
18. Uses <u>wooden</u> <u>mallet</u> to drive chisel . .	2	
19. Pares dado to uniform depth to center of gauged lines.	2	
20. Keeps hands from in front of cutting edge	2	
Total points for laying out and cutting dado. .	40	
III. Locates and bores hole		
1. With rule on edge measures distance from <u>edge</u> <u>2</u> and <u>end</u> <u>3</u>.	2	
2. Measures from 1" mark.	2	
3. With square and pencil lays off light pencil lines whose intersection locates center of whole.	2	
4. Clamps stock in vise horizontally. . .	2	
5. Selects bit of proper size	2	
6. Positions stock to prevent bit from striking metal	2	

Item of Work	Maximum Credit	Credit Earned
7. Starts screw in wood and inspects hole to check location.	2	
8. Holds brace steady and erect	2	
9. Checks alignment	2	
10. Stops bit when screw pierces back side	2	
11. Reverses stock and completes hole from side 6	2	
12. Exercises precaution to prevent splitting as hole is finished	2	
Total points for locating and boring hole . . .	24	

IV. Lays out, cuts, and pares curve		
1. Measures from edge 2 and end 3 to locate center of arc	2	
2. Places rule on edge and measures from 1" mark.	2	
3. With square and pencil lays off light lines whose intersection locates center of arc.	2	
4. Sets and checks dividers or compass. .	2	
5. Scribes light, uniform arc	2	
6. Arc is tangent to end and edge	2	
7. Projects lines from center or measures with rule to determine exact points of tangency	2	
8. Squares lines across end and edge at points of tangency	2	
9. Removes excess stock with saw or with heavy cuts with chisel	2	
10. With 1" chisel, pares curve to center of layout line	2	
11. Keeps bevel up or away from stock. . .	2	
12. Checks for squareness and pares curve until curved edge is square with face 1	2	
13. Keeps hands from in front of cutting edge	2	
Total points for laying out, cutting, and paring curve.	26	

V. Lays out and cuts chamfer		
1. Measures distance from arris to locate chamfer line at one point only	2	
2. Gauges lines by hand or with chamfer stick.	2	

Item of Work	Maximum Credit	Credit Earned
3. Gauges lines with hard pencil, not knife or marking gauge	2	
4. Cuts chamfer along edge first.	2	
5. Takes deep, continuous cuts to remove surplus.	2	
6. Planes with grain.	2	
7. Lightens cut to finish	2	
8. Checks frequently as lines are approached	2	
9. Removes full, uniform shaving on last cut.	2	
10. Places stock low in vise to plane end chamfer.	2	
11. Planes toward chamfered edge	2	
12. Takes shearing cuts.	2	
13. Takes light, continuous cuts to finish	2	

Total points for laying out and cutting chamfer   26

	Maximum Credit	Credit Earned
VI. Demonstrates general competence		
1. Approaches problem deliberately and with confidence	5	
2. Shows evidence at all times of knowing what to do and how to do it	5	
3. Keeps tools orderly arranged.	5	
4. Exercises care in handling tools; permits no cutting edge to strike metal	5	
5. Grasps edge tools by handles, not cutting edges	5	
6. Drops no tools.	5	
7. Keeps hands from in front of cutting edges	5	

Total points for general competence 35

Total points for procedure. 236

QUALITY CHECK LIST
(To be used to record results of evaluation
of completed work.)

I. Measurements and dimensions

Directions:

    1. In checking errors in linear measurements and dimensions, use 1/64" as the unit of measurement.

    2. In checking errors in angular measurement, use 1/2° as the unit of measurement.

3. This check list has been designed to penalize the student: (a) one point for each unit of error made in a direction that will permit correction without spoiling the stock, (b) two points for each unit of error that will not permit correction without spoilage of stock, and (c) two points for each unit of difference between the extremes of a given dimension or measurement. Items of work which bear a penalty of two points per unit of error are marked with an asterisk.

4. In determining penalty for "excess," measure a given student's work at point of greatest distance or at point of largest angle. If the dimension or angle exceeds at no point the specified dimensions or angle the student draws no penalty for this item in the "excess" column.

5. To determine the penalty for "shortage," take measurement at the point of shortest distance or smallest angle. The student draws no penalty in the "shortage" column on items that do not at any point fall under specified dimensions or angles.

6. A double penalty should be given for variations in dimensions. From the measurement taken at the point of greatest distance subtract the measurement taken at the point of shortest distance. Convert the difference to units of error and multiply by two. For example, if the thickness measures 49/64" at the thickest point and 47/64" at the thinnest point the difference is 1/32" (2 units of error) and the total penalty for variation is four.

7. Likewise, subtract the smallest reading from the largest reading for a given angle, convert to units of error, and multiply by two to obtain the penalty for a variation in that angle. If a given angle measures 91° at point of the largest reading and 89 at the point of the smallest, there is a variation of 4 units of error for which the student draws a penalty of 8.

8. Use combination square and bevel protractor for linear and angular measurements.

9. To measure angle of hole, insert a dowel in the hole and measure angle at point of greatest variation.

10. Use template constructed of sheet steel and small numbered drills to check curve.

11. Use surface plate and gauge to test thickness at points other than along ends and edges.

12. Except for thickness as measured with surface plate and gauge, take all measurements from and along or across surfaces 1, 2, and 3.

Measurement	Penalty for Excess		Penalty for Shortage		Penalty for Variation		Credit	
	Maximum	Net	Maximum	Net	Maximum	Net	Maximum	Net
Thickness as measured across ends and edges . .	8		16*		16*		40	
Thickness at points on surface 6. . .	4		8*		8		20	
Width.	8		16*		16*		40	
Length	8		16*		16*		40	
Dado from end 3.	4		4		8*		16	
Width of dado along surface 1.	8*		4		8*		20	
Depth of dado	16*		8		16*		40	
Edge 2 from layout line for hole . . .	4		4		. . .		8	
End 3 from layout line for hole . . .	4		4		. . .		8	
Edge of hole from edge 2. .	4		4		. . .		8	
Edge of hole from end 3 . .	4		4		. . .		8	
End 3 from layout line for center of arc	8*		4		. . .		12	

* Double penalty assessed for variation in dimensions and for errors which cannot be corrected.

Measurement	Penalty for Excess		Penalty for Shortage		Penalty for Variation		Credit	
	Maxi-mum	Net	Maxi-mum	Net	Maxi-mum	Net	Maxi-mum	Net
Edge 2 from layout line for center of arc	8*		4		. . .		12	
Chamfer line on surface 1 from end 3 . .	8*		4		8*		20	
Chamfer line on surface 1 from edge 2. .	8ᵃ		4		8*		20	
Chamfer line on end 3 from surface 1. . .	8*		4		8*		20	
Chamfer line on edge 2 from surface 1	8*		4		8*		20	
Angles formed by sides of dado and sur-face 1	4		8*		8*		20	
Angle formed by side of hole and sur-face 1	16		. . .		. . .		16	
Angle formed by curved edge and surface 1	4		8*		8*		20	
Angle formed by surface 1 and edge 5 . .	4		8*		8*		20	
Angle formed by surface 1 and end 4. . .	4		8*		8*		20	

Total points for compliance with measurements. . . 448

II. Additional evidence of quality of work

<u>Directions</u>:
1. Inspect completed job carefully.
2. Rate the job with respect to each item listed below.
3. Record the appropriate figure to indicate your rating.

Item	Maximum Credit	Credit Earned
1. General appearance of work, expecially smoothness of surfaces 4, 5, and 6	10	
2. Extent to which layout lines are fine and distinct	10	
3. Extent to which stock is free from dents, splits, blemishes, and tool marks.	20	
4. Extent to which all angles are sharp and distinct	10	
Total points.	50	
Total points for quality of completed job . . .	498	

Administering Manipulative-performance Tests

Regardless of how well-constructed a performance test may be, the reliability and validity of results obtained with it remain dependent upon the skill of the examiner who administers the test. The mere fact that a detailed check list has been constructed and specific directions prepared for both the student and examiner will not ensure satisfactory test results. The examiner must be able to bear in mind and look for evidence of application of specific details. (See Chapter Thirteen for specific points on observation.)

In addition to skill in observing the details of performance and in recording the results of the observation, there are other important requirements to be met in administering a performance test. The following are some specific suggestions:

1. If possible, set up a sufficient number of identical stations and make use of assistants necessary to administer the performance test to the entire group to be tested in one class period. The complexity of the operations and the nature of the equipment required will determine the number of students who can be tested at one

time by one instructor. Generally not more than five or six students can be checked at a time. In an hour period an instructor can hardly administer a 12-minute performance test to more than approximately twenty-four students.

2. Make sure that conditions will be the same for each student. Each should have stock of the same quality and working characteristics. Each should have access to tools and equipment of the same kind and condition. There should be nothing at any station which would penalize the particular student assigned to that station.

3. Since the matter of ensuring sufficient difficulty to obtain a significant range of test scores is not generally a problem in constructing performance tests, it is important that tools, materials, and equipment selected for the test be of good quality and in excellent condition. Materials should be of high quality and free of faults which would handicap students. All edge tools should be sharp. All machines and equipment should be carefully checked to make sure that they are in proper condition.

4. Plan profitable activities to occupy the time of students who will be waiting their turn to take the test. These activities should be such that students waiting to take the test will not have an opportunity to do additional studying which may be prompted by the directions to the test. Plan work to be performed by students who will have completed the test early.

5. Carefully read and explain the directions to the entire group. If possible, provide each student with a copy of the directions. Remember that the purposes of the test will determine whether or not the check list will be made available to the students.

6. Do not permit students who have already completed the test to discuss the test with students who are taking or waiting to take the test.

7. Study the check list prior to the administration of the test. Know exactly what to observe and what to record as the student takes the test.

8. If the time element is a factor in the student's score, record his time accurately. As he begins the test, record the exact time; as he finishes, again record the time. The difference in minutes can be computed later.

9. Check all students against the same predetermined standards. As a check against your ability to do this, try filling out a second check list for each of a few students, without reference to the original check list, and then compare the results.

10. If several students are to take the test at one time, arrange the stations to minimize interference. All stations to be supervised by one instructor should be clearly visible from a central point.

11. Evaluate all completed work at one time and by the same predetermined standards.

12. Rather than permit a student to commit an error which would prevent his going on with the test, stop him, give him the instructions necessary to eliminate the difficulty, and allow him to continue. Give him no credit, however, for that part of his performance which required your assistance.

13. After the test has been administered and scored, discuss with the class outstanding strengths and weaknesses noted. Give the students an opportunity to ask questions and clear up any misunderstandings.

SUMMARY

If the development of manipulative skill is one of the objectives for a course, then some means must be devised for measuring and evaluating the extent to which skill has been developed. The performance test is one means of measuring this outcome. It is prepared specifically to measure the student's skill in the performance of selected operations under controlled conditions.

The performance test should be constructed and administered in such a manner as to measure the following important elements of skill:

1. *Speed*—the student's rate of work as compared with a predetermined standard.

2. *Quality*—the precision with which the student works and the extent to which the completed job conforms to prescribed standards.

3. *Procedure*—the extent to which the student follows the accepted method in completing the job and demonstrates his ability to select, care for, and use properly the tools, materials, and equip-

ment required to do the job; his observance of safety precautions; his application of essential facts and principles; and the confidence, deliberation, and self-assurance with which the work is performed.

The following are the major steps involved in the construction of a performance test:

1. Select operations to be incorporated in the performance test.
2. Make a preliminary analysis of each operation selected.
3. Select or design a job which includes the operations selected.
4. Prepare a drawing and/or specifications for the job.
5. List all specific points feasible for testing purposes.
6. Select the specific points to be incorporated in the test.
7. Construct the check list. Usually this will include one section which is to be executed as the student performs and another which is used to record the results of a careful analysis of the student's completed work.
8. Prepare a set of directions to be followed by the student.
9. Prepare a set of directions for administering the test.
10. Select or construct devices for testing the student's completed work.
11. Try out the test, and subject it to the criticism of others.

The performance test, if well prepared and carefully administered, can be used to obtain a highly objective, reliable, and valid measure of the student's ability to perform certain selected operations. It provides a detailed analysis of the student's performance as he makes application of things taught. On the other hand, it has definite limitations and disadvantages. Remember that the mere fact that a given performance test requires actual performance on the part of the student does not necessarily make it a good test. Results are dependent to a great extent upon the manner in which the test is constructed and, especially, upon the training, experience, and skill of the instructor who administers it.

SOME THINGS TO DO AND QUESTIONS TO ANSWER

1. To what extent are the reliability and validity of results obtained with performance tests dependent upon the skill of the person who administers the tests?

2. What factors should be taken into consideration in selecting operations to be incorporated in a performance test? What changes would you suggest in the list of criteria included in this chapter?

3. Describe performance-test situations in which the procedure followed by the student should be given more weight than the quality of the finished job.

4. Prepare a short performance test to measure proficiency in the performance of one or two simple operations selected from one of the practical-arts areas. Have at least five different persons, whom you consider competent to administer the test, observe and score a student's performance and his completed job. Compare the results obtained by the five persons. What are the implications of the results?

5. Aside from the validity of the measurement obtained, what advantages does the performance test have over written tests for the purpose of measuring the student's ability to do manipulative work of a skilled order?

6. Why is it considered unwise to use the performance test as the only means of measuring and evaluating manipulative skills? What other means should be used along with performance tests?

7. How would you check the reliability of a performance test? The validity?

8. Select from the subject-matter area of your own particular interest ten basic operations which might be incorporated in performance tests. Describe jobs into which these operations might be incorporated for testing purposes.

9. How would you obtain group judgments as a basis for weighting various phases of a performance test?

10. What are major difficulties involved in administering performance tests?

SELECTED REFERENCES FOR ADDITIONAL READING

Adkins, Dorothy C., and associates. *Construction and Analysis of Achievement Tests.* Washington, D.C.: Government Printing Office, 1947. Chap. 5.

Brown, Clara M. *Evaluation and Investigation in Home Economics.* New York: F. S. Crofts & Co., 1941. Chap. 8.

Holsinger, James L. "Performance Test—Basic Electricity," *Industrial Arts and Vocational Education,* 36:206–208 (May, 1947).

Hunter, Robert S. "Aptitude Tests for Machine Shops," *Industrial Arts and Vocational Education,* 34:58–63 (February, 1945).

Newkirk, Louis V., and Harry A. Greene. *Tests and Measurements in Industrial Education*. New York: John Wiley & Sons, Inc., 1935. Pp. 116–123, 144–148.

Rosenberger, Homer T. "Testing Occupational Training and Experience," *Educational and Psychological Measurement*, 8:101–115 (1948).

Siro, Einar E. "Performance Tests and Objective Observation," *Industrial Arts and Vocational Education*, 32:162–165 (April, 1943).

CHAPTER
THIRTEEN: OBSERVATION AND
EVALUATION

THERE are certain outcomes of instruction which cannot be adequately measured by either written or performance tests. The finished project and other completed work likewise fail to give the whole story of the individual student's accomplishments and educational growth. To obtain the complete picture of the extent to which changes occur in the student's command of fundamental manipulative skills and in his understanding and ability to apply information relative to materials, tools, and processes, the instructor must observe continually the student's efforts to perform the procedures demonstrated and his attempts to apply the information presented.

The impressions gained by the instructor as he observes the daily performance of students enrolled in courses in which considerable practical work is done constitute, in present practice, one of the most important single considerations and are weighted heavily in the evaluation of achievement and in the assignment of marks in such courses. For evaluating certain outcomes, in practical-arts and vocational industrial courses especially, this is as it should be.

However, a major difficulty lies in the fact that the instructor's impressions of the student's achievement are frequently hazy and nebulous in character and are not based on concrete, objective evidence. Far too many instructors assume that they have an intimate acquaintance with their students' work which automatically provides them with the information and the ability to evaluate readily the progress of each student and to distribute, during the short period of a few minutes normally expended for this purpose, A's, B's, or C's, in such a manner as to assign each student his properly earned mark. Typically, the instructor fails to follow an organized plan for observing student behavior and recording the results of his observations.

If the impressions gained by the instructor as he observes his students at work in a variety of classroom, shop, or laboratory situations are to be considered in evaluating achievement and educational development, observations must be made with that express purpose in mind. For the instructor who proposes to use this technique as a primary means of evaluation there arise such problems as the development of an understanding of the meaning, possibilities, and limitations of observation as a means of evaluation; determining what types of outcomes can be evaluated by this method and what specific elements should be observed in the process; increasing the validity, reliability, and objectivity of observations made and of results obtained; and devising ways of recording and systematizing the results of observation. It is with these and related problems that this chapter is concerned.

Uses and Advantages

Assuming that the instructor has learned to observe objectively, knows precisely what to observe, and follows a workable plan for recording the results of his observations, the observation of the student's daily performance for the purpose of evaluating achievement has the following specific uses and advantages:

1. The observation of the student's daily work as he applies the newly acquired principles and procedures provides a continuous check on the student's achievement. Not only does this close check enable the instructor to remain cognizant of the results of his teaching, to detect and analyze learning difficulties, and to do remedial teaching before undesirable work habits can become established, but the fact that the student is being closely observed

by the instructor will become obvious to that student and thus will, in most cases, serve as an incentive for improvement. The student who knows that his work is receiving the careful attention of the instructor, for the purpose of evaluation, is likely to exert more effort and to make greater improvement than one who knows that his work is never appraised.

2. Observation provides a check on certain important outcomes of instruction without encroaching on instructional time or disrupting training in any way. This is an important consideration. Even though any type of effective test administered has some instructional value, a testing program which consumes as much as 6 or 8 of the 45 hours which might be allotted to a one-semester course should be carefully scrutinized from the standpoint of the time required.

3. The observation of the student's daily performance, if it can be made sufficiently reliable and objective, should result in a more valid measure of the student's ability to use and apply what has been taught than any other measure will provide, the performance test included. In the first place, this technique provides the widest possible sampling of activities to be evaluated. The student's behavior, when observed and evaluated under normal rather than test conditions, provides the most, if not the only, direct measure of certain aspects of his achievement.

4. The time, equipment, and personnel required to administer carefully controlled performance tests make extensive use of them impractical. Observation can be used as a very effective supplement to a few carefully prepared performance tests and written examinations.

5. In addition to the evaluation of such subject-matter outcomes as manipulative skill, care and use of tools and equipment, observance of safety precautions, and the ability to apply previously acquired knowledges and understandings in the solution of concrete problems, observation can be used to evaluate several important concomitant outcomes. Some of these not only defy measurement by written and performance tests but are actually excluded, either at the direction of the instructor, or because of the nature of these outcomes, from the test situation. Such outcomes as ability to get along with people, consideration for others,

initiative, willingness to work, and cooperation can be evaluated only in terms of behavior. In the test situation, none of these traits operates as it would during the course of normal performance in the classroom, shop, and laboratory.

Limitations and Common Faults

The basis of the major limitation associated with observation as a technique of evaluation is inherent not in the fundamental idea itself but in the manner in which observation is frequently used and misused. The major criticism directed at the practice of basing the evaluation of student achievement upon the observation of his daily work during a given course is that this technique relies upon the judgment and opinions of the instructor to the point that the result can be no better than a general, subjective estimate of the extent of progress.

The judgment of the instructor neither can nor should be eliminated. Who is in a better position than the instructor to determine in what respect each student fell below, reached, or exceeded the standards set for him as an individual or for the group? The instructor who has close contacts with his class can become better acquainted with the details of the individual student's performance than anyone else associated with the school. If he cannot evaluate the specific aspects of achievement which are clearly revealed only during class and laboratory periods, no one else can, within practical limitations. The real problem, then, is not one of eliminating the instructor's judgment but that of increasing the validity and objectivity of his observations and evaluations.

Other common faults, no one of which is necessarily inherent in observation as a means of evaluation, are as follows:

1. The instructor's failure to have clearly in mind what to observe.

2. Failure to consider major objectives of the course in determining what to observe.

3. Lack of clearly defined standards. Variation in standards from one instructor to another.

4. Failure to observe. Tendency to observe without paying much attention to the detailed aspects of students' performance.

5. Tendency to give high ratings to students who appear to be

busy without examining critically the quantity and quality of work done.

6. Tendency to let marks previously made by students influence current ratings.

7. Tendency to rate a given student the same on all factors considered.

8. Tendency to give all students in the class approximately the same rating.

9. Attempting to rate students on too many different factors. Trying to use a rating scale which is too elaborate and which calls for closer discrimination than an instructor can actually make.

10. Tendency to base evaluation solely upon either the most recent observations of the student at work or upon one or two striking and vivid instances of exceptionally desirable or undesirable behavior.

11. Tendency to give high ratings to "likable" students—to students who have pleasing personalities—without due regard for the quality and quantity of work performed.

12. Habit of waiting until reports are due and then hurriedly recording marks with little real, honest effort to evaluate achievement.

The common faults enumerated above indicate the scope of the problem which confronts personnel who make use of observation in evaluating student progress. They also identify pitfalls which must be avoided.

Guiding Principles

The instructor who uses effectively the results of observations made in the classroom or laboratory as a major means of evaluation recognizes and applies certain fundamental principles. These may be stated and illustrated as follows:

1. Obtain Prior Knowledge of What to Observe. The instructor must determine in advance what to observe and what types of experiences merit recording. It is a matter of common knowledge that a person who has prior knowledge of what, specifically, he is to look for will observe and remember many more specific features of a situation, picture, activity, or display than can either he or other persons without such prior knowledge. Unless the instructor knows exactly what to observe and has determined in advance the relative importance of the various factors to be considered in evaluating the student's activities, that instructor can make only a rough, subjective estimate of the student's progress. The determining factors in the latter case may be both indefinite and insignificant. He may consider one set of factors in evaluating one student's work and revert to another set for a second student. Without a predetermined list of things to observe and factors to consider, he may evaluate a given student's total achievement on the basis of a limited number of striking incidents which he happens to remember.

2. *Examine General and Specific Objectives to Determine What to Observe.* The major objectives of the school and the specific purposes of the course dictate what should be observed by the instructor. Assume that the school accepts as a major purpose the development of the ability to work cooperatively and amiably with others. Only by observing students in a great variety of situations in which there is an opportunity for cooperative action can instructors or other personnel determine the extent to which this objective is realized. The classroom and laboratory provide many such situations. Instructors should include provisions for recording, for each individual student, on either check list or anecdotal record, instances of student behavior which reveal the extent to which students actually learn to work together cooperatively.

The instructor who accepts as a major objective the development of an appreciation of fine craftsmanship will look for behavior which is indicative of the realization of this objective. Instances in which a student shows respect and admiration for outstanding work performed by other students will be noted. Evidence of the influence of a student's pride in workmanship upon his own work will be sought.

For each of the major objectives of the course, the instructor should have in mind at least, if not on paper, an analysis of the behavior normally expected of students who achieve each of these objectives. In fact, objectives should be stated in this vein. The behavior of a student who achieves on a high level with respect to the "ability to organize and plan his work" might be described as follows:

Prior to formulation of plans, student obtains information necessary to do intelligent planning; plans school activities within framework of limitations imposed by school facilities; considers his own abilities, the time available, equipment and materials accessible, etc., when formulating work plans; shows evidence of knowing precisely what to do first, second, third, etc., before beginning a given job; anticipates and provides for major difficulties; shows evidence of adaptability in that he makes appropriate changes in plans as situation demands.

3. Permit Other Evaluating Devices Used to Influence What Should Be Observed and Recorded. The alert instructor observes, during practical work periods, all aspects of student behavior. Nevertheless, the character and extent of the total program of measurement in effect in his classes will determine in part what particular types of student experiences he should be especially careful to observe and note for purposes of evaluation. If he administers numerous written and performance tests, he may choose to keep a progress chart, on which he records and evaluates the student's performance of the basic operations, but may elect to pay particular attention and give the greatest emphasis to the observation of behavior indicative of the development of certain concomitant outcomes. If observation is to be used as the major if not the only means of measurement, the observations made must encompass all aspects of achievement—the specific subject matter as well as the general outcomes.

4. Devise Method of Recording Results to Conserve Time. While teachers in general would probably agree that the results of observation should be recorded, the time required heads the list of reasons why so many teachers fail to make any record of their observations. Time is an important item. The amount of time required to record the results of observation, however, is by no means as great as is commonly thought. The teacher is prone to assume, for example, that for each of the 100 to 125 students who attend his classes a comment must be entered daily or some type of record made each day. This is not at all necessary. In the first place, check lists can be designed which will keep the amount of writing required to a minimum. Second, the careful selection of instances of student behavior of which a record should be made can reduce the time to a workable minimum. Just as the written test *samples* the specific outcomes, the teacher must select samples of the student's behavior which are representative of his actions. He should make a record of enough instances to establish the pupil's typical pattern of behavior. Beyond that, the teacher should record only the student's actions which show variance from the pattern —changed points of view and other examples of unusual behavior.

5. *Establish and Define Three to Five Levels of Proficiency.* Regardless of the form on which the results of observation will be recorded, it is recommended that three to not more than five levels of proficiency be established for purposes of evaluating the daily performance of students. An alert instructor can learn to identify with reasonably high reliability which of three, four, or five levels of proficiency best fits the performance of each of his students. The difference between any two consecutive levels in a series of five is great enough to keep to a satisfactory minimum the number of errors in classifying students or in rating the various aspects of their achievement. If, however, the range from unsatisfactory work to the best possible performance is divided into fifteen, twenty, or thirty levels, the difference between two consecutive levels of proficiency becomes too small to permit reliable estimates.

Each of the levels of proficiency against which student performance is to be checked should be carefully and concisely described. This description should be formulated in terms of the behavior normally expected at each level of proficiency.

The description of each of the levels of proficiency becomes especially important in situations in which two or more instructors propose to rate the daily performance of students on the basis of a single set of factors. Considerable discussion and much practice will be required to develop a common understanding of the character of performance anticipated under each level of proficiency.

6. *Observe Carefully and Critically.* In order to determine the relative merits of work performed by students, the instructor must observe carefully and critically all aspects of their performance. He must distinguish between students who *appear* to be busy and those whose efforts actually result in worth-while accomplishments.

Typically, the instructor who has not learned to analyze the daily performance of students in the classroom, shop, or laboratory is the one who has made no real, honest effort to observe critically. By thinking through the problem of what to observe, devising a simple means of recording the results of observation, and then deliberately concentrating upon specifics from the beginning of the course, the instructor can promote himself from the ranks of those who merely wait until the time for reporting and then hurriedly rate each student.

7. *Rate Specific Aspects of Achievement Independently.* Teachers are prone to let marks previously made by students influence ratings recorded as the result of observation. In so far as it is possible, each aspect of the student's performance should be evaluated independently. The instructor should purposely avoid reference to previously assigned marks when rating students by observing their daily performance. Although a student who is outstanding in one aspect of achievement is likely to be reasonably high in others, he should not be rated high on one merely because he happens to be high on another.

Frequently instructors fall into the habit of rating a given student the same on all factors to be considered. Rarely would behavior be as consistent as such a marking procedure would indicate. Just as is true with an effective written test, close observation should enable the instructor not only to discriminate between good and poor students but to analyze and to discriminate between the good and poor work or behavior of a given student.

The instructor must be especially careful to guard against the tendency to award unduly high ratings to the performance of "likable" students regardless of the quality of their performance. Give James a high rating opposite "Extent to which he is liked and respected by his fellow students" if he deserves it, but that mark should have no bearing at all on his rating for "Quality of work performed."

8. *Give Appropriate Emphasis to Incidents Observed.* One of the strongest arguments for the practice of keeping a record of observations is the fact that, unless some type of record is kept, the instructor tends to give undue weight to the most recent observations. To be valid, any mark given on the basis of observed be-

havior must be influenced by the student's activities of the entire period for which he is being rated.

There is a tendency to permit one or two noticeable instances of exceptionably good or poor work or of poor discipline to have too much influence on the mark recorded for the student. In rating a student on a given trait, characteristic, or accomplishment, the instructor must consider all items of evidence—all aspects of the student's behavior—which pertain to the outcome being rated. When rating George on the basis of his ability to work cooperatively with others, for example, the teacher must take into consideration not only the fact that two days ago George caused considerable friction when asked to assist with the assembly of a large bookcase but also the fact that except for one other minor incident he has, during the entire course, entered enthusiastically and wholeheartedly into group activities.

Progress Charts

The form used for the purpose of recording the results of observation is of major importance. There have been numerous check lists and rating scales published which may be used effectively for this purpose. Most of these devices are designed for the evaluation of such general outcomes as social sensitivity, creativeness and imagination, emotional stability, and the like. While these are the broad, fundamental outcomes of instruction, we are here concerned primarily with the evaluation of specifics, which for some time to come will probably be measured by teacher-constructed devices.

The progress chart has long been used as a means of recording the results of observation and for the purpose of evaluating the students' achievement with respect to certain outcomes—manipulative skills especially. It is a form of check list.

Progress charts are of two general types. On one will be listed the basic manipulative operations included in the course (see Figure 1). The students' names are arranged on the chart in such a manner as to permit the instructor to check each student against each of the operations listed. On this type of chart provisions may be made for merely indicating what operations the student did or did not perform. Or a system may be employed to show the number of times a given operation is performed. A third possibility is to make provisions for indicating how well or how poorly the student performed each operation. On the second type of progress chart are listed, instead of the basic operations, the jobs or major assignments to be completed by students. Provisions are made either for indicating that a given job was completed or for designating the quality of the work performed by the student in completing it.

Determining What to Evaluate. The most important point to remember in connection with the construction of the progress chart is that it should be designed specifically for the course in which it is to be used. Further, it should be designed by the teacher or teachers of that course. If progress charts are adopted by the entire school system or by a given department, it will be expedient to reproduce blank forms on which individual teachers can enter the names of students and the items against which students are to be checked. Since the items to be entered on the progress chart should be taken directly from the course of study and since the course of study should be changed freely as the situation demands, the practice of printing progress charts, other than in skeleton form, should be discouraged.

One of the controversial issues in connection with the design of progress charts centers in the question of whether jobs (or projects) or operations should be listed on the chart. There is no reason why this problem cannot be readily resolved. What to list on the chart depends entirely upon the manner in which the course is organized and presented. If, for example, the course in question is Industrial Arts Woodworking for senior high school students, in which they will construct only two major projects which together incorporate the seventy-five basic operations included in the course, it becomes quite clear that the operations and not the two projects should be listed on the progress chart. The operations are the constants. They are stable and can be identified. While each of twenty-six students might construct distinctly different pieces of furniture, the operations included will be similar if not the same.

If, on the other hand, the course is Acetylene Welding for tradesmen and taught largely on an exercise basis, the instructor

may choose to list on the progress chart the twenty-eight exercises
or jobs which are to be performed by all students instead of listing
the forty-three basic operations included in the course. In this
case the jobs are little more than exercises, and each includes only
one, two, or three basic operations. All students perform about the
same jobs. The jobs in this instance are specifically assigned and

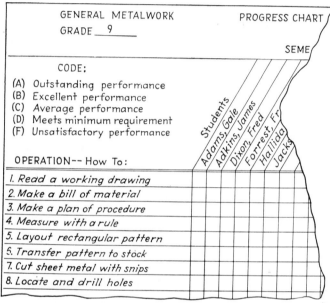

GENERAL METALWORK   PROGRESS CHART

GRADE __9__

SEME

CODE:

(A) Outstanding performance
(B) Excellent performance
(C) Average performance
(D) Meets minimum requirement
(F) Unsatisfactory performance

OPERATION-- How To:

1. Read a working drawing
2. Make a bill of material
3. Make a plan of procedure
4. Measure with a rule
5. Layout rectangular pattern
6. Transfer pattern to stock
7. Cut sheet metal with snips
8. Locate and drill holes

*Fig. 1. An example of a progress chart which makes provisions for checking
student's performance of operations on the basis of five levels of proficiency.*

are of the same stability as the fundamental operations. Either the
operations or the jobs might be listed on the progress chart. If the
method of teaching the course is changed to the extent that students are permitted to select their own projects to be completed,
then the instructor must necessarily list operations on the chart in
order to establish a common basis for evaluation.

Indicating Levels of Proficiency. It has already been suggested
that three to not more than five levels of proficiency should be
used to indicate the quality of the student's performance of each
operation or job listed on the progress chart. Any number of
schemes might be devised for recording the quality of the work

done by students. Figure 1 illustrates one method in which five levels of proficiency are recognized.

If it is considered desirable to keep a record of the number of times a given operation is performed by a student, as well as the quality of his performance, some such code as the following might be employed:

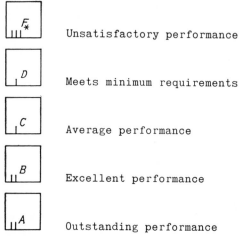

Unsatisfactory performance

Meets minimum requirements

Average performance

Excellent performance

Outstanding performance

*Insert tally marks to indicate total number of times operation is performed by student.

Because the method permits comparisons to be made readily and shows at a glance which students are excelling and which are progressing slowly, many instructors prefer to shade sections of the square to indicate the quality of the student's performance. The code for a system of this type may be as follows:

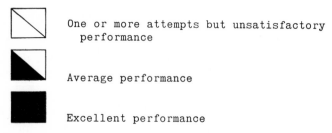

One or more attempts but unsatisfactory performance

Average performance

Excellent performance

Describing Levels of Proficiency. Merely indicating the levels of proficiency to be recognized is not sufficient. The instructor must know precisely what factors, as well as the relative importance to be attached to each, are to be considered in determining the level of proficiency attained by a given student when he performs a particular piece of work. Further, he must have a clear picture of the extent to which work done on each level meets the criteria. A group of instructors might decide, for example, that in evaluating performance the following criteria should be considered and that these criteria should, for most situations, rank in the order listed below:

1. To what extent did the student follow the accepted procedure?

2. What is the quality of the finished work? The student may follow the correct procedure in general and still have the final result of his efforts turn out to be of very poor quality. On the other hand, he may not follow the accepted procedure at all, but his completed work may be of high quality. Both the quality of the finished work and the procedure followed in completing the job should be considered in evaluating his performance.

3. To what extent did he observe all safety precautions? It may be assumed that the student observed all safety precautions if he followed the correct procedure in every detail. Nevertheless, this safety factor is listed separately to lay emphasis upon this important aspect of achievement.

4. To what extent did he use tools and equipment properly?

5. Did he make economical use of time? The speed with which a student works is not as important in a training program as it will be on the job, but it is indicative of the student's probable future rate of work and should be considered in evaluating his performance.

6. How much assistance did he require? After initial instruction, how much help from the instructor, or from other students, did he require in order to complete the work?

With these criteria in mind the various levels of proficiency might be described as shown on the next page.

Remember that these factors and descriptions are only examples. The factors to be considered, and their relative importance, should be determined and descriptions formulated by personnel conducting the course in which they are to be used. The relative impor-

Level of proficiency	*Description*
Unsatisfactory performance	Was unable to follow accepted procedure. Failed to complete work in time available. Failed to observe safety precautions. Misused tools and equipment. Failed to respond to help given.
Meets minimum requirements	Had difficulty in following accepted procedure. Completed work of poor quality. Observed only the most obvious safety precautions. Showed tendency to misuse tools and equipment. Required maximum time to complete work. Required much help.
Average performance	Followed correct procedure in most details. Completed work of average quality. Observed major safety precautions. Used tools and equipment correctly. Worked slowly. Required considerable help.
Excellent performance	Followed accepted procedure in every detail. Completed work of high quality. Observed all safety precautions. Used tools and equipment correctly. Completed operation in average time. Required little help from instructor.
Outstanding performance	Followed prescribed procedure in every detail. Completed work of outstanding quality — accurate and correct. Carefully observed all safety precautions. Used all tools and equipment correctly. Completed operation in minimum length of time. After initial instruction, required no assistance.

tance of factors to be considered and the descriptions of levels of proficiency need not necessarily be the same for all courses or for all phases of a given course.

Advantages, Uses, and Limitations of the Progress Chart. While instructors of practical-arts and vocational subjects have made extensive use of progress charts, there are, with respect to their employment, several issues upon which there is not complete agreement. Some teachers have accepted the progress chart as the most valid means of evaluating achievement and use it exclusively for this purpose. Others question its value. On the positive side, the progress chart has the following uses and advantages.

1. It provides a ready means of keeping a detailed record of the operations performed by each student and of the quality of his performance.

2. The progress chart is especially helpful to the teacher in determining which operations have been learned by the class and which should be practiced further by the students.

3. The progress chart can be adapted for use by the instructor to enable him to keep an accurate record of the operations which he has demonstrated to a given student or groups of students. The

progress chart is especially useful for this purpose in the general shop.

4. The progress chart can be used as one of the strongest possible incentives for greater effort on the part of the student. Students are inclined to put forth effort in order to improve their standing on the progress chart.

5. The fact that the progress chart is displayed in the shop or laboratory tends to make the student keenly aware of what he is to learn in the course. Students tend to plan their work in such a manner as to obtain an opportunity to perform a maximum number of the operations listed.

6. The progress chart likewise stimulates the instructor. When he displays the chart or the analysis chart from which it was derived, he is in a sense promising students that the operations listed on it are the ones which he is going to teach. It is reasonably safe to assume that instructors who display a list of the operations to be taught tend to demonstrate a greater number of the operations included in the course than do teachers who do not use a chart of this type. Students frequently call the instructor's attention to operations which he has overlooked. Rarely would this happen in classes where no progress chart is used.

The major disadvantage of the progress chart centers in the fact that the different levels of proficiency which may be anticipated in connection with each operation or job performed are usually defined in only a general manner. To describe specifically the character of the performance which merits a given rating would result in an awkward and exceedingly cumbersome instrument.

Displaying Progress Charts. The major issue which arises in connection with the use of progress charts is the question of whether the chart should be displayed so that each student can readily see how he and each of the other members of the class have been rated. It is argued that this procedure overstimulates certain students and makes for a type of individual competition which is undesirable. Whether or not the chart results in extreme individual competition depends largely upon the manner in which the instructor handles the situation. It is entirely possible for him to encourage comparisons to the point that certain students, especially the weaker ones, become discouraged. Thus their progress may be retarded. At the same time superior students may attach far too much importance to their high standing in the group.

Instructors frequently assign code numbers to students in an effort to minimize individual competition. Students, however, are prone to reveal their code numbers as they discuss among themselves the achievements of various members of the class. Perhaps the best method of dealing with the problem in trade and other vocational classes is to post the chart with names shown and, through skillful explanations and interpretations, encourage students to compete with their own records. In industrial-arts classes, especially for immature students, the practice of posting progress charts, on which students' names appear and on which the performance of each student is evaluated, should be discouraged. Individual progress records should be kept. There should be no objection in any class, however, to the practice of posting a progress chart on which a record is kept of the specific operations demonstrated to and performed by each student.

Check Lists and Rating Scales

Many of the specific points pertaining to progress charts also apply to the construction and use of check lists and rating scales which might be designed by the instructor for the purpose of evaluating the daily performances of students. The instructor who proposes to use check lists and scales for this purpose should keep in mind two pertinent facts about them. (1) Check lists and scales as generally designed and used tend to be low in reliability. (2) Assuming that the instruments are well constructed, the training and experience of personnel employing them are major factors affecting the reliability of results obtained.

Experience in training instructors to exercise certain supervisory functions over assistant instructors thoroughly convinced the authors of the necessity of providing specific training and experience in the use of check lists to be used in evaluating performance. In conducting a simple experiment to enable instructors to determine for themselves the value of the check list as a means of decreasing the extent of variation from instructor to instructor in evaluating the quality of the same performance, results were obtained which emphasize the importance of training in the use of check lists. As a part of their training, a group of twenty-seven experienced instructors were directed to evaluate each of a series of ten 30-minute demonstrations.[1] The twenty-seven instructors had reviewed thoroughly the principles, techniques, and procedures for giving effective demonstrations. These instructors were directed to evaluate the first, third, fifth, etc., demonstrations by listing the major strengths and weaknesses noted and then recording a numerical mark for each demonstration, the mark to be based upon a 100-point scale with 70 as a critical score. The instructors were directed to evaluate the even-numbered demonstrations by using a detailed check list which they had helped to construct. The total possible points on the check list was also 100, with 70 representing the critical score. After each demonstration was given and evaluated, that particular demonstration was thoroughly discussed. Each instructor had an opportunity to justify his evaluation of the demonstration, point by point.

Table 1. Range and Dispersion of Values Assigned by Twenty-seven Instructors to Five Demonstrations with and Five without the Use of Check Lists

Demonstrations evaluated without use of check list			Demonstrations evaluated by use of check list		
Demonstration no.	Range of values	Standard deviation	Demonstration no.	Range of values	Standard deviation
1	55–90	7.0	2	51–88	8.6
3	65–85	5.1	4	70–91	5.9
5	85–100	3.3	6	78–91	3.2
7	80–100	4.1	8	82–89	1.7
9	80–95	3.7	10	86–92	1.2

Table 1 shows the extent of variation in values assigned the demonstrations. The range and standard deviation of the twenty-seven values recorded for each demonstration are reported. Note that the first attempt at using the check list (demonstration 2) resulted in greater variation in values assigned by the instructors than did their first attempt at evaluating a demonstration without the use of a check list. By comparing notes, discussing standards,

[1] A class under the direction of one of the authors in the Instructor Training Department, Armored School, Fort Knox, Ky., February, 1943.

and receiving instructions as to the meaning and interpretation of items on the check list, and with practice in evaluating demonstrations, the twenty-seven instructors were able to reduce the wide differences in values assigned to demonstrations. Significant improvement was made without the use of a check list. Much greater improvement resulted from use of the check list, however.

Measuring and Evaluating General Outcomes

The progress charts and check lists described in the preceding sections are designed for use in recording the results of observations and in evaluating specific outcomes which have to do with the mastery of subject matter. Instruments of this type must be designed specifically for a given course and preferably by the teachers who are to employ them. Attempts to make progress charts so general that all teachers within a given subject-matter area might be willing to use them will render them valueless. For the areas in which progress charts and check lists of this type might be of value, subject matter neither has nor should become standardized to the point that standardized instruments can be generally employed.

Fortunately, this is not the case in connection with instruments designed for the measurement and evaluation of such general outcomes as social and emotional adjustment, initiative and industry, imagination, dependability, cooperation, attitudes and interests, etc. Considerable research has been conducted in an effort to determine means of measuring these general outcomes. Numerous rating scales, check lists, and inventories—some of which are self-administered—have been standardized. These are designed for use without regard to subject-matter areas. Since, in the opinion of the authors, classroom teachers without special and intensive training in the field of measurement cannot be expected to prepare scales and other rating devices which will compare favorably with the readily available published instruments, no attempt will be made here to describe procedures for their construction. It is strongly recommended that classroom teachers acquaint themselves with the available instruments and that they use these devices in the total measurement program. Some of the references at the end of this chapter contain descriptions of numerous published instruments of this type and include instructions relative to their use and to the interpretation of results obtained.

Anecdotal Records

The *Dictionary of Education* defines the anecdotal record as a "cumulative record consisting of accounts of pertinent, characteristic actions and conversations of an individual as noted and written by the teacher and/or any cooperating officer with whom the individual has had close contact."[2] The anecdotal record as thus defined has been used primarily as a method of recording the results of direct observation of behavior for the purpose of analyzing and evaluating social and emotional adjustment and for obtaining the data necessary to the intelligent planning of a program of activity which might bring about improvement in the personality of the individual pupil. It has been used to some extent by elementary teachers to evaluate pupil growth and by counselors and teachers at all levels in connection with the guidance program.

The following are anecdotes taken from the record kept by a first-grade teacher who uses this technique for obtaining a picture of the personal and social development of individual pupils from the time they enter school:

Name: Nancy R.

September

9th. Appeared to be very unhappy when she came to school the first day. Stood by door of room and refused at first to enter. Upon being questioned said she wanted to be in room with her sister.

10th. Did not enter into games on the playground. Failed to participate in class discussions. When spoken to privately, talked too low to be heard.

13th. Sang song with the group. She has a nice voice. Was not among those pupils who volunteered to sing by themselves or in small groups.

14th. Followed directions very poorly. Her attention span seemed to be very short.

15th. As yet has failed to take part in class discussion. When asked questions, instead of remaining silent she now answers, "I don't know."

20th. She volunteered to bring a knife, fork, and spoon to school. Her group plans to learn to set the table tomorrow.

[2] Carter V. Good (ed.), *Dictionary of Education*. New York: McGraw-Hill Book Company, Inc., 1945, p. 334.

21st. An older girl came in to tell the teacher that Nancy lost the knife and fork she planned to bring to school. Girl reported that, "Nancy asked me to tell you because she did not want to tell her teacher."

22d. Teacher again attempted to start a conversation with Nancy when alone. She turned uneasily and refused to carry on a conversation.

24th. Drew a picture of some things she observed on the excursion but would not share her picture with the group.

27th. Today, for the first time, volunteered to talk to teacher. Told about her sisters and cousins and what they had done over the week end.

28th. Nancy told teacher that her father had run off with another woman and that now her mother and the three children in the family were living in a garage with her uncle.

October

4th. Refused to take part in plans for a culminating activity. Said that she did not want to do anything.

5th. Decided she would like to be in the program.

6th. Told a news story for the first time.

8th. Nancy was excited and enthusiastic about having her picture taken at school. Did not have a pet of her own, so wanted her picture taken with the teacher's dog.

13th. When the culminating program was given for the children in the second grade, Nancy volunteered to tell about the pet of a child who was absent. When the picture of the child and her pet was flashed on the screen, Nancy related with confidence the characteristics of the pet and how to feed and care for it.

It is apparent that such anecdotes as the ones included in the preceding example, which picture in a vivid manner a timid child's adjustment to her first days at school, constitute a valuable record in the hands of a skillful teacher.

Anecdotal records serve very well as evidence in support of the many judgments which must be made by the teacher in evaluating various aspects of the student's adjustment. When kept over a long period of time, the anecdotal record is particularly valuable as a source of data which can be utilized to increase the validity with which rating scales, check lists, and personality inventories can be executed. In filling out rating scales, for example, the instructor frequently finds it quite difficult, without some type of written record, to recall specific instances of behavior which he must have at hand in order to make a valid response to a given item on the instrument.

Anecdotal Records and the Evaluation of Achievement. Teachers of industrial arts and of vocational industrial subjects, because of the unusual opportunities which these fields provide for the observation of students in a variety of work situations, will find the anecdotal record a most useful and effective device.

Entries in the anecdotal record, as it has been commonly used, generally pertain to the concomitant learnings and to general behavior patterns which reflect the personal, social, and emotional adjustments of the individual. This same method of record keeping can be employed to advantage in evaluating the student's achievement—his command of the skills and information included in the course. The anecdotal record as a method of accumulating data of value in connection with the guidance and counseling of individual pupils and in evaluating their over-all adjustment has been adequately treated in several recent publications.[3] The present discussion will be limited, therefore, to the use of anecdotal records for the purpose of evaluating that phase of achievement which has to do with the student's command of the subject.

Just as the instructor feels the need for some type of record of directly observed instances of behavior in evaluating personality development and social and emotional adjustment, he likewise has a need for a record of instances of application and misapplication of the information and skills taught in evaluating the student's daily performance in the shop or laboratory.

Whether the instructor chooses to center his program for the evaluation of the student's performance in the various activities

[3] Among the publications in which these particular uses of the anecdotal record have been described are:

L. L. Jarvie and Mark Ellington, *A Handbook on the Anecdotal Behavior Journal.* Chicago: University of Chicago Press, 1940.

H. H. Remmers and N. L. Gage, *Educational Measurement and Evaluation.* New York: Harper & Brothers, 1943, pp. 377–385.

Arthur E. Traxler, *Techniques of Guidance: Tests, Records, and Counseling in a Guidance Program.* New York: Harper & Brothers, pp. 131–154.

engaged in by the student as he completes a major project or job, or whether he evaluates separately each specific operation performed, he will find that a record of his observations tends to increase the objectivity, reliability, and validity with which he can evaluate the student's daily work. Whether he ultimately makes an abbreviated record of his observations on a progress chart of some type, or whether he chooses to summarize his reactions to the student's performance by executing a check list designed to aid in the evaluation of the work done in completing a major project, the anecdotal record can be used as a primary source of many of the data essential to an intelligent completion of these instruments. Further, the entries in the anecdotal record will serve to remind the instructor of many other instances of performance—errors made, specific instances of exceptionally good work, materials spoiled, etc.—which were not recorded but should be considered in evaluating the student's work.

The following anecdotes, taken from the individual record of a student's performance while enrolled in one of the authors' classes in hand woodwork, illustrate the kinds of observations which might be made and recorded:

Name: Allen S.   Course: Ind. Ed. 181-B

Feb. 9. Failed to present idea for his major problem for the course. Insisted that he cannot think of an object to be constructed which conforms to the general specifications and limitations prescribed and which would be of use to him, his family, or his friends.

Feb. 11. After having failed to decide upon a major problem during the additional time allotted him for that purpose, Allen suggested that the instructor assign him a problem. The table suggested by the instructor was apparently acceptable to him.

Feb. 13. Allen suggested two acceptable changes in the design for his major project, one which would alter the appearance and a second which resulted in an improvement in construction details.

Feb. 18. Especially careful to keep waste to a minimum in getting out stock. Contrary to his plan of procedure, as approved by instructor, Allen starts planing pieces for top of table before squaring stock for legs and rails. Experiences considerable difficulty in adapting normal procedure for squaring stock to solve problem of squaring rails and legs for table. Experiences considerable difficulty in adjusting jack plane.

Feb. 20. Fails to lay off width of all four rails at one setting of marking gauge. Planes one rail $\frac{1}{8}''$ narrower than specified dimension. Rather than discard stock, chooses to decrease other three rails in width and makes appropriate change on drawing.

Feb. 23. Stock squared for rails varied from $- \frac{1}{32}''$ to $+ \frac{1}{16}''$ from specified dimensions for thickness and width, $- \frac{1}{32}''$ to $+ \frac{1}{32}''$ in length. Stock squared for legs varied from $- \frac{1}{32}''$ to $+ \frac{1}{64}''$ in thickness and width; less than $\frac{1}{64}''$ variation in length. One leg and two rails not free of wind. Failed to select best side for face of one rail. Slightly better than average job done in getting surfaces flat and angles 90°.

Feb. 25. Burns chisel slightly in grinding it. Required considerable assistance in whetting chisel. Gauges from wrong side in laying off tenons on one rail.

Feb. 27. Does exceptionally good job in cutting mortises. In one hour of practice, fails to acquire sufficient skill with back saw to cut tenons properly.

From the foregoing excerpts from an anecdotal record in which entries pertain to the work done in completing a major project, it can be seen that this type of record can be used effectively in evaluating the daily performance of students in shop and laboratory situations. A record of this type, together with the instances which a review of the record will enable the instructor to recall, provides a fairly complete picture of that phase of the student's achievement which results from his selection and solution of major shop and laboratory problems.

The preceding example illustrates how the anecdotal record can be adapted to serve as an effective device for the evaluation of achievement. There is no reason why the same record should not include entries pertaining both to social and emotional adjustment and to achievement in the subject-matter area under consideration.

SUMMARY

The impressions gained by the instructor of such subject-matter areas as those represented by the practical-arts and vocational fields, in which provisions are made for a great variety of experiences with tools, materials, and equipment, and in connection with which manipulative skills as well as understandings are developed, constitute an important factor which should be given considerable weight in evaluating achievement. There are certain important evidences of growth which are revealed only during work periods in which students are given an opportunity to make application of information, procedures, and principles taught. This means that the instructor must make careful observations for the expressed purpose of evaluating achievement. His observations must be objective. He must have in mind what to look for and must observe systematically and keep a record of his observations in order to raise his evaluation of growth that occurs to a satisfactory level of reliability and validity.

The following common faults serve to identify pitfalls which must be avoided by the instructor who utilizes the results of his observations in evaluating student progress and in assigning marks:

1. Failure to have clearly in mind what to observe.

2. Failure to consider major objectives of the course in determining what to observe.

3. Lack of clearly defined standards. Variation in standards from one instructor to another.

4. Failure to observe. Tendency to observe without paying much attention to the detailed aspects of student's performance.

5. Tendency to give high ratings to students who appear to be busy without examining critically the quantity and quality of work done.

6. Tendency to let marks previously made by students influence current ratings.

7. Tendency to rate a given student the same on all factors considered.

8. Tendency to give all students in the class approximately the same ratings.

9. Attempting to rate students on too many factors.

10. Tendency to base evaluation solely either upon the most recent observations of the student at work or upon one or two striking and vivid instances of exceptional behavior.

11. Tendency to give high ratings to students who have pleasing personalities without due regard for the quality and quantity of work performed.

12. Habit of waiting until reports are due and then hurriedly

recording marks with little real, honest effort to evaluate achievement.

Many of these weaknesses can be avoided or overcome by examining critically the objectives of the course, outlining the specific types of reactions anticipated, and determining what types of behavior will stand as evidence of the realization of these objectives. The instructor must determine what outcomes can best be measured with the various means at his disposal and list specifically the achievements whose evaluation must rest largely with observation. He must devise a method of recording results of his observations which will not be too time consuming and must establish and define the various levels of proficiency in terms of which evaluations are to be made. He must learn to observe carefully and critically the specific aspects of performance and acquire the habit of rating each independently and with appropriate emphasis.

Progress charts, check lists and rating scales, and anecdotal records are some of the devices which may be used to increase the objectivity, reliability, and validity of the results of observations made by the instructor. It must be remembered, however, that, regardless of how well these are prepared, the results are dependent upon the instructor's skill in employing them.

SOME THINGS TO DO AND QUESTIONS TO ANSWER

1. What are some of the outcomes of instruction which cannot be measured in testing situations but must be evaluated during activity periods?

2. Aside from the use which can be made of the results of observation for purposes of evaluation, why is it important that the instructor be able to observe carefully and critically the performance of students and to keep records of his observations?

3. What are some of the common faults of observation as used for purposes of evaluation?

4. How are the specifics which should be observed by the instructor during practical work periods related to the objectives of the course?

5. Design a simple check list which can be used for recording the results of observations made during practical work periods. Have several

competent persons execute the check list while observing the same student participating in group activities. Compare the results. To what extent are the ratings similar? What are the implications of this simple experiment?

6. How may an instructor improve his ability to judge student performance?

7. How may anecdotal records be used in conjunction with progress charts and check lists?

8. Under what conditions would you recommend that progress charts be displayed in the classroom?

9. Should anecdotal records be accessible to the student? Why? How may these records be used to serve as a basis for a teacher-student conference?

SELECTED REFERENCES FOR ADDITIONAL READING

Brown, Clara M. *Evaluation and Investigation in Home Economics.* New York: F. S. Crofts & Co., 1941. Chap. 8.

Henry, Nelson B. (ed.). *The Measurement of Understanding,* 45th Yearbook, National Society for the Study of Education, Part I. Chicago: University of Chicago Press, 1946. Chaps. 13–16.

Newkirk, Louis V., and Harry A. Greene. *Tests and Measurements in Industrial Education.* New York: John Wiley & Sons, Inc., 1935. Chap. 13.

Remmers, H. H., and N. L. Gage. *Educational Measurement and Evaluation.* New York: Harper & Brothers, 1943. Chap. 16.

Siro, Einar E. "Performance Tests and Objective Observation," *Industrial Arts and Vocational Education,* 32:162–165 (April, 1943).

Smith, Eugene R., and Ralph W. Tyler. *Appraising and Recording Student Progress,* Vol. III of *Adventures in American Education.* New York: Harper & Brothers, 1942.

CHAPTER

FOURTEEN: EVALUATING MAJOR
PROJECTS

CERTAIN teachers may administer neither written nor performance tests. Others may make little or no effort to evaluate the daily performance of students, either by executing check lists and rating scales or by keeping progress charts up to date. Practically all teachers of subjects involving manipulative skills as well as understandings do, however, evaluate the projects and other major jobs completed by their students. The machine-shop instructor evaluates and assigns a mark to a drill-press vise completed by a student. The instructor of mechanical drawing evaluates each major problem solved and each drawing executed. The auto-mechanics instructor evaluates each job performed by the members of his class. The home-economics instructor evaluates each project completed by her students. Each of the projects completed by his students is evaluated by the instructor of a course in woodwork.

Not merely because shop and drawing teachers make wide use of this means of evaluating progress, but because the evaluation of projects has a definite place in the total program of evaluation. and because there is a definite need for improvement in the validity and reliability of procedures in current use, the problem of evaluating major projects is treated here.

While there may not be at hand extensive, objective evidence to substantiate this point, the authors will venture a statement to the effect that the marks assigned to projects completed by students in shop and drawing courses are given far more weight by the teacher in determining final course marks than any other single factor. Further, on the same basis, it can be stated that the mark assigned a given project by the instructor is all too frequently based almost exclusively upon the quality of the finished product with little or no consideration for the designing and planning and for the procedure followed by the student completing the job.

The Function of Projects

Before presenting in some detail a plan for the evaluation of projects in shop and drawing courses and prior to suggesting its place in the total program of measurement and evaluation, let us examine briefly the function of projects in the instructional program.

Frequently, shop teachers are criticized, and justly so, on the basis that they merely have students "make things." The project should be considered as a means to an end. It is a means employed by the teacher to develop certain desirable habits, skills, knowledges, and appreciations. The project serves as a vehicle of instruction. It becomes a problem which tends to aid students in organizing and integrating their experiences as they direct their efforts toward its solution. As contrasted with the exercise, the project, when carefully selected and planned, can be effectively employed to develop and sustain a high degree of interest.

Objectives and the Evaluation of Projects

Assuming that the function of the project as thus conceived is acceptable, the question to what extent the completed project stands as evidence of the realization of stated objectives then arises. As stated earlier, instructors frequently base course marks almost entirely upon the quality of finished products. The fallacy of this procedure comes into sharp focus when one considers the fact that a given student might eventually produce a project of extremely high quality, and yet, in the process of its construction, he might have committed any one or all of the following:

1. Consumed an unjustifiable amount of time in the completion of the project.

2. Asked for and obtained more assistance from the instructor and from his fellow students than any other member of the group.

3. Wasted an undue amount of materials.

4. Performed inaccurate and faulty work which was concealed when the project was assembled.

5. Abused tools and equipment; failed to use them properly.

6. Persistently violated safety rules.

7. Failed to follow the general procedure as initially planned.

8. Failed to accept the challenge to design a project of his own or even select and adapt a design but waited for the instructor to assign him a design to execute.

9. Showed no evidence of having developed an appreciation of good design and skilled workmanship.

10. Failed to learn the related information about tools, materials, and processes which was assigned as a part of his project.

The completed project, then, if taken as it stands, without regard for the designing, the planning, the performance of specific operations and other activities which resulted in its completion, does not provide definite and valid evidence of the student's achievement. It cannot be considered as final and positive evidence of even the one important aspect of achievement with which the quality of the completed project has been considered synonymous: the development of manipulative skill. If, as Selvidge and Fryklund[1] define it, "Skill is a thoroughly established habit of doing a thing in the most economical way," then the behavior exhibited as the student completes a project must be examined along with the concrete results of his efforts. Assuming the development of skill to be the only objective for which projects were completed, the practice of assigning marks solely on the basis of the quality of these completed projects is open to question.

The instructor usually lists several objectives which he hopes to achieve. He plans several types of activities through which these objectives may be realized. The construction of projects or the completion of similar jobs constitutes one of the major activities.

[1] R. W. Selvidge and Verne C. Fryklund, *Principles of Trade and Industrial Teaching*. Peoria, Ill.: Manual Arts Press, 1946, 2d ed., p. 170.

This type of activity may be the major, if not the only, means through which certain objectives are to be achieved. The completion of projects may play a part, along with such activities as reading assignments, class discussions, and field trips, in the realization of other objectives.

Any activity included in the course should be evaluated in terms of the objectives for which that particular activity was planned. For example, the instructor of electricity in the high school program of industrial arts might plan to have students design and construct several small projects in the hope that this work would contribute to the realization of the following objectives:

1. The acquisition of certain elementary, basic skills involving tools and materials used in the electrical field.

2. The development of an understanding of certain principles of electricity and of their application to electrical appliances used in the home.

3. The development of appreciation of good design and craftsmanship as applicable to the construction and especially to the selection of electrical appliances.

The instructor of bench woodwork might designate the following as the objectives which are to be achieved, at least in part, by the planning and execution of projects in the shop:

1. The acquisition of skill in the performance of operations involving the common hand woodworking tools and materials.

2. The ability to design and plan useful objects which can be made by hand from the common cabinet woods and the ability to make and follow a detailed plan of procedure in constructing them.

3. The ability to apply specific knowledge of the characteristics and properties of woodworking materials and tools in the completion of useful objects.

4. The development of an appreciation of good design and fine craftsmanship as applicable to woodwork.

5. The development of pride in individual accomplishment and an interest in shop activities which might lead to the selection of some phase of industrial activity as either an occupation or a hobby.

What to Evaluate

The objectives which the instructor has in mind when he encourages students to plan and construct projects give the clue to what should be evaluated. In evaluating the outcomes which result from this type of activity, he must look for and consider any and all evidence of the realization of these objectives. A part of that evidence is revealed as the student works out or selects and adapts a *design* for the project. Additional evidence comes to light as the student makes a *plan* for its construction. The *execution* of the plan provides still more evidence. The *finished product* reveals other things about the student's performance.

Evidence Revealed during Designing Phase. As the student designs or chooses and adapts a design for his project, the teacher may be able to secure the answers to such questions as the following or to similar ones which the stated objectives may suggest:

1. Did the student choose to construct a project which is useful to him or to his associates?

2. To what extent did he evidence sensitivity to the elements of good design—proportion, balance, mass, weight, texture, color, blends and contrasts, surface and line enrichment, etc.?

3. Is the material selected appropriate?

4. To what extent did he adapt his design to take advantage of the strength, appearance, and working characteristics of the materials selected, and how effectively did he provide for or overcome weaknesses inherent in the material?

5. To what extent is the design his own work?

6. To what extent did he seem to attach importance to the whole problem of selecting or evolving a design of high quality for the project?

7. Was his initial design feasible with respect to (1) his ability, (2) cost, (3) facilities available, (4) time available, and (5) accessibility of materials?

8. Were his sketches and drawings neat and orderly and generally indicative of good workmanship? Did they show sufficient detail?

Evidence Revealed during Planning Stage. The manner in which the student formulates his plans for the construction of the project reflects the extent to which he achieves certain desirable objectives. With respect to his planning activities, the instructor should seek answers to such questions as the following:

1. Did the student obtain the basic information about materials, tools, and processes essential to intelligent planning?

2. To what extent was he able to work out his own plans?

3. Was his plan for the construction of the project orderly and logical? To what extent did the steps of procedure outlined by the student follow in a logical and systematic order?

4. Did he plan in such a manner as to conserve time and materials?

5. Was his bill of materials adequate in terms of his plan?

6. To what extent did he take into consideration in formulating his plan the time, materials, tools, and equipment available?

Evidence Revealed during the Execution Stage. The activities engaged in by the student as he carries out his plan for the completion of each project are especially important to his progress toward course objectives. In connection with the evaluation of the student's execution of his plan, the instructor will need the answers to such questions as the following:

1. To what extent did the student follow the detailed steps of his plan?

2. In how many instances did he have to retrace steps because of failure to follow his plan?

3. In how many instances did the student spoil work or ruin materials because of failure to follow his plan?

4. To what extent did the student follow the approved procedure in performing specific operations?

5. To what extent did he exhibit skill in the use of tools and equipment? Did he exhibit satisfactory progress in the development of skill?

6. Did he observe all safety precautions?

7. Did he select the proper tools for each operation? Did he use them properly?

8. To what extent did he exhibit initiative in revising his plan or working schedule to get around difficulties which arose—lack of a specific tool at a given time, lack of proper materials, etc.? To

what extent was he able to revise his plan of attack to make the most advantageous use of his time?

9. To what extent did the student practice those operations with respect to which he needed additional skill in order to minimize the possibility of spoiling materials or doing a poor job?

10. To what extent did he exhibit an understanding of the limitations and capabilities of tools and materials?

11. In the light of the quality of his performance, how did the total time required to complete the project compare with the amount of time consumed by the average student? Did the student keep busy? Did he use his time profitably? Did he maintain a fair balance between the quality of work performed and the time required to reach the standard which he attempted to meet?

12. How much help from the instructor and from other members of the class was needed?

Evidence Revealed by the Finished Product. In examining the completed project to determine the extent to which it reveals evidence of the realization of the objectives which prompted its construction, such questions as the following might be considered:

1. To what extent is the finished product an embodiment of the original plan? Did the student complete the project as planned?

2. Does the general appearance of the project reflect neat, orderly, and accurate work?

3. How do the actual dimensions of the project compare with those on the drawing? Did the student work to dimensions within reasonable tolerances?

4. How do angular measurements check with those specified?

5. Of what quality is the finish?

6. Were materials used to best advantage? (Grain matched, best sides exposed, etc.)

7. Did the students' interest continue throughout the work on the project?

8. Does the student have a desirable attitude toward the finished product? Does he exhibit pride in accomplishment? Is this justified?

9. Do all joints fit properly? Are all margins uniform; are curved and irregular lines properly executed, etc.?

Means of Evaluating Achievement Resulting from Projects

The project, as contrasted with the exercise, poses for the student a problem whose solution calls for the acquisition of new information and skills and for the integration of these with facts and skills previously learned. The outcomes which result from designing, planning, and completing a project are highly complex. The problem of measuring and evaluating these outcomes is no less complicated. In courses in which individual choices play an important part in the selection of projects, the problem becomes so involved as to render precise measurement in terms of objectives practically impossible. And yet there must be considerable freedom in the selection of projects if individual needs are to be considered and if objectives, as generally stated, are to be achieved.

In many courses the greater portion of the student's time is devoted to activities centering in the designing, planning, and completion of projects. Teachers organize their instructional programs around the project work carried on by the students. The teacher may find it advantageous, from the standpoint of motivation and other elements of good teaching, to organize a major portion of his program of evaluation around these same activities.

For the most part, such an organization for purposes of evaluation requires a combination of techniques already presented. The major emphasis should be on the observation of the student's behavior as he perfects the design, formulates his plan, and completes the project. In addition to the observation and evaluation of his behavior, the physical results of the student's efforts—the final design, the plan formulated, and the finished project—should be checked and evaluated.

In so far as the work performed in connection with projects is concerned, there are several techniques and devices which may be used to increase the objectivity of the instructor's observations and to provide an accurate, detailed record of the results of his observations. Among these are the anecdotal records, progress charts, and check lists and rating scales treated in Chapter Thirteen. Check lists, rating scales, and quality scales may also be devised for the evaluation of the actual design, the student's final plan, and the completed project.

The progress chart on which are listed the specific operations included in the course may be used effectively to keep a record of the operations performed by each student. It may be used to keep a record also of the degree of skill with which the student performed each operation involved in completing a given project. The progress chart does not, however, provide for an evaluation of the over-all procedure followed in completing a project or job. It makes no provision for recording and evaluating the manner in which the operations were grouped and for indicating whether or not the student arranged and performed the operations in the same order as planned. The typical progress chart certainly would make no provisions for reporting and evaluating the proficiency and initiative exhibited by the student when confronted with situations requiring changes in initial plans. Some type of check list or rating scale will be needed to supplement the progress chart. The anecdotal record may be used effectively to accumulate information required to execute these instruments.

The Development and Use of Rating Scales

It is with full realization of the low reliability of the results frequently obtained with check lists and rating scales that a treatment of their development is included and their use is recommended at this point. Even if the reliability cannot be increased beyond that obtained in making purely subjective estimates of the student's achievement without the aid of any instrument, the use of rating scales can be justified on the basis that these instruments do call to the attention of the instructor, and may to the student as well, detailed aspects of the student's achievement. They are thus effective instructional aids.

Further, this presentation of the construction and use of rating scales by-passes, for the following reasons, the statistical processes normally utilized in scaling the items included in them: (1) The various scaling processes are cumbersome and laborious. (2) The application of the necessary statistical procedures would require more training in statistical manipulation that we are here assuming. (3) The individual classroom teacher has not the time required to scale the various items so that statistically the various possible responses will be uniformly spaced. (4) Assuming that

projects will be individually selected or designed by the students
and that plans of procedure will likewise be individually formulated, the construction of rating scales with the amount of detail
that standardization procedures would require is out of the question. (5) The use of a rating device on which numerical values
have been more or less arbitrarily set will enable the teacher to
rate his own students, on the basis of his own standards, about as
reliably as will the use of a standardized scale. Eliminating large
differences in ratings given comparable work by two different
teachers or differences in two independent ratings given the same
work by the same teacher is largely a matter of training in the *use*
of the rating device involved and not the refinement of the instrument.

Constructing Rating Scales

The following are suggestions which should prove helpful to
teachers in constructing rating scales to be used in evaluating the
outcomes which result from the designing, planning, and completion of projects:

1. The more limited and restricted the course, the more specific
can be the rating scales designed for use in the course. To obtain
the specificity which at first glance might appear to be essential, it
would probably be necessary to construct a separate rating device
for each individual project undertaken by the members of the
class. This procedure would be practical only in those situations
in which all the students plan and construct the same projects. In
the more wholesome setup, in which there is considerable freedom
in the selection of projects, the instructor must include in a limited
number of scales, or preferably in one, the points which should
be considered in evaluating the typical projects. Or, in order to
make provisions for the evaluation of the full range of project
activities conducted in the course, the instructor may need to design a separate scale for each of the major types of projects selected by students.

2. Bear in mind that while the work performed by students in
connection with projects may be a major part of the course it is
not the only activity conducted and does not necessarily achieve
or contribute to the realization of all the objectives of the course.

3. To determine what specific items should be incorporated in the scale, first list the specific course objectives to which classwork in the form of projects contributes. With these objectives in mind, make an analysis of the detailed aspects of the work done in designing, planning, and completing projects. This analysis should reveal the specific points to be included in the rating scale.

4. If, as has been assumed here, emphasis is placed upon the designing and planning of projects as well as upon the procedure followed and upon the completed project, these four phases of the work define logical divisions in the rating scale. If projects are assigned and plans of procedure are prepared in advance for the student, the scale would include items relating only to the procedure that is followed by the student and to the completed job itself.

5. If the rating scale is to be used for the purpose of converting evaluations to a numerical basis or to some other quantitative or qualitative form, each item should be designed to permit of numerical ratings. This may be accomplished either through (1) the listing of numerous detailed requirements of approximately the same relative value, with one point being granted for each requirement with which the student complies, or (2) making provisions for choosing among three to five degrees or levels of compliance or quality of results obtained.

6. Remember that, for most projects, the general procedures followed and the skill with which each operation is performed are the most important phase of the whole performance. Therefore, more points should be included in this section of the scale concerned with the execution of the plan than any other. If values are assigned to entries made on a progress chart to indicate the skill with which each operation is performed and if these entries are considered in computing course marks, the procedures followed can readily be weighted appropriately.

7. Generally the same system of indicating values should be used throughout the scale. The relative weight of a given section of the scale can be increased or decreased by adding or eliminating specific items in that section.

The following rating scale is included to illustrate the points enumerated above:

RATING SCALE FOR PROJECTS IN
BENCH WOODWORK COURSE

Name:_____ Course:_____

Project:_____ Score:_____

Instructor:_____ Date:_____

Number of items which do not apply:_____

Directions: Each of the items in this scale is to be
rated, if it applies, on the basis of 4 points for outstanding quality, degree, compliance, or performance,
3 points for better than average, 2 points for average,
1 point for inferior, and 0 for unsatisfactory or failure.
Encircle the appropriate number to indicate your rating.
Draw a horizontal line through the row of numbers opposite
each item which does not apply. Enter the total points
earned under each major phase. Enter the composite total
in the space at the top of this sheet. Also indicate the
number of items which do not apply.

I. Designing Phase: (Total Points____)
   1. To what extent is the project designed or selected of
      value to him or to his associates?   0 1 2 3 4
   2. To what extent did he evidence sensitivity to the
      elements of good design?
      A. Size, proportion, balance, relative weight of
         parts?   0 1 2 3 4
      B. Texture, color, surface and line enrichment?
                                                 0 1 2 3 4
   3. Is the material selected appropriate?   0 1 2 3 4
   4. To what extent did he adapt his design to take ad-
      vantage of the strength, appearance, and working
      characteristics of materials specified?   0 1 2 3 4
   5. To what extent is the design his own work?
                                                 0 1 2 3 4
   6. To what extent did he seem to attach importance to
      the problem of selecting or evolving a design of
      high quality?   0 1 2 3 4
   7. Was his initial design feasible with respect to:
      A. His ability and the time available?   0 1 2 3 4
      B. Cost, materials, and facilities available?
                                                 0 1 2 3 4
   8. To what extent were his sketches and drawings orderly
      and generally indicative of good workmanship?
                                                 0 1 2 3 4
II. Planning Stage: (Total Points____)
   1. Did he obtain the basic information about tools,
      materials, and processes essential to intelligent
      planning?   0 1 2 3 4
   2. To what extent did he prepare his own plan of pro-
      cedure?   0 1 2 3 4
   3. To what extent was his plan orderly and logical?
                                                 0 1 2 3 4

4. Did he plan in such a manner as to conserve time and
   materials?   0 1 2 3 4
5. Was his bill of materials adequate in terms of his
   plan?   0 1 2 3 4
6. To what extent did he take into consideration the
   time, materials, equipment, and tools available?
                                                 0 1 2 3 4

III. Execution Stage: (Total Points____)
   1. To what extent did he follow the detailed steps of
      his plan?   0 1 2 3 4
   2. To what extent did he avoid having to do work over
      because of failure to follow his plan?   0 1 2 3 4
   3. To what extent did he refrain from spoiling ma-
      terials by working accurately and care-
      fully?   0 1 2 3 4
   4. To what extent did he follow approved procedures in
      performing specific operations?   0 1 2 3 4
   5. To what extent did he exhibit skill in the use of:
      A. Layout and measuring tools?   0 1 2 3 4
      B. Cutting edge tools?   0 1 2 3 4
      C. Boring and drilling tools?   0 1 2 3 4
   6. To what extent did he show improvement in the use of
      tools?   0 1 2 3 4
   7. Did he select the proper tool for each operation?
                                                 0 1 2 3 4
   8. Did he use all tools properly?   0 1 2 3 4
   9. To what extent did he exhibit initiative in revising
      his plan as required by changing conditions?
                                                 0 1 2 3 4
   10. Did he practice difficult operations to minimize
       material spoilage and poor workmanship?   0 1 2 3 4
   11. To what extent did he keep profitably employed?
       Busy?   0 1 2 3 4
   12. To what extent did he maintain a fair balance
       between quality of work performed and time consumed?
                                                 0 1 2 3 4
   13. To what extent was he able to do his own work with-
       out assistance from instructor or other students?
                                                 0 1 2 3 4

IV. Completed Project: (Total Points____)
   1. To what extent is finished product an embodiment of
      original plan?   0 1 2 3 4
   2. Does the general appearance of the project reflect
      neat, orderly work?   0 1 2 3 4
   3. Are the dimensions of the actual project the same as
      those on the drawing, within reasonable tolerances?
                                                 0 1 2 3 4
   4. How do angular measurements check with those
      specified?   0 1 2 3 4
   5. Of what quality is the finish?   0 1 2 3 4

6. To what extent were materials used to best advantage?
                                                       0 1 2 3 4
7. Do all joints fit properly?   0 1 2 3 4
8. Are all margins uniform, curved and irregular lines
   properly executed, etc.?   0 1 2 3 4

Using Rating Scales

In executing the rating scale, the instructor will need to take advantage of all information about the student's work which is at his disposal.

He should study the student's drawings and specifications along with his plan of procedure prior to issuing stock for the project. The preliminary phases of the rating scale can be executed at this time. If he keeps anecdotal records, the information recorded will be of value, especially in completing the section pertaining to procedures followed by the student in executing his plan. The progress chart will provide him with additional information relative to the procedure followed and the degree of skill exhibited.

In evaluating the completed project, the instructor should inspect it carefully in every detail. He should have at hand, in addition to the rating scale, a list of factors and specific points to be considered in evaluating that particular project. He should make use also of any measuring instruments—such as rules, calipers, squares, and straightedges—which may enable him to determine accuracy and quality of work. Further, he may design and construct special devices which will magnify errors to the point that finer discriminations can be made.

For the same reasons that statistical procedures for refining rating scales have not been included, the construction and validation of quality scales have not been treated. However, the instructor may find that by selecting samples of work of various qualities and using them as a basis for his evaluations he can improve and refine his judgments of the quality of projects.

Two other techniques for increasing the reliability of ratings are as follows: (1) Rate a series of projects, using a project rating scale, one copy for each project. After a lapse of two or three days, rate the same projects, using the same scale but not referring to the original ratings until all projects are rated twice. Compare the results obtained on the two independent ratings. (2) After each of a series of similar projects has been rated, but before totaling the scores, place the projects in descending order as evaluated on the basis of a list of factors which should be considered in evaluating the projects. Then total the scores on the rating scales used originally. Arrange the scales in descending order, and compare this arrangement with the order in which the actual projects have been arranged on the basis of an independent rating.

SUMMARY

The project is not an end but rather a means of developing certain desirable habits, skills, attitudes, and appreciations. It is a vehicle of instruction. The completed project does not constitute adequate evidence of the extent to which these objectives have been realized. Even though the finished job may be outstanding in terms of predetermined criteria for its evaluation, the student who completed it may have consumed an undue amount of time in doing so. He may have received considerable assistance from others, done faulty work which was later concealed, abused tools and equipment, violated any number of safety rules, failed to follow a definite plan, failed to take the initiative in selecting or designing the project, failed to develop the habits and appreciations anticipated, and failed to learn and apply the facts and principles related to the planning and completion of the job. Not only, then, must the instructor look for evidence of growth and achievement in the completed project itself, but he should consider and evaluate the activities of the student as he selects or adapts a design for the project, as he makes plans for its completion, and as he executes his plans.

Among the techniques and devices which can be used to systematize observations and aid in the evaluation of the activities related to projects are anecdotal records, progress charts, check lists, and rating scales. Whether or not their utilization increases the objectivity, reliability, and validity with which evaluations are made is dependent upon the skill of the observer.

SOME THINGS TO DO AND QUESTIONS TO ANSWER

1. What is the function of projects as utilized in courses involving both understandings and manipulative skills?

2. What is the importance, from the standpoint of the realization of the objectives of the course, of completed projects as compared with the educational gains made by the student as he designs, plans, and completes the project? Evaluate this statement: "Too much emphasis is placed upon the evaluation of the completed project, not enough upon the activities incidental to its completion."

3. Design a check list, and outline the procedure to be followed in evaluating a given completed project. Have several persons who are competent to do so evaluate this project by executing check lists and following the procedure recommended. What are the range and dispersion of the results? What are the implications of this elementary experiment?

4. What are quality scales? How would you proceed to develop a quality scale which might be used to evaluate specific projects in your field of work? Under what conditions would you recommend their development and use? Under what conditions would their utilization be impractical?

5. Evaluate and assign numerical marks to a series of twelve or more projects of the same general type by using a check list designed for that purpose. Record the results. Then arrange the projects in order from best to poorest without reference to the results obtained with the check list. To what extent are the projects now arranged in the same order as their rank order on the basis of scores obtained with the check list? What are the implications?

6. Select a given practical-arts course generally offered on the junior high school level, and state the objectives for this course. Explain the relative weights that you would attach to the designing, planning, and execution phases of project work and to the finished projects completed in this course. Show how changes in emphasis in the statement of objectives would influence the weighting of these four aspects of the project work of the course.

SELECTED REFERENCES FOR ADDITIONAL READING

Adkins, Dorothy C., and associates. *Construction and Analysis of Achievement Tests.* Washington, D.C.: Government Printing Office, 1947. Chap. 5.

Brown, Clara M. *Evaluation and Investigation in Home Economics.* New York: F. S. Crofts & Co., 1941. Chap. 8.

Caveny, C. C., and J. A. Weichelt. "Reliability of Shop Grades," *Industrial Arts and Vocational Education,* 34:233–236 (June, 1945).

Dolan, Frank D., and Harold A. Schulz. "Machine Shop Grading in the Ordnance School," *Industrial Arts and Vocational Education,* 33:403–405 (December, 1944).

Henry, Nelson B. (ed.). *The Measurement of Understanding,* 45th Yearbook, National Society for the Study of Education, Part I. Chicago: University of Chicago Press, 1946. Chaps. 13–16.

Newkirk, Louis V., and Harry A. Greene. *Tests and Measurements in Industrial Education.* New York: John Wiley & Sons, Inc., 1935. Chap. 12.

Remmers, H. H., and N. L. Gage. *Educational Measurement and Evaluation.* New York: Harper & Brothers, 1943. Chap. 11.

CHAPTER

FIFTEEN: INTERPRETING TEST DATA
AND ASSIGNING MARKS

A PERSISTENT problem in teaching is that related to marks and marking.

Whether letter marks, or "Satisfactory" and "Unsatisfactory," or a detailed descriptive check list is used to report the student's progress, the instructor must determine the extent that each student has achieved with respect to each of the factors upon which the report is based. Should Joe receive "A" or "B"? Should Martha be checked "Satisfactory" or "Unsatisfactory"? Should "Pass" or "Failure" be recorded for Bill? Does James's work merit a strong favorable comment opposite "Command of Fundamental Processes," or should an unfavorable remark be recorded? Each of these questions involves the same basic problem—that is, how to determine, on the basis of their achievement, what students have placed themselves in what particular categories.

It is to this and related problems that the current chapter is devoted. Among the specific questions to be considered are: (1) How should the school's policy concerning the type of report to submit be determined? (2) What factors should affect marks? (3) What is a valid basis for establishing standards? (4) How may test data be grouped and treated to facilitate their interpretation?

Determining the School's Policy Relative to Types of Report

While teachers serve on committees appointed by school administrators to study the problem of marking and to make recommendations concerning its solution, the individual teacher generally does not determine independently what type of achievement report he will make or when and how frequently it will be submitted. Through cooperative action, teachers and administrators establish a policy with respect to marking. The teacher is expected to follow that policy until it is modified.

The school's policy usually centers in one or a combination of two or more of the following methods of reporting achievement in a given course:

1. Letter marks based on a four-, five-, or six-letter system.

2. Numerical marks based on a 100-point scale (percentage).

3. Rank order, a number assigned to each student to indicate where he stands—first, second, third, etc.—in the group in which he has been included for the purpose of reporting achievement.

4. Percentile rank, a number assigned to each student which indicates what percentage of his group he has excelled.

5. Descriptive reports written by the teacher.

6. Descriptive reports completed by executing a prepared check list.

7. A report involving only two categories, "Pass" and "Failure" or "Satisfactory" and "Unsatisfactory."

Factors Affecting Marks

The need for uniformity with reference to the type of report to be used within a given school is obvious. Equally obvious is the necessity of having all teachers in the system base marks upon the same set of factors, in so far as differences in subject-matter areas will permit. Each factor to be considered should be given the same relative value by all teachers of a given course taught in the school system. Further, until schools of the same type throughout the country adopt uniform marking policies, the school mark is likely to remain relatively low in validity.

The factors considered by instructors in assigning marks are as numerous and as varied as are the types of reports in current use.

In addition to actual achievement in the subject, teachers frequently consider and give weight to such factors as (1) willingness to work, industry, effort, and initiative; (2) the extent to which the student improved during the course; (3) regularity of attendance; (4) personality factors; (5) deportment; (6) innate ability; and (7) the student's attitude toward the course and toward the instructor. In regard to the factors which *should* be considered in assigning marks, the authors accept the point of view (which is held by an increasingly large number of specialists in the field of measurement) thus clearly expressed by Ross:[1]

> . . . *In determining any mark, only those factors should be taken into account which afford evidence of the degree to which the pupil has attained the objectives set up for that particular course.* Daily work, class tests, oral quizzes, and final examinations are examples of factors which indicate progress toward the objectives of instruction. In other words they may be accepted as evidence of scholarship. Attendance, effort, attitude, conduct, and the like, on the other hand, should receive no direct consideration, since indirectly and automatically they affect the pupil's test scores anyway.

Many teachers will object to leaving out of consideration such factors as the pupils' attitude, effort, conduct in the class, and various personality traits. These are certainly important and should be taken into account some way. But if only one mark is given, it should be a mark in *scholarship,* and not a hodgepodge of miscellaneous items.

As Ross points out, this certainly does not mean that such items as personality factors, attitude, and effort should not be incorporated in some type of report to be made available to all teachers and guidance personnel directly concerned with the pupil's educational and social growth. It does mean that factors of this type cannot be reduced to a numerical basis (for the same reason that dollars and horses cannot be added to obtain a meaningful number) and incorporated in a mark that will be interpreted as an index of the student's mastery of the subject.

The results obtained through the employment of certain devices and techniques planned to measure achievement, then, be-

---

[1] C. C. Ross, *Measurement in Today's Schools.* New York: Prentice-Hall, Inc., 1947, 2d ed., p. 405.

come the basic factors which should be considered in assigning achievement marks. For the course in which the direct subject-matter objectives center in the development of manipulative skills as well as understandings, the results to be considered might include:

1. Scores on quizzes and short written tests.
2. Scores on performance tests.
3. Scores on comprehensive tests and term or final examinations.
4. Data pertaining to the students' daily performance in the classroom, shop, or laboratory—data recorded on certain observation check lists and progress charts.
5. Marks on completed projects.
6. Marks on written assignments, special reports, etc.

The relative values to be assigned to each measure to be considered in computing periodic or final course marks again become a problem requiring the cooperative action of school administrators and the teachers concerned. While the combined judgments of all teachers to be affected may not be any more valid than the judgment of a single member of the group who has made a special study of the problem of evaluating achievement, the decision to use a set of cooperatively assigned values will probably be more readily accepted and followed than any other.

After a careful consideration and a thorough discussion of the merits of the various measures by the teachers and administrators concerned, the group will probably bring to light and agree to observe, in assigning relative values, such guideposts as the following:

1. Objective measures which can be expressed and recorded numerically should be given more weight than subjective measures whose validity is dependent upon the teacher's ability to remember details for an extended period of time.
2. Comprehensive examinations should be given more weight than short quizzes which are administered primarily for instructional purposes.
3. While extremely important, work done outside of class and work on a cooperative enterprise within the class should generally be given less weight, because of the indeterminate amount of as-

sistance which may have been obtained, than individual performance during the regular class period.

4. The relative amount of time devoted to the acquisition of informational content and to the development of manipulative skill is probably as valid as any other basis for weighting measures of the two types of outcomes.

5. As a general rule, no one measure, except perhaps the quite comprehensive and completely validated final examination, should be given a weight sufficient to spell failure for a student who "falls down on" this measure, regardless of how high his scores may be on other measures to be considered.

Determining Standards

Along with the problem of determining the type of report to be used and of selecting the various measures to be considered in assigning marks belongs the question of the establishment of a satisfactory set of standards in terms of which marks may be assigned. Traditionally, achievement has been reported as though it were an absolute quantity. The student received a given percentage score, which was by no means an absolute measure, however. It was indeed relative, dependent in part upon the difficulty of the test and how "hard" the teacher graded.

The problem of setting standards is relatively simple in highly specialized training programs designed to teach students to perform only a few specific operations. For instance, competent personnel can come to agreement as to the number of words that an army radio operator must be able to send and receive per minute in order to perform effectively. The problem becomes extremely difficult and involved, however, in programs in which the student's total achievement is made up of a large number of knowledges and skills.

There are two basic principles which should be considered before attempting to work out a system for establishing standards and for assigning marks in a program in which proficiency is dependent upon mastery of a large number of knowledges and skills. First a standard should be set which is based on what a large number of students have been able to accomplish. Second the procedure for assigning marks should take into consideration the fact that tests and other measuring devices vary greatly in difficulty. Experience shows that the difficulty of tests cannot be controlled accurately unless revisions are made upon the basis of a thorough analysis of a large number of test papers.

Recognizing the futility, as well as the undesirability, of attempting to establish absolute standards in terms of which the achievement of all students can be evaluated, educators have turned deliberately to some type of relative basis for the assignment of marks. There are several possibilities. In establishing policy, the school may elect to adopt one or more of the following bases for the assignment of marks:

1. Norms on standardized tests.

2. The student's current achievement as compared with his past record.

3. His command of the subject at the end of the course as compared with his status at the beginning of the course—the extent of his improvement.

4. The student's achievement as compared with his intelligence or aptitude for the type of work covered in the course.

5. The student's achievement as compared with the achievement of other members of his class.

6. The student's achievement as compared with the members of other current classes and with members of previous classes that completed the same course.

Statistical Treatment of Test Data

From the preceding discussion it is obvious that there is an almost unlimited number of combinations of specific policies which might be adopted by a given school system in establishing its own pattern for the assignment of marks. Regardless of what pattern is established, individual teachers must be able to interpret test data, not only for the purpose of assigning marks, but in order to fulfill other purposes of testing as well. Intelligent interpretation is dependent not only upon an understanding of the possibilities and limitations of measuring devices but upon the ability to systematize data and to make comparisons within and between groups of test scores.

While the systematic treatment of test data for the purpose of interpreting them and using them as a basis for assigning marks necessarily involves some use of elementary statistical procedures, there is no real justification for the typical instructor's attitude toward the procedures and techniques required.

With the expressed purpose of reviewing for some readers the minimum essentials and for others of presenting a few elementary techniques which can be readily applied, the authors have included the following brief treatment of methods of handling test data. It is hoped that this brief introduction will serve to motivate teachers who have not as yet seen fit to make use of statistical analyses of test data to the point that they will utilize the most precise methods that their busy schedules will permit.

Determining Rank Order

Determining rank order simply involves listing the scores in order from the highest to the lowest score in the series. The high score receives the rank of 1, the next highest 2, and so on. When there is a small number of students in the class, this can be done easily by arranging the individual test papers or answer sheets so that the highest score appears on top with the remaining papers in descending order.

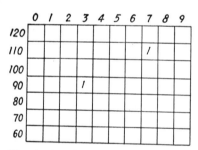

Fig. 1. A tally chart conveniently arranged for placing a large series of scores in descending order.

If the number of papers exceeds twenty or twenty-five, it will probably be easier to tally the scores on a simple chart than to shuffle and reshuffle the papers. For illustrative purposes let us assume that for a particular test you know the high score is around 125 and the low score is in the 60's. Some such tally chart as the one shown in Figure 1 provides a ready means of arranging the scores in descending order. Let us suppose that the first paper happened to have a score of 93. For this score a tally mark would be made in the 90 line and in column 3. A score of 117 would be tallied opposite 110 and 7.

When the papers have been arranged from high to low or the scores have been tallied on the chart, the scores can be written in descending order. Rank orders would then be assigned as in the following example:

Score	Rank order
126	1
117	2
114	3
102	4
93	5
88	6
85	7
71	8
69	9
61	10

In the case of tie scores the procedure is the same except that the assigned rank is the average of the ranks displaced by the tie scores. An easy means of accomplishing this is to rank the scores in descending order, including tie scores. Then list a tentative rank for each score as in the following illustration:

Score	Tentative rank	Assigned rank
62	1	1
59	2 ⎫ Average	2.5
59	3 ⎭	2.5
57	4	4
56	5	5
55	6 ⎫	7
55	7 ⎬ Average	7
55	8 ⎭	7
54	9 ⎫ Average	9.5
54	10 ⎭	9.5

The assigned rank for tied scores becomes the average of the tentative ranks that are affected. If this simple procedure is followed it will be found useful in minimizing the chances of careless errors.

Another suggestion might be considered at this point. If a particular test has been given to previous classes, you may want to establish a second rank-order group on the basis of all persons who have taken the test. Very often this will make possible some useful and interesting comparisons, and the total grouping can be utilized in each of the succeeding steps described below. This is especially helpful in small classes, where it is sometimes difficult to determine the relative positions of particular individuals. By comparing test results with those of previous classes it is possible to obtain a better idea of just where the various students stand. Individual test scores will tend to have more meaning when related to the achievement of several classes. If we know that a student ranked third in a group of 125, we have a good indication of how he compares with other students. If we only know that among 8 students he ranked third, we have no idea whether he is likely to rank third in a larger group or whether he will rank fifth from the bottom.

Uses and Limitations of Rank Order. As a means of comparing scores within a group, rank order is a simple, readily obtained measure which has some value. It is widely used.

There are two major disadvantages associated with rank order.

1. The first is psychological. Many educators feel that the use of rank order tends to overemphasize individual competition even to a greater extent than the practice of assigning letter marks.

2. The second limitation centers in the fact that rank order fails to indicate the extent or amount of difference in the achievement of students who are compared. For example, consider the rank order of the following scores:

	Score	*Rank order*
Difference	96	1 ⎱ Difference of 1
of 1 point	95	2 ⎰ in rank order
Difference	94	3 ⎱ Difference of 1
of 13 points	81	4 ⎰ in rank order
	80	5

While there is a difference of 1 between scores 95 and 96 and also a difference of 1 in their rank order, there is a difference of 13 between scores 81 and 94 but still only a difference of 1 in their rank order. A change of one or two points in a student's score may mean a drastic change in his standing in the class, while a change of several points in another student's score may not alter his relative rank. To illustrate, assume that the following scores were made on an English test.

Student	Score	Rank order	Student	Score	Rank order
A	107	1	A	107	1
B	104	2	C	103	$3\frac{1}{2}$
C	103	$4\frac{1}{2}$	D	103	$3\frac{1}{2}$
D	103	$4\frac{1}{2}$	E	103	$3\frac{1}{2}$
E	103	$4\frac{1}{2}$	F	103	$3\frac{1}{2}$
F	103	$4\frac{1}{2}$	B	102	6
G	101	7	G	95	7
H	94	8	H	94	8

If student B makes a score of 102 instead of the 104 that he obtained, his rank falls from 2 to 6. On the other hand, student G can drop from 101 to 95 without changing his relative order in the group.

How to Arrange Scores in a Frequency Distribution

Test scores alone have little meaning. For example, if a student received a score of 63 on a test, what does this mean? He may appear to have a low score. Actually the test may have been so difficult that no student received a higher score. It may be that the best possible score he could have attained was 65. In such a case he may be considered to have done well. Because so many meanings may be applied to a single score when no other information is given, it becomes necessary to provide additional facts that will aid in correctly interpreting the score. One of the first steps in such a treatment is to place the scores in a frequency distribution.

A frequency distribution shows how the scores are distributed and how many times each score appears. This not only gives a picture of the distribution but prepares the scores for ready calculation of several important statistical measures. The arrangement of scores in a frequency distribution, together with the techniques presented on succeeding pages, can be accomplished by following a definite series of steps.

1. Frequency Distribution with Step Intervals of 1. When the range of the scores is small, they may be arranged into a frequency distribution with step intervals of 1. As an example consider the following 29 test scores:

82, 87, 83, 80, 83, 86, 89, 85, 81, 83, 82, 86, 84, 83, 80, 85, 87, 83, 81, 84, 86, 87, 85, 83, 85, 87, 81, 84, 87

The highest score is 89 and the lowest is 80.

The first step in placing these scores in a frequency distribution is to arrange vertically and in descending order all possible scores from 89 to 80. These possible scores are the class intervals of the frequency distribution.

After arranging the class intervals of the frequency distribution, it is necessary to tally the scores. This is done by placing a short vertical line (1) after each interval as the score is read from the original list of scores. Every fifth score is indicated with a cross tally mark. The tally marks are then totaled and placed in a frequency column. The number of times a score occurs is called the frequency, and the column of numbers showing the frequency of each score is headed with the small letter f. The tallying of the raw scores previously presented has been completed in Table 1.

When the frequencies are added, the total (N) obtained should check with the original number of scores. The entire solution appears in Table 1.

Table 1. Illustration of the Method of Tallying Scores and of Indicating Frequencies in a Frequency Distribution

	Possible scores	Tally marks	f
Highest score.......	89	1	1
	88		0
	87	⊥⊦⊦⊤	5
	86	111	3
	85	1111	4
	84	111	3
	83	⊥⊦⊦⊤ 1	6
	82	11	2
	81	111	3
Lowest score.......	80	11	2
			N = 29

2. Frequency Distribution with Step Intervals Greater than 1. Step intervals of 1 are inconvenient and have little meaning when used with large groups of scores that are well scattered. It is usually necessary to construct the distribution with step intervals of more than 1. For example, if the scores on a test range from 32 to

136, they may be recorded by listing the numbers from 32 to 136 in a column and by placing a tally mark for each score in the group. It is obvious that the distribution would be unwieldy. The method used to shorten and simplify such a distribution is to bunch or combine the scores into groups. This makes it possible to arrange the scores in a convenient and workable form.

The first step in grouping the scores is to select the appropriate step or class interval. The number of class intervals depends on the range of the test scores. There is no fixed or set rule governing the number of intervals of a frequency distribution, although for ordinary purposes 10 to 20 intervals are used. For example, in the series of scores mentioned above (32 to 136), the range is 104 (136 — 32 = 104). If the scores were placed in intervals of 1, the distribution would have 105 intervals. If they were placed in intervals of 2, there would be 53 intervals; by fours, there would be 27 intervals; by fives, 21 intervals; by tens, 11 intervals; by twenties, 6 intervals. In this case it would ordinarily be best to choose the class interval of 10. It is usually considered good practice to select, from among those which can be used, the interval which works the most conveniently. Class intervals of 5 and 10 are considered convenient and are used more often than any other size.[2]

After the interval size has been selected, the class intervals are arranged vertically from high to low (see Table 2). The tally marks are then placed in the table and totaled in the frequency column as was done for the distribution with step intervals of 1. The frequency column (*f*) is then totaled.

To illustrate the preceding points, let us assume that the following are test scores to be arranged in a frequency distribution table:

80, 80, 61, 63, 58, 55, 71, 68, 73, 63, 55, 68, 76, 71, 69, 68, 65, 78, 80, 74, 88, 80, 66, 63, 58, 68, 54, 71, 78, 63, 55, 68, 70, 71, 69, 68, 65, 78, 80, 74, 92, 97, 50, 49, 46, 44, 93

The steps involved are as follows:
1. Locate the highest and the lowest scores (97 and 44).
2. Determine the range (97 — 44 = 53).

[2] The reader should keep in mind that the experienced statistical worker will often use more refined techniques than those described in this chapter.

3. Determine appropriate interval size ($53 \div 5 = 10+$; a class interval of 5 will result in more than 10 intervals but less than 20).

4. Determine the limits of the intervals, and arrange them vertically.

5. Tally the scores.

6. Total the number of scores in each interval, and record in f column.

7. Total the frequency column.

Table 2 illustrates this entire procedure.

Table 2. Example of a Frequency Distribution with Class Interval of 5

Interval	Tally Marks	f
95–99	1	1
90–94	11	2
85–89	1	1
80–84	̶H̶H̶	5
75–79	1111	4
70–74	̶H̶H̶ 111	8
65–69	̶H̶H̶ ̶H̶H̶ 1	11
60–64	̶H̶H̶	5
55–59	̶H̶H̶	5
50–54	11	2
45–49	11	2
40–44	1	1
		$N = 47$

Interval Mid-point. If further treatment of the scores is desired, it is also necessary to know how to locate the mid-point of a specific step interval. This is the point exactly in the middle of the step interval. It is found by adding half the interval size to the lower limit of the interval. For example, the mid-point of the step interval 65–69 would be 67.5. The reason it is 67.5 and not 67 becomes clear if we remember that the top extreme of the interval is 69.99+, or up to but not including 70. The location of the interval mid-point is shown graphically in Figure 2.

The Mean and How to Calculate It

The mean is one statistical measure which is useful in describing how a class performed as compared with other groups or how an individual's achievement compares with that of other members of his own group. The mean is the common, or arithmetic, average—the most widely understood of the various types of averages, or measures of central tendency.

The most direct way to obtain the mean of a series of scores is to add the scores and divide their sum by the number of scores. When the number of scores is large and other statistical measures also must be computed, time can be saved by grouping the scores in a frequency-distribution table. It is then possible to estimate where the mean falls and by simple calculations correct the error to obtain the actual calculated mean.

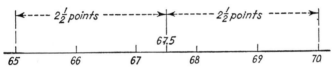

Fig. 2. Graphic illustration of the mid-point of the interval 65–69.

The procedure for computing the mean from a frequency-distribution table may be illustrated by a typical problem. This is called the "assumed-mean" method. Assume that the following numbers represent test scores:

54, 92, 7, 98, 56, 48, 86, 59, 32, 39, 26, 18, 41, 73, 64, 39, 16, 58, 70, 61, 50, 11, 71, 36, 37, 28, 78, 47, 10, 74, 66, 59, 68, 72, 56, 44, 33, 67, 79, 51, 34, 76, 65, 54, 38

The steps in calculating the mean for this series of scores are as follows:

1. Place the scores in a frequency distribution. The range is from 7 to 98, or 91 points. If an interval size of 10 and a top interval of 90–99 are used, the frequency distribution shown in Table 3 is the result. The scores have been tallied, the tally marks have been summed up, and the f column has been added.

2. By inspection select the interval in which it is assumed that the mean will fall. The interval in which it falls is called the "midinterval." In this case it appears that the mean might fall in the interval 50–59. Mark it as indicated in Table 3. (Any interval may be selected, but by selecting the one in which the mean might fall the calculations will be less complex.) Draw a line above and below this interval to mark it clearly.

3. Determine the mid-point of the interval selected in step 2. This mid-point is the *assumed mean,* in this case 55 (one-half of the distance between 50 and 59.99).

Table 3. Setting Up a Frequency Distribution Is the First Step in Determining the Mean by the "Assumed-mean" Method

Interval	Tally Marks	f
90–99	11	2
80–89	1	1
70–79	‖‖‖ 111	8
60–69	‖‖‖ 1	6
50–59	‖‖‖ 1111	9
40–49	1111	4
30–39	‖‖‖ 111	8
20–29	11	2
10–19	1111	4
0– 9	1	1
		N = 45

4. Record deviation values for each interval. Each interval is assigned a deviation value on the basis of its distance from the mid-interval. The mid-interval has a deviation value of 0 as may

Table 4. Deviation Values Are Assigned to the Intervals

Interval	Tally marks	f	d
90–99	11	2	4
80–89	1	1	3
70–79	‖‖‖ 111	8	2
60–69	‖‖‖ 1	6	1
50–59	‖‖‖ 1111	9	0
40–49	1111	4	−1
30–39	‖‖‖ 111	8	−2
20–29	11	2	−3
10–19	1111	4	−4
0– 9	1	1	−5
		N = 45	

be noted in the column headed "*d*" in Table 4. The interval above the mid-interval is one interval away; therefore we say it has a deviation of 1, and the figure 1 is placed in the *d* column. The second interval above the mid-interval has a deviation value of 2, the third interval 3, and so on. In like manner the intervals below the mid-interval are assigned deviations *except that a minus sign precedes each number* because the intervals are below the mid-interval.

5. Multiply the frequency opposite each interval by the deviation value of the interval ($f \times d$), and record the product. In the interval 90–99, the frequency of 2 is multiplied by its deviation of 4. The result is 8. This is done for each frequency and deviation, and the results are placed in a column headed "fd," as shown in Table 5. Be sure to maintain plus and minus signs.

Table 5. The "*f*" and "*d*" Values Are Multiplied to Form an "*fd*" Column

Interval	Tally marks	f	d	fd
90–99	11	2	4	8
80–89	1	1	3	3
70–79	⊥⊥⊤ 111	8	2	16
60–69	⊥⊥⊤ 1	6	1	6 (+33)
50–59	⊥⊥⊤ 1111	9	0	0
40–49	1111	4	−1	− 4
30–39	⊥⊥⊤ 111	8	−2	−16
20–29	11	2	−3	− 6
10–19	1111	4	−4	−16
0– 9	1	1	−5	− 5 (−47)
		N = 45		Σfd = −14

6. The next step is to add the *fd*'s algebraically. This is done by first adding the plus values, then adding the minus values, and finally adding algebraically the two totals obtained. In this case, when the plus values are added we get +33. For the minus values we get —47. Adding these two we obtain the sum —14 (—47 + 33 = —14). This total, —14, is called the sum of the *fd*'s and is written Σ*fd* (capital sigma is the symbol which means "the sum of").

7. The preliminary calculations are now completed, and it is possible to find the mean by substituting in the following formula:

$$M = AM + \frac{\Sigma fd}{N} \times i$$

1. AM is the assumed mean, or the mid-point of the interval which has the zero deviation (55).
2. Σfd is computed by adding the "fd" column algebraically (—14).
3. N is the number of scores (45).
4. i is the interval size (10).

Substituting in the formula, the equation is solved in the following manner:

$$M = AM + \frac{\Sigma fd}{N} \times i$$

$$M = 55 + \frac{-14}{45} \times 10$$

$$M = 55 - \frac{140}{45}$$

$$M = 55 - 3.11$$

$$M = 51.89$$

The steps necessary to compute the mean may be summarized as follows:

1. Place the scores in a frequency distribution.
2. Select the mid-interval.
3. Assign the deviations.
4. Multiply each frequency by its deviation value, and total the fd column.
5. Compute Σfd.
6. Substitute in the formula.
7. Solve the formula.

The Median and How to Compute It

The median is a second measure of central tendency, or average, which is commonly used. It is a point above which 50 per cent of the cases fall and below which the other 50 per cent fall. If 44 is the median of a given series of scores, then 50 per cent of the scores are greater than 44 and 50 per cent are lower.

When test papers are arranged in order from the highest score to the lowest, a rough median may be found by locating the middle paper. If there are 37 test scores arranged in order, the score on the nineteenth will be the rough median or, more correctly, the mid-score. In case the number of test scores is even, the average of the two middle scores is taken as the rough median. If, for example, the eighteenth and nineteenth scores in a series of 36 scores are 90 and 96, the rough median or mid-score is their average, 93.

The true median is a point, not a given score, and is usually calculated from a frequency distribution. To illustrate, consider the following series of test scores:

52, 60, 57, 46, 41, 56, 57, 58, 59, 64, 66, 56, 55, 55, 54, 50, 49, 43, 47, 48, 51, 53, 54, 56, 61, 58, 65, 58, 60, 60, 56, 55, 43, 44, 53, 50, 52, 55, 57, 54, 57

1. The first step in calculating the median is to place the scores in a frequency distribution as was done in computing the mean. The range in this case is from 41 to 66, and an interval size of 3 is used to tally the test scores in the frequency distribution shown in Table 6.

Table 6. A Frequency Distribution Is Made and the Frequencies Are Added Cumulatively to Complete the First and Second Steps in Computing the Median

Interval	Tally marks	f	cf
66–68	1	1	42
63–65	11	2	41
60–62	1111	4	39
57–59	JHHT 111	8	35
54–56	JHHT JHHT 11	12	27
51–53	JHHT	5	15
48–50	1111	4	10
45–47	11	2	6
42–44	111	3	4
39–41	1	1	1
		$N = 42$	

2. Add the frequencies cumulatively, starting at the bottom and recording opposite each interval the sum of the number of scores included in that interval and in all intervals below it. In Table 6 this has been recorded in the column headed "*cf.*" The frequency of the lowest interval is 1. The 3 cases in the second interval from the bottom are added to the 1 in the lowest interval to account for

the 4 appearing in the *cf* column opposite the interval 42–44. This number is increased by 2—the number of cases in the next interval—to obtain the 6 recorded opposite the interval 45–47, and so on.

3. Locate the interval in which the median falls. This is done by dividing *N* by 2 and inspecting the *cf* column to determine in what interval the mid-score occurs. One-half of 42 is 21. Going up

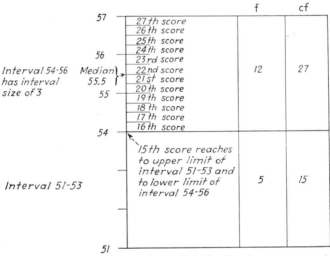

Fig. 3. Graphic illustration of the theoretical distribution of scores within the interval.

the *cf* column, we see that the twenty-first score falls in the interval 54–56.

4. Add to the lower limit of the interval in which the median falls the proportionate amount of this interval which is used to reach the exact point of the median. In performing this step, it is assumed that the scores within the interval consume equal distances on a vertical scale. This is illustrated graphically in Figure 3. In the example, 15 scores were consumed to reach the upper limit of the interval 51–53. There are 12 cases in the interval 54–56. Six of these $(21 - 15 = 6)$ are required to get us just past the twenty-first $(^N\!/_2)$ case. Therefore six-twelfths, or exactly one-half, of the interval is used to reach the point located when $^N\!/_2$ cases are passed. The lower limit of the interval in which the median

falls is 54. The interval size is 3. One-half of 3 added to 54 is 55.5, the calculated median.

The steps in computing the median may be summarized as follows:

1. Place the scores in a frequency distribution.
2. Add the scores cumulatively.
3. Locate the interval in which the median falls.
4. Add to the lower limit of the interval in which the median falls the proportionate amount of the interval required to reach the point just beyond the mid-score.

The above procedure for computing the median is the same as that required to clear the following formula for the median:

$$Md = L + \frac{\frac{1}{2}N - fb}{f} \times i$$

where L = lower limit of interval containing point desired
N = number of cases
fb = cumulative frequency below interval containing point desired
f = frequency in interval containing point desired
i = size of interval in frequency-distribution table

Comparison of the Mean and Median

Frequently, for purposes of interpreting data and in assigning marks, you as an instructor will need to determine whether the mean or the median should be calculated and reported. Each has its advantages and disadvantages as revealed by the following comparison:

1. The mean is affected greatly by extreme scores, while the median is not. The influence of extreme scores upon the mean is illustrated by the "teeter-totter" in Figure 4.

2. While the median is not influenced by extreme scores, in cases where there are gaps in the distribution it may be changed drastically by adding one score to the series. For example, in the following series of scores the median is 39:

28 36 37 39 63 64 78
Median

Add a score of 65 to the series, and the rough median becomes 51.

$$28 \quad 36 \quad 37 \quad 39 \quad 63 \quad 64 \quad 65 \quad 78$$

Median: 51

(mid-point between 39 and 63)

3. The mean is more commonly understood than the median.
4. The median is easier to compute than the mean.

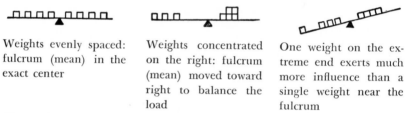

Weights evenly spaced: fulcrum (mean) in the exact center

Weights concentrated on the right: fulcrum (mean) moved toward right to balance the load

One weight on the extreme end exerts much more influence than a single weight near the fulcrum

Fig. 4. The "teeter-totter" helps to explain the influence of extreme scores on the mean.

Quartiles, Deciles, and Percentiles

Except for the proportion of the number of scores falling below the point desired, these measures are computed in the same manner as the median. They are interpreted similarly. Whereas the

Table 7. Frequency Distribution Arranged to Illustrate the Calculation of the Median, Quartiles, and Percentiles

Interval	f	cf
95–99	1	25
90–94	2	24
85–89	5	22
80–84	5	17
75–79	4	12
70–74	3	8
65–69	2	5
60–64	2	3
55–59	1	1
	$N = 25$	

median is a point above and below which the two halves of the distribution fall, quartiles divide the distribution into four equal parts. The first quartile, written Q_1, is a point below which 25 per

cent of the cases fall and above which the remaining 75 per cent
fall. Q_2 is the same as the median. Q_3 is the point which separates
the upper 25 per cent from the lower 75 per cent. *Deciles* divide
the distribution into tenths, while *percentiles* divide it into hun-
dredths. The first decile is the same as the 10th percentile; the
25th percentile is the same as Q_1; the 50th percentile is the same as
the median; etc.

Assume that, for purposes of interpreting the scores tabulated
in Table 7, the median, Q_1, Q_3, and the 70th percentile are desired. The frequencies have been added cumulatively.

To find the median, we follow the same procedure as before or
substitute in the formula

$$Md = L + \frac{\frac{1}{2}N - fb}{f} \times i$$

$\frac{1}{2}N = 12\frac{1}{2}$
   $L = 80$, the lower limit of the interval in which the median
     falls
 $fb = 12$, the number of scores below this interval
  $f = 5$, the number of scores in the interval
  $i = 5$, the size of the interval
Substituting in the formula, we have

$$Md = 80 + \frac{12\frac{1}{2} - 12}{5} \times 5 = 80.5$$

To find Q_1 or the 25th percentile, the formula is modified as
follows:

$$Q_1 = L + \frac{\frac{1}{4}N - fb}{f} \times i$$

The data in Table 7 give the symbols in the formula the following
values:

$\frac{1}{4}N = 6\frac{1}{4}$
   $L = 70$, the lower limit of the interval in which Q_1 falls
 $fb = 5$, the number of scores below this interval
  $f = 3$, the number of scores in the interval
  $i = 5$

Substituting in the formula, we have

$$Q_1 = 70 + \frac{6\frac{1}{4} - 5}{3} \times 5 = 72.08$$

To determine Q_3, $\frac{3}{4}N$ is used in the formula. The symbols have the following values in this case:

$$\frac{3}{4}N = 18\frac{3}{4}$$
$$L = 85$$
$$fb = 17$$
$$f = 5$$
$$i = 5$$

Substituting, we find that

$$Q_3 = 85 + \frac{18\frac{3}{4} - 17}{5} \times 5 = 86.75$$

To determine the 70th percentile $\frac{70N}{100}$ is used in the formula. The symbols now have the following values:

$$\frac{70}{100}N = 17.5$$
$$L = 85$$
$$fb = 17$$
$$f = 5$$
$$i = 5$$

Substituting,

$$P_{70} = 85 + \frac{17.5 - 17}{5} \times 5 = 85.5$$

Percentile Graphs

When all the percentiles for a distribution have been computed, they may be shown in the form of a percentile graph. The percentile rank (P.R.) for each score can be plotted on graph paper. If the distribution is normal, the line connecting the several percentile ranks will appear as in Table 8. When this method is used, it is necessary to compute the percentile rank for each of the scores in the distribution. For a large distribution this is a laborious task.

A simpler method is to construct a percentile curve (cumulative-frequency curve). In this method it is necessary only to find the percentile of the *lower limit* of each interval. These points are then connected by a continuous line. The curve derived by this technique will not be as accurate as that obtained by computing each P.R., but for ordinary test data it will be entirely adequate. The illustrations, in Tables 8 and 9, show the appearance of a percentile graph for a normal and a skewed distribution, respectively.

Procedure for Constructing Percentile Graphs

The percentile curve is plotted by locating the value of the lower limit of each class interval of the frequency distribution and then connecting these points to form the graph. Refer to Table 8 as each of the following steps is explained.

Table 8. Percentile Graph for a Normal Distribution

Intervals	0 10 20 30 40 50 60 70 80 90	Intervals	f	cf	Per-cent
95 – 100		95 –100	2	80	100.0
90 – 94		90 – 94	4	78	97.5
85 – 89		85 – 89	7	74	92.5
80 – 84		80 – 84	11	67	83.8
75 – 79		75 – 79	16	56	70.0
70 – 74		70 – 74	16	40	50.0
65 – 69		65 – 69	11	24	30.0
60 – 64		60 – 64	7	13	16.2
55 – 59		55 – 59	4	6	7.5
50 – 54	A	50 – 54	2	2	2.5

0 10 20 30 40 50 60 70 80 90 100
Percentiles

1. Write in the class intervals at the left of a sheet of graph paper. Copy these from the frequency distribution that has been made. Space the intervals in such a manner as to make the over-all height of the graph approximately $4\frac{1}{2}$ inches, or about three-fourths of the width of the completed graph. For convenience, the intervals can also be written on the right, as shown in Tables 8 and 9. Number the vertical lines 0, 10, 20, etc., to represent every 10th percentile.

2. Enter the frequencies directly from the frequency distribution. Compute the cumulative frequency (cf) and the cumulative percentages. Put these in three columns to the right of the inter-

vals, as shown. Head the columns "*f*," "*cf*," and "*per cent*." The per cent values are found by dividing each *cf* value by *N* (80 in the example).

3. Plot the theoretical 0 and 100 percentiles. The theoretical 0 percentile is the lower limit of the bottom class interval. The 100 percentile falls at the top of the top interval.

4. Plot the points that represent the position of the lower limit of each class interval. Use the cumulative-percentage column at the right, and determine the position on each horizontal line. For example, the lowest interval (50–54) contains 2.5 per cent of the cases. The 0 percentile has already been located. Count over 2.5 percentiles on the base line, and place a mark above this point and on the base line of the next highest interval or the line dividing the first two intervals (as at *A* in Table 8). For the interval 55–59 the point would be placed above the 7.5 percentile and on the base line of the interval 60–64. Continue this process for each of the intervals. You will then have a point on each horizontal line.

5. Connect these points with a curved line. If the distribution is near normal, the curve will approximate that shown in Table 8. If the distribution is skewed, the curve may not be symmetrical. It may take the shape of the curve shown in Table 9, which has been smoothed to aid interpretation. The smoothing can be justified only if one considers the sample from which the data are taken as being representative of a larger group.

When the curve is completed, it is possible to determine the percentile rank of any score in the distribution and also the score which is necessary in order to attain any percentile rank. For example, a person receiving a score of 76 on this particular test would receive an approximate percentile rank of 52. The dotted line in Table 8 illustrates the procedure to be followed in determining the percentile rank of the score of 76. From the score 76 on the vertical scale project a horizontal line until it cuts the percentile curve, and drop a perpendicular line to the percentile scale on the base line. Use the reverse procedure to find the score for a given percentile.

There are certain limitations that must be kept in mind in using percentiles. It will be remembered that in a normal group the scores tend to cluster about the mean of the distributions. This will mean that the range of values of the scores between the 45th and 50th percentiles is much less than the range of values between the 90th and 95th percentiles.

Table 9. Percentile Graph Made from Test Scores in a Skewed Distribution

Intervals	f	cf	Per-cent
95 – 100	13	136	100.0
90 – 94	15	123	90.4
85 – 89	21	108	79.4
80 – 84	15	87	63.9
75 – 79	16	72	52.9
70 – 74	16	56	41.2
65 – 69	6	40	29.4
60 – 64	6	34	25.0
55 – 59	3	28	20.6
50 – 54	7	25	18.4
45 – 49	8	18	13.2
40 – 44	4	10	7.3
35 – 39	2	6	4.4
30 – 34	1	4	2.9
25 – 29	1	3	2.2
20 – 24	1	2	1.5
15 – 19	1	1	.7

Percentiles

The Standard Deviation and How to Compute It

While the mean and the median indicate how scores tend to cluster, they tell nothing about the scatter, or spread, of raw scores. Fifty is the mean score of 49, 50, and 51. Fifty is also the mean of 10 and 90. In interpreting test data and in assigning marks, there is a definite need not only for measures which reveal average accomplishment but also for a measure which will indicate the extent to which scores vary from a central point. The range gives us some idea about the scatter. The *standard deviation* is a measure which has far more meaning. It is defined as the *square* root of the *mean of the squares of the deviations* of a series of numbers from their mean. A short series of numbers can be utilized to illustrate its mathematical meaning.

For example, consider the following numbers:

2,   4,   6,   8,   10

Their mean is 6. Each number varies from 6 as follows:

10 deviates from 6 a distance of   4.

8 deviates from 6 a distance of   2.

6 deviates from 6 a distance of   0.

4 deviates from 6 a distance of —2.

2 deviates from 6 a distance of —4.

Square each of these deviation values, and we have: 16, 4, 0, 4, and 16. The sum of this series is 40. This is the sum of the squares of the deviations of the numbers from their mean. Divide 40 by 5 to get the mean of the squares (8). The square root of 8 (2.8+) is the standard deviation of the series 2, 4, 6, 8, and 10. The small Greek letter sigma (σ) is used as the symbol for this measure.

You will recall that the mean may be computed by arranging scores in a frequency distribution, assuming the mean to be the mid-point of a given interval, and then correcting for the error. After the mean has been computed in this manner, only one additional step is required to obtain values from this same frequency distribution which can be substituted in a formula for the standard deviation. In computing the mean the following steps were taken:

1. Arrange scores in a frequency distribution.

2. Select the mid-interval.

3. Assign the deviation values.

4. Multiply each frequency by its deviation value, and add algebraically the fd column to obtain Σfd.

5. Substitute in the formula, and solve.

With the exception of solving the formula, these steps have been taken in Table 10.

Since the standard deviation is the *square root* of the *mean* of the *squares* of the deviations of a series of numbers from their mean, the one additional step required is to square the deviations. This has been done in Table 10 by multiplying the fd values by the d values ($d \times fd = fd^2$), and the results have been recorded under the fd^2 column. For example, in the interval 90–94, the fd value is 4, and the d value is 2. Their product, 8, is recorded in the fd^2 column.

Table 10. Frequency Distribution Arranged for the Purpose of Computing the Mean and the Standard Deviation

Interval	f	d	fd	fd²
95–99	1	3	3	9
90–94	2	2	4	8
85–89	5	1	5	5
80–84	5	0	0	0
75–79	4	−1	−4	4
70–74	3	−2	−6	12
65–69	2	−3	−6	18
60–64	2	−4	−8	32
55–59	1	−5	−5	25
	N = 25		$\Sigma fd = -17$	$\Sigma fd^2 = 113$

The table now contains all the data needed to find both the mean and the standard deviation. Substituting in the formula $M = AM + (\Sigma fd/N) \times i$, we find the mean to be 79.1. To obtain the standard deviation we may substitute in the formula

$$\sigma = i \sqrt{\frac{\Sigma fd^2}{N} - \left(\frac{\Sigma fd}{N}\right)^2}$$

where σ = standard deviation
i = size of the interval
N = number of scores
Σfd^2 = sum of the fd^2 column
Σfd = algebraic sum of the fd column
Clearing the formula, we get

$$\sigma = 5 \sqrt{\frac{113}{25} - \left(\frac{17}{25}\right)^2} = 10.1$$

The steps in finding the standard deviation may be summarized as follows:

1. Place the scores in a frequency distribution.
2. Assign deviations.
3. Multiply each interval's deviation value by its frequency, and add the products algebraically to obtain Σfd.
4. Multiply the fd value of each interval by its d value, and add to obtain Σfd^2.
5. Substitute in the formula, and solve.

Uses and Limitations of the Standard Deviation. As a measure of dispersion, or scatter. the standard deviation has certain distinctive uses and limitations. The following points clarify its meaning and uses and point out some of its limitations.

1. Whereas the range shows the distance between the highest and the lowest score in a series, the standard deviation is a measure which shows the extent to which scores are grouped about the mean.

2. Extremely high and low scores influence the standard deviation to an even greater extent than is true of the mean. Remember that the deviations are *squared* during the process of calculating the standard deviation. A score which lies 16 units from the mean exerts 4 times as much influence on the standard deviation as one only 8 units away.

3. In addition to its many other uses the standard deviation can be employed effectively in establishing standard scores and for assigning letter marks.

Assigning Letter Marks

The preceding sections have been devoted to a discussion of (1) the importance of determining marking policies through cooperative action of the school's faculty, (2) the factors which should affect marks, (3) the types of reports which might be submitted, and (4) statistical procedures which are helpful in interpreting test data. The specific problem of assigning letter marks is the subject of this section.

One of the major reasons given for the measurement of achievement is to obtain data which might serve as a basis for the assignment of marks and reporting progress. In assigning marks and reporting achievement there has been for the last quarter of a century a noticeable trend, especially in the elementary grades, toward the use of some type of descriptive report to serve either as a substitute for or supplement to the letter mark. Many teachers are still confronted, however, with the problem of distributing A's, B's, C's, D's, and F's in such a manner as to assign each student a mark in keeping with his actual achievement.

Some teachers do not attempt to assign letter marks until all the test results are accumulated for a given marking period. If letter marks are to be assigned at the end of a given interval or at the end of the semester, however, letter marks should also be assigned for each major test given and for each major project in order that students may be aware of their achievement and understand where they stand in terms of the school's marking system.

Assignment of Marks in Small Classes. The assignment of letter marks in *small* classes is a problem whose solution is usually dependent almost entirely upon the considered judgment of the instructor. If objective statistical procedures are to be employed at all, they can do no more than provide facts which may substantiate or which may prove helpful in exercising this judgment.

Assuming that marks are to be assigned on the basis of a five-letter system, the first major step in assigning marks to a small class is to determine the school's policy with respect to the percentage of students in a *normal* class who would normally receive each of the letter marks. It should be emphasized here that, whether statistical procedures are or are not to be used, there is no reason for assigning a certain percentage of the members of a given class A's, B's, etc. Neither the innate abilities nor the achievements of the students of a small class are likely to be normally distributed.

Any number of different distributions of A's, B's, C's, D's, and F's might be adopted by a given school to use as a point of departure in assigning marks. Because they make for easy computation and at the same time approximate a normal distribution, the following percentages are suggested: A's—10 per cent; B's—20 per cent; C's—40 per cent; D's—20 per cent; F's—10 per cent.

Remembering that this is only a starting point, let us examine the distribution of scores on page 444 to which letter marks have been assigned on this basis.

These particular scores are somewhat similar to a normal distribution. The scatter of the scores above the mean is much the same as that below the mean. In this particular case the considered judgment of the instructor might be to leave the distribution as it stands without any changes. In most cases it will not be this easy to justify the allocation of marks. In considering whether some adjustment should be made in the allocation of marks, the instructor should ask himself such questions as:

1. Are there, within the distribution, any natural groupings or

clusters of scores? Since measuring devices are not accurate to within one point, the instructor is hesitant, and rightly so, about including in the B category, for example, a score which is only one point above the highest score in the C group. As another example, assume that there were a score of 93 in the preceding distribution

Letter mark	Score	Percent
A	$\left.\begin{array}{c} 99 \\ 94 \end{array}\right\}$	10
B	$\left.\begin{array}{c} 90 \\ 89 \\ 87 \\ 87 \end{array}\right\}$	20
C	$\left.\begin{array}{c} 85 \\ 84 \\ 81 \\ 80 \\ 80 \\ 80 \\ 78 \\ 76 \end{array}\right\}$	40
D	$\left.\begin{array}{c} 73 \\ 71 \\ 70 \\ 67 \end{array}\right\}$	20
F	$\left.\begin{array}{c} 63 \\ 59 \end{array}\right\}$	10

of scores. The 94 *and* the 93 would probably be placed in the same category, either with the A's or in the B classification.

2. Is the class in question a normal group, or is it unusually high or low in abilities and accomplishments? If the class is unusually capable, the instructor might justify the assignment of A's to as many as 20 or 30 rather than 10 per cent of the students. At this point it should be mentioned that many instructors are inclined to assume that their classes are superior and attempt to justify the assignment of higher marks than the situation warrants.

One way of determining the relative standing of the group in question is to compare the mean scores made by its members on specific tests with the mean scores made by other groups who have taken the same tests.

3. What is the range of the scores? What is the mean score?

How are the scores grouped around the mean? If the range of scores is very small, the instructor has little basis for assigning letter marks.

Table 11. Two Examples Showing How the Approximate Percentage Distributions Might Be Modified on the Basis of Considered Judgment

Approximate percentage distribution	Scores	Adjusted letter marks	Approximate percentage distribution	Scores	Adjusted letter marks
10	{ 58 } 52	A-5%	10	{ 75 }	A
			20	74 73	
20	52 51 50 50 50	B-25%		69 68	
			40	68 67 67 66	B
40	49 48 48 47 47 46 45 45 45 45	C-45%	20	64 64 63 63 63	C
			10	{ 62 }	
20	43 40 40	D-12½%			
10	32 21 28	F-12½%			

The two examples in Table 11 illustrate the fact that the use of the suggested percentage distribution is only a starting point that establishes five arbitrary groupings. Following this it is necessary to inspect the distribution and to consider all known facts about the students and about the nature of the subject which should have a bearing upon their marks. This will usually result in a revision of the arbitrary percentage distribution.

Use of Standard Deviation in Assigning Marks

As has been pointed out earlier, marks should be based on standards which are set by the accomplishments of a large number of students. It has also been noted that tests employed to measure achievement usually vary greatly in difficulty. The procedure described here is one method commonly used to assign marks in terms of standards set by the group. Further, this same method tends to compensate for variations in the difficulty of examinations.

Since different forms of the same test vary in difficulty, a student who can answer only 60 per cent of the items on one form of a test might be able to answer 70 or even 80 or 90 per cent of the items on another form of the same test. It has been found, however, that the mean score on one form is usually equivalent to the mean score on another. In other words the student who makes a mean score on one will make a mean score on the other forms of the test, provided that all forms are good tests.

In Table 12 are recorded numbers which represent roughly the scores made by a group of students who took three forms of the same test. The mean of the scores made on Form A is 80; Form B, 80; Form C, 60. A student who makes 80 on Form A also made approximately 80 on Form B and 60 on Form C.

It would seem on first observation that the student who makes 20 points less than the mean on one form of a test should also make 20 points below the mean on another form. However, the various forms of the same test are usually of such a nature that the range and distribution of scores about the mean will be different for each. After giving the forms to several hundred students it might be found that all students taking one form make scores which fall within 10 points of the mean, while on the other form of the test the scores might range from 30 to 40 points above and below the mean. This makes it necessary that some measure of distance from the mean be used which will describe the wide differences in distribution of test scores about the mean. One such measure is the standard deviation.

A student who takes three forms of the same test will make scores which fall approximately the same σ unit distance from the means of the three forms. The raw scores may vary tremendously. Observe that in Table 12 the σ values for the raw scores are listed. Reading across from left to right, observe that the raw scores, other than the mean scores on Form A and B, are different but that the σ values are the same.

By using the mean and σ, it is possible to establish uniform standards of achievement and to express each student's achievement in terms of uniform units of measurement from the mean.

There are certain basic conditions which must be met before at-

Table 12. Standard-deviation Values for Raw Scores on Three Forms of the Same Test

Student number	Form A		Form B		Form C	
	Raw percent-age scores	σ units from mean	Raw percent-age scores	σ units from mean	Raw percent-age scores	σ units from mean
1	95	1.96	86	1.96	90	1.96
2	90	1.30	84	1.30	80	1.30
3	90	1.30	84	1.30	80	1.30
4	85	0.65	82	0.65	70	0.65
5	85	0.65	82	0.65	70	0.65
6	85	0.65	82	0.65	70	0.65
7	80	0.00	80	0.00	60	0.00
8	80	0.00	80	0.00	60	0.00
9	80	0.00	80	0.00	60	0.00
10	80	0.00	80	0.00	60	0.00
11	80	0.00	80	0.00	60	0.00
12	75	−0.65	78	−0.65	50	−0.65
13	75	−0.65	78	−0.65	50	−0.65
14	75	−0.65	78	−0.65	50	−0.65
15	70	−1.30	76	−1.30	40	−1.30
16	70	−1.30	76	−1.30	40	−1.30
17	65	−1.96	74	−1.96	30	−1.96
Mean =	80		80		60	
σ =	7.67		3.07		15.34	

tempting to use the mean and standard deviation to set standards and assign marks:

1. Calculations must be based upon scores made by a large number of students.

2. On the basis of ability, the students must be representative of students who take the course.

3. The subject matter must be of such nature that it will cause students to achieve different amounts.

4. The test and other measuring devices used must measure small differences in achievement.

5. The students must put forth effort.

6. The instruction must be uniformly good.

The greater the extent to which these conditions obtain, the greater the accuracy with which this technique can be applied.

The following points should be observed in using the mean and standard deviation to set standards and assign marks:

1. This technique *does not* relieve responsible personnel of the necessity for exercising judgment in setting standards and assigning marks. If the six basic conditions listed above do not obtain to a high degree, certain adjustments, in line with the combined judgments of competent individuals, will have to be made.

2. Ordinarily the critical score is located by subtracting $1\frac{1}{2}\sigma$ units from the mean. This is the arbitrary feature of this technique. If it seems advisable to set higher or lower standards, some other σ unit distance from the mean should be adopted.

3. The scores of each new class should be combined with scores of all other classes which have taken the *same* test or tests. This should be continued until the critical score no longer is affected significantly by the addition of another class to the accumulated scores. Each class does not necessarily set its own standard, but it may have a slight influence upon the standard.

4. If a large number of students are dropped at the end of each semester, some consideration should be given to the fact that the class becomes a more highly selected group as it makes progress through the training program.

5. If marks for practical work and other requirements are to be considered in computing periodic final marks, they should be added before the mean and standard deviation are computed.

6. There should be complete understanding of the fact that tests simply do not measure the full range of achievement in a training program. A raw score of 70 on a 100-point test *does not* represent 70 per cent of perfect achievement.

The standard deviation is frequently used to convert raw scores to some type of standard scores. It is also used in conjunction with the mean to assign letter marks. When marks are assigned in this manner, the usual procedure is to use a five-letter system and to let one σ on the base line of a normal distribution curve encompass all scores to be assigned a given letter mark, as is shown in Figure 5. For example, assume that A. B. C. D. and F are to be used as letter marks. The mean and σ would be calculated. To determine which scores are to be assigned A's $1\frac{1}{2}\sigma$ is added to the mean. All scores greater than this value receive A's (see Figure 5). The scores falling between the values $M + \frac{1}{2}\sigma$ and $M + 1\frac{1}{2}\sigma$ are assigned B's. To determine the limits of the C group,

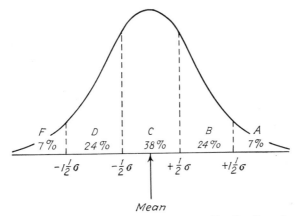

Fig. 5. *Percentages of marks assigned to a normally distributed group when one σ on the line is used to encompass each letter mark.*

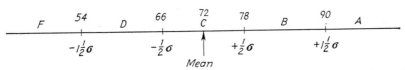

Fig. 6. *Location of limits of letter marks in distribution whose mean is 72 and whose σ is 12.*

$\frac{1}{2}\sigma$ is added and subtracted from M. The scores to be assigned D's are those falling between $M - \frac{1}{2}\sigma$ and $M - 1\frac{1}{2}\sigma$, and the ones which fall below $M - 1\frac{1}{2}\sigma$ are assigned F's. To illustrate further, assume that the mean of a series of scores is 72 and the standard deviation is 12. As shown in Figure 6, all scores falling above $72 + (1\frac{1}{2} \times 12)$, or 90, would receive A's. The B's would go to scores falling between 78 and 90, the C's to those between 66 and 78, etc.

In a perfectly normal distribution, as shown in Figure 5, only 7 per cent of the scores would fall above $M + 1\frac{1}{2}\sigma$, 24 per cent between $M + \frac{1}{2}\sigma$ and $M + 1\frac{1}{2}\sigma$, 38 per cent between $M - \frac{1}{2}\sigma$ and

$M + \frac{1}{2}\sigma$, and 24 per cent between $M - 1\frac{1}{2}\sigma$ and $M - \frac{1}{2}\sigma$, and 7 per cent would fall below $M - 1\frac{1}{2}\sigma$. In such a distribution, letter marks would be distributed as follows: A, 7 per cent; B, 24 per cent; C, 38 per cent; D, 24 per cent; F, 7 per cent.

Rarely would marks be so neatly distributed. The scores listed in Table 13 were made by students in a course in metalwork and are as near the normal distribution as might be expected. Observe that there are only slight differences in the percentages of the letter marks assigned and percentages in a perfectly normal distribution.

Table 13. Typical Series of Test Scores Approximating Normal Distribution

Scores		Letter marks	
7%	108 105	A A	7%
24%	98 97 96 94 93 92 90	B B B B B B B	24%
38%	89 89 87 86 85 85 83 83 82 81 80 80	C C C C C C C C C C C C	38%
24%	78 77 77 76 73 72	D D D D D D	20%
7%	68 67 61	F F F	11%

$$M = 84.4$$
$$\sigma = 10.3$$

If the assumption can be made that the class to be assigned marks is a typical class, or if the marking policy dictates that each student is to be marked in terms of the achievement of his particular class, the marks can be readily assigned by computing the mean and standard deviation as indicated above without making significant adjustments. If, however, the distribution varies drastically from the normal probability curve, or if the class is considerably above or below average and must be compared with other classes in the school, drastic adjustments may be necessary. If marking is to be done in terms of the achievement of a *normal* class, the mean of the scores made by such a class should be taken as the starting point for determining letter marks for a new class being tested. For example, assume that a current class makes a mean score of 76 on a test on which a *typical* class is known to have averaged 80. Obviously the new class is below average. Instead of adding $1\frac{1}{2}\sigma$ to 76 to determine the point at which the A's should start, $1\frac{1}{2}\sigma$ is added to 80. This will decrease the number of A's and increase the number of F's to be assigned the new class. If only two or three classes have taken the test, the scores of all should be thrown together for purposes of determining a mean score. At least this will increase the chances of obtaining a standard which is based on normal accomplishment.

SUMMARY

The procedures used by teachers in assigning marks are many and varied. In this chapter certain guiding principles have been set forth, and selected procedures have been described and illustrated. It has been pointed out that the marking policies for a given school should be determined through the cooperative action of the members of the teaching and administrative staffs and that any one or a combination of two or more methods might be adopted.

Regardless of the method selected, the group should plan to base the mark upon valid measures which are indicative of the extent to which the student has achieved the objectives established for the course. Scores on quizzes or short written and oral tests, scores on performance tests, results on comprehensive tests, data pertaining to the student's daily performance in the classroom,

shop, or laboratory, and marks on completed projects, written assignments and special reports are indicative of achievement and
should affect course marks. Such factors as interest, effort, and attitude should be incorporated in separate descriptive reports.

As far as standards in terms of which marks might be assigned
are concerned, the school's marking policy might take into consideration (1) norms on standardized tests, (2) the student's achievement as compared with his past record, (3) the extent of improvement made by the student during the course, (4) his achievement
as compared with his aptitude, (5) his relative standing in the
class, and (6) his achievement as compared with that of large
numbers who have previously completed the course.

The several statistical procedures presented in this chapter by
no means eliminate the necessity of the instructor's exercising considered judgment in interpreting test data and assigning marks.
The extent to which the instructor should rely upon these procedures is dependent upon: the number of scores involved, the
distribution of student abilities, the nature of the subject matter,
the sensitivity of measuring devices used, effort put forth by the
students, and the character of the instruction.

SOME THINGS TO DO AND QUESTIONS TO ANSWER

1. What advantages do you see in the practice of determining marking policies for a given school through the cooperative action of the
faculty? What disadvantages?

2. What are the arguments for and against the practice of permitting such factors as effort, interest, and attitudes to affect school marks?
Assuming this policy to be in effect in your school, what would you
recommend as a procedure for taking into account such factors in calculating and assigning marks?

3. As possible means of reporting relative achievement which measure do you consider the more desirable, rank order or percentile rank?
Why?

4. Describe a procedure for assigning marks which takes into consideration (1) the student's ability and (2) the amount of improvement
he made during the course.

5. What are some things that the teacher might do, other than assign marks, to help the student appraise his progress at frequent intervals during the school year?

6. Assuming that the instructor calculates the mean and standard deviation and uses these measures to determine the range of each of the letter marks to be assigned, what factors should he take into consideration in "adjusting" these ranges?

7. What merit is there in having the students appraise each other's progress? In appraising their own progress?

8. How may the instructor get students to appraise their own individual accomplishments?

9. What are the advantages and disadvantages of a marking system which merely indicates that a student either passes or fails?

10. What are some of the disadvantages of a marking system in which all aspects of educational development and social and personal growth are incorporated in a single course mark?

11. What can a teacher do to eliminate unwholesome competition among members of a class?

12. What is wrong with permitting the final examination to determine a student's mark in a course?

SELECTED REFERENCES FOR ADDITIONAL READING

Caveny, C. C., and J. A. Weichelt. "Reliability of Shop Grades," *Industrial Arts and Vocational Education,* 34:233–236 (June, 1945).

Greene, Harry A., Albert N. Jorgensen, and J. Raymond Gerberich. *Measurement and Evaluation in the Secondary School.* New York: Longmans, Green & Co., Inc., 1946. Chaps. 25, 26.

Hall, D. M. "A New Technique for Assigning Class Grades," *Journal of Educational Research,* 41:214–221 (November, 1947).

Remmers, H. H., and N. L. Gage. *Educational Measurement and Evaluation.* New York: Harper & Brothers, 1943. Chaps. 21, 22.

Rinsland, Henry Daniel. *Constructing Tests and Grading.* New York: Prentice-Hall, Inc., 1945. Chap. 7.

Ross, C. C. Measurement in Today's Schools. New York: Prentice-Hall, Inc., 1947. 2d ed., Chaps. 8, 14.

Smith, Homer J. "Grading Pupils in Industrial Subjects," *Education,* 65:600–605 (June, 1945).

Strong, Ruth. *Reporting to Parents.* New York: Bureau of Publications, Teachers College, Columbia University, 1947.

Tiegs, Ernest W. *Tests and Measurements in the Improvement of Learning.* Boston: Houghton Mifflin Company, 1939. Chap. 7.

Wrinkle, William L. *Improving Marking and Reporting Practices.* New York: Rinehart & Company, Inc., 1947.

CHAPTER
SIXTEEN: ANALYZING AND
IMPROVING TESTS

ALL tests can be improved. It is with this thought in mind that we turn to a consideration of several techniques that will be useful in the improvement process. Two broad steps point up what must be done:

1. The total test results must be arranged in a logical manner, analyzed, and evaluated.

2. Each item must be studied to determine whether or not it is doing what is expected of it.

This chapter provides suggestions for carrying out each of these steps. A determined effort has been made to keep in mind the busy teacher who does not have the time (let alone the experience) to manipulate refined statistical procedures in analyzing, evaluating, and improving his tests. For that reason the first sections contain rule-of-thumb suggestions wherever possible, with statistical considerations held to a minimum.

This does not mean that statistical procedures are impractical and useless. On the contrary, they are absolutely necessary in obtaining refined and precise data. The final section of this chapter outlines several statistical procedures that can be used in test analysis. As a teacher grows in his ability to make effective measuring instruments, he should be learning more and more about the refined techniques.

It is possible, however, to utilize approximation methods for obtaining usable facts upon which the teacher can base his reflective thinking. Test improvement, as well as original test construction, is a creative process which makes use of all pertinent data. The use of the techniques presented here will provide data sufficient for the purposes of most classroom teachers.

Analyzing and Evaluating Total Test Scores

The typical teacher, after correcting a test, invariably will look over the scores to see how well his class has done as a group. Sometimes he assigns letter marks to the scores without much rhyme or reason. At other times he spends a great deal of effort mulling over the scores while trying to decide who should receive what marks. Perhaps he wonders what the scores really mean and how valid the test is. Whatever his thoughts, it is logical to review the test results in terms of the original intentions for the test.

Let's skip to the second person now and consider several ideas that should be helpful to you in studying total test scores. In Chapter Fifteen you learned how to arrange scores, distribute marks and report achievement. The suggestions that follow carry the process one step further. Let's assume that you have prepared a summary sheet similar to the one shown on the next page.

After the scores have been assembled, distributed, and recorded, it will be helpful to sit back and reflect on the results obtained by the total group on the test. The first step is to reexamine the objectives that the test purports to measure. It was suggested that the objectives should be written down. If you were not sufficiently impressed with the logic of this suggestion, it should begin to be apparent that written objectives are very useful after a test has been given as well as when it is being constructed. Not only do they make easier the job of test evaluation, but there will be many times when student inquiries can be answered easily by referring to the written objectives.

At this stage we are interested in reviewing the objectives in terms of the total test results (the next section deals with individual items). In most instances a careful comparison of the objectives and the scores made on the test will provide the instructor with considerable food for thought. Simple subjective reflection

Code No.	Score	Rank	Letter mark
1	80	11	C
2	73	15	D
3	85	7	C
4	84	8	C
5	89	4	B
6	59	20	F
7	63	19	F
8	94	2	A
9	71	16	D
10	67	18	D
11	99	1	A
12	87	5.5	B
13	70	17	D
14	78	13	C
15	87	5.5	B
16	90	3	B
17	76	14	C
18	80	11	C
19	81	9	C
20	80	11	C

Total possible score, 103.
Range, 99–59 (40 points).
Mean score, 80 (approximate).
Median score, 80.

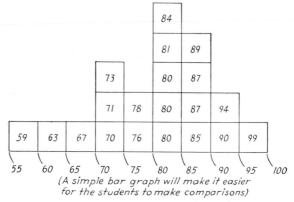

(A simple bar graph will make it easier
for the students to make comparisons)

Fig. 1. A simple summary sheet is helpful in further evaluation of the total sheet.

will usually bring forth interesting information about the total test and class accomplishments in terms of the test.

It is difficult (and perhaps unwise) to attempt to prescribe a precise step-by-step procedure that should be followed in this reflective process. Every test and every class will be different. A variety of factors will always be present. However, two general questions will be helpful in getting your train of thought under way:

1. Does this test really measure the objectives that I set out to measure?[1]

2. Do the scores on the test provide me with information that is really useful in evaluating my students' achievement and my teaching efforts?

As these two questions are considered carefully and conscientiously, it will be helpful to review the summary of test results. Examine the extreme scores. Study the manner in which the scores are scattered. As you observe a score that is particularly high or low or a group that is clustered together, translate the scores into names. Jot down significant thoughts that come to mind as you look at the scores of particular individuals. You will come out with a reminder for a word of encouragement here, an admonition there, a check into this cumulative record, a question to be asked of these students, a brief conference with other students, and so on.

Before the process is finished, you will want also to check on the difficulty of the test. One method of doing this is to compare the average score with the total possible score. A general rule for standardized tests is that the average score should be about 50 per cent of the total possible score. Most informal achievement tests will not approach this percentage—the average score is likely to be higher. Mastery tests, such as a recall test on safety practices, should not be judged on this basis, as the intent of such tests is to have all students obtain a perfect mark.

A simple, and more useful, variation of the above rule suggests that the range of scores should be from slightly less than half the

[1] For a refined method of establishing the validity of a test see Dorothy C. Adkins, and associates, *Construction and Analysis of Achievement Tests*, pp. 160–180.

items right to practically all (but not all) the items right. For example, a test of 60 items, according to this rule, would have a low score in the 20's and a high score in the 50's. This is only a very general rule, however, and a test that happens to meet this criterion is not automatically a good test.

This suggestion will have its greatest value in calling quick attention to the negative aspects of a test. If the range of scores is small—if all the scores are grouped near the top or bottom or center of the distribution—the first interpretation would perhaps be that the test does not discriminate sufficiently to be of much value. If all the scores are at the top, you may have "taught the test." That is, you may have emphasized points because you knew they would be in the test. If all the scores are clustered near or at the bottom, this may indicate some omissions in your teaching.

For most teachers, studying the total test results, then, is a subjective process. There are no simple steps that will automatically result in a completely objective appraisal. Much depends upon the type of student, the type of class, the type of subject matter, and the type of teacher. Nevertheless, these very factors make such a study interesting as well as useful if the effort is careful and conscientious.

We pass now to a consideration of the individual items in the test. An analysis of their adequacy will often be more revealing than what is found in studying the total test scores. Sometimes it will be well to postpone a critical consideration of the total test scores until the individual items have been evaluated. If you know something about how the individual items are performing, this will provide a better understanding of the adequacy of the total test.

Item Analysis

It is appropriate at this point to repeat again that the value of an examination is dependent largely upon two factors: (1) how well the test samples the objectives being measured; (2) how well each item discriminates, that is, whether it distinguishes between the good students and the poor students.

Positive aspects of both factors should be present in a good examination. It is conceivable that a test might sample certain objectives broadly, but if the items do not discriminate positively, the results will have little value (both good and poor students would get the items right). On the other hand, a particular test may discriminate highly between good and poor students but may cover such narrow objectives as to provide a poor indication of the intended measurement. Neither test would be valid.

An item analysis will also be useful in performing the following functions:

1. It may make the instructor think twice about his ability to make good test items. Questions that he considers to be excellent will sometimes turn out to be poor when analyzed, whereas doubtful items will sometimes prove to be of high value.

2. The information obtained will prove to be useful in the construction of later tests. Methods of phrasing statements, vague words to be avoided, the types of questions that only take up space —these are some of the things to be learned from a thorough analysis.

3. Interesting and useful information may be provided on the achievement of individual students. This can be extremely valuable in diagnosing individual difficulties and prescribing remedial measures.

4. Improvement in teaching methods and teaching resources will often be suggested by the analysis. It may be the means of impressing upon the teacher the need for improvement.

5. When a long test has been constructed, an item analysis will indicate the items that can be discarded without impairing the value of the test. Thus it serves as a means for saving time. An extreme example is that of a college examination of 664 items that required 5 to 6 hours of student time to complete.[2] After an item analysis had been made, practically the same results were obtained by selecting 228 of these items which could be answered in roughly 2 hours' time.

There are refined statistical techniques that can be used in determining the value of particular items (see page 472). However, approximation methods will enable you to do three things:

(see page 472)

---

[2] *Studies in College Examinations,* University of Minnesota, Committee on Educational Research, 1934, p. 126.

1. To determine the items that do not discriminate between the good and the poor students.

2. To discover items that are too easy, even for the poor students.

3. To discover if any items are too difficult, even for the best students.

The procedure described below is similar to that used in most item-analysis techniques. The details differ in that rough indices are used (with a resultant increase in the amount of error). For informal tests this possible increase in the amount of error is not fatal when it is remembered that test construction is largely a creative undertaking. The manipulation and use of statistical data will not, per se, guarantee a good test. The process of item analysis is only a means to an end. In other words, the best technique of item analysis will not counteract or make up for the inclusion of poor items in a test. It will only point out the existence of such items.

Basically, item analysis is a process of dividing the test scores into two groups and then comparing the individual item responses of each group. More specifically, it can be carried out by the following six steps.

1. Determine the criterion of comparison.

2. Divide the papers into comparison groups.

3. Tally the individual responses to each item for each group.

4. Convert each figure to its equivalent percentage.

5. Compare and interpret the group responses.

6. Record the results on an individual item card.

Determine the Criterion of Comparison. The usual criterion for grouping the papers is the total test score. When this is done, you assume that the best students are those who get good scores on the test and the poor students are those with low scores. This is an easy criterion to use, and it will be sufficient for most purposes, although it assumes that the test has been carefully constructed and reviewed before it is taken by the students.

In certain instances other criteria may be used. You may have a test made up, let us say, of three distinct parts that are not closely related. A student who does well on one part might do very poorly on another part. The total test score might therefore be misleading as to the achievement on a specific part. In such instances the grouping would be on the basis of the scores made on each part (subtest) .

Sometimes it may be desirable to group the papers on the basis of marks made during the previous term or marks on several examinations, term papers, or completed projects. For example, all students who received A's in a previous course might be grouped together and their test papers compared with those students who received C or D. Sometimes it might be desirable to make the comparison on several different bases.

Divide the Papers into Comparison Groups. There are several methods of grouping the papers for purposes of comparison. In most instances two groups are selected for study, although three are sometimes used. The grouping may be in terms of equal thirds, the upper and lower quarters, or the upper and lower quarters and the middle 50 per cent of the papers. Sometimes the upper and lower halves are compared (see page 477) .

Very often the upper and lower quarters are compared and the middle group disregarded. Some teachers select the top 25 and the bottom 25 papers in large classes, and others select 100 papers, representing the full range of scores. This makes it easy to convert to percentages. The trend in the validation of standard tests seems to be to use the upper and lower 27 per cent, with the middle group disregarded.[3]

If you have followed the explanation to this point, you will visualize three sets of test papers before you, separated on the basis of total scores. On the left will be one-fourth of the papers—papers of those students receiving the highest scores on the test. On the right will be the lowest one-fourth. This means that the middle pile will contain one-half the papers. We are now ready to do some simple tabulating.

Tally the Individual Responses to Each Item for Each Group. The purpose of this step is to record how many people in each group get the item right, how many get it wrong, and how many omit it. A simple tally sheet can be used. The nature of the tally

[3] Truman L. Kelley, "The Selection of Upper and Lower Groups for the Validation of Test Items," *Journal of Educational Psychology,* 30:17–24 (January, 1939) .

sheet will depend upon the type of item being analyzed. For two-response items, such as true-false, a sheet such as that in Figure 2 might be used.

	High Group – 25%			Middle Group – 50%			Low Group – 25%		
Item	Right	Wrong	Omit	Right	Wrong	Omit	Right	Wrong	Omit
1	JHT ////	///	/	JHT ////	JHT JHT JHT	//	//	JHT ////	//
2	//// 4	JHT /// 8	/ 1	// 2	JHT JHT JHT JHT // 22	// 2		JHT JHT 10	/// 3
3									

Fig. 2. *A tally sheet that can be used in recording responses on two-response items.*

As each item is inspected, a simple tally mark is made in the appropriate column. The total figure in each cell can be added later and underlined (or encircled) as was done for item 2.

When a multiple-response item, such as multiple-choice, is analyzed, it will be advisable to use a slightly different column arrangement that provides additional information. It is possible to determine not only how many get the item right but also how many times an alternative choice was made. The method followed will be readily understood by studying the following example, which uses only the upper and lower quarters. The middle group could easily be added. For purposes of illustration one of the items (No. 2) has been included just above the tally sheet. It will be noted that the A, B, C, D, E columns refer to the alternative choices for answering the item. Column O includes the number of persons omitting the item.

The value of this type of tally sheet for multiple-response items is shown in item 3. Neither the high group nor the low group selected choices D and E of this item. This provides very useful data to the test maker, since it indicates that very probably choices D and E should be modified or changed. They are not sufficient detractors. Such interpretations will be considered in more detail shortly. The point to remember at this stage is that the tally sheet for multiple-response items should indicate how many students selected each choice.

Convert Each Figure to Its Equivalent Percentage. This is an optional step, although it will be easier for most persons to make comparisons on the basis of percentages. This will be especially

Horizon

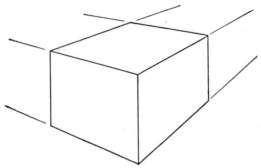

1. The drawing above is an example of
   A. an oblique drawing.
   B. a parallel perspective drawing.
   C. an isometric drawing.
   D. an angular perspective drawing.
   E. a cabinet drawing.

Item No.	High Group – Choices						Low Group – Choices					
	A	B	C	D	E	0*	A	B	C	D	E	0
1	0	1	1	<u>40</u>	1	0	4	4	2	<u>22</u>	5	6
2	8	<u>23</u>	2	0	6	4	11	<u>13</u>	7	3	6	3
3	0	0	<u>37</u>	0	0	6	4	2	<u>36</u>	0	0	1
4	<u>17</u>	13	11	0	2	0	<u>6</u>	6	18	2	11	0

  * Omissions.

Fig. 3. Tally sheets that can be used with multiple-response items (43 persons in each group—correct response underlined).

true if the middle group is included, for it will contain one-half the papers and therefore twice as many as either the upper or lower group.

The easiest method of converting to percentages is to prepare a simple reference table in which is included the equivalent percentage of each number. This will save time and a great deal of arithmetic. For example, suppose the upper and lower groups contain 43 papers each, as in Figure 3. The equivalent of one forty-third is roughly 2.3 per cent. Therefore, if only one person answered a particular item correctly, the figure 2.3 would be substituted for the 1. A simple chart could be made for reference purposes, as shown in Figure 4.

```
        Total papers..43

        Number
        Correct      |      %

           1         |     2.3
           2         |     4.6
           3         |     6.9
           4         |     9.2
           5         |    11.5
           6         |    13.8
```

Fig. 4. An example of a reference table that can be developed to facilitate the conversion to equivalent percentages.

It would take only a few minutes to prepare similar equivalent tables for any particular set of papers. This step is desirable because percentage figures will have more meaning for most people. If this were done for the several examples in Figure 3, the equivalent percentages would appear as in Figure 5.

Item No.	High Group – %						Low Group – %					
	A	B	C	D	E	0	A	B	C	D	E	0
1	0	2	2	92	2	0	9	9	5	50	12	13
2	10	53	5	0	15	7	25	30	16	7	14	8
3	0	0	85	0	0	15	9	5	82	0	0	4
4	40	30	25	0	5	0	14	14	41	5	25	0

Fig. 5. When equivalent percentages are substituted for raw scores it becomes easier to make comparisons (using the same data as in Fig. 3).

One caution should be heeded when percentages are used, especially in connection with test scores for small classes. The percentages are apt to be misleading unless the raw numbers are kept in mind. For example, if there are only ten papers in a group the percentage will advance by tens. The difference between 50 and

60 per cent, then, would be the difference of only one paper. This would not be as significant as one might tend to believe if he considers the percentage scores only.

Compare and Interpret the Group Responses. Two questions will be useful as guides in the process of comparing and interpreting the group responses to each item:

1. Does the item discriminate positively?
2. What is the relative level of difficulty?

An item discriminates positively when the good students get the item right significantly more often than the poor students. Conversely, when the poor students get the item right and the good students mark it wrong, it is said to discriminate negatively. A great many items in the typical informal test will show very little if any discrimination. An example of each of these points is shown in Figure 6, which contains data on selected multiple-choice items. The figures in each column are rough equivalent percentages.

Item	High Group								Item	Low Group					
	A	B	C	D	E	O				A	B	C	D	E	O
1	2	82	4	4	8	0		Positive	1	4	14	4	10	68	0
2	56	11	0	25	8	0		Negative	2	10	5	3	75	7	0
3	0	0	85	0	0	15		No Discrimination	3	9	5	82	0	0	4

Fig. 6. An illustration of the results on three items tending to indicate positive, negative, and no discrimination.

It can be seen by inspection of the first item that a large number (82 per cent) of the good students have selected the correct response, while a relatively small number (14 per cent) of the poor students have made the correct selection. Such an item discriminates positively. In the second example the opposite is true. Only 25 per cent of the good students marked the item correctly, while 75 per cent of the poor students were right in their choice. This item would be discriminating negatively. In the third example both groups answer the item about equally well. There is no discrimination. On the surface, at least, the item would be of little value.

An invariable question at this point is how great the difference must be between the upper and lower groups before the extent of discrimination can be said to be significant. In other words, how much difference should there be between the high group and the low group in order to have a good item? It would be gratifying to be able to give a specific figure (in terms of raw numbers or percentages) that would act as a criterion of comparison. But this is not possible, for there are several factors that must be considered in making a statistical determination.

There are precise methods for determining whether a difference is significant (see next section, page 477). However, the authors suggest once again that careful, considered judgment will be sufficient for the tests made and used by the typical classroom teacher. While it is true that this suggestion encourages subjectivity in the analytical process, it is also true that it helps to avoid the placement of blind faith in a statistical coefficient which in reality may have little real meaning.

After you have made the simple comparison chart, it will be up to you to study the group responses to determine whether or not the item is discriminating as it should. In many cases this will be relatively easy because of a very wide difference. In other instances your best judgment will have to be exercised, for there will be a question as to whether an item is really discriminating.

Most of the examples thus far in this section have been based on only the upper and lower groups. The suggestion still holds that it will usually be wise to include also the middle group in making the comparison and interpretations.[4] The procedure need be no different except to add the middle group to the chart. The example shown in Figure 7 includes the middle group. The analysis, in this case, has been in terms of a two-response item; therefore it has been necessary to include only a single column for each group (the percentage of students answering correctly).

As an aid in further describing the interpretation of item-analysis data four examples (Figures 8 to 11) have been selected to illustrate certain points. These examples do not contain all the ramifications that will be forthcoming from the analysis, but they will be sufficient to indicate the type of reasoning that should be followed by the test maker in his efforts at test improvement. The

[4] The next section contains a description of a statistical method for comparing on the basis of the upper and lower halves.

chart of Figure 8 includes the results from an entire class divided into three groups (upper and lower 25 per cent and middle 50 per cent). The other examples (Figures 9 to 11) use only the upper and lower 25 per cent. In each instance the percentages used have

	Item	% Responding Correctly		
		Upper Group– 25%	Middle Group– 50%	Lower Group– 25%
Positive discrimination.	1	75	54	36
Negative discrimination.	2	46	48	64
No discrimination.......	3	82	84	86

Fig. 7. An analysis chart for a two-response item that illustrates the manner in which three groups can be compared.

been reduced to round numbers, and the correct choice has been underlined. No attempt has been made to include an example illustrating negative discrimination.

Which one of the following sets of words is associated
primarily with foundry work?
A. expansion and extension
B. cope and drag
C. tap and die
D. flange and fuse
E. hollow mandrel and blowhorn

	Upper 25%						Middle 50%						Lower 25%					
Choice	A	B	C	D	E	0	A	B	C	D	E	0	A	B	C	D	E	0
% right	0	95	0	0	5	0	0	55	17	13	15	0	10	42	15	8	20	5

Fig. 8. An example of an analysis chart for a particular multiple-choice item showing positive discrimination.

Interpretation

1. The item is discriminating positively (95 per cent of the upper group answered correctly, 55 per cent of the middle group, and 42 per cent of the lower group).

2. It does not discriminate within the upper group. Almost the entire group selected the correct response.

3. This is not a particularly difficult item. In the middle and

lower groups approximately half the students selected the correct response.

4. There is little difference between the middie group and the lower group on this item.

5. The several detractors appear to be functioning reasonably well, except in the upper group. Each of the choices was selected by several students in the lower group and, with the exception of choice A, in the middle group.

6. Only five per cent omitted the item. It is probable that the omissions were caused by a lack of knowledge on the part of the students and not because of the ambiguity of the item.

7. For this particular test and this particular group of students this item is performing well.

```
The principle of the wedge is applied in
A. pounding with a hammer
B. setting screws with a screwdriver
C. smoothing a board with sandpaper
D. cutting metal with a cold chisel
E. glazing a window sash with a putty knife
```

	Upper 25%						Lower 25%					
Choice	A	B	C	D	E	0	A	B	C	D	E	0
% right	0	12	0	88	0	0	0	12	0	60	14	14

Fig. 9. Item-analysis data showing positive discrimination.

Interpretation

1. This item discriminates positively although it appears to be relatively easy for each group. Most of the upper group and more than half of the students in the lower quarter made the correct choice.

2. Choices A and C are dead-weight in the item. They might as well be left out since none of the students who missed the item selected them. In other words, they are not sufficient detractors. Other choices should be substituted in the item. For example, they might be changed to read as follows:

    A. pulling nails with a claw hammer
    C. smoothing concave curves with a wood file

A supercharger is an air-blowing device used to
A. supply air to the carburetor.
B. force additional fuel through the carburetor.
C. supplement the electrical system at high speeds.
D. force air into the cylinders.
E. facilitate the distribution of exhaust gases.

	Upper 25%						Lower 25%					
Choice	A	B	C	D	E	0	A	B	C	D	E	0
% right	58	15	0	27	0	0	38	2	24	28	2	6

Fig. 10. Item analysis data showing no discrimination but providing important information for the use of the instructor.

Interpretation

1. About one-fourth of each group selected the correct response. Therefore, there is no discrimination at all on this basis.

2. In each group more of the students selected choice A than the correct choice. At first glance it might appear that this is a poor item. A careful study should be made of choice A and the correct choice, D. In this instance the correct choice *is* the one shown. The students who selected choice A did not have correct information.

3. Choice E does not seem to be a good detractor. It should be modified or changed.

4. Students in both groups should be asked why they marked choice A especially. While the figures indicate the item to have no discriminating power, it is doubtful that it need even be modified, let alone discarded. From this point it would appear that the teaching is at fault and further investigation is necessary before coming to any conclusion about the item.

5. This example has been inserted to illustrate the fact that something more than a manipulation of figures is necessary in interpreting the results of an item analysis. Though this item may not appear outwardly to be discriminating, it may, in reality, be a perfect measure of discrimination between those who know the point in question and those who do not. The nature of the item is such that the authors would doubt the advisability of making any change on the basis of the data at hand.

Industrial arts activities in the high school
A. will sometimes be of a prevocational nature.
B. should be primarily prevocational in nature.
C. should never be presented in terms of vocational
   objectives.
D. should be carried on primarily by those students who
   expect to become tradesmen.
E. should be more general in nature than the junior high
   school offerings.

Choice	Upper 25%						Lower 25%					
	A	B	C	D	E	0	A	B	C	D	E	0
% right	<u>36</u>	26	24	0	14	0	<u>12</u>	12	40	5	31	0

Fig. 11. Item-analysis data showing positive discrimination in an item that is relatively difficult.

Interpretation

1. This item seems to be discriminating positively.

2. It is relatively difficult since less than half of the upper group has selected the correct response. It can be said that this item is discriminating at the upper levels.

3. The discrimination is by no means perfect, since 12 per cent of the lower group selected the correct response. Of course, it might be that the 12 per cent guessed at this answer. (The procedure described here makes no attempt to correct for guessing.)

These four examples and the several interpretations should indicate the variety of meanings that might be attached to the results on an individual item. It should be repeated that the process is more than one of comparing numbers. As each item is examined, critical attention should be given to the objective which the item purports to measure. That is, you should ask two questions:

1. What objective is this item supposed to measure?

2. Do the results indicate that it is being measured adequately?

If the items are checked in this manner against the objective being measured, this will provide a good indication of the adequacy of the sampling. While this aspect should be given careful consideration during the construction of the test, it should also receive attention during the analysis and improvement phase. For example, it may be found that the two or three items used to measure a stated objective are poor items. If this happens very often, the sampling becomes inadequate and the value of the test is decreased.

Very often a poor item can be improved considerably by changing a word or phrase or modifying one of the choices. When the item analysis points to a doubtful item, it will be well to consult several of the students who have taken the test and ascertain their reactions to the questionable items. Very often they will provide information that would not have been readily apparent to the test maker. This does not mean that all items can be improved by slight changes or modifications. Items often have to be discarded, and an effort has to be made to devise new ones for measuring the objective.

Most teacher-made tests contain a significant number of items that are of little value in the test. One study on this problem showed that roughly one-third of the items were discarded after an item analysis had been made.[5] The tests used in this study were carefully constructed, which would seem to indicate that in the ordinary classroom test an even larger percentage of the items might be practically worthless. An item analysis is the means for identifying the "deadwood" in a test.

Record the Item-analysis Results on an Individual Item Card. In order to have a record of the discriminating power and relative difficulty of each item the item-analysis information should be placed on an individual item card. If a card file of test items is being developed the same card can be used for this record (see Card-file Test Building, page 129). Each time the item is used in a test, data can be added. The continuance of this practice will provide useful information on the value of the item. It also will be helpful as later tests are constructed. In other words, if your card file contains item-analysis data on a large number of items, it will be a relatively easy task to construct a test using the items that you know to be satisfactory.

The data for two-response and multiple-response items may be recorded as in the examples of Figure 12. You may wish to have the item itself on one side of the card with the analysis data on the other.

[5] *Studies in College Examinations, op. cit.,* p. 119.

__(alcohol)__ Shellac is thinned with_____...

	Upper 25%	Middle 50%	Lower 25%	
% right	75	54	36	11/15/47–9th Gr.–48 students

_____ A threaded bolt illustrates the principle of the

A. lever
B. wheel and axle
C. wedge
D. inclined plane
E. pulley

	High Group*						Low Group*					
Choice	A	B	C	D	E	0	A	B	C	D	E	0
No. right	0	1	3	38	1	1	3	4	12	15	3	7
% right	0	2	6	86	2	2	7	9	27	34	7	16

*N = 44 each group.

Fig. 12. Illustrating two methods of recording item-analysis data on individual item cards.

A Statistical Procedure for Evaluating Test Results

In the previous section we considered a subjective method for evaluating total test results and making an item analysis. It was stated that there are statistical procedures which will provide more precise data for evaluating the test. One such procedure is described below in step-by-step form.

This procedure, using the analysis-of-variance technique,[6] will provide the following:

1. An estimation of the test reliability.
2. An indication of the significance of the test scores.
3. A convenient form for making an item analysis.

No attempt will be made to describe the background material necessary to a thorough understanding of the analysis-of-variance

[6] Cyril Hoyt, "Test Reliability Estimated by Analysis of Variance," _Psychometrika,_ 6:153–160 (June, 1941).

technique. Rather, actual results from a test[7] will be used to illustrate how the procedure is carried out.

This particular test consisted of 40 items and was given to 42 students in Freshman Electricity at the Stout Institute. The procedure follows in step-by-step form:

1. Arrange the Test Papers in Descending Order. The paper having the highest total score should be placed on top. The paper with the lowest score will be on the bottom.

2. Construct a Student-item Chart (see Table 1, page 478). The numbers across the top relate to the individual test items (there were 40 items in this test). The numbers in the left-hand column relate to the test scores of students who took the test (42), with the highest score on top.

For each student check the items which he marked correctly. For example, student 1 missed only item 40. Therefore an X is

Source of variance	df	Sum of squares	Mean of squares	F	Hypothesis tested
Between individuals					
Between items					
Residual					
Total					

Fig. 13. Illustrating the analysis-of-variance table.

placed in each square except that under item 40. Do this for each test paper. When this step is completed, it will provide a graphic presentation of the test results.

3. Add the Individual Columns and Rows. These are labeled t_i and p_i (see Table 1). Add the column t_i and row p_i. Identical results should be found for each addition (in this example, 1,187). This figure is labeled Σt_i and Σp_i (Σ = summation).

[7] Adapted from John A. Jarvis, "Evaluation of Test Results," *Industrial Arts and Vocational Education,* 38:41–44 (February, 1949). Used by permission.

4. Square Each t_i and p_i Value. The results are posted in column t_i^2 and row p_i^2. Add the column and the row separately. The totals are labeled Σt_i^2 (35,577) and Σp_i^2 (38,041).

5. Construct a Variance Table. The headings will be as in Figure 13.

6. Using the Data at Hand, Complete the Table. The formulas for determining the necessary data are given in Figure 14 ($k =$ number of individuals; $n =$ number of items).

Source of variance	Degrees of freedom — df	Sum of squares	Mean of squares	F	Hypothesis tested
Between individuals	$k-1$	$\dfrac{1}{n}\Sigma t_i^2 - \dfrac{(\Sigma t_i)^2}{nk}$	$\dfrac{\text{Sum of squares}}{df}$ ⓐ	↗$\dfrac{a}{c}$	Reject (2.11)
Between items	$n-1$	$\dfrac{1}{k}\Sigma p_i^2 - \dfrac{(\Sigma t_i)^2}{nk}$	$\dfrac{\text{Sum of squares}}{df}$ ⓑ	↗$\dfrac{b}{c}$	Reject (2.11)
Residual	$(n-1)(k-1)$	Total − (between individuals + between items)	$\dfrac{\text{Sum of squares}}{df}$ ⓒ		
Total	$nk-1$	$\dfrac{(\Sigma t_i)(nk-\Sigma t_i)}{nk}$			

Fig. 14. An analysis-of-variance table with the formulas for computing the values under each heading.

By substituting in the formulas in Figure 14 and using the results of the test in electricity, the following results are forthcoming:

Degrees of freedom between
$$\text{individuals} = k - 1$$
$$= 42 - 1$$
$$= 41$$

$$\text{Degrees of freedom between items} = n - 1$$
$$= 40 - 1$$
$$= 39$$

$$\text{Residual} = (n - 1)(k - 1)$$
$$= (40 - 1)(42 - 1)$$
$$= 41 \times 39$$
$$= 1,599$$

$$\text{Total degrees of freedom} = nk - 1$$
$$= (40 \times 42) - 1$$
$$= 1,679$$

Sum of squares between individuals $= \frac{1}{n}\Sigma t_i^2 - \frac{(\Sigma t_i)^2}{nk}$

$$= \frac{1}{40} \times 35,577 - \frac{(1,187)^2}{40 \times 42}$$

$$= 54$$

Sum of squares between items $= \frac{1}{k}\Sigma p_i^2 - \frac{(\Sigma t_i)^2}{nk}$

$$= \frac{1}{42} \times 38,041 - \frac{(1,187)^2}{40 \times 42}$$

$$= 69$$

Total sum of squares $= \frac{(\Sigma t_i)(nk - \Sigma t_i)}{nk}$

$$= \frac{(1,187)(42 \times 40 - 1,187)}{42 \times 40}$$

$$= 348$$

Residual sum of squares $=$ total $-$ (between items $+$ between individuals)

$$= 348 - (54 + 69)$$
$$= 225$$

The mean-of-squares column is now computed by dividing each sum of square by its degree of freedom:

Mean square for individuals $= \frac{54}{41} = 1.316$
Mean square for items $= \frac{69}{39} = 1.77$

Residual $= \frac{225}{1,599} = .1408$

The F column is computed by dividing the mean square by the mean square residual as follows:

$$F_a = \frac{a}{c} \qquad\qquad F_b = \frac{b}{c}$$

$$= \frac{1.316}{.1408} \qquad\qquad = \frac{1.77}{.1408}$$

$$= 9.35 \qquad\qquad = 12.60$$

By substituting the several results the variance table can now be completed (see Figure 15). The significance of the test results is determined by using the figures in F_a and F_b. If these values are sufficiently high, it is assumed that the test is sufficiently reliable to be used for marking purposes. The comparison figure may be found by referring to a table of F values in a statistics text.[8] Using

Source of variance	df	Sum of squares	Mean of squares	F
Between individuals	41	54	1.316 ⓐ	9.35ⓐ
Between items	39	69	1.77 ⓑ	12.60ⓑ
Residual	1,599	225	.1408 ⓒ	
Total	1,679	348		

Fig. 15. The analysis-of-variance table with computed values.

the example of Figure 15 (with 41 and 39 degrees of freedom), the F value in the table is found to be 2.13. In this case the F values (9.35 and 12.60) are greater than 2.13, and hence we can assume that the test is significant.

7. *Compute the Reliability Coefficient for the Test.* An estimation of the reliability coefficient of the test can be obtained by using the following formula:[9]

$$r_{tt} = \frac{a - c}{a}$$

$$= \frac{1.316 - .1408}{1.316}$$

$$= .893$$

Remember, reliability refers to the accuracy or dependability of a test (see Chapter Four). A test that has perfect reliability will yield the same relative score each time the test is given. This goal is seldom if ever reached, although the reliability of some tests may approach perfection. The above formula is but one of various methods that can be used.[10]

[8] E. F. Lindquist, *Statistical Analysis in Educational Research,* p. 62. This also will be a useful reference for the person who is interested in developing a further understanding of the analysis-of-variance technique.

[9] Hoyt, *op. cit.*

[10] A common method is to correlate the odd-even scores on the test and then use a step-up formula.

The invariable question is to ask how high the reliabili;y coefficient must be before it is acceptable. No hard and fast rule can be stated. The validity of the test must be considered. However, a very crude rule is to suggest that for most purposes an achievement test should have a reliability coefficient of .90 or above.[11] In general the reliability can be increased by lengthening the test (or shortening the time of administration) and improving those items in which chance factors operate.

8. Using Table 1, Complete the Item Analysis. Draw a line dividing the test results in two equal parts (in this instance between rows 21 and 22).

To this point we know two things: the test results are significant and the scores are arranged in descending order. Therefore, it can be said logically that, when the lower half of the class gets an item right more often than the upper half of the class, that item should be eliminated from the test or revised.

This is exactly the same procedure as was described in the earlier section of this chapter, although the charting technique was not used. However, in this procedure it is possible to determine statistically whether the difference is significant between the upper and lower groups on a single item. This is done by finding the percentage difference between the two groups and dividing by the standard error of the difference. This computation must be done for each of the items. The procedure is illustrated by using the results for the first item taken from Table 1. This same procedure is then followed for each of the remaining items.

Let N_1 = number in upper group marking item correctly

X_1 = total number in upper group

P_1 = percentage of upper group marking item correctly

Q_1 = percentage of upper group marking item incorrectly

N_2, X_2, P_2, Q_2 = same designations for lower group

[11] For a more complete description of the procedures used in determining reliability, together with an interpretation of their usefulness, see the references at the end of this chapter.

Table 1. Tabulation of Items Answered Correctly by Each Student

Items

Student	1	2	3	4	5	6	7	8	9	10	11	12	13	14	15	16	17	18	19	20	21	22	23	24	25	26	27	28	29	30	31	32	33	34	35	36	37	38	39	40	t_1	t_1^2
1	X	X	X	X	X	X	X	X	X	X	X	X	X	X	X	X	X	X	X	X	X	X	X	X	X	X	X	X	X	X	X	X	X	X	X	X	X	X	X		39	1521
2	X	X	X	X		X	X	X	X	X	X	X	X	X	X	X	X	X	X	X	X	X		X	X	X	X	X	X	X	X	X	X	X	X	X	X	X	X		37	1369
3	X	X	X	X	X	X	X	X	X	X	X	X	X	X	X	X	X	X	X	X	X	X		X	X	X	X	X	X	X	X	X	X	X	X	X	X	X	X	X	36	1296
4	X	X	X		X	X	X	X	X	X	X	X	X	X	X	X	X	X	X	X	X	X	X	X	X	X		X					X	X	X	X	X	X	X	X	36	1296
5		X	X	X	X	X	X	X	X	X	X	X		X	X	X	X	X	X	X	X		X	X	X	X	X	X	X			X	X	X	X	X	X	X	X	X	35	1225
6	X	X	X	X	X	X	X	X	X	X	X	X	X	X	X	X	X	X	X	X	X	X	X	X	X	X	X	X	X			X	X	X	X	X	X	X	X	X	35	1225
7	X	X	X	X	X	X	X	X	X	X	X	X	X	X	X	X	X	X	X	X	X		X	X	X		X	X	X		X	X	X	X	X	X	X	X			35	1225
8	X	X	X	X	X	X	X	X	X	X	X	X	X	X	X		X					X	X	X	X	X	X	X	X	X	X	X	X	X	X	X	X	X	X	X	35	1225
9	X		X	X	X	X	X	X	X	X	X	X	X	X	X	X	X	X	X		X	X	X	X	X	X	X	X	X	X	X	X	X	X	X	X	X	X	X	X	35	1225
10	X	X	X	X	X	X	X	X	X	X	X		X	X	X	X	X	X	X	X		X	X	X	X	X	X	X	X		X	X	X	X	X	X	X	X	X	X	34	1156
11	X		X	X	X	X	X	X	X	X	X	X	X	X	X	X	X	X	X	X		X	X	X	X	X	X	X	X		X	X	X		X	X		X	X	X	33	1089
12	X	X	X	X	X	X	X	X	X	X	X	X	X	X	X	X	X	X	X	X		X	X	X	X	X	X	X	X		X	X	X	X	X	X	X	X	X	X	33	1089
13	X	X	X	X	X	X	X	X	X	X	X	X	X	X	X	X	X	X		X	X	X		X	X	X	X	X	X		X		X	X	X	X	X		X	X	33	1089
14	X	X	X	X	X	X	X	X	X	X	X	X	X	X	X	X	X	X	X	X	X	X		X		X	X	X	X	X		X	X	X	X	X			X	X	33	1089
15			X	X	X	X	X	X	X			X	X	X	X	X		X	X	X		X	X	X	X	X	X	X	X			X	X		X	X	X		X	X	32	1024
16	X	X	X	X	X	X	X	X	X	X	X	X	X	X	X	X	X	X	X	X	X	X		X	X	X	X	X	X	X	X	X	X	X	X	X			X	X	32	1024
17		X	X	X	X	X	X	X	X	X	X	X	X	X	X	X	X	X	X	X	X	X	X	X	X	X	X	X	X		X	X	X	X	X	X	X	X	X		32	1024
18			X	X	X	X	X	X	X						X	X	X	X	X	X		X	X	X		X	X	X	X		X	X	X	X	X	X	X		X	X	31	961
19	X	X	X	X	X	X	X	X	X	X	X	X	X	X	X	X	X	X	X	X	X	X		X	X	X	X	X					X	X	X	X	X	X	X	X	31	961
20		X	X	X	X	X	X	X	X	X	X		X	X	X	X	X	X	X	X	X	X	X	X	X	X	X	X					X	X	X	X	X	X	X	X	31	961
21	X	X	X	X	X	X	X	X	X	X	X		X		X	X	X	X	X	X		X	X			X	X	X	X			X	X	X	X	X	X	X	X	X	31	961
22	X	X	X	X	X	X	X	X	X		X	X	X	X	X	X	X	X	X	X	X		X	X	X	X		X	X				X	X	X	X	X		X	X	29	841
23	X	X	X	X	X	X	X	X	X		X	X	X	X	X	X	X	X	X	X	X	X	X	X	X	X	X	X	X		X	X	X	X	X	X	X	X	X	X	29	841

	24	25	26	27	28	29	30	31	32	33	34	35	36	37	38	39	40	41	42	Σt_i	Σt_i^2
$\Sigma t^2 \to$	841	841	784	784	784	625	625	576	529	484	484	441	400	400	324	324	289	289	36	35577	38041
$\Sigma t_i \to$	29	29	28	28	28	25	25	24	23	22	22	21	20	20	18	18	17	17	6		
	X	X	X	X			X	X	X	X		X	X			X	X			29	841
	X	X	X	X	X	X	X	X	X	X		X	X	X	X	X	X	X		40	1600
	X	X	X	X	X	X		X				X		X	X	X	X			32	1024
	X	X	X	X	X	X	X			X		X	X	X				X		31	961
	X	X	X	X	X	X	X	X	X	X		X	X	X	X	X		X		39	1521
	X	X	X	X	X	X	X	X	X	X		X	X	X	X	X		X		39	1521
	X	X	X	X	X	X	X	X	X			X	X	X		X	X	X		35	1225
	X	X	X	X	X	X	X	X	X	X	X	X	X	X	X	X		X		40	1600
			X	X	X	X				X				X		X				19	361
			X	X				X				X	X	X		X				20	400
																				6	36
	X		X	X	X	X	X	X	X	X	X									33	1089
	X		X	X	X			X	X	X	X		X		X		X			34	1156
	X	X	X		X		X		X		X					X	X			25	625
	X	X	X		X	X	X	X	X		X	X	X	X	X	X				37	1369
	X		X		X	X			X											22	484
	X	X	X	X	X	X		X		X		X	X			X	X			34	1156
		X				X		X												13	169
	X		X	X			X	X	X		X		X	X	X	X	X			31	961
							X			X										12	144
	X	X	X	X	X	X	X	X	X		X	X		X		X				34	1156
		X					X			X	X									20	400
	X	X	X			X		X	X	X		X	X		X		X			32	1024
	X		X	X	X	X	X	X	X	X	X	X	X		X					31	961
	X	X	X	X	X	X		X	X		X	X		X	X	X	X	X		34	1156
	X	X	X	X	X	X	X	X		X	X	X		X	X	X		X	X	39	1521
	X	X		X	X		X	X	X	X		X	X		X	X				31	961
		X	X		X		X		X		X		X			X				30	900
	X				X		X			X		X			X					21	441
	X	X	X	X	X	X	X		X	X	X	X	X	X	X	X	X	X		39	1521
		X		X	X		X	X												22	484
	X	X	X	X	X	X	X		X	X				X	X	X				34	1156
	X	X	X	X	X	X	X	X	X	X	X		X	X		X				37	1369
	X	X	X	X	X	X	X	X	X	X		X	X		X	X	X	X		39	1521
	X	X	X	X	X	X			X	X	X	X						X		32	1024
	X	X	X	X	X	X	X	X	X	X	X	X	X		X	X	X			39	1521
		X	X	X		X	X		X			X								27	729
	X	X			X	X	X	X			X	X			X					32	1024
	X			X		X	X								X					23	529
																	X			20	400
$\to$	24	25	26	27	28	29	30	31	32	33	34	35	36	37	38	39	40	41	42	P_i	Σp_i^2

Students

The first step is to find the percentage figures for both groups:

$$P_1 = \frac{N_1}{X_1} = \frac{16}{21} = 76\% \qquad Q_1 = 100 - P_1 = 100 - 76 = 24\%$$

$$P_2 = \frac{N_2}{X_2} = \frac{4}{21} = 19\% \qquad Q_2 = 100 - P_2 = 100 - 19 = 81\%$$

The formula for finding the standard error of the difference is

$$SD_{\text{diff}} = \sqrt{\frac{P_1 Q_1}{X_1} + \frac{P_2 Q_2}{X_2}}$$

By substituting in the formula the result will be as follows:

$$SD_{\text{diff}} = \sqrt{\frac{76 \times 24}{21} + \frac{19 \times 81}{21}}$$

$$= 12.65$$

The final step is to divide the percentage difference between the two groups by the standard error of the difference:

$$\frac{P_1 - P_2}{SD_{\text{diff}}} = \frac{76 - 19}{12.65} = \frac{57}{12.65} = 4.51$$

If the resultant ratio exceeds 2, the item is said to discriminate. All items having a ratio of less than 2 should be revised or eliminated from the test. Item 16 in Table 1 (page 478) is used to illustrate such an item. In the upper group, 18 (86 per cent) answered the item correctly; in the lower group, 16 (76 per cent). The standard error of the difference is computed as follows:

$$SD_{\text{diff}} = \sqrt{\frac{P_1 Q_1}{X_1} + \frac{P_2 Q_2}{X_2}}$$

$$= \sqrt{\frac{86 \times 14}{21} + \frac{76 \times 24}{21}}$$

$$= 12.0$$

Then

$$\frac{P_1 - P_2}{SD_{\text{diff}}} = \frac{86 - 76}{12} = \frac{10}{12} = .83$$

These figures might be put into table form for ready reference. The nature of such a table can be illustrated by using figures from the above examples.

Table 2. Illustrating the Table Headings That Might Be Used for Summarizing the Data on Individual Items

Item no.	Upper half		Lower half		$P_1 - P_2$	SD_{diff}	$\dfrac{P_1 - P_2}{SD_{\text{diff}}}$
	N_1	P_1	N_2	P_2			
1	16	76	4	19	57	12.65	4.51
16	18	86	16	76	10	12.0	.83

Using a Nomograph to Assign Discriminating Values to Test Items

Lawshe[12] has developed a nomograph that can be used in assigning D values (discrimination values) to individual test items. It simplifies the procedure described in the previous section in that it is not necessary to divide the percentage difference by the standard error of the difference. The nomograph (see Figure 16) is used for this purpose.

The first step is to divide the class into two groups (high and low) as before. Second, compute the percentage of each group marking the item correctly. Next, locate these percentage points on the left and right sides of the nomograph. Place a straightedge across these two points. The discrimination value will be found on the middle line at the point where it is crossed by the straightedge. In Figure 16 the first item in the electricity test again has been used to illustrate the procedure (the dotted line represents a straightedge). In the high group 76 per cent marked the item correctly. In the low group the figure was 19 per cent. By joining these two points with a straightedge it is possible to read off the D value on the middle line—in this case 1.6. Lawshe suggests that items having a D value of less than .4 should be eliminated or revised.[13]

A comparative study of these two procedures will show discrepancies in certain instances. That is, the results of both methods will be similar for most items while differing on a few. The use of the nomograph will save considerable time, and for most purposes the results will be sufficiently precise.

[12] C. H. Lawshe, Jr., *Principles of Personnel Testing.* New York: McGraw-Hill Book Company, Inc., 1948, p. 190.
[13] *Ibid.*

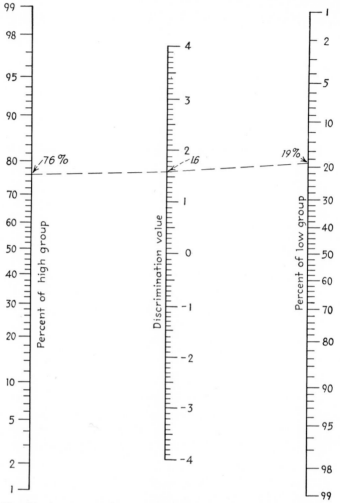

Fig. 16. A nomograph for assigning D values to test questions.

SUMMARY

A first step in evaluating the total test is to arrange the scores in a logical manner. A summary sheet will be helpful for this. The test objectives should then be studied in relation to the test results, keeping in mind to jot down significant notes or reminders about individual students. Two questions will be useful in this reflective process:

1. Does this test really measure the objectives that I set out to measure?

2. Do the scores on the test provide me with information that is really useful in evaluating my students' achievement and my teaching efforts?

A general rule in judging the difficulty level of a test is that the range of scores should be from slightly less than half the items right to practically all (but not all) the items right.

Item analysis is a process of dividing the test papers into two or three groups (usually on the basis of high scores and low scores) and comparing the results of each group on each item. It is useful in determining the discriminating power and difficulty level of each item. It also provides additional information that can be useful in the improvement of instruction.

One method for carrying out an item analysis is described by the following steps:

1. Determine the criterion of comparison.
2. Divide the papers into comparison groups.
3. Tally the individual responses on each item for each group.
4. Convert the total responses to percentages.
5. Compare and interpret the group responses.
6. Record the results on an individual item card.

Subjective methods can be used in making the comparisons, and these will be sufficient for many purposes. However, more precise methods will add to the effectiveness of the item analysis, and individual test makers should strive to understand and adopt such methods in improving their examinations.

SOME THINGS TO DO AND QUESTIONS TO ANSWER

1. From your experiences in taking examinations what are some of the weaknesses that should be looked for as any test is being analyzed and improved?

2. If all the students get an item right on a test, do you think that it should be left out of later tests? Why?

3. In what ways will an item analysis provide information that will be helpful in the improvement of instruction?

4. Why is it stated that in a good achievement test none of the students should obtain a perfect score?

5. Without referring to the text (at least, to begin with) describe

what item analysis is. This is a good exercise for collecting your
thoughts and summarizing the concepts you have to this point.

6. Explain how you would make an item analysis of a manipulative-
performance test.

7. What are your interpretations of the results on the several multiple-choice items listed on the accompanying tally sheet (the correct
choices are underlined) :

Item	High Group – %						Low Group – %					
	A	B	C	D	E	0	A	B	C	D	E	0
1	9	6	_60_	6	19	0	16	6	_16_	26	28	8
2	_34_	44	3	9	0	10	_23_	39	5	16	0	17
3	0	0	7	0	_93_	0	3	0	0	7	_81_	9
4	_14_	4	55	2	25	0	_10_	7	46	7	30	0

8. When does an item discriminate positively?

9. What is your thinking with respect to the difficulty level of individual items? For example, how many students should get an item
right before it is retained in a test?

10. To what extent would the chart in Table 1 (page 478) be useful
to a test maker even though he did not wish to carry out the statistical
computations?

SELECTED REFERENCES FOR ADDITIONAL READING

Adkins, Dorothy C., and associates. *Construction and Analysis of
Achievement Tests.* Washington, D.C.: Government Printing Office,
1947. Chap. IV.

Davis, Frederick B. *Item-analysis Data, Their Computation, Interpre-
tation and Use in Test Construction,* Harvard Education Papers,
No. 2. Cambridge, Mass.: Graduate School of Education, Harvard
University, 1946. P. 42.

Guilford, Joy Paul. "New Standards for Test Evaluation," *Educational
and Psychological Measurement,* 6:427–438 (1946).

Hawkes, Herbert E., E. F. Lindquist, and C. R. Mann. *The Construction and Use of Achievement Examinations,* Part I. Boston: Houghton Mifflin Company, 1936.

Lindquist, E. F. *Statistical Analysis in Educational Research.* Boston:
Houghton Mifflin Company, 1940. Pp. xi and 266.

CHAPTER

SEVENTEEN: IMPROVING YOUR INSTRUCTION —A CHALLENGE

THIS final chapter is in the form of a very brief recapitulation—in a sense, the "so what" part of the book.

To this point you have studied various kinds and types of measuring instruments. You have read dozens of suggestions for constructing tests. You have viewed many illustrations of good and poor practices. You have been admonished on certain points in a variety of ways.

All these efforts will have been successful to the extent that your teaching becomes more effective. That is another way of repeating that tests are not ends in themselves. They have little value unless the results are used to improve the teaching and learning that take place.

What does this mean as far as your teaching activities are concerned? In brief, it means you must study the results of the tests you give. Use them to bring about better student growth. Make the results a basis for improving your instruction. Be critical of your teaching efforts, but don't stop there. Start to build. Do it by asking questions such as the following:

1. Who is achieving as well as I had hoped?
2. In what ways can he be encouraged to make even greater progress?
3. Who is having trouble?

4. Where is he having trouble?
5. Why is he having trouble?
6. What method (s) might aid in improvement?
7. How can the method (s) best be carried out?

After you have given a test to your students, come back to this page and review these questions. Perhaps you will think of others that are even more helpful. The important point is that such questions will guide your thinking, if you are really interested in doing a better job of teaching.

Do not make the mistake of thinking that test results will supply all the answers to all these questions. It may be necessary to consult other sources—the cumulative-record folder, data from the counselor, marks in other courses, and so on. But a study of your own test scores can start you on the way in a systematic, organized manner.

All your evaluation efforts should be systematic and continuous. They are not something to be tacked on about report-card time and then forgotten. Most teachers know this, but too many continue to be thus casual.

What can be done to combat this weakness? When you plan your teaching, plan your testing. Remember, it is an integral part of the teaching process. Knowing what you want to measure will be an invaluable help in knowing what and how to teach. This is another way of saying that your testing program must be closely related to the objectives you are striving to achieve (Chapter Three). In other words, as you set forth your objectives, you should also be asking yourself how their attainment will be measured. This will help to put meaning into your objectives, and in turn your testing will be more effective.

In the years ahead we shall witness significant improvements in detailing exactly what we are trying to measure. You can contribute to this improvement process by developing precise characterizations of the changes you want your students to make. Effort spent in this direction will make your teaching not only easier but much more effective.

Such an approach also will help you to develop test items that measure application, insight, and understanding of things learned (Chapter Five). It will be a useful means of keeping your measuring instruments practical and realistic rather than academic and farfetched. These thoughts are among the most important to carry with you in your teaching efforts.

With this in mind you will keep telling yourself that pencil-and-paper tests cannot do the whole job. Observation will probably be your most important evaluating tool (Chapter Thirteen). You will be observing every day. Make the process objective. Know what you are observing and why. Develop the simplest possible means for recording your observations.

Perhaps the above statement implies that written tests should be used little, if at all. This is not the case. The point to remember is that pencil-and-paper tests can be devised to measure much more than a knowledge of facts (Chapters Six to Ten). We have just begun to scratch the surface of possibilities in this direction. With some ingenuity and hard work you can make significant contributions to this process.

Explore the uses to which object tests can be put (Chapter Eleven). You will want to experiment with the actual objects in various ways and for measuring different outcomes. Well-prepared object tests are one of the best means of bringing real-life situations into your evaluation efforts.

In some instances you may want to develop manipulative-performance tests (Chapter Twelve). Remember, all tests should be tests of performance, but we are thinking here of instruments for measuring the attainment of manipulative skills. Like all tests they demand careful organization and development.

Whatever the type of device, it should be constructed in terms of the two basic questions that have been repeated again and again (Chapter One):

Exactly what am I trying to measure?

How can I best do the measuring?

This brings us back to the matter of objectives, but that is as it should be. In all phases of teaching, including evaluation, there is constant need to refer back to the goals that have been established. Perhaps it is better to say that the objectives should be before you at all times. Naturally, they must be stated in such a manner as to have real meaning. Once again, this is a phase of evaluation in which a great deal of work needs to be done.

When you know exactly what it is you are trying to measure, it will be much easier to develop an instrument that is valid, reliable, objective, discriminating, comprehensive, and easy to administer and score (Chapter Four). These qualities are the marks of a good test. They should characterize all your evaluating efforts.

Finally, do not lose sight of the fact that evaluation is based on reflective judgment, using all the pertinent data that can be gathered. Tests and testing are only a means to an end. They will be useful only in so far as they bring about better teaching and thus better student growth.

Many of these points about teaching and testing can be summed up by repeating the classic story William James first told some fifty years ago. It might be considered as a final admonition:

A friend of mine, visiting a school, was asked to examine a young class in geography. Glancing at the book she said: "Suppose you should dig a hole in the ground, hundreds of feet deep, how should you find it at the bottom—warmer or colder than on top?" None of the class replying, the teacher said: "I am sure they know, but I think you don't ask the question quite rightly. Let me try." So, taking the book, she asked: "In what condition is the interior of the globe?" and received immediate answer from half of the class at once: "The interior of the globe is in a condition of igneous fusion."[1]

[1] William James, *Talks to Teachers on Psychology and to Students on Some of Life's Ideals.* New York: Henry Holt and Company, Inc., 1899, p. 150.

INDEX